D0907761

STUDIES IN SOVIET HISTORY AND SOCIETY

edited by Joseph S. Berliner, Seweryn Bialer,
and Sheila Fitzpatrick

THE CULTURAL FRONT

POWER AND CULTURE IN REVOLUTIONARY RUSSIA

SHEILA FITZPATRICK

CORNELL UNIVERSITY PRESS

Ithaca and London

First published 1992 by Cornell University Press.

International Standard Book Number 0-8014-2196-9 (cloth)
International Standard Book Number 0-8014-9516-4 (paper)
Library of Congress Catalog Card Number 92-52752
Printed in the United States of America
Librarians: Library of Congress cataloging information appears
on the last page of the book.

⊗ The paper in this book meets the minimum requirements of the American National Standard for Information Sciences—Permanence of Paper for Printed Library Materials, ANSI Z39.48-1984.

To Jerry Hough,
a companion in arms,
and the memory of two veterans
of the cultural front:
Brian Fitzpatrick (1905–1965)
I. A. Sats (1903–1980)

Contents

Preface

This book explores the subject of power and culture in Soviet Russia. It focuses on the relationship between the Bolshevik (Communist) Party and the Russian intelligentsia in the three and a half decades that began with the Bolshevik Revolution of 1917 and ended with Stalin's death in 1953. For almost half of that period, the relationship was one of actual or potential confrontation—a struggle for "hegemony" on the one side and for "autonomy" on the other, as the protagonists expressed it. What they were really struggling for, who was struggling, and what was the outcome are the big questions that this book addresses.

An overview of the book's themes is presented in Chapter 1. The following chapters take up various aspects of the subject, proceeding chronologically from the period of the Revolution and Civil War (Chapter 2) through the 1920s (Chapters 3–5) and the watershed of the Cultural Revolution (Chapters 6–7) to the Stalin era (Chapters 7–10), where the main focus of attention is the prewar period. Some sections of Chapters 8 and 10 look ahead to the postwar drive for cultural conformity known as the *zhdanovshchina*.

Chapters 1 and 8 are published here for the first time, and Chapter 9 ("Becoming Cultured") is a substantially revised and reworked version of an essay published elsewhere. The other chapters are based on essays that were published separately as articles and book chapters in the 1970s and 1980s. With one exception (Chapter 10), they appear here without major alteration: I have made small stylistic

changes and corrections, altered usage and terminology to conform
with other parts of the book, and deleted material that was repeated
in other chapters, but I did not make substantive changes in the argument or in its manner of presentation. The body of the text of Chapter 10 ("Cultural Orthodoxies under Stalin") is essentially unchanged since its first publication, but I have removed the original
concluding section and part of the original introduction, which put
the essential argument in a frame that does not fit the present volume.

Several of the chapters written in the 1970s introduced concepts
that were unfamiliar at the time—cultural revolution, for instance,
and the upward mobility of working-class *vydvizhentsy*, those who
were "drawn out" for training and promotion—and the careful
reader will still find a few of those little flags with which scholars
attempt to stake a new claim: "Historians have unaccountably neglected . . . " and the like. For the most part, these topics are no
longer neglected, but I left the flags there anyway, for reasons of nos-
talgia and pride. The articles that came out in the 1970s were part of
the so-called revisionist movement in American Sovietology which
was associated both with repudiation of Cold War scholarship, particularly the totalitarian model, and with a challenge from social historians to the dominance of political scientists.

Controversies over these issues were fierce, and anyone who
wishes to know more about them should consult Abbott Gleason's
article "'Totalitarianism' in 1984," *Russian Review* 43 (April 1984);
the exchange of opinions prompted by my article "New Perspectives
on Stalinism," *Russian Review* 45 (October 1986) and 46 (October
1987); or the survey by Jane Burbank, "Controversies over Stalinism:
Searching for a Soviet Society," *Politics & Society* 19, no. 3 (1991). I
am not going to rehearse those controversies here because I do not
want to encourage readers to approach these essays within the old
polemical framework. When paradigms start to shift, scholars always
argue and even insult each other. The controversies often prove
ephemeral and go stale; the work, with luck, does not. For better or
worse, the dominant paradigm in our field has long ago shifted away
from the totalitarian model.

I think the reader will find considerable consistency of theme, argument, and approach throughout this book. I have intentionally excluded work that is concerned primarily with other issues (though
Chapter 2, "The Bolsheviks' Dilemma," stands at the transition point
between the "power and culture" studies that are represented in this
volume and my more recent work on social identity). All the same,
this book was written over almost two decades, and one's thinking is

bound to evolve over such a period. People change, and so to some degree do their ideas and tastes, as well as the direction of their curiosity. No doubt today I would not—and probably could not—write "The 'Soft Line' on Culture and Its Enemies" (the article on which Chapter 5 is based)—the same way I wrote it in 1973, any more than I would have or could have written Chapter 9 ("Becoming Cultured") back in 1973; but that does not mean I have any real disagreements with its argument.

On the assumption that it is neverthless interesting and important for readers to know when the various chapters were first conceived, I have indicated the original date of writing (not of publication, which sometimes gives a misleading impression of the intellectual sequence) at the end of each chapter. The year and place of first publication are listed (for all but the two chapters that are published here for the first time) in the Acknowledgments.

Many people contributed in many ways to the writing of this book and the essays on which it is based. My interest in Soviet history, and specifically in the "power and culture" theme, developed toward the end of my undergraduate days in Australia, when I wrote my fourth-year history honors thesis on Soviet music. But no doubt I should go further back to explain it fully, for undoubtedly the example of my father, Brian Fitzpatrick, a radical Australian historian and civil libertarian, had something to do with it. When I went to Oxford to do a D. Phil. in the mid-1960s, Max Hayward, my adviser at St. Antony's College, was interested in the theme of intelligentsia and revolution, albeit from a different angle than mine and as a literary scholar rather than as a historian. Two British scholars from whom I learned a great deal in this period—because of as much as in spite of their sharp differences in outlook—were Leonard Schapiro and E. H. Carr. My 1970 book, *The Commissariat of Enlightenment*, a revised version of my dissertation, represents my first attack on the issue of power and culture.

The eighteen months I spent doing research in Moscow as a British Council exchange student between 1966 and 1970 were extremely important in the development my ideas on Soviet history. Without doubt the major formative influence was Igor Aleksandrovich Sats, a member of the editorial board of Aleksandr Tvardovsky's *Novyi mir* in the 1960s and at an earlier period literary secretary (and brother-in-law) of Anatoly Lunacharsky. Irina Anatolevna Lunacharskaia, Lunacharsky's daughter, also helped me a great deal; in general I lived in a very Lunacharskian world in Moscow as a young scholar. For years I had very little to do with professional historians (not counting archivists) in the Soviet Union. The first one I met with whom I found real interests in common was V. Z. Drobizhev, but that was more than a decade later, when I was working mainly on social mobility.

I did not know much about American Sovietology before I came to the United States in the early 1970s. Stephen F. Cohen, future biographer of Nikolai Bukharin, was one of the first Sovietologists I encountered; it was from him I learned that there were Sovietological revisionists and that I was one of them. Later we were often at odds on matters of interpretation, and in this way he was a major influence on me in the 1970s (for example, Chapter 5, "The Soft Line on Culture and Its Enemies," is the product of an argument with Cohen).

An important milestone for me was the conference on cultural revolution that I organized at Columbia University, with the encouragement of Loren Graham and S. Frederick Starr, in 1974. The idea was one I had started to develop earlier, during and partly in reaction to the Chinese Cultural Revolution as reported in the Soviet press (for want of other sources of information in Moscow), but it was only at this point that it became fully formulated. Chapter 6 of this book—originally published in my edited volume *Cultural Revolution in Russia, 1928–1931* (1978)—is a revised version of the paper I wrote for the 1974 conference.

The period of my greatest involvement in Sovietological controversy, on the one hand, and social science theory, on the other, ran from the mid-1970s to the early 1980s, the years of my marriage to Jerry Hough. Chapters 3, 4, 7, and 10 of this volume were written in that period, as well as my books *Education and Social Mobility in the Soviet Union* (1979) and *The Russian Revolution* (1983), Hough and Merle Fainsod's *How the Soviet Union Is Governed* (1979), and Hough's *Soviet Union and Social Science Theory* (1981). There was a lot of cross-fertilization in all this work. I see a strong influence of Hough in my non- or even anti-Marxist approach to Russian labor history as well as on such issues as totalitarianism and social mobility.

"The Bolsheviks' Dilemma," Chapter 2 of this book, was inspired by a workshop on popular culture that I organized with Marc Ferro at the University of Texas in the late 1980s; its deconstructionist approach to class provoked objections from Ronald Suny (*Slavic Review* 47 [Winter 1988]) similar to those expressed by the German historian Geoff Ely in the *Russian Review* exchange on Stalinism two years earlier. Chapter 9 grew out of an essay written at Terry Thompson's request for a festschrift for Vera Dunham in the mid-1980s.

Chapter 8 was written on the occasion of a Shostakovich conference in Toronto organized by R. Sterling Beckwith and Peter Solomon.

I thank John Ackerman, my editor at Cornell University Press, for encouraging me to put together this volume; John McCannon, a graduate student at the University of Chicago, for help in preparing the manuscript for publication; and my husband, Michael Danos, for reading the whole manuscript, making very useful comments from the perspective of a theoretical physicist, and persuading me to keep the preface short.

SHEILA FITZPATRICK

Chicago, Illinois

Acknowledgments

"The Bolsheviks' Dilemma: The Class Issue in Party Politics and Culture" was first published as "The Bolsheviks' Dilemma: Class, Culture, and Politics in Early Soviet Years" in *Slavic Review* 47 (Winter 1988): 599–613. Copyright © 1988 by the American Association for the Advancement of Slavic Studies, Inc. Reprinted by permission of AAASS.

"Professors and Soviet Power" was first published as Chapter 5 of Sheila Fitzpatrick, *Education and Social Mobility in the Soviet Union, 1921–1934* (Cambridge and New York, 1979). Copyright © 1979 by Cambridge University Press. Reprinted by permission of Cambridge University Press.

"Sex and Revolution," first published as "Sex and Revolution: An Examination of Literary and Statistical Data on the Mores of Soviet Students in the 1920s" in *Journal of Modern History* 50 (June 1978). Copyright © 1978 by the University of Chicago. Reprinted by permission of the University of Chicago Press.

"The Soft Line on Culture and Its Enemies," first published as "The 'Soft' Line on Culture and Its Enemies: Soviet Cultural Policy, 1922–1927," *Slavic Review* 33 (June 1974): 267–87. Copyright © 1974 by the American Association for the Advancement of Slavic Studies, Inc. Reprinted by permission of AAASS.

"Cultural Revolution as Class War" was published in *Cultural Revolution in Russia, 1928–1931*, edited by Sheila Fitzpatrick (Bloomington, Ind., 1978). Copyright © 1978 by Indiana University Press. Reprinted by permission of Indiana University Press.

"Stalin and the Making of a New Elite" was first published as "Stalin and the Making of a New Elite, 1928–1939" in *Slavic Review* 38 (September 1979): 377–402. Copyright © 1979 by the American Association for the Advancement of Slavic Studies, Inc. Reprinted by permission of AAASS.

An earlier version of "Becoming Cultured: Socialist Realism and the Representation of Privilege and Taste" was published as "'Middle-class Values' and Soviet Life in the 1930s" in *Soviet Society and Culture: Essays in Honor of Vera S. Dunham*, edited by Terry L. Thompson and Richard Sheldon (Boulder, Colo., 1988). Copyright © 1988 by Westview Press.

An earlier version of "Cultural Orthodoxies under Stalin" was published as "Culture and Politics under Stalin: A Reappraisal" in *Slavic Review* 35 (June 1976): 211–31. Copyright © 1976 by the American Association for the Advancement of Slavic Studies, Inc. Reprinted by permission of AAASS.

A Note on Spelling

I have followed the system established by the Library of Congress for transliteration of Russian words and names. I have made exceptions, however, for well-known persons and places whose names are more familiar to readers in other spellings: for example, Gorky, Kazan, Lunacharsky, Mayakovsky, Meyerhold, Mikoyan, Pokrovsky, Rimsky-Korsakov, Stanislavsky, Tchaikovsky.

Glossary

ASM   Association for Contemporary Music
bourgeois specialist   member of non-Communist intelligentsia (1920s term)
Cheka   security police (Civil War period)
First Five-Year Plan   state economic plan, 1929–1932
Glaviskusstvo   chief arts administration under Narkompros
Glavlit   government agency for literary censorship
Glavrepertkom   government agency for theater censorship
GPU (OGPU)   security police (1920s and early 1930s)
gubkom   provincial party committee
khoziaistvenniki   industrial administrators and managers
komchvanstvo   Communist conceit
Komsomol   League of Young Communists (14–23 age group in 1920s)
kulak   rich (exploiting) peasant
kul'tpokhod   cultural campaign
kul'turnost'   culturedness, good taste, as distinguished from the high culture of the bourgeois intelligentsia
meshchanstvo   petty-bourgeois philistinism
Narkompros   People's Commissariat of Enlightenment (= Ministry of Education and Culture), Russian Republic
NEP   period of the New Economic Policy, 1921–1928
NKVD   security police (from 1934)
Pioneers   Communist youth organization for 10–14 age group
Proletkult   nongovernmental association for proletarian culture (most important in Civil War period)
rabfak   "workers' faculty"; a school to prepare young workers for entrance to higher education

Rabkrin   People's Commissariat of Workers' and Peasants' Inspection

RAPM   Russian Association of Proletarian Musicians

RAPP (VAPP)   Russian Association of Proletarian Writers

Sovnarkom   Council of People's Commissars

spetseedstvo   specialist baiting, anti-intellectualism

spetsialisty (abbr. *spetsy*)   non-Communist professionals employed by the state

Stakhanovites   workers and peasants rewarded for overfulfilling work norms, in the manner of a highly publicized coal miner named Stakhanov (term in use from 1935)

TsIK   Central Executive Committee of All-Union Congress of Soviets

VAPP   see RAPP

Vesenkha   Supreme Council of the National Economy (= Ministry of Industry), 1920s

vydvizhentsy   workers and peasants "promoted" to white-collar, professional, and managerial work, especially the cohort selected for higher education during the Cultural Revolution

zhdanovshchina   the campaign launched by Andrei Zhdanov in the late 1940s against writers, musicians, and other artists in whose work he detected Western influence

The Cultural Front

CHAPTER 1

Introduction:
On Power and Culture

Power and culture were inevitably intertwined in Soviet Russia in the first two decades after the Bolshevik Revolution. The words "power" and "culture" can be interpreted in several ways, but let us start with their meanings for contemporaries. In Soviet usage of the 1920s, "power" (*vlast'*) meant state power and its exercise by the ruling Bolshevik Party.[1] For the Bolsheviks, the form of state power they had introduced in Soviet Russia was a dictatorship of the proletariat, and the Bolshevik Party was the proletarian vanguard. For most members of the intelligentsia, the new regime was a dictatorship of the Bolshevik Party pure and simple.

"Culture" (*kul'tura*) meant high culture in the usage of the 1920s. The concept embraced literature, scholarship, and the arts, Russian and Western and past and present; and it was generally accepted that the Russian intelligentsia was the guardian of culture and of "cultural values" (*kul'turnye tsennosti*). Bolsheviks sometimes tried to argue that this high culture that was protected by the intelligentsia was actually only "bourgeois culture," as opposed to a largely hypothetical "proletarian culture." Often, however, they talked about culture as an absolute, classless entity—the opposite of that "lack of culture" (*beskul'tur'e*) that had historically characterized backward

---

[1] Until 1918 the Communists were known as Bolsheviks, and "Bolshevik" remained part of the party's official title throughout the 1920s and 1930s. Both terms were used in the 1920s, but in the 1930s the term "Communist" was used in most contexts. I follow the prevailing usage of the group and period under discussion.

1

Russia. In the 1930s, the concept of "culturedness" (*kul'turnost'*) came into common use as a second antonym for "lack of culture," especially in the sphere of everyday life, but it did not displace *kul'tura* from its preeminent position.

"Power" was sometimes a synecdoche for the Bolshevik Party, "culture" for the intelligentsia. In this usage, "power" might threaten "culture" or seek an alliance with it.

But "culture" was also one of the primary spheres of revolutionary contestation, like politics and economics. It was a locus of struggle, an arena in which power (hegemony) could be won or lost. From the standpoint of Marxist theory, the two great protagonists in the struggle were the proletariat, the new ruling class, and the bourgeoisie, the old one, still resisting its defeat. The standard-bearer for the proletariat was the Bolshevik Party, which was at the same time the embodiment of power, while the standard-bearer for the bourgeoisie was the Russian intelligentsia, simultaneously the embodiment of culture. Thus, in the terminology of the 1920s, "power" fought "culture" for power in culture. The Bolsheviks, lovers of military metaphor, soon dubbed the location of these conflicts "the cultural front."

In the 1920s, the thinking of the Bolshevik Party was framed in terms of binary oppositions: proletarian/bourgeois, revolutionary/counterrevolutionary, ally/enemy, thesis/antithesis. Lenin's famous question "*Kto kogo?*" (which can be roughly translated as "Who will beat whom?") epitomizes this tendency. The Bolsheviks conceptualized their conflicts with the intelligentsia in terms of class struggle, identifying their party with the proletariat and the intelligentsia with the bourgeoisie. This was certainly how it should have been according to Marxist theory, but in practice neither class label fitted its subject very well. The Bolshevik Party had links with the industrial working class, it was true, but these links were much more tenuous than they had seemed in the heady days of October 1917. As for the Russian intelligentsia, it had virtually no historic or present connection with a capitalist bourgeoisie.

The intelligentsia were not far behind the Bolsheviks in their mastery of dialectical—not to say Manichean—thinking. For the intelligentsia, the conflicts with the Soviet state of the 1920s were a continuation of the prerevolutionary struggle for "freedom" against tsarist "autocracy." In its framing of the conflict, each side managed to deliver a deadly insult to the other. The Bolsheviks called the intelligentsia "bourgeois," though the intelligentsia considered themselves to be the very antitheses of bourgeois philistines. The intelligentsia treated the Bolsheviks as heirs of the repressive, unenlightened tsarist state, though in Bolshevik terms there could be no greater gulf than that between autocracy and revolution.

True to their respective premises, the Bolsheviks and the intelligentsia often had radically different notions of the underlying meaning of any specific conflict between them. Their repeated clashes over university governance and admissions policies are a good example. From the intelligentsia's (professors') standpoint, the key issue at stake was freedom—preservation of university autonomy against the state's efforts to impose political control. From the Bolsheviks' standpoint, the key issue was class—that is, whether "bourgeois" professors should be allowed to frustrate the democratization of higher education by blocking the admission of large numbers of working-class students who had not graduated from high school.

Of course, the great binary oppositions of Soviet discourse in the 1920s often obscured as much as they revealed. It is always an oversimplification, even if one necessary for the purposes of exposition, to reduce social entities as complex as the Bolshevik Party and the Russian intelligentsia to monolithic unities. A variety of cultural values and opinions on cultural policy were represented within the Bolshevik Party. Most notable was the split between Old Bolsheviks of moderate, eclectic views and conciliatory spirit such as A. V. Lunacharsky, whose values had much in common with those of the (non-Bolshevik) Russian intelligentsia, and Bolshevik "Young Turks," such as those represented in the Russian Association of Proletarian Writers (RAPP)[2] and other militant Communist cultural organizations, who favored forcible politicization of culture and the establishment of Communist and proletarian "hegemony" in the various branches of scholarship and the arts. Among the Bolshevik Young Turks, a "leftist" subgroup shared the belief of avant-garde artists such as the poet Vladimir Mayakovsky and the theater director Vsevolod Meyerhold that revolutionary art and revolutionary politics had a natural affinity.

It was the aim of the militant Young Turks in the 1920s to seize control of the Bolshevik agenda on culture from party moderates such as Lunacharsky. They succeeded in doing so at the end of the decade, at least temporarily, when Cultural Revolution enthroned the militant agenda. Even before that, however, they had managed to pull the definition of Communist values in culture into their own corner. Thus in the debates on cultural policy in the mid-1920s, the militants often appeared to be arguing for "Communist" principles, while the moderates seemed to be resisting them on grounds of expediency, cost, or (most damningly) "softness" on the intelligentsia. In the latter part of the 1920s, accordingly, Lunacharsky and the moder-

---

[2] RAPP's activities are discussed in chaps. 5 and 6.

ates might prevail on a given issue because their views had considerable support in the upper echelons of government, but their victory was likely to be understood either as a defeat for Communist principles or, at best, as a necessary compromise. The "Communist" idea in culture had been effectively defined by the militants as the antithesis of the "bourgeois" (intelligentsia) idea.

Within the creative intelligentsia, similarly, there were profound splits between avant-gardists, traditionalists, preservationists, realists, symbolists, Marxists, and those who either were or were not prepared to be "fellow travelers" of Soviet power. In fact, it was a period of intense sectarian struggle in all branches of culture; and probably the main reason that it is possible to speak of the intelligentsia as a coherent social entity with common values is that the Bolshevik militants framed the conflict in these terms. Just as the idea of an intelligentsia had been constructed in the mid–nineteenth century in the process of struggle with the tsarist autocracy, so that idea—which by the early twentieth century had shown signs of disintegration, as separate professional identities took over—was revived and reconstructed in the years after the October Revolution in a similar process of abrasive interaction between educated non-Bolshevik professionals and the new holders of state power.

The intelligentsia also had its Young Turks—the avant-gardists of the artistic left—who were trying to seize control of the agenda in the early 1920s. They were much less successful than their counterparts on the Bolshevik side, partly because of their stridency, intolerance, and willingness to allow politics to invade the sphere of culture. They also labored under a disadvantage similar to that of the Bolshevik moderates: their own side (the intelligentsia) suspected them of consorting with the enemy. Competition from the equally aggressive and intolerant "proletarians" in the arts also took its toll, and in the course of the 1920s the artistic left became increasingly marginalized. It was the "eternal" cultural values of the non-avant-gardist mainstream—preservationist, humanist, apolitical, more or less pluralist—that came to be accepted as *the* intelligentsia values. Among these values, intellectual and artistic freedom and professional autonomy were high on the list. But it was the untrammeled independence of solid traditional institutions such as the Academy of Sciences, not of fringe groups with dubious professional credentials, that was of primary concern.

The two great protagonists in the struggle on the cultural front, the Bolshevik Party and the intelligentsia, had more in common than either cared to admit. For all the party's claims to be proletarian, almost all its early leaders came from the intelligentsia, had spent years in emigration in Europe, and shared the culture of other Europeanized Russian intellectuals. The (non-Bolshevik) intelligentsia, moreover, had a long radical and revolutionary tradition, and even those segments of it that were most strongly opposed to the Bolsheviks and their Marxist-Leninist ideology had absorbed a good deal of Marxism over the years.

The Bolshevik Party and the intelligentsia shared an idea of culture as something that (like revolution) an enlightened minority brought to the masses in order to uplift them. There was no sense on either side that the culture that was best for the masses was the culture that the masses liked. What would now be called urban popular culture was condemned out of hand by the culture-bringers inside and outside the party as "vulgar," "trivial," and "petty-bourgeois" (*meshchanskaia*), the last epithet being equally derogatory whether it came from the lips of a wellborn liberal intellectual or those of a militant proletarian Bolshevik.

The protagonists resembled each other, too, in having a highly developed sense of historical mission and moral superiority. The collective self-consciousness that created the Russian intelligentsia in the mid–nineteenth century was, above all, consciousness of a mission to enlighten, to serve the people, to act as critic and conscience of the state. This sense of avocation translated easily into belief in a historical mission of leadership. But the Bolshevik Party had an equally strong sense of destiny and mission derived from Marxist theory and a sense of identification with the forces of history. In its own eyes, the party had recognized the historical necessity of proletarian revolution in Russia and led the proletariat to victory. Now it had the further mission of leading the country through the perils of the transition to socialism. Though the Bolsheviks expressed their claims to leadership in scientific-historical terms, those claims rested as solidly on a sense of moral entitlement and duty as did those of the intelligentsia.

Perhaps the most important thing the Bolsheviks and the Russian intelligentsia had in common was that each was an elite group in Soviet society and neither wanted to admit it. With equal indignation, Bolsheviks and intellectuals flatly denied that their own group could conceivably be seen as possessing or claiming elite status; the very idea was a travesty, politically motivated and intended to defame. Of course, each group added, it was absolutely true that the *other* group was an elite. But that just proved the point, dialectically speaking: if "culture" was the elite, "power" must be, however paradoxically, the underdog; if "power" was the elite, "culture" must be its servant.

To the intelligentsia and to most of the outside world, it was self-evident that the Bolsheviks were a new privileged, superior class in Russian society by virtue of the fact that they were its new rulers. This perception rested on the realities of power, and was unaffected by Bolshevik arguments about the party's ascetic traditions and repudiation of privilege (the "party maximum," for example, which kept the salaries of cadres below those of professionals in the 1920s).

To the Bolsheviks and to most of the outside world, it was equally self-evident that the intelligentsia was an elite that had possessed high social and economic status under the old regime and, to a surprising degree, had managed to hang onto these advantages under Soviet power. In the opinion of working-class Bolsheviks in particular, the intelligentsia still behaved like a privileged class, treating party members like social inferiors and mocking their lack of education. Hence the reiterated complaint in party circles that, despite the Revolution, Bolshevik "power" still had to tip its cap to intelligentsia "culture."

In fact, the complex relationship between the Bolshevik Party and the Russian intelligentsia in the decade after the Revolution is probably best understood as two competing elites, resentfully interdependent, jealously jockeying for position, and withal constituting the only possible claimants for leadership in a fragmented and unsettled postrevolutionary society. It was a cliché of the 1920s that the Soviet regime could not survive without the collaboration of "bourgeois specialists."[3] Lenin laid down the law firmly on this point, insisting that Communists lacked the expertise and experience to run the state and therefore had no choice but to "use" (a favorite, intentionally demeaning term) the experts, even though their loyalty could not be relied on. Many Communists resented this dependence, but of course the dependence (as well as the resentment) worked the other way as well. The intelligentsia needed the goodwill or at least the tolerance of the party leaders to preserve their collective status and well-being, and individual bourgeois specialists relied on the protection of Communist patrons, usually their immediate bosses, to give them some security in a very uncertain world.

In the period of Cultural Revolution, Communists offered a new reading of the relationship between the party and the intelligentsia. The essence of the new reading was that the experts were using the Communists more effectively than the Communists were using the experts. Despite their exclusion from political power, it was argued,

---

[3] In the 1920s, this was the contemporary term for non-Communist professionals employed by the Soviet state. *Spetsialisty*, sometimes abbreviated to *spetsy*, was often applied by extension to the intelligentsia as a whole.

bourgeois specialists were managing to push through their own agendas because they knew more about their subjects than the Communists under whom they worked. In the melodramatic version of this reading popular with the militants of Cultural Revolution, these agendas were no less than counterrevolutionary: the specialists were plotting to wreck the Soviet economy and overthrow Soviet power! The counterrevolutionaries must be caught and punished. "Bourgeois hegemony" in culture must be overthrown, and a new proletarian intelligentsia, combining expertise and political loyalty, must be trained to replace the bourgeois, counterrevolutionary wreckers.

Ironically, the Russian intelligentsia's collective attitude toward the Communist Party and the regime on the eve of the First Five-Year Plan was probably more positive than it had been at any earlier time, since the party appeared to be preparing to embark on a course of economic and cultural modernization and building of national strength of which most intellectuals approved. Thus the Cultural Revolution, whose unexpected onset in 1928–1929 coincided with the adoption of the First Five-Year Plan, was a double blow, and the climactic conflict of culture and power was almost totally one-sided. Members of the intelligentsia were harassed, humiliated, removed from their jobs, and in some cases arrested. They found no effective way to fight back, and (outside the small circles of ceaselessly warring "proletarians" and "leftists" in the arts) most seemed too intimidated even to try. A sense of powerlessness and vulnerability, familiar from the Civil War, returned. But this time the threat was more psychological then physical, and the victims often seemed pained and surprised that the Soviet regime did not recognize their (comparative) loyalty to it. The whole episode left the intelligentsia deeply intimidated and insecure, silencing those who had been most inclined to challenge state authority and causing the rest to develop new techniques of individual self-protection and ingratiation with "power."

Cultural Revolution was the high point of the "*Kto kogo?*" representation of Soviet society and politics, in which proletarian "power" and bourgeois "culture" were locked in a mortal combat on whose outcome rested the fate of the Revolution. "*Kto kogo?*" was essentially a call to battle rather than a heuristic method, and it was an axiom of this approach that conflicts had to end in outright victory for one side and total defeat for the other. The fallacy of this assumption is obvious. Indeed, even Marxist dialecticians knew in their calmer moments that the outcome of a conflict between thesis and antithesis is synthesis.

The notion of some kind of synthesis of Communist and traditional (or middle-class) Russian values in the Stalin period has been explored by a sociologist, Nicholas Timasheff, writing in the 1940s, and more recently by a literary scholar, Vera Dunham. Timasheff's hypothesis was that a "great retreat" from revolutionary values occurred in the 1930s.[4] It was exemplified in a revival of prerevolutionary patterns of schooling, respect for the Russian past, appreciation of the classics of nineteenth-century Russian literature and music, and traditional family values. In sum, as Jerry Hough has pointed out, it represented a sharp reaction against and repudiation of the ultraradicalism of Cultural Revolution.[5]

Vera Dunham noted a similar shift, but identified it as a turn toward middle-class values, notably those of propriety, culture, and good taste (*kul'turnost'*), and placed it in the immediate postwar period rather than the 1930s. Dunham conceptualized this shift as the product of a "big deal" struck by the Stalinist regime and an emergent middle class, by which the regime provided privilege and accommodation of middle-class values in return for loyalty and support.

Timasheff characterized the alien values absorbed by the regime in the 1930s as traditionally Russian (with no specific social location); Dunham saw them as "middle-class" (with strong pejorative overtones).[6] But it is not too difficult to recognize them as close relatives—albeit coarsened and debased, particularly in Dunham's account—of the very values that the mainstream of the Russian intelligentsia upheld under the banner of "culture" in the 1920s.

It may perhaps be straying too far from Dunham's conception to suggest that her notion of the "big deal" might equally well be applied to the Russian intelligentsia. Yet if anyone cut such a deal with the Stalinist regime, in many respects the intelligentsia seems a more likely party to it than Dunham's "middle class"—an entity that seems too intimately linked with the regime, like Trotsky's "bureau-

---

[4] Nicholas S. Timasheff, *The Great Retreat: The Growth and Decline of Communism in Russia* (New York, 1946); Vera S. Dunham, *In Stalin's Time: Middle-Class Values in Soviet Fiction* (Cambridge, 1976).

[5] See Jerry F. Hough, "The Cultural Revolution and Western Understanding of the Soviet System," in *Cultural Revolution in Russia, 1928–1931*, ed. Sheila Fitzpatrick (Bloomington, Ind., 1978), pp. 242–44.

[6] In Dunham's usage, the English term "middle class" has a lot in common with the Russian word *meshchanstvo*. The latter, often translated as "petty bourgeoisie," was the name of an urban social estate in tsarist times. As used by Russian intellectuals, it has always had strong connotations of vulgarity and philistinism. Dunham, who shares this usage, presents *meshchanstvo* and intelligentsia as diametrically opposed concepts (*In Stalin's Time*, pp. 19–23). For her, therefore, the intelligentsia (that is, the old Russian intelligentsia, called "bourgeois" by Bolsheviks in the 1920s) did not become part of the Stalinist "middle class" because its members did not have "middle-class values."

cracy," to be in a position to make deals with it.[7] If one hypothesizes something like a deal between the Russian intelligentsia and the Stalinist regime in the 1930s, it would presumably involve the intelligentsia's pledge of loyalty and service to the regime in exchange for privilege and social status for themselves and the regime's support for major traditional cultural institutions such as the Academy of Sciences; and an agreement that the two sides would cooperate in disseminating a popularized form of the intelligentsia's culture among the masses.

There are many indications that something of this sort was occurring. The stage was set in 1931–1932 with Stalin's assurance that the intelligentsia had now abandoned their habits of sabotage and counterrevolution and the Central Committee's abrupt dissolution of the militant "proletarian" organizations that had spearheaded Cultural Revolution in the arts. In effect, the party was repudiating just those cultural values that, thanks to the militants' efforts in the 1920s, had previously been identified as specifically Communist. This shift left a vacuum of values as well as leadership; and, predictably, that vacuum was often filled by the formerly disgraced bourgeois intelligentsia.

When Mikhail Pokrovsky's Marxist school of history was discredited, for example, bourgeois historians of the old school recovered their dominance of the profession. When the Russian Association of Proletarian Musicians (RAPM) lost its grip on musical affairs, works from the classical repertoire beloved of the Russian intelligentsia—Beethoven, Tchaikovsky, Rimsky-Korsakov—came flooding back to the concert halls and opera houses. The apogee of the regime's endorsement of the high culture of the intelligentsia came in 1937, when every newspaper and cultural organization in the Soviet Union carried extravagant celebrations of the Pushkin centenary and acclaimed the poet (whom the futurist Mayakovsky had compared to a White general in 1918) as a great humanist and hero of the socialist state.

The repudiation of Cultural Revolution left the small self-consciously Communist intelligentsia that had emerged in the 1920s in disgrace and total disarray. Those members of the cohort that sur-

---

[7] Dunham does not attempt a rigorous definition of her "middle class," but the following passage suggests that it is essentially equivalent to Trotsky's "bureaucracy," with the possible addition of *arriviste* professionals (that is, the group I refer to as *vydvizhentsy*): "The middle class had the great advantage of being 'our own people': totally stalinist, born out of Stalin's push for the industrialization, reeducation, and bureaucratization of the country, flesh of the flesh of Stalin's revolutions from above in the thirties, and ready to fill the vacuum created by Stalin's Great Purge and by the liquidation of the leninist generation of activists" (ibid., p. 13).

vived the debacle might become cultural administrators or even professors, but they did not henceforth aspire to cultural leadership as a
group, and neither they nor anyone else proposed a new system of
Communist cultural values to replace the old ones that had been
discredited as a result of the Cultural Revolution. There were no further attempts in the Stalin period to establish "Communist hegemony"—in the sense of hegemony of Communist values—in culture;
the regime settled for the less ambitious goal of strict administrative
and censorship controls over culture, supplemented by the intelligentsia's dutiful self-policing.

The great cultural arbiter of the 1930s was Maxim Gorky, a writer
with an international reputation who was neither a Communist nor a
Marxist, despite his prerevolutionary association with Lenin. He had
spent most of the 1920s in quasi-emigration in Europe. During the
Civil War, Gorky had used his influence with Lenin to protect pre-
cisely those segments of the Russian intelligentsia that the Bolsheviks found least congenial; during the Cultural Revolution, his
work and opinions had been harshly criticized by the militant Communists of RAPP. After Gorky's much-publicized return to the Soviet
Union in the early 1930s, however, Stalin conspicuously and deferentially consulted Gorky on a wide range of cultural questions, while
Gorky, a self-made intellectual from a humble social background,
conspicuously and deferentially took counsel with the most highly
respected representatives of the conservative mainstream of the Russian intelligentsia.

New orthodoxies to which practitioners were required to conform
emerged in the various branches of the arts and scholarship in the
course of the 1930s. This was not the result of conscious planning by
Gorky or Stalin: indeed, the dissolution of the proletarian organizations in 1932 was meant to put an end to repressive factional cultural dictatorships such as RAPP's in literature, and Gorky's new slogan of "socialist realism" was intended to allow greater diversity
rather than to impose a new straitjacket. All the same, "Arakcheev
regimes" (to use Stalin's term of the early 1950s) kept appearing in
various cultural professions and disciplines.[8] Leaving aside for the
moment the systemic reasons for this development, we must note
that the cultural orthodoxies established in the 1930s virtually never
had any Marxist (or Marxist-Leninist) content and often involved the

---

[8] The name of Count A. A. Arakcheev, organizer of the notorious "military colonies"
in the 1820s, is associated with authoritarian, army-style discipline imposed in a non-
military context. Stalin criticized "Arakcheev regimes" in science in "On Marxism
and Linguistics" [Otnositel'no marksizma i iazykoznanii), in his Sochineniia, ed. Robert H. McNeal, 3 vols. (Stanford, 1967), 3:114–48.

canonization of a *non-Communist* authority figure who was held in respect within the profession and belonged to the intelligentsia's conservative mainstream.

The old artistic "left" associated with such figures as Meyerhold and Mayakovsky (who committed suicide in 1930) fared scarcely better than the militant Communist "proletarians." Its decline in the 1930s—symbolized by the increasingly embattled situation of Meyerhold, which culminated in the closing of his theater and finally, in 1939, his arrest—was not the result of any abrupt withdrawal of official favor (as was the case with the "proletarians"). Nevertheless, the climate turned increasingly hostile to modernism, an artistic movement that Gorky and many others saw as a product of the corruption and decay of Western capitalism. In the mid-1930s a major campaign was launched against "formalism" (that is, modernism) in all branches of art; Dmitrii Shostakovich's new opera, *Lady Macbeth of the Mtsensk District*, was the primary victim.

There are obvious analogies with the contemporary condemnation of "*entartete Kunst*" (degenerate art) in Nazi Germany, whose leaders, like those of the Soviet Union, had a stake in contrasting the decadence of the liberal democracies with their own healthy, life-affirming society. All the same, it is doubtful that the sad fate of modernism in the Soviet Union can be attributed solely to the cultural policies of political leaders. (It was Stalin, after all, who posthumously canonized the archmodernist, Mayakovsky, as a great Soviet poet.) In the Soviet Union, as elsewhere in the world, the avant-garde consisted of small, vulnerable fringe groups—albeit vociferous ones in the 1920s—that were unpopular both with audiences and within the artistic professions. The Soviet avant-garde had won a particularly bad reputation among fellow professionals in the early Soviet years, not only by breaking intelligentsia ranks to ally themselves with the Bolsheviks but also by trying to use Bolshevik power to crush their artistic opponents. Within the intelligentsia, therefore, many people had scores to settle with the left, just as they did with the "proletarians."

By the mid-1930s, the sociological and political configuration of the intelligentsia was being changed by the emergence of a new cohort of graduates from Soviet institutions of higher and technical education. These were the *vydvizhentsy*—"yesterday's workers and peasants," many of them Communists, who had been mobilized for further education during the First Five-Year Plan in a crash program initiated by Stalin and Viacheslav Molotov. The announced purpose of this program was to train a new "worker-peasant intelligentsia" to replace the old "bourgeois" one, which in 1928–1929 was under collective suspicion of counterrevolution and sabotage. By the time the *vydvizhentsy* began to graduate, however, these accusations had been dropped and the old intelligentsia welcomed back into the Soviet fold. Instead of replacing bourgeois intellectuals in the professions, some of the *vydvizhentsy* found themselves abruptly seconded to political and administrative jobs in 1937–1938, replacing Communist bureaucrats and managers who had fallen victim to the Great Purges.

The remaining *vydvizhentsy* settled down to work as engineers, teachers, agronomists, chemists, architects, and so on in the professions for which they had been trained. Their arrival caused problems for the old intelligentsia. In the first place, they were so numerous in some professions, such as engineering, that they tended to swamp the older group. In the second place, they were poorly trained by the old intelligentsia's standards: many had not been high school graduates when they were sent to college; their years at college coincided with the high point of cultural-revolutionary disruption of curricula and methods of instruction; and, for the Communists of the cohort in particular, schooling was often interrupted by short-term assignments to help with collectivization and other party tasks. In the third place, their basic social and political values at the time they graduated were usually quite different from those of the old intelligentsia. *Vydvizhentsy* were generally very loyal to the Soviet regime and enthusiastic about its goals. Coming from lower-class backgrounds, they perceived themselves as beneficiaries of the Revolution, owing to it their opportunities and education.

The social and attitudinal gulf that separated old and new intelligentsia remained for many years. But we should not overlook the important fact that values and behavior patterns were being transmitted across the gulf. What the old intelligentsia absorbed from the *vydvizhentsy* belonged mainly to the realm of political values and organizational behavior (since *vydvizhentsy* often served as party or trade union secretaries in their institutions and ended up in professional-administrative rather than purely professional jobs). What was transmitted in the other direction, however, was of equal or greater volume and importance. The *vydvizhentsy* cohort, although largely composed of either Communists or people committed to the regime, was very different from the young Communist intelligentsia that emerged during the years of the New Economic Policy (NEP) and flourished briefly during the Cultural Revolution. That earlier Communist cohort, trained in Marxism, with polemical skills honed in the party faction fights of the 1920s, was composed of militant, highly politicized intellectuals who were missionaries for a Communist Idea in culture. The *vydvizhentsy*, by contrast, were practical people from humble backgrounds who knew little of Marxist theory and were politically loyal rather than politicized. They had no specific cultural agendas when they were mobilized for higher education and the professions. Their purpose was to learn; and their teachers, inevitably, were members of the old intelligentsia.

The need to learn applied specifically to the body of knowledge associated with their new disciplines and professions, and more generally to the broader culture and mores that society expected educated people to possess. Like any other upwardly mobile individuals, the *vydvizhentsy* were eager to acquire the cultural and social expertise appropriate to their new status, anxious not to contravene upper-class norms, and fearful that they might involuntarily do so. They were both wary and respectful of the old intelligentsia: these people, after all, had "real culture," and furthermore, being products of a prerevolutionary bourgeois upbringing for the most part, they knew how to behave in a cultured manner in good society.

Marxist critics have generally explained the signs of growing embourgeoisement of Soviet society and mores in the Stalin period in terms of Thermidor—the classic image of revolutionary degeneration. But it can also be explained in less loaded terms as a natural consequence of the rise of a large cohort of *vydvizhentsy* into the Soviet elite. Old Bolsheviks may have lost some of their revolutionary idealism in the 1930s, but it was not they who yearned for orange lampshades (to borrow Vera Dunham's memorable image) and *kul'turnost'*. This was the domain of the upwardly mobile *vydvizhentsy*; it was their—and their wives'—striving for culture that made *kul'turnost'* a hallmark of the era. By the same token, they were undoubtedly the unwitting cause of much of the vulgarization and debasement of high culture in the Stalin period. The oppressive cultural orthodoxies and deadening spirit of conformity that took root in the professions in the 1930s must in part have reflected the needs and insecurities of the *vydvizhentsy*: it is the poorly trained and inexperienced professional, after all, who wants to be told exactly how to do a job and what model to follow.

Terror was also a powerful stimulus to orthodoxy. As Aleksandr Solzhenitsyn points out, terror in the Soviet Union came in waves, and each wave affected different groups in the population.[9] A big wave, the Cultural Revolution, hit the intelligentsia at the beginning of the 1930s. Then another wave, the Great Purges, hit in 1937–1938.

[9] Aleksandr I. Solzhenitsyn, *The Gulag Archipelago, 1918–1956: An Experiment in Literary Investigation*, trans. Thomas P. Whitney, 2 vols. (New York, 1973), 1:24–26.

The first episode left the intelligentsia shaken, humiliated, and cowed, though the battering lasted only a few years and was followed by a collective rehabilitation. In the second episode, it was the Communist elite rather than the intelligentsia that took the heaviest impact, but the intelligentsia also suffered substantial losses. The intelligentsia subgroup that was hardest hit in the Great Purges was the cohort of young Communist and Komsomol militants associated with the Cultural Revolution. Then came the old (formerly "bourgeois") intelligentsia—the Cultural Revolutionaries' victims in the earlier episode. The *vydvizhentsy*, sent to study during the First Five-Year Plan and entering the professional and administrative elites from the middle of the 1930s, were more typically beneficiaries of the Great Purges than victims.

It is clear that the sequence of blows in the Cultural Revolution and the Great Purges was psychologically devastating to members of the old intelligentsia. A sense of powerlessness, humiliation, and even martyrdom took hold of them, and they were left cowering in expectation of further blows. This was one aspect of the intelligentsia's reality, and it dominated the consciousness of the Soviet Russian intelligentsia for half a century. At the same time, however, the intelligentsia never lost the privileged social and economic status they had recovered and acquired in the aftermath of the Cultural Revolution. This aspect of the intelligentsia's reality tended to be ignored in the group's mythology because it made their situation more ambiguous and their suffering less pure.

The new (post–Cultural Revolution) status of the intelligentsia was indicated in many ways, both material and symbolic. Through their workplaces and unions, the professional and cultural elites had access to networks of privilege similar to those that served Communist administrators, though only a small minority were party members in the prewar period. The major traditional cultural and scientific institutions, such as the Bolshoi Theater and the Academy of Sciences, were particularly favored, as were members of the Unions of Soviet Writers, Composers, Architects, and so on. Material rewards and acclaim were heaped on the chess players, pianists, and violinists who won international competitions, as well as the engineers associated with high-profile construction projects and the aviators who broke long-distance flying records.

The pejorative terms "bourgeois specialist" and "bourgeois intelligentsia" dropped out of use after the Cultural Revolution. But this was not the most significant change in nomenclature. The term "intelligentsia," historically resonant and used with pride within the group itself, not only came back into favor but was also appropriated by Stalin in his analysis of the basic class composition of Soviet socialist society in 1936.[10] Stalin's comments and the new usage of the term led to several remarkable developments. In the first place, Stalin identified the intelligentsia as one of the three basic corporate entities of Soviet society, the others being the working class and the peasantry.[11] Although he spoke of the three groups as having equal rights, it was not long before Soviet public and popular usage arranged them in the natural hierarchical order, with the intelligentsia at the top. In the second place, "the intelligentsia" as it was now defined was a much broader group than it had been earlier,[12] including not only the old intelligentsia and the newly risen *vydvizhentsy* but also, remarkably, the entire corpus of Communist administrative and managerial cadres. Thus Stalin and all his Politburo colleagues were now (if they had not been before) officially members of the intelligentsia. The word "intelligentsia" had unmistakably become a Soviet synonym for "elite."

Undoubtedly the old intelligentsia resented Stalin's appropriation of its name, believing that the inclusion of the *vydvizhentsy* debased the concept and dismissing the inclusion of Communist officialdom as simply ridiculous and inappropriate. From a more detached perspective, however, it is hard to imagine a more eloquent symbolic gesture of rapprochement with culture from the side of power. Battered and intimidated as the intelligentsia was in the Stalin era, the outcome of the great *"Kto kogo?"* conflict between Communists and the intelligentsia was by no means clear-cut: the intelligentsia had lost freedom and self-respect along the way, though it had won the battle of culture, while the Communists had lost confidence in the relevance of Communism to culture, though it had won the battle of power. To be sure, the two sides agreed to call it a victory for the party, but any other public verdict would have been inconceivable. Indeed, it could be argued that the Communists' determination to claim victory was equaled only by the intelligentsia's determination to concede it and claim the martyr's crown.

(1991)

[10] I. V. Stalin, "O proekte konstitutsii Soiuza SSR: Doklad na Chrezvychainom VIII Vsesoiuznom syezde Sovetov (25 noiabria 1936 g.)," in his *Sochineniia*, ed. McNeal, 1:142–46, 168–70.

[11] Both workers and peasants were "classes" in Stalin's terminology, while the intelligentsia was a "stratum" (*prosloika*).

[12] Just how broad depended on the context. For statistical purposes, white-collar clerical workers were sometimes included in the intelligentsia category in the 1930s. In common and even official usage, however, they continued to be called *sluzhashchie* (employees) and were treated as a social group that was quite distinct from the intelligentsia.

CHAPTER 2

The Bolsheviks' Dilemma: The Class Issue in Party Politics and Culture

The Bolsheviks' dilemma had to do with proletarian identity. In their own eyes, before and during 1917, their party was the vanguard of the proletariat. During the decades of struggle with tsarism, this self-image had always been questionable: the party was led by Marxist intellectuals who believed in the working class but had no real reason to believe that the working class believed in them. But in 1917 for a few crucial months the image corresponded with reality. To the astonishment and joy of the Bolshevik Old Guard, the Bolshevik Party became the standard-bearer for a workers' and soldiers' revolution.

In October 1917 the Bolsheviks seized power in Petrograd and established a "dictatorship of the proletariat." But it turned out that the working class was volatile and even fickle in its loyalties. Within six months of taking power, the new Bolshevik rulers were experiencing problems with the working class that were similar in kind if not in degree to those of previous governments. The Bolsheviks' commitment to the proletariat, it appeared, was not an absolute guarantee of reciprocal proletarian commitment to the Bolsheviks. As rulers in a time of national crisis, the Bolsheviks were bound to take actions that would disappoint or alienate their working-class constituency. They therefore had either to find new ways of demonstrating their right to the status of vanguard of the proletariat or to devise a new justification of their right to rule. Their dilemma as a revolutionary ruling party was a dilemma of identity: to be or not to be proletarian—and, if to be proletarian, how.

The mirage of class

The Bolsheviks were Marxists, and class analysis was their basic tool for understanding Russian society and politics. They believed Russia had entered the capitalist phase in the last prewar decades, so that the major protagonists in the political struggle of 1917 were the capitalist bourgeoisie and the industrial proletariat. The maturity of the Russian proletariat—that is, its character as an urban class, divorced from the land and separated from the peasantry by a distinctive proletarian consciousness—was an article of faith for the Bolsheviks. Without a mature proletariat, there could be no successful proletarian revolution.

The irony of the situation in the Bolsheviks' first years of power was that Marxist class analysis proved so inappropriate to Russian social reality. By comparison with Western Europe (the model for the Marxist analysis), Russia's class structure had been weak and undeveloped even in 1914. Its capitalist bourgeoisie emerged late, and remained under the shadow of the state on the one hand and of foreign capitalist investors in Russian industry on the other. Its urban working class retained ties to the peasantry in the early twentieth century, though the strength and significance of those ties was a matter of dispute. Its urban petty bourgeoisie was a shadowy class, conceptualized by Russian social observers mainly as a target for contemptuous abuse. The peasantry was still traditional, showing only the first signs of the class differentiation that the Marxists predicted and that the tsarist government's prewar agrarian reforms were supposed to encourage.

This weak class structure crumbled under the impact of war, revolution, and civil war. The old upper classes (landowning and service nobility, capitalist bourgeoisie) were destroyed by revolutionary expropriation, peasant land seizures, and emigration. The merchant, shopkeeping, and small manufacturing middle classes were put out of business under War Communism. The peasantry, reasserting the traditional communal organization, dragged the Stolypin "separators" back into the village, conducted an egalitarian redistribution of land, and, for the time being, eliminated the incipient differentiation of the late imperial period.

The collapse of the old upper classes was so thorough that the new rulers faced no significant threat from "the class enemy." The Bol-

sheviks were thus left in an awkward situation, for revolutionary regimes precariously balanced in power need rhetorical enemies. Of
Russia's old elites, only the intelligentsia (a professional bourgeoisie,
in Marxist terms) survived, despite the privations of War Communism and significant losses through emigration, as a coherent social
group. The Bolsheviks turned it into a surrogate bourgeoisie for rhetorical purposes—the surviving symbol of the old world and its exploitation, privileges, and injustices. For the first decade of Soviet
power, members of the intelligentsia were known, insultingly, as
"bourgeois specialists."[1]

For the Bolsheviks, the appalling aspect of postrevolutionary social disintegration was that it extended to the Bolsheviks' "own"
class, the industrial proletariat. At the beginning of 1917, Russia's
industrial working class (including workers in the non-Russian regions of the empire) was about 3.5 million strong, with an additional
million or so railroad workers.[2] These 4 to 5 million people represented a tiny fraction of Russia's total population (around 144 million), but they accounted for about one-fifth of the urban population—not an insignificant proportion. In 1917, moreover, 7 million
men were in the Imperial Army, most of them conscripted for the
European war. The Bolsheviks, and indeed other Marxists of the
time, counted the soldiers as proletarians, whose class consciousness
(regardless of social origins) had been forged through service in the
armed forces and exploitation by the officer corps. In fact, the Bolsheviks and the October Revolution drew much of their support from
soldiers and sailors.

The industrial working class began to disintegrate in 1918 because
factories had closed and hunger stalked the towns. Many workers
left the towns and went back to their native villages. There, it suddenly became clear, they not only retained close family ties but were
often still considered commune members by other peasants and received allotments in the land distribution. Perhaps a million workers
turned back into peasants for the duration of the Civil War,[3] con-
founding Bolshevik assumptions about the maturity of the working
class. In addition, Red Army mobilization and assignment of workers

---

[1] The term "bourgeois" was as pejorative to the intelligentsia (to whom it connoted
philistinism, vulgarity, and materialism) as it was to the Bolsheviks. Moreover, the
intelligentsia had radical traditions (as witness their prominence in the Bolshevik
leadership), regarded themselves as "above class," and considered themselves to be
linked not by professionalism (as the word "specialist" suggests) but by moral commitment and critical thinking.

[2] E. G. Gimpelson, *Sovetskii rabochii klass, 1918–20* (Moscow, 1974), pp. 80–81.

[3] V. M. Selunskaia, "Rukovodiashchaia rol' rabochego klassa v sotsialisticheskoi revoliutsii v derevne 1918 g.," *Voprosy istorii*, 1958 no. 3, p. 10.

to "cadre" jobs as organizers and administrators removed hundreds of thousands of workers from factories and mines; and the malfunctioning of industry forced many workers who remained to turn their hands and the factories' lathes to small-scale private enterprise for the black market.

By the end of the Civil War, the total number of industrial workers in Russia had dropped to just over one million—a third of what it had been in 1917.[4] There were still, to be sure, 5.5 million "proletarians" (including half a million former workers) serving in the Red Army;[5] but as the Civil War drew to a close, that proletarian bastion was also due to crumble through demobilization. For the Bolsheviks, the situation was ominous and extraordinary. Against the odds, they had made a workers' revolution. Then, in the hour of victory, the Russian proletariat had disappeared, leaving only its vanguard, like the smile of the Cheshire cat, behind.

"Fantasies of proletarian culture"

In cultural matters, the historic relation of intellectuals to workers in the Bolshevik Party was one of tutelage. The Old Bolshevik intellectuals had established their earliest connection with actual workers through adult education classes in factory districts, and saw themselves not just as revolutionaries but as enlighteners of the people. One of the great battles of the Bolshevik prerevolutionary emigration had been over an émigré party school for workers.[6] This quarrel provoked the 1909 break between Lenin and the Vpered (Forward) group, which included the philosopher Aleksandr Bogdanov and the litterateur and future commissar of enlightenment, Lunacharsky.

In the relationship of teachers and taught, the assumption is that the teachers possess a higher culture, which the students need and wish to acquire. That was the view of Bolsheviks and other Russian Marxist intellectuals for all practical purposes; and it was a matter of

---

[4] A. G. Rashin, "Dinamika promyshlennykh kadrov SSSR v 1917–1958 gg.," in *Izmeneniia v chislennosti i sostave sovetskogo rabochego klassa* (Moscow, 1961), p. 9.

[5] Gimpelson, *Sovetskii rabochii klass*, p. 37.

[6] The issue was the Capri school, organized for Russian revolutionary worker students in 1909 by Bogdanov and Lunacharsky, and opposed by Lenin (then in Paris) because of his philosophical differences with Bogdanov. Thirteen workers, at least one a police spy, were smuggled with great difficulty and expense out of Russia to attend the school; five were ultimately won over to Lenin's side. For an entertaining account of this storm in a teacup, see S. Livshits, "Kapriiskaia partiinaia shkola (1909 g.)," *Proletarskaia revoliutsiia*, 1924, no. 6 (29), pp. 33–74.

pride when their working-class students acquired so much love of learning and the higher culture that they became "worker-intellectuals." But a complication arose out of Marxist theory. In Marxist terms, culture is not a classless phenomenon: each class generates its own culture, and the culture of the ruling class has hegemony in the society as a whole. Thus Russia's Marxist intellectuals shared in the aristocratic-bourgeois culture that was dominant in the society that reared them. The proletariat was presumably developing its own class culture, which would one day supersede that of the bourgeoisie.

In mid-1917 a number of the former Vperedists created an organization to further the development of proletarian culture, Proletkult. (About the same time, some of them, including Lunacharsky but not Bogdanov, rejoined the Bolshevik Party.) The basic theoretical premise of Proletkult was that the working class must spontaneously develop its own culture, distinct from the culture of the formerly dominant bourgeoisie. This apparently simple concept turned out to be extremely problematic. In the first place, why were intellectuals setting up this organization, if the aim was spontaneous development of proletarian culture? In the second place, what was true proletarian culture, and how would it be recognized? In the third place, what was the proper relationship between Proletkult, aspiring to be the cultural organization of the proletariat, and the Bolshevik Party and Soviet state, claiming to represent the proletariat in the political sphere?

To the first question—the role of intellectuals in Proletkult—there was basically no satisfactory answer. Although the idea was seemingly incompatible with their theories on the class nature of culture, the Proletkult intellectuals took it for granted that workers were comparatively uncultured on some universal, classless scale of cultural achievement. Intellectuals, who were higher on the cultural scale, therefore had something to offer.[7] In practical terms, no doubt, the answer was that intellectuals like to teach, and socialist intellectuals like to teach workers. Furthermore, as Nadezhda Krupskaia pointed out, Proletkult (which was well funded by a variety of Soviet government and other institutional sources) was a haven for intellectuals who needed jobs—particularly, she claimed, socialist intellectuals with anti-Bolshevik leanings.[8]

The determination of what proletarian culture was presented simi-

---

[7] The Proletkultist V. Kunavin wrote that Proletkult, like the Bolshevik Party in its different sphere, based itself on the proletarian vanguard, "the more cultured and more advanced stratum" of the working class. Unfortunately, "as is well known, our proletariat stands on a rather low level of development in a cultural sense" (*Proletarskaia kul'tura*, 1920 no. 17–19, p. 74).

[8] Protocol of meeting of State Commission on Education, 13 April 1918, in *Voprosy literatury*, 1968 no. 1, p. 120.

lar problems. All Marxist intellectuals agreed, without even thinking about it, that proletarian culture had little or nothing to do with observable popular lower-class habits and cultural tastes. "Vulgar," "tasteless," or "trivial" culture was obviously not proletarian;[9] and if workers liked it, obviously they had been infected with petty-bourgeois attitudes. Religion, similarly, was by definition not part of proletarian culture, and if workers put up icons in the house, that was not part of their real culture but a manifestation of peasant superstition that had not yet been outlived.

For all Bolsheviks, not just Proletkultists, proletarian consciousness—the wellspring of proletarian culture—was an object of reverence, not fully susceptible to empirical investigation. "Proletarian consciousness" was defined in tautologies. What the Bolsheviks (and other Marxist intellectuals) meant by the term the consciousness of a "conscious" worker; and a "conscious" worker was a worker who fitted the intellectuals' idea of what a worker ought to be. Pragmatically, from the Bolshevik standpoint, the most "conscious" workers in 1917 were those who were revolutionary. (After that date, as we shall see, the question became more complicated.) Emotionally, the Bolsheviks associated proletarian consciousness with toughmindedness (*tverdost'*), which was often favorably contrasted to the intelligentsia's softness (*miagkost'*).

Bogdanov, probably the most influential Proletkult theorist, identified the dominant characteristics of proletarian culture as collectivism and the unity of "physical" and "spiritual" elements;[10] and he evidently accepted the idea, widely current in Proletkult, that Proletkult's purpose was to be a "laboratory" for the development of proletarian culture. Others objected to the laboratory concept and argued that proletarian culture was something that "grows in the struggle with bourgeois culture," in the environment of the "revolutionary, political, and economic struggle and the organization of a new society."[11]

The question of what proletarian culture was received no definitive answer during the Civil War period, despite the flourishing (as long as state subsidy continued) of theater workshops, studios, literary circles, and adult education classes under Proletkult auspices.

[9] See Jeffrey Brooks, "Competing Modes of Popular Discourse: Individualism and Class Consciousness in the Russian Print Media, 1880–1928," in *Culture et révolution*, ed. Marc Ferro and Sheila Fitzpatrick, pp. 71–81 (Paris, 1989).

[10] A. A. Bogdanov, "Puti proletarskogo tvorchestva (Tezisy)," *Proletarskaia kul'tura*, 1920 no. 15–16, p. 50.

[11] *Proletarskaia kul'tura*, 1920 nos. 17–19, p. 76. This view, reported as an unattributed dissenting one at the Proletkult congress, foreshadows the emphasis on class struggle and hostility to bourgeois cultural specialists later characteristic of RAPP, the Russian Association of Proletarian Writers.

For the sad truth was that those who organized the circles and taught the classes were not proletarian, and neither, in many cases, were their students. As a Proletkult spokesman commented in 1920, Proletkult had to draw in office workers and peasants because the real proletarians had disappeared—some to responsible cadre positions, some to the front with the Red Army, and others back to the villages.[12]

The third thorny problem of Proletkult was its relation to the Soviet state and the Bolshevik Party. Proletkult claimed autonomy in the cultural sphere, rejecting outright the idea of subordination to any state institution, and more cautiously (on the part of its Bolshevik members) asserting autonomy on cultural questions vis-à-vis the Bolshevik Party, whose sphere was defined as political. This stance created problems with the Soviet Commissariat of Enlightenment, headed by Lunacharsky, and even greater problems with Lenin and the Bolshevik Central Committee.[13]

Lenin thought proletarian culture was a fantasy and Proletkult an organization where futurists, idealists, and other undesirable bourgeois artists and intellectuals addled the minds of workers who needed basic education and culture ("culture," for Lenin, being the opposite of "beskul'tur'e," or lack of culture). Part of Lenin's problem with Proletkult was Bogdanov, a past and perhaps future political rival who might use it as an organizational base. Another political problem was Proletkult's link with left Communism and its possible connection to workers' opposition movements inside the Bolshevik Party.[14] But, even apart from politics, Lenin regarded the whole enterprise with contempt and irritation.

"Proletarian culture = Communism. . . . Are we all agreed on that?" he wrote testily to Bukharin, a Proletkult supporter, during the Politburo meeting that discussed Proletkult in October 1920.[15] At an adult education congress in 1919 attended by many Proletkultists, he argued vigorously that "the basic task of 'proletarian culture' is proletarian organization," meaning acquisition of the skills necessary to run the country and save the Revolution. This task was urgent and

[12] Kunavin, in Proletarskaia kul'tura, 1920 no. 17–19, p. 74.

[13] See Sheila Fitzpatrick, The Commissariat of Enlightenment: Soviet Organization of Education and the Arts under Lunacharsky, October 1917–1921 (New York, 1971), chap. 5; V. V. Gorbunov, "Bor'ba V. I. Lenina s separatistskimi ustremleniiami Proletkul'ta," Voprosy istorii KPSS, 1958 no. 1, pp. 29–39.

[14] Soviet historians suggest such a connection existed, but cite only the manifesto "My—kollektivisty," composed by "an underground intelligentsia group of Bogdanov's adherents" in the spirit of the banned Workers' Opposition, and circulated at the Proletkult's second congress in November 1921. E. V. Primerov, Bor'ba partii za leninskoe edinstvo svoikh riadov (1921–1924) (Na materialakh partorganizatsii krupneishikh promyshlennykh tsentrov strany) (Lvov, 1979), pp. 134–35.

[15] Cited in Gorbunov, "Bor'ba V. I. Lenina," p. 30.

overwhelming. "That is why I regard all intellectual fantasies of 'proletarian culture' with such ruthless hostility."[16]

Class and party

Within the Bolshevik Party, the two traditional social groups were workers and intellectuals, the latter often generically referred to as "students" by the workers. The workers came from the factory, the students from institutions of higher education. But even in the prerevolutionary party, the terms did not necessarily indicate present occupation. It was common for workers to be fired from their jobs for political activity, and sometimes to be banned from future employment in factories. It was even more common for students to be expelled from university, technical college, or seminary, and those who were expelled rarely had an opportunity to return to their studies (unless they went abroad to a European university). A proportion of the fired workers and expelled students became full-time, professional revolutionaries by occupation, but they were still regarded in party circles as either "workers" or "intellectuals" by social class.

At the time of the February Revolution, "workers" (that is, persons who were workers by occupation, or had been until they were removed from the factory by arrest, revolutionary activity, or military draft) constituted about 60 percent of Bolshevik Party members; and almost all the rest were intellectuals, students, and other white-collar people.[17] The same ratio of two workers to every intellectual or white-collar person continued to hold through the large party enrollments of 1917, but for the first time in 1917 a significant number of new party recruits (12 percent) were peasants, obviously coming in from the Imperial Army. Worker recruitment continued during the Civil War, but peasant recruitment (now via the Red Army) rose every year in both absolute and proportional terms, and white-collar recruitment was also substantial in 1919–1920.[18]

By the end of the Civil War, in a party that was now over half a

---

[16] V. I. Lenin, *Polnoe sobranie sochinenii*, 5th ed., 55 vols. (Moscow, 1958–1965), 38:368–69.

[17] This is the official Soviet figure (see T. H. Rigby, *Communist Party Membership in the U.S.S.R., 1917–1967* [Princeton, 1968], p. 85), and it appears to be confirmed by more reliable data from the 1922 party census, which show that, of those who were party members in 1922 and entered the party before 1917, 63% were workers and 31% intelligentsia and white-collar people: *Vserossiiskaia perepis' chlenov R.K.P., 1922 goda*, vyp. 4 (Moscow, 1923), p. 27.

[18] *Vserossiiskaia perepis'*, p. 27. The white-collar category includes intellectuals (professionals), but by all accounts most of the new white-collar recruits were office workers.

million strong, only a little over 40 percent of members were classified as workers, with the rest of the membership more or less equally
divided between peasants and white-collar people.[19] But a new complication had to be taken into account when one assessed the social
composition of the party: large numbers of its members no longer
engaged in the occupations they had had in 1917, typically because
they had become cadres, whose new occupation (not necessarily recognized as permanent in 1921) was management and administration.
It was the party's policy to use "our own proletarian executants" to
run the country, Grigorii Zinoviev said in 1919, citing Lenin's "Can
the Bolsheviks Retain State Power?" This was the way to make sure
that the new "directing stratum" did not become "a service intelligentsia of Soviet *chinovniki* [functionaries]" but remained proletarian.[20]

Intellectuals predominated in the party leadership, in contrast to
the membership of the party as a whole. At the Sixth Party Congress
in August 1917, the delegates elected a Central Committee of twenty-
one full members: two workers, one peasant, and eighteen intellectuals.[21] The Bolshevik intellectuals, characteristically from privileged
backgrounds, were men of letters rather than professionals,[22] and
many of them had spent years in emigration under the tsar. About
half the intellectuals in the party leadership were Russian; about a
third were Jewish.[23] In general, the upper echelon of the party was

[19] Rigby, *Communist Party Membership*, pp. 52 and 84.
[20] Organizational Report, *VIII s"ezd RKP(b): Mart 1919 goda. Protokoly* (Moscow,
1959), p. 281.
[21] Central Committee as listed in Robert V. Daniels, *The Conscience of the Revolution: Communist Opposition in Soviet Russia* (New York, 1969), app. II; biographical
data from *Entsiklopedicheskii slovar' Russkogo Bibliograficheskogo Instituta Granat*,
7th ed. (Moscow, 1927–9), vol. 41 ("Deiateli SSSR i Oktiabr'skoi Revoliutsii"); *Who
Was Who in the USSR*, compiled by the Institute for the Study of the USSR, Munich
(Metuchen, N.J., 1972); and other sources. Fifteen of the eighteen intellectuals had
entered, though not always graduated from, universities or higher technical schools.
The remaining three (Ia. A. Berzin, Iakov Sverdlov, Stalin), who were of lower social
origin, had gone to seminaries or middle schools.
[22] Of fifty-one intelligentsia delegates to the Sixth Congress, twenty (including
Lenin) gave their profession as *literary*, twelve as teachers, seven as medical professionals, six as lawyers, four as statisticians, and two as technicians (*tekhniki*). Three
others not classified as "intelligentsia" listed their profession as "officer, Junker"
(*Shestoi s"ezd, RSDRP [bol'shevikov], avgust 1917 g.: Protokoly* [Moscow, 1958], p.
274).
[23] In the Central Committee elected in August 1917, ten of twenty-one members
were Russian, six Jewish, two Latvian, and one each Polish, Georgian, and Armenian;
and in the Central Committee elected in March 1921, of twenty-four full members,
fourteen were Russian, five Jewish, two Latvian, two Georgian, and one Polish. The
working-class members of the Central Committee were more likely than the intellectuals to be Russian and less likely to be Jewish: of the CC's "workers" in 1921, 80%

both more Jewish and less Russian than the party membership as a whole in the Civil War years.[24]

More workers came into the Central Committee during the Civil War—that is, more *former* workers, since all had been professional revolutionaries before 1917, and all were currently full-time party, soviet, or trade union officials.[25] But the proportion of workers diminished sharply at the top of the party hierarchy. Workers constituted 42 percent of full Central Committee members in 1921 but only 33 percent of the members and candidate members of the superior party bureaus. And in the Politburo, with eight full and candidate members, only one had been a worker and the rest were all intellectuals.[26]

Class tensions within the party

The Civil War was the great period of factional struggle in Bolshevik history. The main issues under debate were the Brest peace, the use of "bourgeois specialists" in the Red Army and elsewhere, "appointmentism,"[27] labor conscription, and the status of trade unions. The main factions involved—apart from the dominant Leninist faction—were the Left Communists in 1918, the Military Opposition in 1919, and the Democratic Centralists, Workers' Opposition, and Trotsky's faction in 1920–1921. The period of overt factional struggle ended at the Tenth Party Congress in 1921, when Lenin's faction pushed through a resolution "on party unity" banning factions.

Western historians have generally interpreted the whole episode of factions as a struggle between the principle of party democracy on

---

were Russian and none Jewish; of its intellectuals, 43% were Russian and 36% Jewish (calculated from sources cited in n. 21, above).

[24] Of all party members in 1922, 72% were Russian, 7% Ukrainian and Belorussian, and 5% Jewish (*Sotsial'nyi i natsional'nyi sostav VKP[b]* [Moscow, 1927], p. 114). Cf. full members of the Central Committee in January 1922, of whom 58% were Russian and 21% Jewish (calculated from sources cited in n. 21, above.)

[25] Of twenty-four full members of the Central Committee elected at the Tenth Congress in the spring of 1921, ten (42%) were workers and fourteen were intellectuals (calculated from sources cited in n. 21, above). All delegates to the Ninth Party Congress (March–April 1920), including the "worker" group, were on full-time party (35%) or soviet (65%) work (*Deviatyi s"ezd RKP[b], mart-aprel' 1920 g.: Protokoly* [Moscow, 1960], pp. 484–86).

[26] Party bureaus = Politburo, Orgburo, and Secretariat (fifteen persons in all) (calculated from sources cited in n. 21, above).

[27] The practice of filling responsible party positions by appointment (strictly speaking, nomination by the Central Committee's Secretariat in Moscow) rather than by local election.

the one hand and the Leninist imperative of authoritarian centraliza-
tion on the other.[28] But this emphasis on the primacy of the democratic issue may reflect the historians' values more accurately than it
does the Bolsheviks'. For Bolsheviks, party democracy and centraliz-
ation of authority were important, but class issues were the ones that
aroused real passion. With the exception of the Brest peace debate,
all the factional discussions of the Civil War period involved a class
issue, and the last great factional struggle—the three-cornered fight
between Lenin's faction, Trotsky's faction and the Workers' Opposition in 1920–1921—amounted to a virtual class confrontation within
the party.

The use of bourgeois specialists was the first class issue that surfaced in the factional struggles. It began with the Left Communists,
mainly intellectuals filled with revolutionary idealism and intolerant
of compromise, who questioned the use of specialists in the economy. The issue was picked up by the Military Opposition (probably
less intellectual and more lower class, though evidence is scanty),
which violently attacked Trotsky's policy of giving Red Army com-
mands to former tsarist officers.

By 1920, however, the bourgeois specialist issue was primarily associated with the Workers' Opposition, and party opinion seemed to
be dividing very much on class lines. Bolshevik intellectuals generally thought it was both necessary and possible to work with the
specialists. Working-class Bolsheviks, however, tended to be very
suspicious of the specialists, stressing their past membership in the
privileged classes and doubting their loyalty to the Soviet regime. At
its most extreme, this position was known in Social Democratic circles as the heresy of *makhaevshchina*—a creed of total repudiation
of intellectuals and their contribution to the revolutionary movement
drawn from the turn-of-the-century writings of the Polish socialist
Jan Machajski.

In September 1919 Zinoviev referred to "a dissatisfaction" of
"broad dimensions" with the leadership's policy of using bourgeois
specialists. A worker Bolshevik put it more bluntly: "Comrades, people say that I hate specialists. Yes, that's true, and I'll go to my grave
hating them. . . . We have to hold them in a grip of iron, the way they
used to hold us."[29] According to the trade union leader Tomskii, this
attitude was common in the working class, so that Bolsheviks had a

---

[28] See, for example, Daniels, *Conscience of the Revolution*, and Leonard Schapiro,
*The Origin of the Communist Autocracy: Political Opposition in the Soviet State:
First Phase, 1917–1922* (Cambridge, Mass., 1955).

[29] *IX konferentsiia RKP(b), Sentiabr' 1920 goda: Protokoly* (Moscow, 1972), pp. 143,
187.

hard time defending party policy on specialists before factory audiences:

> If Communists at party meetings, and even at nonparty meetings, speak against specialists, that means following the line of least resistance. Because of course the mood of the masses—as a result of hunger, aspirations to equality at any cost—has been against the specialists. The specialist lives better, he is paid better; the specialist gives orders, makes demands; the specialist is an alien entity, the specialist did not make the October Revolution. That is how people evaluate the specialists.[30]

Working-class Bolsheviks sometimes hinted that the party's policy on specialists reflected a class bias, or unconscious sense of class solidarity with the bourgeois specialists on the part of the intellectuals in the party leadership. Timofei Sapronov, a worker Bolshevik in the Democratic Centralist group, indicated this suspicion in a harsh exchange with Aleksei Rykov, an intellectual who was then chairman of the Vesenkha, the government agency responsible for managerial appointments in industry. From Sapronov's standpoint, bourgeois specialists were members of the old privileged classes, potential counterrevolutionaries. He complained that now, "with a mandate from Vesenkha," they were coming back to the factories as managers and oppressing the workers just as they used to do. When Rykov accused him of "hating" the specialists, Sapronov counterattacked:

> Yes, I have that sin. But Comrade Rykov also has a sin, and from a proletarian point of view it is a worse sin. Comrade Rykov loves the *spetsy* too much and gives them too much scope, and those privileges that Comrade Rykov gives the *spetsy* are too blatantly obvious to the workers. . . . Basically there is a lot to reproach Rykov for—giving *spetsy* too large rations, colossal salaries, and so on.[31]

Class tensions within the Bolshevik Party were most acute in 1920–1921, the heyday of the Workers' Opposition. One party intellectual, a member of the Democratic Centralist faction (which was generally sympathetic to the Workers' Opposition), complained that "the 'Workers' Opposition' is busy with intelligentsia baiting."[32] The

---

[30] *XI s"ezd RKP(b), Mart–aprel' 1922 g.: Stenograficheskii otchet* (Moscow, 1961), p. 279.

[31] *IX konferentsiia*, p. 193.

[32] R. Rafail, *Desiatyi s"ezd RKP(b), Mart 1921 g.: Stenograficheskii otchet* (Moscow,

forthcoming party purge became the focus of bitter arguments, because many working-class Bolsheviks wanted to make class the major criterion, and the party leadership was less enthusiastic.[33]

According to Iaroslavskii, the Workers' Opposition wanted to use the party purge to "get rid of the intelligentsia. . . . Under the pretext of making the party healthy, they are even suggesting that we draw up special lists of party members, where the [social] genealogy of each is shown in detail; on the basis of this genealogy we will now be able to purge our party." Moreover, he added, the Oppositionists were representing their disagreements with the party leadership as a class conflict: Bolshevik working class against Bolshevik intelligentsia. They regarded worker Bolsheviks who supported Lenin's faction as traitors to their class.[34]

Anti-semitic undertones could be heard in this "intelligentsia baiting," or so Iaroslavskii and Rafail, both Jewish intellectuals, implied. Rafail said the Workers' Opposition blamed everything on intellectuals in the same way people used to blame it on "the Yids." To Iaroslavskii it sounded as if some "provincial comrades" were leaning toward adoption of "Beat up the intellectuals!" as a slogan.[35] The phrase *"Bei intelligentov!"* was clearly intended to recall the pogrom rallying call, *"Bei zhidov!"*

It was not only at the center that class tension and class divisions within the party were evident. The same phenomenon was observed in the provincial party organizations in 1920–1921. N. N. Krestinskii, the party secretary in 1921, reported a series of local conflicts, many of which "took the form of a struggle between the working-class segment of various gubkoms [district committees] and the

---

1963), p. 274. Rafail used the term *intelligentoedstvo*, an impromptu variant of the more familiar *spetseedstvo*, which referred only to harassment of the bourgeois specialists.

[33] According to guidelines published in *Pravda*, 30 June 1921, the purge commissions should look particularly carefully at party members who had formerly belonged to other political parties or held official positions under the old regime or the Provisional Government, and at those who were white-collar employees of Soviet institutions (a group suspected of "careerist" reasons for party membership) or held Soviet offices "linked with some sort of privileges." In implementation, the purge hit hardest on peasants (45% of those expelled) and then white-collar employees (35%); only 20% of those expelled were classified as workers (V. M. Molotov, Organizational Report, in *XI s"ezd*, p. 47).

[34] *XI s"ezd*, p. 105. The Workers' Oppositionist Perepechko similarly reported that workers at the Moscow power station had demanded that the party be purged of the intelligentsia (ibid., p. 90).

[35] *Desiatyi s"ezd*, pp. 274, 263. Both Iaroslavskii and Rafail seem to be using Aesopian language, and there are signs that the text has been edited at points where the issue of anti-Semitism is raised.

intelligentsia segment."[36] Sometimes these conflicts were inflamed by Moscow's appointment of an "outsider" to head the local party organization, as in Tula and Nizhny Novgorod,[37] but the danger seems to have been greatest when Moscow's appointee was an intellectual and the local committee strongly working class. In other cases, the local party organization split along class lines in a situation of intense competition with the Mensheviks for local working-class support.[38] In Petrograd, working-class Bolsheviks criticized Zinoviev for his authoritarian rule, and he denounced them in his turn as "Makhaevists and fourth-rate Workers' Oppositionists."[39]

Class tensions were almost always present in Bolshevik debates about authority in the Civil War period. Critics of the leadership alleged that the party was becoming divided into two groups: the bosses (party leaders, officeholders, "commissars") and the rank and file.[40] As we have already noted, the leadership and party elite contained a disproportionate number of intellectuals, while the party's rank and file was mainly lower class. This *class* division was so much stressed by the Workers' Opposition that it was at times difficult to judge whether the Oppositionists were objecting primarily to the existence of an elite group in the party per se or to the existence of an elite group in which working-class Bolsheviks were inadequately represented.

Workers' Oppositionists reportedly complained that "there are intellectuals everywhere you look" in the party, and regarded the party's Central Committee and bureaus (where intellectuals predominated) as the root of all evil.[41] They said that the Bolshevik Party had become "a nonproletarian party [that] does not give power to the workers," Anastas Mikoyan reported to the party organization in

[36] Ibid., pp. 45–46.

[37] Primerov, *Bor'ba partii*, pp. 99–101. In Tula the conflict arose out of the opposition of local working-class Bolsheviks to the appointment of Zh. Meerzon, an outsider who was Jewish (a former Bundist) and probably an intellectual, as secretary of the gubkom in 1922. Conflict arose in the Nizhny party organization when Molotov was head of the gubernia soviet in 1920. Anastas Mikoyan, his successor as senior, Moscow-appointed Bolshevik in this important industrial city, attributes it to the fact that Molotov, an intellectual, "was weakly linked to [the Bolsheviks in] the working-class districts (his main support came from [the Bolshevik organization in] Gorodskoi raion)" (A. I. Mikoian, *V nachale dvadtsatykh* . . . [Moscow, 1975], p. 25). Later Mikoyan, a lower-class semi-intellectual who, like Stalin, was a member of Lenin's faction in the party struggles, had a long struggle with the Workers' Opposition in Nizhny Novgorod.

[38] E.g., the Mariupol party organization in the Donbass, which in 1922 was split between "the city [gorodskaia] part, where petty-bourgeois elements predominated, and the factory part, where workers predominated" (Primerov, *Bor'ba partii*, p. 108).

[39] Ibid., 77–78.

[40] T. Sapronov, in *IX konferentsiia*, pp. 159–60.

[41] *Desiatyi s"ezd*, p. 274.

Nizhny Novgorod in 1922. This complaint could be understood in various ways, but Mikoyan interpreted it as an accusation that there were not enough working-class Bolsheviks among the party cadres. The charge was unfounded, he said: in Nizhny, "workers" held 60 percent of the senior cadre positions, as against 26 percent held by intellectuals and 14 percent by persons of peasant or white-collar background.[42]

"Vanguard of a nonexistent class"

The Kronstadt revolt in March 1921, erupting while the Tenth Party Congress was in session in nearby Petrograd, became an immediate symbol of crisis in the Revolution. It followed weeks of workers' strikes in Petrograd and scattered disturbances in factories and garrisons in other parts of the country. With the Mensheviks' influence reviving in the working class, the Workers' Opposition challenging the Bolshevik Party leadership, trouble with the unions, and disputes about Proletkult's status, the class issue had come to the fore with a vengeance. Many people, Bolsheviks among them, saw the situation as a parting of the ways between the Bolshevik Party and the working class.

The leadership's response to the crisis was firm. The Kronstadt revolt was subdued by military force, the Workers' Opposition was outlawed by the ban on factions, and within a few months War Communism was abandoned and the New Economic Policy legalized the market. Proletkult, now formally subordinated to the state's Commissariat of Enlightenment, lost most of its state subsidy as a by-product of the New Economic Policy and shrank into insignificance.[43]

Despite their firm actions, the Bolsheviks were stunned and appalled by the turn of events. Their own sense of legitimacy depended on the belief that the working class supported them. Moreover, their analysis of politics indicated that a regime without a base of class support must fall. While publicly denying that Kronstadt was a symbol of rejection by the proletariat, the Bolsheviks inwardly feared that it was.[44] Anguished discussion on the working class and the Bol-

---

[42] Primerov, Bor'ba partii, p. 76. Mikoyan was referring here to the "platform of the 22," an offshoot of the defeated and banned Workers' Opposition.

[43] See Fitzpatrick, Commissariat of Enlightenment, pp. 238–41, 269–70.

[44] The Bolshevik press asserted that the revolt was instigated by "White Guards" and that in any case the Kronstadt sailors, many of whom were conscripted peasants, were not truly proletarian. The latter argument was logical, but it was not a logic that the Bolsheviks had previously followed with regard to the class definition of soldiers and sailors.

sheviks' relationship with it took place within the party in 1921 and 1922. For the first time, some Bolsheviks began to speak slightingly of Russian workers as a class, and to doubt their commitment to the Revolution.

At the Tenth Party Congress, the Workers' Oppositionist Iurii Milonov stated that a gulf was opening between the working class and "a certain section of our Party" (presumably the intellectuals of the Leninist faction). He warned that "our Party is ceasing to be a workers' party," and sketched an alarming picture of the perils before it:

> Once the peasantry is not with us, once the working class is falling under the influence of various petty-bourgeois anarchist elements and tending to move away from us, what can the Communist Party now depend on? . . . An awful situation has been created; we find ourselves above an abyss, between the working class, which is infected with petty-bourgeois prejudices, and the peasantry, which is petty-bourgeois in essence; [and] it is impossible to depend solely on the soviet and party bureaucracy.[45]

The image of the abyss was vivid to all his Marxist listeners. Nevertheless, not all Bolsheviks wanted to dwell on it, and the emotions of many were turned against the working class. Unprecedentedly critical and jaundiced remarks were being made by Bolshevik cadres: for example, that "the working class has turned out to be a turncoat [*shkurnik*] in the revolutionary and political struggle," that the proletariat had become "déclassé."[46] Faced with hostile and insubordinate workers, the Bolsheviks were now less inclined to respect their class credentials. The Bolsheviks were becoming increasingly aware of the thin lines that separated peasant from worker and worker from petty bourgeois; and sometimes Bolshevik cadres even set out to make a sociological case against particular working-class groups that offended them. In Tula, for example, Bolshevik investigators of the pro-Menshevik workers at the Armaments Plant gathered data on

[45] *Desiaty s"ezd*, pp. 85, 74. Milonov, working in Samara, had been actively campaigning there against appointmentism and the increasing separation of the party's elite from its rank and file. In August 1920 he had argued publicly in Samara that the Bolsheviks were degenerating "from a party of the ruling proletariat into a party of its administrative stratum, the labour bureaucracy" (Robert Service, *The Bolshevik Party in Revolution: A Study in Organisational Change, 1917–1923* [London, 1979], pp. 141, 146–47).

[46] Milonov, describing the opinion of "some people in the provinces," in *Desiatyi s"ezd*, p. 74; Riazanov, implicitly attributing this opinion to the party leadership, in *XI s"ezd*, pp. 37–38.

their ties with the land and the peasantry on the one hand and their "petty-bourgeois" acquisitiveness and aspirations on the other to demonstrate that they were not true proletarians.[47]

The foremost articulator of this new skepticism about the Russian working class was Lenin, whose extraordinary remarks to the Eleventh Party Congress indicted not only the working class of 1922 but also the working class of 1917—that is, the proletarian cohort that had made the Revolution.

> Very often when people say "workers" they think that means factory proletariat. But it doesn't mean that at all. In Russia, since the war, people who are not proletarian at all have come to the plants and factories. They came to hide from the war, but are our social and economic conditions now really such that real proletarians come to the factories and plants? That is not true. It's true in Marx's terms, but Marx was not writing about Russia but about all capitalism as a whole, starting from the fifteenth century. Over the course of six hundred years it is true, but for present-day Russia it is not true. Often the people coming to the factory are not proletarians but all kinds of accidental elements.[48]

Even for Lenin, with his enormous authority and prestige in the party, this was going too far. Riazanov, an Old Bolshevik intellectual of independent views and moral authority in the party, implicitly rebuked Lenin for repeating "the fashionable attack on workers for being *déclassés*." It was pointless, Riazanov believed, to go into a panic and label the working class as *shkurniki* and *déclassés*.

> After all, we have a dictatorship of the working class—a dictatorship of the proletariat. That not all factory workers are born Communists, and that not all factory workers are workers, we know very well from the classic texts. [Nevertheless,] we must tell ourselves that we must make every effort to ensure that those workers that we still have, who remained in our big enterprises, join the Communist Party."[49]

Shliapnikov, leader of the defeated Workers' Opposition, was even more withering in his response to Lenin's speech: "Vladimir Il'ich said yesterday that the proletariat as a class, in the sense that Marx meant, does not exist. Permit me to congratulate you on being the vanguard of a nonexistent class." Shliapnikov complained of the "very unflattering" remarks about the proletariat—"our own class, of

[47] Primerov, *Bor'ba partii*, pp. 100–101.
[48] *XI s"ezd*, pp. 37–38.
[49] Ibid., p. 80.

which we consider ourselves the vanguard"—that Lenin, Lev Kamenev, and other Bolshevik intellectuals were making. "We need to remember once and for all that we will not have another and 'better' working class, and we have to be satisfied with what we've got," he warned.[50] Despite his dubious standing in the party since the Workers' Opposition was banned, the delegates applauded his remarks.

Conclusion

The political and economic traumas of 1921–1922 left the air thick with spoken and unspoken accusations of betrayal. Embattled Bolshevik cadres were thinking the unthinkable: *The working class has betrayed the Revolution.* Disgruntled workers reversed the accusation: *The Bolsheviks have betrayed the working class.* For the former Workers' Oppositionists, it was not the party but the intellectuals in the party leadership who had betrayed the workers. And others were ready to point out that the Bolsheviks' "proletarian" spokesmen, who had failed to defend the Kronstadt rebels,[51] were not workers at all but cadres—people who had left the working class to become revolutionary bosses.

But in a sense all these accusations were beside the point. Given the context of the party's relationship with the working class, there was no realistic possibility that the Bolsheviks would not betray it. In the first place, they had made an absurd, undeliverable promise to the working class when they talked of a "dictatorship of the proletariat." The oxymoron of a "ruling proletariat," appealing though it might be to dialectical thinkers, was not realizable in the real world. It was a proposition that the Bolshevik intellectuals did not think out carefully in advance, and for good reason.

In the second place, as a result of the spontaneous deconstruction of the industrial proletariat during the Civil War, the Bolsheviks found themselves at least temporarily "the vanguard of a nonexistent class" in 1921. Marx was no guide in this situation, as Lenin indicated in his remarks to the Eleventh Congress. Even Engels' well-known warning about premature seizure of power covered only part of the problem, and failed to suggest a solution acceptable to a regime that had just won a revolutionary civil war.

When one reads the Bolsheviks' debates of the early 1920s, it is

---

[50] Ibid., pp. 103–4.
[51] Paul Avrich, *Kronstadt 1921* (Princeton, 1970), p. 183.

hard to feel that in the short term the Bolsheviks had any real alternative to maintaining the proletarian connection. The party's identity and sense of legitimacy were closely linked to the proletariat.
Moreover, it was the Bolsheviks' firm belief that all political parties,
revolutions, and regimes have a class base. What class other than the
proletariat could the Bolsheviks choose? What historical meaning
had their revolution if it were not proletarian?

Thus the phase of sharp Bolshevik criticism of the working class
was short-lived. By April 1923, when the Twelfth Party Congress met
(with Lenin ill and absent), Kamenev came close to apologizing for
Lenin's harsh remarks a year earlier, and Zinoviev said firmly that
"declassing" was a problem of the past, and a healthy relationship
between party and proletariat had been reestablished.[52] As NEP took
hold, factories went back into production, the industrial work force
expanded, and former workers began to return from the villages to
mines and factories.[53]

In the months after the Twelfth Party Congress, party organizations
in big industrial centers such as Donetsk and Nizhny Novgorod
launched local drives to recruit factory workers into the party.[54] In
January 1924 the Central Committee plenum announced a general
campaign (later known as the "Lenin levy") to enroll hundreds of
thousands of workers from the bench as party members.[55]

The stated objective of this policy was to make workers at the
bench the majority group in the party. This aim was never achieved,
mainly because the policy had a second and partly contradictory objective: to draw the newly enrolled Communist workers out of the
factory and turn them into administrative cadres. The latter objective
was judged to be so urgent and important that, according to the Thirteenth Party Congress's resolution of May 1924, it "cannot be put off

[52] *XI s"ezd,* pp. 161, 37. Kamenev referred to the "accusation" that had surfaced in
precongress discussions that "Comrade Lenin underestimates the forces of the proletariat" and exaggerates its lack of culture. He did not repeat or attempt to defend
Lenin's argument. Note that the text on "exaggeration of lack of culture" appears to be
garbled in the transcription.

[53] On this process, and the appeals to workers who had taken refuge in the village to
come "home" to the factory, see A. I. Vdovin and V. Z. Drobizhev, *Rost rabochego
klassa SSSR, 1917–1940 gg.* (Moscow, 1976), p. 88.

[54] Primerov, *Bor'ba partii,* pp. 186–87.

[55] "O prieme rabochikh ot stanka v partiiu," 31 January 1924, *Pravda,* 1 February
1924. The campaign was named in honor of Lenin because of his death in the month
of its initiation. However, given Lenin's desire in 1922 to restrict enrollment of new
party members, even of workers (see Rigby, *Communist Party Membership,* pp. 102–
3), it is quite possible that he would have opposed the campaign. Of all the party
leaders, he was by far the most cautious on questions of proletarianization.

until some future time."[56] Thus, faced with a choice between having more Communist workers in the factories and more Communist former workers in the apparats, the party firmly opted for the latter. This was how the party of the 1920s set about resolving the Bolshevik dilemma of proletarian identity.

The new approach to proletarian identity (which had its precedents in pre- and immediate postrevolutionary Bolshevik practice) emphasized class origins, not class as measured by current occupation. This approach was partly "genealogical," as Iaroslavskii complained in 1922. Since comparatively few proletarians had proletarian fathers, however, a major indicator used in the 1920s was "class position."[57] This term referred to an individual's basic occupation either in 1917 or (for purposes of party registration) at the time of entry into the party.

Adult mobility between classes—typically from blue-collar to white-collar managerial class or from peasant to industrial working class—was so widespread a phenomenon in the Soviet Union of the 1920s and early 1930s that it was normal to use at least two indicators ("class position" and current occupation) to determine an individual's position in society. "What were you before?" was considered as necessary a question as "What are you?" in the first postrevolutionary decade. Not only did the proletarian credentials of cadres need to be recognized, but members of the old privileged classes, no doubt still hostile to Soviet power, might be hiding their true social identity behind an innocuous current occupation.

The then-and-now components of class identity raised potentially complex theoretical questions about class consciousness and class culture. Fortunately, however, the Bolsheviks kept the argument on a relatively simple level in the 1920s. "Proletarian consciousness," which to the Bolsheviks had meant active support of the revolutionary movement before and during 1917, now meant active involvement in the building of a new socialist society, whether at the factory bench or elsewhere. Thus workers did not lose their proletarian consciousness by leaving the factory bench, as many people had feared earlier.[58]

---

[56] "Ob ocherednykh zadachakh partiinogo stroitel'stva," May 1924, in Kommunisticheskaia Partiia Sovetskogo Soiuza v rezoliutsiiakh i resheniiakh s"ezdov, konferentsii i plenumov TsK, vol. 3 (Moscow, 1970), pp. 46–47.

[57] The great majority of Russian workers, both before and after the war, were the children of either peasants or peasant-workers (the father spent all or part of the year in industrial employment outside the home village).

[58] When Zinoviev spoke in 1919 about using "proletarian executants" to run the country (VIII s"ezd: Protokoly, p. 281), he noted in passing that after six months away

As for culture, a militant cohort of young Communist intellectuals demanded "proletarian hegemony" in culture in the late 1920s.[59] But their problem, like Proletkult's, was that they had no real proletarian culture to offer. Though a Russian working class was reconstituted in the NEP years, it did not generate an identifiable class culture. The latter-day "proletarian" intellectuals had no real roots in the working class, and occupied themselves largely with denunciation of "bourgeois" culture and literary faction fighting during their short period of cultural power.

From the standpoint of "conscious" workers, in any case, proletarian culture was bound to be only a sideshow. The conscious workers of the 1920s cohort were the ones who joined the party during the Lenin levy and, in all probability, shortly thereafter accepted promotion to cadre status (that is, moved upward into a higher social class). Proletarian culture was simply not on the minds of most of this group, not even as a fantasy of intellectuals. Had they known about it, however, it would have had little appeal. They were after real culture, not any ersatz proletarian version. And real culture, after all, was what most Old Bolshevik intellectuals thought workers deserved.

(1988)

---

from the factory, the worker might lose touch with the proletariat. This was a commonly voiced concern at the beginning of the 1920s, but it dropped out of Bolshevik discussions after about 1922.

[59] The most prominent such group was RAPP, the Association of Proletarian Writers. The phenomenon of Cultural Revolution as a whole is discussed in chap. 6.

CHAPTER 3

Professors and
Soviet Power

In the Civil War years almost all professors regarded the new regime with deep hostility.[1] In the provinces reached by the White
armies, the professors simply voted with their feet. Virtually the entire faculty of Perm University fled east as the Red Army approached
Perm in 1919.[2] Of the faculty of Tomsk University, three of thirty-
nine full professors were actually ministers in Admiral Kolchak's
Siberian government.[3] Eighty professors left Kazan with the Czechs
in the autumn of 1918; and both the Kazan and Perm faculties established short-lived universities-in-exile in Tomsk under Kolchak.[4] In
southern Russia, most of the faculty of the former Imperial University of Warsaw (evacuated to Rostov on Don in 1919) retreated with
the White armies in 1920 and took a boat to Constantinople.[5]

Soviet historians attribute this hostility to the bourgeois political
affiliations of the professors; émigré writers ascribed it to the hostile
and provocative actions of the Soviet government. Much can be said
for both views. Many of the professors were Kadets (Constitutional
Democrats), some had been active in politics before October, and

[1] Unless I specify otherwise, the term "professor" is used for the two senior categories of faculty, *professor* and *dotsent*.
[2] *Permskii Gosudarstvennyi Universitet* (Perm, 1966), pp. 22–23.
[3] *Tomskii Gosudarstvennyi Universitet* (Tomsk, 1934), p. 16.
[4] *Krasnoe studenchestvo*, 1927–1928 no. 4–5, p. 118; *Tomskii Gosudarstvennyi
Universitet*, p. 16.
[5] S. E. Belousov, *Ocherki istorii Rostovskogo Universiteta* (Rostov on Don, 1959), p.
163.

some undoubtedly continued covert political activity against the new regime. Yet "bourgeois" political affiliations were not necessarily a barrier to cooperation with the Bolsheviks: S. F. Oldenburg, a former member of the Provisional Government and secretary of the Academy of Sciences, quickly established a working relationship with the new government; and Mikhail Novikov, rector of Moscow University during the Civil War years, seems to have been prevented from doing so mainly by the recalcitrance of his colleagues.

Within the government and the Bolshevik Party, the official policy toward the professors was relatively conciliatory but the rhetoric was often belligerent.[6] In particular Mikhail Pokrovsky, the deputy commissar of enlightenment, went out of his way to offend the sensibilities of the professors. Unlike Lunacharsky, he had no instinctive tact and saw no reason to drop the vicious polemical tone he had always used against liberal academic colleagues just because he was now a powerful figure in the new government. Nor did he disdain the tactic of rhetorically invoking the Cheka to frighten and humiliate the professors.

The most important conflict between the professors and the new regime broke out in Moscow University on the issue of the autonomy of institutions of higher education. Until the autumn of 1920, Narkompros (the People's Commissariat of Enlightenment) and Novikov, the elected rector of the University, were trying to reach an accommodation.[7] They were prevented from doing so, essentially, by the persistence of the Kadet professors in dabbling in anti-Soviet conspiracy (or perhaps simply engaging in anti-Soviet conversation) and the persistence of the Cheka in arresting them. The final hardening of Narkompros's attitude toward university autonomy directly followed the trial in which members of the Kadet "Tactical Center," including the former liberal leader Petr Struve and Professors G. V. Sergievskii, S. P. Melgunov, S. A. Kotliarevskii, M. S. Feldshtein, and N. K. Koltsov, were found guilty of anti-Soviet conspiracy.[8]

The issue of autonomy was formally settled by the new university constitution of 1921.[9] The higher schools were to be directly under Narkompros's control. Narkompros was to appoint the rector, who was president of a governing body of three to five members, and to approve professorial appointments; the governing body appointed

---

[6] On the early relations of the universities and the Soviet government, see Sheila Fitzpatrick, *The Commissariat of Enlightenment* (New York, 1971), chap. 4.

[7] See Novikov's own account in M. M. Novikov, *Ot Moskvy do N'iu-Iorka* (New York, 1952).

[8] N. V. Krylenko, *Sudebnye rechi* (Moscow, 1964), pp. 57–60.

[9] The term "university" is used here and subsequently as a translation of the Soviet acronym "VUZ," meaning institution of higher education.

deans and junior faculty.[10] This arrangement was seen as an infringement of democracy not only by the professors but also (from a quite different point of view) by the Communist students, whose participation in the running of the higher school was now theoretically limited to electing representatives to departmental committees, curriculum commissions, soviets to advise the dean, and so on. Both professors and revolutionary students sincerely believed that democracy required an electoral system that their own group—and no other—could monopolize. Thus Narkompros found itself in the unenviable position of violating "bourgeois" and "revolutionary" democracy at a single stroke.

The formal constitution, however, tells us little about how the higher schools actually operated in the 1920s. In the first place, it gives no sense of the heavy real-life involvement of Communist students in university administration. Narkompros appointed rectors, but their functions were often taken over by Communist students, either on the initiative of the students (who suspected that administration "bureaucrats" might collaborate with the old professors) or because the rectors were too busy to do their jobs. In the Moscow Mining Academy, for example, A. P. Zaveniagin (later a major industrial administrator) served as deputy rector from his freshman year; the rector, I. M. Gubkin, was simultaneously a member of Vesenkha (the Supreme Council of the National Economy) in charge of the oil industry and had little time for the routine administrative tasks of the academy.[11] Communist students who served as school or departmental secretaries, as many of them did, were too busy to study.[12] All through the 1920s party spokesmen complained about this situation, and the agitprop department and other bodies issued dozens of fruitless instructions telling students to keep out of university administration. Bukharin made the point with characteristic sharpness (and some exaggeration) in 1924: "Our Komsomols in the universities often appoint professors and purge students—but look at their academic performance: 80 percent fail. A lot of independence and not the slightest real knowledge . . ."[13]

In the second place, the constitution was silent on the whole question of interference by local party committees and soviets in univer-

[10] *Sobranie uzakonenii i rasporiazhenii rabochego i krest'ianskogo pravitel'stva RSFSR*, 1921 no. 65, art. 486; 1922 no. 43, art. 518.

[11] V. S. Emelianov, *O vremeni, o tovarishchakh, o sebe*, 2d ed. (Moscow, 1970), p. 55.

[12] See *Permskii Gosudarstvennyi Universitet*, p. 31; *Istoriia Leningradskogo Universiteta: 1819–1916. Ocherki* (Leningrad, 1969), p. 268; L. Milkh in *Pravda*, 3 April 1928, p. 4.

[13] *Partiia i vospitanie smeny* (Leningrad, 1924), pp. 122–23.

sity life. Provincial universities were vulnerable to this kind of pressure. Even the more prestigious universities of the capitals were frequently buffeted by conflicts between local authorities who wanted to appoint Marxists to teach the social sciences and professors who tried to rebuff them. (Outside the social sciences, however, it seems that professorial appointments in the universities of the capitals were usually made by the departments and schools concerned, with Narkompros providing more or less automatic ratification.)

From a Soviet standpoint, the old university faculty was as socially and politically alien as the old student body. But it was more difficult to replace, and during NEP the regime made little attempt to replace or even rejuvenate it. Despite the belligerence of *rabfak* students—workers and peasants being prepared for university entrance—and some Communist officials,[14] the official policy was to employ and conciliate "bourgeois specialists," including professors. When the professors of Moscow Higher Technical School (later the Bauman Institute) went on strike in the spring of 1921, after the appointment of an unacceptable governing body, Narkompros and the Politburo jointly revoked the appointment and instructed Communist students at the school to behave less aggressively toward the professors.[15] The next year, when professors of Moscow Higher Technical School went on strike again, together with those of the physics and mathematics school of Moscow University and some from Petrograd and Kazan Universities, two high-level commissions investigated the circumstances and offered concessions to the professors.[16]

The professors, implies V. V. Stratonov, head of the physics and mathematics school of Moscow University, were not fooled by the Bolsheviks: they knew what promises of "almost autonomy" meant.[17] But really nobody, not even the Bolsheviks, knew what those promises meant or would mean. To the scholars deported in 1922, the situation of "old" professors in Soviet universities understandably looked very gloomy. The crucial event, from their point of view, was

[14] Among such Communist officials was Evgenii Preobrazhenskii, co-author with Bukharin of *Azbuka kommunizma*, economist, and organizer of the Trotskyist Opposition campaign in 1923–1924, who at this time was head of Narkompros's administration of higher and technical education, and was at loggerheads with others in the Narkompros collegium. He was blamed, probably rightly, for provocative handling of the professors in both 1921 and 1922. After the second strike he was reprimanded and removed from the job.

[15] See V. I. Lenin, *Polnoe sobranie sochinenii*, 5th ed., vol. 52 (Moscow, 1965), p. 388.

[16] See *Istoriia Moskovskogo Universiteta* (Moscow, 1955), 2:88–89, and V. V. Stratonov, "Moscow University's Loss of Freedom," in *Moskovskii Universitet, 1755–1930*, ed. V. B. Eliashevich, A. A. Kizevetter, and M. M. Novikov (Paris, 1930), pp. 226–35.

[17] Stratonov, "Moscow University's Loss of Freedom," p. 218.

the loss of the autonomy that the Provisional Government had been conferred on the higher schools. For different reasons, Soviet historians have tended to give similar emphasis to the "consolidation of Soviet power" in higher education, implying that the old professors' sphere of internal political influence was reduced virtually to nothing.

But it is clear, if only from the events of 1928–1929, when the higher schools lost their autonomy for the second time, that the professors' sphere of influence did in fact survive the events of 1921–1922. The pattern that emerged in the NEP period was a separation of powers in the universities between "new" Communist students and "old" professors, with Narkompros and the appointed rectors playing a mediating role. Between the deportations of 1922 and the campaign against bourgeois specialists which began in 1928, the old professors lived increasingly comfortable and relatively independent lives in their own sphere, dealt with the Soviet government as negotiators rather than petitioners, and enjoyed privileges that, mutatis mutandis, put them in much the same position vis-à-vis the society as a whole as they had had before the Revolution.

Marxism and the social sciences

Social science was the area of greatest conflict, repression, and violation of scholarly autonomy. From 1918 to 1923, relations between the Soviet government and "bourgeois" professors in the social sciences, humanities, and law were extremely strained. Both sides perceived the conflict as a matter of ideology. The party leaders, who intervened infrequently in other spheres of university life, exerted the greatest efforts to introduce Marxism and create social science schools capable of training a new Soviet elite. The old professors resisted; and, as we shall see, the outcome was by no means a clear victory for Marxism and Soviet power.

During the Civil War, Narkompros began to reorganize the existing schools of history, philology, and law as social science schools (*fakul'tety obshchestvennykh nauk*), to which Communist professors were appointed. Narkompros invited the Socialist (later Communist) Academy, then little more than a Marxist debating club with a library, to work out the bases of a new social science program by introducing Marxist methodology and developing the concepts of scientific socialism.[18]

[18] *Istoriia Leningradskogo Universiteta*, p. 211; Eliashevich et al., *Moskovskii Universitet*, pp. 122–23.

The old faculty reacted with indignation, noncooperation, and demonstrative contempt for the Marxist professors. At Moscow University, Narkompros's first initiative foundered when a "bourgeois" professor (A. M. Vinaver) was elected dean of the new social science school.[19] In Petrograd, leadership was assumed by the flamboyant "leftist" but non-Communist academician N. Ia. Marr, who gave the school an unusual bias toward ethnology and linguistics but not much in the way of orthodox Marxism.[20]

The situation changed, however, when Narkompros's initiative was taken up by Lenin and the party leadership in 1920. At this time the system of party schools and Communist universities (institutions specifically for the training of Communists and outside the Narkompros education system) was still in its infancy.[21] In the early 1920s the Central Committee and Narkompros treated the new Communist universities and the social science schools of the old universities as institutions of a similar type, issuing instructions to them jointly and sending the same small group of Communist intellectuals to lecture at both. But the social science schools, unlike the new Communist universities, had a hard core of committed anti-Communists and non-Marxists on their existing faculties. Of all "bourgeois" professors, people these had the strongest objection to Communists and their beliefs, included the largest proportion of former Kadet politicians, and had the least ground for ideologically neutral cooperation with the new regime.

Lenin, who was extremely interested in university teaching of Marxist social science, was not discouraged by this situation, and even devised a cunning scheme to make the old professors teach Marxism in spite of themselves. "Bind them to a firm program," he told Pokrovsky.

> Give them themes that will objectively force them to take our point of view. For example, make them teach the history of the colonial world: there, after all, even bourgeois writers can only "expose" each other in all kinds of dastardly behavior: the English expose the French, the French the English, and the Germans both at once. "The literature of the subject" will oblige your professors to recount the atrocities of capitalism in general. As well, require of each of them a basic knowledge of Marxist literature; announce that anyone who does not pass a special Marxist exam will be deprived of the right to teach. I assure you

[19] Eliashevich et al., *Moskovskii Universitet*, pp. 122–23.
[20] *Istoriia Leningradskogo Universiteta*, pp. 211–12.
[21] On the early history of party schools, see L. S. Leonova, *Iz istorii podgotovki partiinykh kadrov v sovetsko-partiinykh shkolakh i kommunisticheskikh universitetakh (1921–1925 gg.)* (Moscow, 1972).

that even if they still do not become orthodox Marxists, they will nevertheless assimilate things that were completely excluded from the
program of their courses before; and then it will be the business of the
students, under our political guidance, to use that material as it ought
to be used.[22]

Clearly Lenin was still thinking in terms of a prerevolutionary situation, in which Marxism as an intellectual system tended to influence even non-Marxists, and nonpolitical intellectuals were in general sympathy with the revolutionary cause. But all that had changed,
even by 1920. For non-Marxists, Marxism had become the ideology
of the ruling group; and in the universities there were already signs
that religious philosophy was acquiring the seductive antiregime appeal that before the October Revolution had belonged to Marxism.

The non-Marxist professors were never in fact required to pass an
exam in Marxism. But in the early 1920s a rich variety of covertly
anti-Soviet courses were being taught, by both old professors and
new. The old professors in the Moscow University social science
school, managed to include no fewer than nine courses on the history of religion and church law in the program. Of the new Marxist
professors, those who taught full-time were almost all Mensheviks or
political deviants of some kind: that was the reason they were teaching full-time instead of carrying out more important government and
party work. The anarchist Judah Grossman-Roshchin lectured on
ethical sociology.[23] Lenin's old rival Aleksandr Bogdanov lectured on
political economy and "some sort of cloudy idealist 'organizational
science.'"[24] Of the Mensheviks, B. I. Gorev "replaced the concept of
dictatorship of the proletariat with that of dictatorship of the party in
his lectures," and Nikolai Sukhanov "tried to 'disprove' the Leninist
theory of the possibility of the victory of socialism in one country,
propagating his own opportunist 'theory of productive forces,' which
led to the conclusion that there were no objective economic precon-
ditions for socialism in Russia."[25]

---

[22] M. N. Pokrovskii, "Chem byl Lenin dlia nashei vysshei shkoly," *Pravda*, 27 January 1924, p. 2.

[23] L. V. Ivanova, *U istokov sovetskoi istoricheskoi nauki: Podgotovka kadrov isto-
rikov-marksistov, 1917–1929* (Moscow, 1968), pp. 13–14. Early in 1921 Pokrovsky
asked Lenin's opinion about the desirability of employing Mensheviks (naming V. G.
Groman, O. A. Ermanskii, N. N. Sukhanov, F. A. Cherevanin, and Iulii Martov) in the
Moscow University School of Social Sciences. Lenin's answer was: "I am very doubtful, and think it had better be put before the Politburo of the Central Committee"
(ibid., p. 22). Whether or not there was a Politburo resolution, a number of Mensheviks were in fact employed.

[24] *Iz istorii Moskovskogo Universiteta* (Moscow, 1955), p. 118.

[25] *Istoriia Moskovskogo Universiteta*, 2:82–83.

Under these circumstances, it seemed hopeless to rely on the university social science schools to teach Marxism; and even before the first appearance of significant numbers of Communist students in the universities in 1921, the concept was changed. The social science schools, it was decided, should be training institutions for Soviet government personnel, with departments of economics, Soviet law, and "social pedagogy."[26] In effect, the instruction they would offer would be technical rather than ideological.

Following the new conception, government agencies began to send students and offer special stipends for the training of specialized personnel. The Moscow University social science schools, which had the special function of serving the central commissariats, added departments of statistics and international relations: in the early 1920s it received forty stipends from the Central Cooperative Union for the training of future specialists for the cooperative network, thirty from the Finance Commissariat for future financial experts, and 25 from Vesenkha for future economists.[27] To some extent, this pattern seems to have been duplicated in the provinces. In 1924, for example, 88 of 300 students in the Saratov University social science school were cadres seconded from local administrative bodies to raise their qualifications as members of the new Soviet bureaucracy.[28]

The social science schools remained acutely short of Communist teachers. Even in Moscow, where they could call on Old Bolshevik intellectuals in government work—Lunacharsky, Pokrovsky, and V. N. Meshcheriakov from Narkompros; the historian F. A. Rotshtein; I. I. Skvortsov-Stepanov, editor of *Izvestiia*; the jurists N. V. Krylenko, D. I. Kurskii, P. I. Stuchka, and others—to give occasional lecture courses in their areas of expertise, the supply of Communist teachers was scanty.[29] The same Bolshevik names are repeated in the lists of the Communist Academy, the Institute of Red Professors, the Sverdlov Communist University in Moscow, the Moscow University social science school, and the Plekhanov Economics Institute. Not surprisingly, the amount of time that any of these men could give to any individual institution was extremely limited. There were constant

[26] Sovnarkom resolution of 4 March 1921, "On the plan of organization of schools of the social sciences in Russian universities," *Sobranie uzakonenii*, 1921 no. 19, art. 117.

[27] *Iz istorii Moskovskogo Universiteta*, p. 113.

[28] *Saratovskii Universitet, 1909–1959* (Saratov, 1959) p. 33.

[29] For lists of Communists sent to the Moscow University School of Social Sciences, see Ivanova, *U istokov*, pp. 23, 25–26; V. Ukraintsev, *KPSS—organizator revoliutsionnogo preobrazovaniia vysshei shkoly* (Moscow, 1963), p. 115; *Istoriia Moskovskogo Universiteta*, 2:250–51; *Moskovskii Universitet za 50 let* (Moscow, 1967), pp. 57, 457; G. D. Alekseeva, *Oktiabr'skaia revoliutsiia i istoricheskie nauki v Rossii (1917–1932 gg.)* (Moscow, 1968), p. 260.

complaints that Communists ordered to teach in one of the higher
schools by the Central Committee were not in fact doing so.[30]

The old professors still provided the basic faculty of the social
science schools and were responsible for most of the teaching. In
1923 Moscow University reported that 21 percent of the teachers in
its social science school were Communists, but almost certainly they
were doing less than 21 percent of the teaching.[31] In the provinces
the situation was worse. Kazan University opened a social science
school with departments of law and politics, economics, and history
in April 1919, but "the teaching personnel transferred almost without change from the [old] law school and in part from the history
school."[32] At Lenin's suggestion, the Marxist scholar V. V. Adorat-
skii—like Lenin, a prerevolutionary graduate of the Kazan law
school—was sent to teach in the Kazan social science school, but by
1921 he was back in Moscow.[33] Later the Central Committee did not
even try to get leading Communists to go to provincial universities
on a long-term basis, but simply sent them out to give a few lectures
and organizational advice.[34] The problems in some provincial schools
were more basic than a lack of Marxists. The Tomsk social science
school, for example, collapsed after a year as a result of "the departure of a large number of professors from the city of Tomsk."[35]

In 1922 the Central Committee decided that there were just not

---

[30] Detailed instructions on the subject were published in *Izvestiia TsK* in 1922 and
1923. The Twelfth Party Congress resolved "to draw all members of the old party
guard completely into service in both the Communist universities and universities in
general. The casual attitude of some of the most responsible comrades toward the
business of teaching in the higher schools must stop" (quoted in *Izvestiia TsK*, 1923
no. 6 (54), pp. 53–54).

[31] *Iz istorii Moskovskogo Universiteta*, p. 134. In 1922 V. P. Volgin, N. M. Lukin,
M. N. Reisner, and I. D. Udaltsov were the most prominent Marxists on the faculty of
the Moscow University School of Social Sciences. Reisner and Lukin may have been
teaching full-time (though not only at Moscow University), but Udaltsov and Volgin
(who was rector of the university as well as holder of a responsible position in
Narkompros) certainly were not. The faculty included such notable non-Marxists as
the jurists A. M. Vinaver and S. A. Kotliarevskii, the medieval historial D. M. Pe-
trushevskii, the philosopher P. F. Preobrazhenskii, the linguist A. M. Selishchev, and
the formalist literary scholar M. D. Eikhengolts. See the list of faculty members in
*Otchet o sostoianii i deistviiakh I-go Moskovskogo Gosudarstvennogo Universiteta za
1922 g.* (Moscow, 1923), pp. 22–32.

[32] M. K. Korbut, *Kazan'skii Gosudarstvennyi Universitet imeni V. I.
Ul'ianova-Lenina za 125 let: 1804/5–1929/30* (Kazan, 1930), 2:309.

[33] *Rabochii fakultet Kazanskogo Gosudarstvennogo Universiteta imeni V. I. Lenina:
Na putiakh k vysshei shkole: Vosem' let raboty 1919–1927* (Kazan, 1927), pp. 156–57;
Alekseeva, *Oktiabr'skaia revoliutsiia*, p. 260.

[34] See, for example, *Izvestiia TsK*, 1923 no. 2 (50), p. 20: in 1922 Vazgen Ter-Vagan-
ian was sent as a lecturer to Kursk; Shalom Dvolaitskii to Voronezh; Ivan Skvortsov-
Stepanov to Kharkov, Ekaterinoslav, and Kiev; and Feliks Kon to Briansk.

[35] *Tomskii Gosudarstvennyi Universitet*, p. 17.

enough Marxists to go round, and abolished all the university social science schools except those in Moscow, Petrograd, Saratov, and Rostov.[36] Most of the provincial universities reestablished the law schools and teachers' colleges that the social science schools had briefly replaced.[37] The four remaining social science schools continued to struggle to assemble an acceptably Marxist, or at least pro-Soviet, faculty. In Rostov an investigation ordered by a bureau of the Central Committee found a total of thirteen Communists (including instructors and other junior teaching personnel) on the faculty. Forty-eight of the fifty-six full professors were classified as the "old reactionary" type, and the remainder apparently belonged to the intermediate group of non-Communists prepared to cooperate with the Soviet regime. According to a Soviet historian, "there were Kadets among the reactionary professors. Some of them had completely mastered Soviet phraseology and even acted as delegates to the city soviet, but at the same time worked with the reactionary groups linked with the reactionary professoriate of Novocherkassk and Moscow."[38]

As the Communist University system developed, the presence of "reactionary professors" put the old universities at an increasing disadvantage as centers of Marxist social science training.[39] The deportations of 1922 demoralized the social science schools of the old universities, with which many of the deportees had been associated. The commissariats turned out to be too disorganized to predict their own need for personnel and make effective use of the schools as a service training facility. In 1924, accordingly, a commission of the Orgburo of the Central Committee recommended dissolution of the university social science schools over a two-year period, and cessation of enrollment after the 1924–1925 academic year.[40]

This did not mean that the universities, or even the schools and departments that had been incorporated in the social science schools, lost their function as elite training institutions. They continued, after the 1925 break for reorganization, to enroll high-quality "Soviet" stu-

[36] Ivanova, U istokov, pp. 23–24.

[37] The Kazan school of social sciences reverted to a law school (Korbut, Kazan'skii Gosudarstvennyi Universitet, p. 311) and the Perm school of social sciences to teacher training (Permskii Gosudarstvennyi Universitet, p. 35). Konstantin F. Shteppa, then a historian at Kiev University, says that the second course was more common (Shteppa, Russian Historians and the Soviet State [New Brunswick, N.J., 1962], p. 11).

[38] Quoted in S. E. Belozerov, Ocherki istorii Rostovskogo Universiteta (Rostov, 1959), pp. 164–65.

[39] See the comment by V. N. Iakovleva at a meeting of university rectors, Ezhenedel'nik NKP, 1924 no. 1 (22), p. 18.

[40] Ivanova, U istokov, p. 35. Members of the commission included M. N. Pokrovsky, A. S. Bubnov, and K. A. Popov.

dents. But these students were taught by "old" professors, more or less in the traditional disciplines of law, history, philology, and so on. The schools were ideological training institutions only in the most marginal sense—and in fact, given the predominance of "bourgeois" students preparing for academic careers in the graduate schools, they probably transmitted the professors' ideology more effectively than that of the regime. They were service training facilities only in the very general sense in which the old universities had been for the old regime.

The Orgburo's decision of 1924 allowed the university social science schools to break up into their traditional constitutent parts and the old professors to resume their traditional role of leadership. In Moscow University the reorganization, which took place in 1925, created schools of ethnology (the *etnofak*) and law. The *etnofak*, in spite of its name, was a revival of the old historical-philological school. The main subject taught was not ethnography (which was in fact taught in the geography department of the school of physics and mathematics) but history.[41] Economics, statistics, and sociology seem to have vanished from Moscow University as separate academic disciplines at this time, no doubt because they had not been taught before the Revolution and the social science teachers had been borrowed from the old Moscow Commercial Institute.

In Leningrad, similarly, the old historical-philological school reemerged under the attractive title of *iamfak* (a contraction of *iazykoznanie*, linguistics; *material'naia kul'tura*, material culture, the term favored by Professor Marr for the disciplines of history, archaeology, and anthropology; and *fakul'tet*, faculty). The law department was officially dissolved, presumably because its faculty, unlike Moscow's, had not acquired an energetic Marxist or Soviet-oriented group. But it continued to function normally under the title of "the former law department" until it was reestablished as a law school in the autumn of 1926.[42] The economics department of the social science school was transferred to the Leningrad Polytechnical Institute and the social-pedagogical department to the Herzen Pedagogical Institute.

The teaching of ideology

It was Lenin's belief that all university students should take a basic social-science-cum-civics course called "the general scientific

[41] *Moskovskii Universitet za 50 let*, pp. 60, 563–65.
[42] *Istoriia Leningradskogo Universiteta*, pp. 226–29.

minimum." The course was to be primarily informational, covering Marxist sociology, elements of natural science, and the government and economy of the USSR.[43] Lenin's very long list of compulsory subjects (including the Soviet electrification plan) was later reduced to three: historical materialism, capitalism and proletarian revolution, and the political structure and social tasks of the Russian Soviet Republic.[44]

Although the scientific minimum was officially introduced for all students, there is very little indication that it was actually taught in the higher schools in 1922–1923. The people who were supposed to teach it were those same Old Bolshevik intellectuals to whom the Central Committee delegated all Marxist theoretical work, and they simply did not have the time. At the Timiriazev Agricultural Academy, Bukharin said in 1924, "I have been told that ten Communist lecturers have been appointed—Stuchka, Miliutin, Teodorovich, and others—but not one of them gives lectures. They are there on paper but not in fact."[45] (But Bukharin, also a member of the Marxist theoretical pool, was in the same position as those he criticized: he was too busy to teach Marxism in the universities.)

The situation changed, however, after the battle between Stalinists ("the Central Committee majority") and Trotskyists in the winter of 1923–1924, when a distressingly large proportion of Communist cells in the universities voted for Trotsky. At that point it became clear to the dominant Stalinist group that the younger generation of Communists, including those in higher education, were ill informed about the history of the party before the October Revolution and Civil War, and unaware of important and damaging facts in Trotsky's biography. Trotsky, after all, had been first a Menshevik and then a conciliator, and had joined the Bolsheviks only in the summer of 1917. He and Lenin had engaged in acrimonious exchanges in emigration, from which very useful quotations could be culled. Accordingly, the resolution of the Thirteenth Party Conference early in 1924 "on the results of the discussion and on petty-bourgeois deviation in the party" stated:

> One of the most important tasks is raising to the necessary level the study of the history of the Russian Communist Party, and above all the basic facts of the struggle of Bolshevism and Menshevism, the role of separate factions and trends during the course of that struggle, in par-

[43] For the first version, drafted by Lenin, see Sovnarkom resolution of 4 March 1921, "On the establishment of a general scientific minimum compulsory for teaching in all higher schools of the RSFSR," *Sobranie uzakonenii*, 1921 no. 19, art. 119.

[44] Sovnarkom resolution of 1 November 1922, signed by L. B. Kamenev, *Sobranie uzakonenii*, 1922 no. 75, art. 929.

[45] *Partiia i vospitanie smeny*, p. 104.

ticular the role of those eclectic factions that tried to "reconcile" Bolsheviks with Mensheviks. The party Central Committee must take a series of steps to facilitate the publication of the appropriate textbooks on the history of the All-Russian Communist Party, and also make the teaching of its history obligatory in all party schools, universities, political study circles, and so on.[46]

An explanatory circular spelled out the political implications by recommending that "special attention be paid to the illumination of Trotskyism in the past and present," and that Lenin's writings and other literature be used "to expose the intellectual essence of Trotskyism."[47]

Stalin took a leading part in introducing the study of the new subject of "Leninism." Two months after Lenin's death, Stalin was lecturing to students of the Sverdlov Communist University in Moscow on "the foundations of Leninism"; and a month later he published "A Plan for Seminars on Leninism" in a new journal for Communist students edited by Molotov.[48] Seminars on Leninism were being held in Moscow University as early as the 1924–1925 academic year.[49] In January 1925 the Central Committee secretariat instructed all "big pedagogical and socioeconomic universities" to establish chairs of party history and Leninism. The technical universities were to create departments to teach what was now called "the social minimum." Local party committees were to be responsible for directing the work of these departments. The new subjects were to be compulsory, and students would be examined on them.[50]

The elite universities made some effort to keep the new courses at a reasonable intellectual level. The Moscow University seminars, for example, made relatively little use of textbooks—which in Pokrovsky's view led to blind and dogmatic memorization of material—and studied the newly published collections of Lenin's works.[51] A similar approach was taken in Sverdlov Communist University, and the fictionalized memoirs of a former student made it clear that the discov-

[46] *Pravda*, 19 January 1924, p. 5.

[47] Quoted in Leonova, *Iz istorii podgotovki partiinykh kadrov*, p. 115.

[48] Robert C. Tucker, *Stalin as Revolutionary* (New York, 1973), pp. 316–19; *Krasnaia molodezh'* (monthly journal of the Central Moscow Bureau of Proletarian Students), 1924 no. 1 (May), pp. 45–49.

[49] *Iz istorii Moskovskogo Universiteta*, p. 141.

[50] Ukraintsev, *KPSS—organizator*, p. 114.

[51] Pokrovsky: *Krasnaia molodezh'*, 1924 no. 1, p. 103; Lenin's works: Ivanova, *U istokov*, p. 39; *Programmy po istorii klassovoi bor'by v Rossii, istorii klassovoi bor'by na zapade, istorii VKP(b): Na fakul'tete sovetskogo prava I-go MGU* (Moscow, 1928). The *programmy*, unlike those for secondary schools, included bibliographies. Lenin's works predominate in the course on party history, though it also includes some Marx, Engels, Pokrovsky, and Stalin (*Voprosy leninizma* and his speech to the Fourteenth Party Congress).

ery of old controversies involving current political figures was genuinely exciting (even scandalous) for the young Communists preparing themselves for future leadership.[52] Excitement was perhaps less of a factor in Leningrad. It took Leningrad University two years to put together a course on party history and Leninism, though when it finally was introduced, it included a special seminar for physics and mathematics students on "Darwinism and Marxism" which was apparently not taught in Moscow.[53]

For most higher schools and most students, however, the new courses were dreary in the extreme. Both in content and in student reaction, they bore more than a passing resemblance to the social studies taught in high school. True, the university courses included attacks on Trotsky, but they were of interest only to students who cared about Trotsky in the first place. The "social minimum" subjects were learned by rote, and often were reduced to an almost meaningless catechism: "To the question 'What is a trade union?' one gets the laconic reply that 'It is a school of communism'; imperialism is 'the best path to socialism.'"[54] In 1926 Mikhail Kalinin told a meeting of rectors that "our teaching of social sciences has become something like the teaching of the Law of God in the old gymnasia"; and when this remark was quoted by the Trotskyist Lev Sosnovskii in a debate at the Communist Academy, it produced cries of approval and prolonged applause.[55]

Professorial organizations and attitudes

For the old professors the teaching of Marxism and party history was not really important so long as they did not have to teach it. What was important to them was their own teaching and research—in which they achieved relative independence in the very years when party history was being effectively introduced into the university curriculum—and the general conditions of life and work within the profession.

The question of professional organization was a very lively political issue at the beginning of the 1920s. The professors wanted an

[52] See V. Astrov, Krucha (Moscow, 1969), pp. 173–74, 210–11, 288–89, 403–5, and passim.

[53] Istoriia Leningradskogo Universiteta, p. 282.

[54] N. I. Loboda in Nauchnyi rabotnik, 1927 no. 10, pp. 57–58.

[55] Izvestiia, 18 May 1926, p. 3; Upadochnoe nastroenie sredi molodezhi (Moscow, 1927), pp. 68–69.

"autonomous" form of professional organization; and the regime assumed that they wanted it for primarily political purposes. There seem to be some grounds for this assumption. The group of Moscow liberals with which V. V. Stratonov was associated strongly resisted Soviet pressure to join the new regime-sponsored teacher's union, Rabpros. They tried to organize concerted action against the Soviet proposals on a national scale. They attempted to use such organizations as the Commission for Improving the Life of Scholars, established during the Civil War on Gorky's initiative, and the All-Russian Committee of Aid to the Starving as fronts for non- and probably anti-Soviet professional organization.[56]

Soviet authorities, the Cheka in particular, interpreted these activities as counterrevolutionary. Émigré memoirists do not actually admit to conspiracy, though they do indicate deep hostility to the Soviet regime. Stratonov's memoirs, for example, deny conspiracy while expressing attitudes that would make absence of political resistance apparently dishonorable and cowardly. They were written in 1930, and it is possible that he was afraid of compromising colleagues who had remained in the Soviet Union.[57] The confusion is compounded by the fact that the major Soviet reprisals against the liberal professors—the Tactical Center trial of 1920 and the deportations of 1922—were apparently exemplary actions designed to intimidate the group rather than responses to specific offenses.

In the autumn of 1922, 100 to 150 "anti-Soviet lawyers, literati, and professors" were deported from the Soviet Union.[58] They seem to have been randomly chosen from among the leaders of the liberal intelligentsia. Some were historians and philosophers who either were teaching in the university social science schools of Moscow and Petrograd or had taught there—A. A. Kizevetter, S. L. Frank, I. A. Ilin, N. A. Berdiaev, F. A. Stepun, L. P. Karsavin, N. O. Losskii, S. P. Melgunov, and Pitirim Sorokin among them. Others in the group of deportees were the biologist Mikhail Novikov, former rector of Moscow University; V. V. Stratonov, dean of the Moscow University school of physics and mathematics and later memoirist; Ovchinnikov, the former rector of Petrograd University; Professors Troshin and I. A. Stratonov of Kazan University; and Professor V. Iasinskii

---

[56] Stratonov, "Moscow University's Loss of Freedom," pp. 214–18; *Nauchnyi rabotnik*, 1925 no. 1, pp. 160–61. On the committee and its dissolution, see Fitzpatrick, *Commissariat of Enlightenment*, pp. 233–34, and Bertram D. Wolfe, *The Bridge and the Abyss* (London, 1967), pp. 109–18.

[57] The memoir is cited in n. 16.

[58] *Izvestiia TsK*, 1922 no. 11–12, pp. 47–48.

of Moscow Higher Technical School, who had been effectively in charge of the Commission for Improving the Life of Scholars.[59]

The Central Committee report for 1922 justified the expulsions on the grounds of the ideological competition the old intelligentsia was offering the Marxists:

> The growing influence of a revitalized bourgeois ideology in the young Soviet Republic made it necessary for us to apply decisive measures in the struggle against this evil. . . . The Soviet government took administrative measures to deport a considerable group of ideologists of the "new" bourgeoisie beyond the borders of the Soviet Republic. In the current situation, the expulsion of some dozens of old bourgeois activists and ideologues of the petty bourgeoisie from the largest cities was a necessity.[60]

The deportations no doubt intimidated the scholars who remained and facilitated their acceptance of the new university constitution and the new Soviet Teachers' Union. But these people did not become permanent outcasts, and during NEP there were no further punitive actions against the liberal intelligentsia as a group. At the end of 1923, in fact, Zinoviev announced that a breakthrough had been achieved: both the intelligentsia and the party understood the need to work together, and "we will no longer remember the past."[61] The assembled intellectuals must have felt reasonably secure at this point, since they drew Zinoviev's attention to "the pitiful position of Russian scholars living in emigration and prepared to return to Russia to work in the service of Soviet power." Zinoviev's response was quite sympathetic. "So far as the Soviet government is concerned," he replied, "there are no obstacles to the return from abroad of those scholars who are sincerely prepared to break with the White emigration. They will meet the same kind of attentive treatment on the part of Soviet power as the scholars in Russia receive."[62]

---

[59] For members of the group expelled and information on their academic disciplines and institutional affiliations, see P. Sorokin, *The Long Journey* (New Haven, 1963), p. 192; Stratonov, "Moscow University's Loss of Freedom," pp. 241–42; *Istoriia Moskovskogo Universiteta*, p. 118; *Istoriia Leningradskogo Universiteta*, p. 244; Korbut, *Kazan'skii Gosudarstvennyi Universitet*, p. 318; Aleksandr I. Solzhenitsyn, *The Gulag Archipelago 1918–1956*, trans. Thomas P. Whitney (New York, 1973), p. 372.

[60] *Izvestiia TsK*, 1923 no. 4 (52), p. 25: Central Committee report to the Twelfth Party Congress.

[61] Speech to First Congress of Scientific Workers, November 1923, *Pravda*, 24 November 1923, p. 4.

[62] Report to the Petrograd *guberniia* conference of scientific workers, *Pravda*, 9 November 1923, p. 4. This statement was greeted with great approval by the Petrograd intelligentsia, and Zinoviev was elected a member of the Scientific Workers' Section of the Teachers' Union.

Apparently with this encouragement, some members of the Berlin emigration, such as the writer Viktor Shklovskii, did return, and were in fact treated in the same way as other members of the literary intelligentsia.[63] Within a year the professors received permission to publish a thick monthly journal, the contents of which included a long list of scholars who had perished in the postrevolutionary years.[64] Scholars who had emigrated or been deported remained members of the Academy of Sciences and other scholarly organizations without protest from the regime.[65]

The professors had bitterly objected to their inclusion in the Teachers' Union, since the expressed purpose of bringing them in was to democratize the professorial aristocracy through contact with the cultural proletariat of rural primary school teachers and, for that matter, school cleaners and janitors, who also were enrolled in the union. As a "transitional measure" before full absorption, they were allowed to form a separate section within the union—the Section of Scientific Workers.[66]

The section in fact turned into a permanent institution whose links with the Teachers' Union were minimal. It became possible to enroll in the section without becoming a member of the Teachers' Union: of the section's 9,000 members in the Russian Republic in 1926, more than 60 percent were not registered members of the Teachers' Union.[67] The section had its own independent local branches; and by 1927 its secretary, N. I. Loboda, was writing of the section's nominal subordination to the Teachers' Union as a pure formality. In the past, he said,

> many people looked on the section as a temporary organization, whose basic function was to unite scientific workers (a category of worker that yields to professional organization only with the greatest difficulty) within its ranks, so that this mass could be poured into a single Union of Education Workers. . . . This is a completely incorrect view. Life has shown that the Section of Scientific Workers is the only possible union for scientific workers and the most flexible means to meet their needs.[68]

[63] On Shklovskii's return, see Victor Erlich, *Russian Formalism: History-Doctrine*, 2d ed. (The Hague, 1965), p. 136.

[64] *Nauchnyi rabotnik*, 1925 no. 2, pp. 185ff., and 1925 no. 3, pp. 160ff.: "Losses to Russian science."

[65] See ibid., 1930 no. 3, p. 58; and Loren R. Graham, *The Soviet Academy of Sciences and the Communist Party, 1927–1932* (Princeton, 1967), p. 88.

[66] Resolution of First Congress of Workers in Education and Socialist Culture (1920), quoted in *Nauchnyi rabotnik*, 1928 no. 2, p. 44.

[67] *Nauchnyi rabotnik*, 1927 no. 1, p. 7.

[68] Ibid., p. 21.

A "scientific worker" was defined as a member of a higher educational or scholarly research institution. But membership in the section was on an individual and not an institutional basis, and scholars without institutional affiliation could join if the section considered their work meritorious. University administrators could not join the section unless they happened also to be scholars. *Rabfak* professors were included at the discretion of the section, which required evidence that they had the appropriate credentials and had published scholarly work.[69]

The section was as exclusive an institution as could be desired; and it seems to have elected its own officers and represented its members' interests with a success that is in striking contrast to the situation in the Teachers' Union as a whole.[70] But the caste spirit of the professoriate and old intelligentsia was manifest even more strongly in another institution, the Commission for Improving the Life of Scholars.

The commission, originally established during the Civil War for the purpose of distributing the special "academic ration" issued to scholars and prominent members of the intelligentsia, provided salary supplements and a variety of rest and recreational facilities to scholars during NEP. Financed from the mid-1920s by the government of the Russian Republic,[71] the commission ran the Scholars' Club in Moscow, where local and visiting scholars crowded to hear scholarly lectures and concerts by the finest Russian artists. At its disposal were, appropriately, a number of monuments of aristocratic culture that were used as resorts and sanatoria for the scholars, among them the Uzkoe estate near Moscow, the Gaspra estate in the Crimea, and sanatoria in Detskoe Selo, near Leningrad, and Kislovodsk.[72]

Before 1929, Communist or Soviet influence on the internal workings of the commission seems to have been minimal. At Uzkoe, whose facilities included a functioning church, Easter was celebrated but May Day was not. The commission's register of scholars—

[69] Ibid., pp. 4, 7.

[70] See Sheila Fitzpatrick, *Education and Social Mobility in the Soviet Union, 1921–1934* (London and New York, 1979), pp. 30–31.

[71] Earlier the commission had been on the Narkompros budget. When Narkompros decided in 1924 to liquidate the institution and transfer its assets to the Section of Scientific Workers, Sovnarkom RSFSR took it over. See Tsentral'nyi gosudarstvennyi arkhiv oktiabr'skoi revoliutsii i sotsialisticheskogo stroitel'stva SSSR (TsGAOR), f. 2306, op. 1, d. 2101 (meeting of presidium of Narkompros collegium, 3 and 10 September 1924), and f. 2306, op. 1, d. 3328 (meeting of Narkompros collegium, 1 September 1924); *Piat' let raboty tsentral'noi komissii po ulushcheniiu byta uchenykh pri Sovete Narodnykh Komissarov RSFSR (TseKUBU)* (Moscow, 1927), p. 8.

[72] *Piat' let raboty*, pp. 19–25, 28–35.

divided into status categories ranging from "young scholars at the beginning of their careers" to "outstanding scholars whose work has international significance"—included not only scholars who had emigrated or been deported but also (in 1930) eighteen scholars who had been sent to Solovki or otherwise exiled within the Soviet Union.[73] "Among middle and lower scientific workers," one member of the Section of Scientific Workers said, "the commission is regarded as an aristocratic institution because it is the milieu of certain circles of old scientific workers—old not in the sense of years, but as a characterization of attitude."[74]

Professorial salaries and privileges

When professorial salaries were low in the early 1920s (in the range of 28 to 33 rubles a month in 1924, not much higher than a schoolteacher's salary),[75] the Commission for Improving the Life of Scholars provided additional salary supplements. In 1923–1924, 9,000 scholars received salary supplements ranging from 7.5 rubles a month for young scholars to 40 rubles for the highest category of established scholars.[76] From 1924–1925, the commission paid salary supplements only to the two highest categories on the professorial scale. But professorial salaries had already begun to rise sharply: in January 1925 the average professorial salary was given as 80 rubles, and an estimate at the end of the year put the average at 120–150 rubles.[77]

Given the instability of the currency and the different types of ruble being quoted, not much can usefully be said about pre-1925 salaries in comparative terms.[78] But it should be pointed out that throughout the 1920s virtually all university faculty in the capitals and big cities held down two or even three jobs, either working in various government agencies or in several higher schools simul-

---

[73] *Nauchnyi rabotnik*, 1930 no. 3, pp. 61, 58; *Piat' let raboty*, p. 11.

[74] *Vecherniaia Moskva*, 5 February 1930, p. 2.

[75] Iosif Khodorovskii, in *Narodnoe prosveshchenie*, 1923 no. 5–6, p. 3; Lunacharsky, in *Krasnaia molodezh'*, 1924 no. 1, p. 96.

[76] *Piat' let raboty*, p. 18.

[77] *Narodnoe prosveshchenie*, 1925 no. 5–6, p. 3; *Krasnaia molodezh'*, 1925 no. 5 (9), p. 118, quoted in Ukraintsev, *KPSS–organizator*, p. 134.

[78] Salaries as expressed in *biudzhetnye* rubles were about 60% of what was actually paid in *chervonnye* rubles (see, for example, tables in *Itogi desiatiletiia sovetskoi vlasti v tsitrakh, 1917–1927* [Moscow, 1927], pp. 342–43). Most writers do not differentiate, and there was an obvious temptation for Narkompros and professorial spokesmen asking for salary increases to use the budgetary measure for pathetic effect.

taneously.[79] Since a professor in a Russian university had a six-hour teaching load, even three appointments were quite feasible,[80] and the shortage of teaching personnel left many jobs available. In real terms by 1925 we are dealing with professorial incomes in the bracket of 200 to 350 rubles a month.[81] This figure compares rather favorably with the 30 rubles that Narkompros was currently trying to secure for rural teachers, with the average of 55 rubles received by workers in census industry in 1925–1926, and even with the average 141 rubles received by employees in the central government bureaucracy (the most highly paid category of state employee) in the same year.[82]

Yet the professors were not happy with what they earned. The nonscientists in particular resented the fact that the "government specialists" earned more than they did. As Professor G. V. Sergievskii wrote, the incomes of those who worked only in the higher schools remained lower than those of the engineers, chemists, agronomists, financial experts, and so on who worked for economic agencies of the Soviet government on a full- or part-time basis. The financial incentive was such that

> the majority of professors who have even the slightest opportunity to apply their knowledge in some field of production prefer not to load themselves with teaching work in the higher school but, taking care to keep their connection with the university, construct their material well-being on the salary from enterprises of Vesenkha, the Commissariat of Agriculture, or the Commissariat of External Trade.[83]

The professorial organizations were vigilant in defending and extending the rights of their members, especially in the material realm. In Moscow, where a good proportion of the academic population was concentrated, one of the main social problems of the 1920s was an acute housing shortage. The formal housing privileges of scientific workers—secured through the activity of their organizations and the cooperation of Sovnarkom and the Moscow Soviet—included the right to extra space for study purposes and the right to

[79] An investigation of 268 section members throughout the USSR showed that they held 466 academic jobs, an average of 1.66 per person. *Nauchnyi rabotnik*, 1925 no. 3, p. 113.

[80] *Nauchnyi rabotnik*, 1925 no. 1, p. 176; 1925 no. 2, p. 145.

[81] Professor G. V. Sergievskii in 1925 gave 200–350 rubles as an average professorial income (*Nauchnyi rabotnik*, 1925 no. 1, p. 177); 350 rubles was the level at which the commission discontinued salary supplements (*Piat' let raboty*, p. 18).

[82] See Fitzpatrick, *Education and Social Mobility*, p. 30; *Itogi desiateliia sovetskoi vlasti*, pp. 342–43, 347.

[83] *Nauchnyi rabotnik*, 1925 no. 1, p. 177.

samouplotnenie; that is, the right to choose the other people who would occupy the family apartment if the number of square meters per family member exceeded the number permitted.[84]

Their actual privileges went further, since the old Muscovites were still living in their bourgeois prerevolutionary apartments, and most of them managed to satisfy the space norms by bringing in relatives or domestic servants. (Employment of a servant remained the norm in the professorial milieu throughout NEP, and indeed beyond it.) They had constantly to fear arbitrary eviction, however, or illegal orders to share the apartment with unknown lower-class families, since local authorities desperate for housing space were less sensitive to professorial privilege than Sovnarkom. The Commission for Improving the Life of Scholars had a special office of legal consultants handling housing problems at the rate of thirty a day.[85]

But for all their efforts, disasters occurred. "The people's judges showed a tendency toward restricted interpretation of the housing rights of scientific workers," and the professors themselves found violation of their domestic privacy the most difficult of all Soviet impositions to bear.[86] Housing problems, according to the Old Bolshevik S. I. Mitskevich (deputy head of the housing section of the commission), had led to the premature death of many scholars, including Mikhail Gershenzon, the last surviving *Vekhi* contributor in Russia. The linguist Dmitrii Shor, returning from a trip abroad in the summer of 1926, found his room already inhabited by new occupants and his possessions thrown out of the apartment. Professor D. S. Krein of the Moscow Conservatorium shot himself two hours before the court hearing that was to decide whether local authorities had violated his rights by settling strangers in his apartment.[87]

Job security was not an important issue for scholars during NEP, despite the fact that in formal terms professors did not have indefinite tenure but were supposed to be reviewed for reappointment at the ends of terms that ranged from five to ten years.[88] There are no reports that this procedure was followed in practice, or that professors were dismissed by this means, between 1922 and 1928. Evi-

[84] Resolution of VTsIK and Sovnarkom RSFSR of 31 July 1924, *Nauchnyi rabotnik*, 1925 no. 1, pp. 212–13.

[85] *Piat' let raboty*, p. 43.

[86] *Nauchnyi rabotnik*, 1927 no. 1, p. 41. See, for example, the story "Nalët" in Lidia Seifullina, *Izbrannye proizvedeniia* (Moscow, 1958), 1:387ff.

[87] S. I. Mitskevich, letter to the editor, *Izvestiia*, 31 August 1926, p. 4.

[88] Decree of Sovnarkom RSFSR of 21 January 1924, *Sobranie uzakonenii*, 1924 no. 7, art. 44; and Narkompros instructions reminding higher educational institutions of the Sovnarkom decree in *Nauchnyi rabotnik*, 1925 no. 3, p. 165.

dently the shortage of qualified teachers and the delicacy with which they were normally handled by Narkompros in this period made the law a dead letter (as is confirmed by the outrage of the professoriate in 1928–1929, when the law was actually and punitively applied).

Children of faculty were exempt from payment of university fees, whatever their parents' income.[89] But since the social selection process put some obstacles in their way, the Scientific Workers' Section was allotted a quota of places.[90] Apparently the number of places reserved for scholars' children was more than adequate in the provinces but not in Moscow and Leningrad, where two-thirds of the professors were concentrated. Besides, provincial scholars also wanted their children to go to the prestigious institutions.

The section was naturally concerned about the training of new scholars; and on this question the professors' interest in self-perpetuation seems to have come into conflict with the party's interest in bringing in Communists. Local party committees were instructed to be alert for vacancies at the junior faculty level and to select candidates among the graduating Communist students.[91] But there is no evidence of Communist success in this realm. In 1926 a large proportion of both senior and junior faculty were from intelligentsia families (53 percent of senior faculty, 48 percent of junior). But proportionately more senior faculty members were Communists (6 percent, as against 4 percent of junior faculty), and the only real differential was by sex: 32 percent of junior faculty members but only 4 percent of senior faculty members were women.[92]

From 1925 a formal system of graduate studies (aspirantura) replaced the old system of informal apprenticeship to a professor. Stipends were available for about 60 percent of the graduate students, but they were small, and Communist students were neither attracted nor energetically recruited into graduate studies.[93] The professors effectively had control of the system of graduate studies in the latter years of NEP, and the only really controversial issue was whether

[89] Decree of VTsIK and Sovnarkom RSFSR of 15 December 1924, in Nauchnyi rabotnik, 1925 no. 1, p. 217.

[90] In the 1924 enrollment for Russian higher educational institutions, the section was allocated 350 places. For the 1926 enrollment it got 560 places, 164 of them in Moscow and 135 in Leningrad. Nauchnyi rabotnik, 1925 no. 2, pp. 172–73; 1926 no. 4, pp. 36, 95.

[91] Izvestiia TsK, 1923 no. 6 (54), p. 83.

[92] Statisticheskii sbornik po narodnomu prosveshcheniiu RSFSR 1926 g. (Moscow, 1927), pp. 38–39.

[93] M. N. Pokrovsky in Izvestiia, 11 April 1926, p. 3, and 19 May 1926, p. 3, and speech to Fifth Plenum of the Soviet of Scientific Workers, December 1928, Nauchnyi rabotnik, 1929 no. 1, p. 20.

their overwhelmingly non-Communist graduate students should have to study Marxism.[94]

Accommodation with the Soviet regime

Some Communists thought the old professors were being altogether too successful in upholding "bourgeois" academic tradition in higher education. Communist students resented the informal alliance of "bourgeois" students and professors. In 1927 a speaker at the All-Russian Congress of Soviets warned against the local dominance of "lords of the *kafedra* [university department]." "There are individuals," he said, "quite important ones, who think they can monopolize the leadership of all scientific fields. We must struggle with these individuals, who do after all have influence. . . . We must take the most energetic measures to bring new young forces into the ranks of scientific workers."[95]

But during NEP the party leadership did very little to encourage this view. When students were purged in 1924, the professors were untouched. Communist students were repeatedly instructed not to harass the professors. Andrei Lezhava, the deputy head of the government of the Russian Republic, sharply rebutted the criticism of the "lords of the *kafedra*": Such criticism might conceivably apply to the extreme right wing of the professoriate, but "we already have a large body of scholars and teachers who are completely devoted to the construction of the worker-peasant state."[96]

No doubt the technical specialists were more willing to make peace with the Soviet regime than professors in the humanities and the social sciences, for whom opportunities and potential rewards were less. Nevertheless, a general accommodation was reached in the mid-1920s. As Professor P. N. Sakulin pointed out:

> When the party attained victory, it could neither expect nor demand a lightning change of attitude in the intelligentsia. It seems to me that the intelligentsia would even have lowered its dignity if it had at once run after the victor's chariot. . . . The intelligentsia . . . waited to see what political circumstances would be established for its creative work.[97]

---

[94] There was, at least formally, a "compulsory Marxist minimum" for all graduate students between 1925 and 1927 (*Istoriia Leningradskogo Universiteta*, p. 252). For Pokrovsky's defensive comments on it to the Section of Scientific Workers, see *Nauchnyi rabotnik*, 1927 no. 3, pp. 41–43.

[95] *Izvestiia*, 17 April 1927, p. 5. The speaker was B. P. Pozern.

[96] *Ibid.*, p. 6.

[97] *Sud'by sovremennoi intelligentsii* (Moscow, 1925), p. 17.

But this view was perhaps too highminded even for the majority of professors. If the professorial organizations accurately reflected the concerns of their members, what was crucial was improvement of material circumstances from the low point of the Civil War and confirmation of the group's social status and privileges. A great deal was achieved in this direction during NEP, and more was promised and expected.

As for the political circumstances, there were both pluses and minuses. The Soviet government exercised censorship but permitted the reestablishment of private publishing in the early 1920s. Scholars appear to have been affected comparatively little by the censorship, in contrast to writers of fiction and drama. The regime required Marxism to be taught in the higher schools but did not require the old professors to teach or study it. (Those who did teach Marxism complained bitterly of the contemptuous attitude of their scholarly colleagues.) Preference in admissions was given to Communist students, and the professors sometimes said they felt obliged to pass such students even if they were academically below standard. But the professors' children also had preference in admissions from 1924, and the reintroduction of entrance examinations suggests that the regime was beginning to listen to the experts.

During NEP the leadership behaved in a conciliatory manner toward bourgeois specialists, but lower-level officials usually did not. But a situation in which prominent members of the intelligentsia were conventionally allowed to appeal over the heads of underlings to the top political leadership was, in its own way, flattering. In personal terms, the party leaders treated intelligentsia leaders with respect. Professors were not simply offered conciliation by second-level Communists such as Lunacharsky and Public Health Commissar Nikolai Semashko (who, as the professors obviously appreciated, had goodwill but no political clout); they were publicly approached by such "real" leaders as Zinoviev, Aleksei Rykov, and Bukharin.

The high intelligentsia, indeed, was a part of Soviet high society, and its members had relatively free access to the holders of power. They might be invited to Olga Kameneva's salon, rub shoulders with the military and GPU leadership at the Meyerholds', breakfast with Sergei Kirov or Valerian Kuibyshev for a discussion of scientific research prospects. Such get-togethers did not necessarily imply political influence or security. But for the intelligentsia leaders the situation held personal and status advantages that had never been equaled under the old regime, with the possible exception of the years of Count Sergei Witte's ascendancy.

Of all party leaders, Bukharin was probably closest to the intelligentsia—not because he was the most conciliatory (Rykov was far more so) but because he was the most involved in the spiritual and psychological problems that members of the old Russian intelligentsia discussed among themselves. In 1924 he devoted two long articles to dissection of Ivan Pavlov's views on society and politics.[98] His own views were sharply at variance with Pavlov's, but the argument led to a relationship of respectful friendship between the two men.[99] The next year Bukharin took part in a public debate on the fate of the intelligentsia. It was on this occasion that Professor Sakulin, defending the principles of intellectual and creative freedom, mentioned the lack of dignity that would have been involved if the intelligentsia had immediately "run after the victor's chariot"—a remark, directed at Bukharin, that suggests the peculiar mix of intimacy and role playing that sometimes characterized the intellectuals' exchanges with the politicians in the latter years of NEP.

In the debate on the intelligentsia, Bukharin played the role of Bolshevik commissar to the hilt. "We will not repudiate our Communist aims," he thundered. "We must have cadres of the intelligentsia ideologically conditioned [*natrenirovy*] in a particular way. Yes, we will put our stamp on intellectuals, we will process [*vyrabatyvat'*] them as in a factory."[100]

Of course, a serious advocate of such a policy would not have engaged in debate with intellectuals on "the fate of the intelligentsia" in the first place; and one might also remark that Bukharin was using the language of the artistic avant-garde rather than the language of Soviet politicians.[101] But it is particularly interesting to discover that this debate was used to substantiate the claim (which in general terms was almost certainly correct) that Bukharin supported the intelligentsia's aspirations. According to Sakulin's later recollection of the debate, Bukharin "promised in the name of the party" that at some future time the regime would relax ideological controls and allow greater intellectual freedom.[102]

---

[98] N. I. Bukharin, "O mirovoi revoliutsii, nashei strane, kul'ture i prochem: Otvet akademiku Pavlovu," *Krasnaia nov'*, 1924 nos. 1 and 2. I. P. Pavlov's text, which Bukharin quotes extensively, was apparently not published.

[99] Stephen F. Cohen, *Bukharin and the Bolshevik Revolution* (New York, 1973), p. 237.

[100] *Sud'by sovremennoi intelligentsii*, p. 27.

[101] *Trenirovka* (conditioning) was a word much used by the theater director Vsevolod Meyerhold in connection with the "biomechanical" preparation of actors. It was also used by A. K. Gastev, the poet and theorist of the scientific organization of labor.

[102] P. N. Sakulin, writing in *Nauchnyi rabotnik*, 1928 no. 5–6, p. 45, said that Bukharin had promised that concessions would be made "when we deem it politically appropriate." This remark does not appear in the published stenogram of the debate, *Sud'by sovremennoi intelligentsii*.

It would be a mistake, however, to regard the issue of intellectual freedom as the central concern either of the regime in its dealings with the intelligentsia or of the intelligentsia leaders themselves. In political terms, the intelligentsia leadership came from the Academy of Sciences and the high-salaried specialists and consultants associated with the government commissariats; and for these men intellectual freedom was secondary to the issue of political influence and specialist input in government policy making. It was impossible for scholars to refuse all contact with politics, wrote S. F. Oldenburg, chief negotiator with the regime for both the Academy of Sciences and the Section of Scientific Workers. To do so, in Oldenburg's view, was not only impossible but shortsighted. How else but through contact with politics was a working partnership of intelligence and power to be established?[103]

At the Second Congress of Scientific Workers, held in 1927, the leading scholars appeared not only confident but demanding. The demands were for money, and the terms in which they were put both emphasized a special relationship with the political leadership and made claims on it. This stance marked a change in the conventions of public discourse: bourgeois specialists had previously spoken aggressively only from an anti-Soviet position. But Academicians Oldenburg and Marr, who led an attack on Narkompros for its failure to obtain adequate financing for higher education and scholarly research, appeared to speak not only from a Soviet position but from a position of special access to the highest authorities. Their treatment of Lunacharsky, in fact, had the mixture of condescension and intimidation characteristic of commissars in their dealings with politically inferior bourgeois specialists in the old days.

In his speech to the Congress, Lunacharsky rather plaintively defended Narkompros's record of asking for money: "Almost every year Narkompros warns of the danger [that industrialization may be held up for lack of specialists]. These warnings are quite sensitively received, and the government will act the moment it becomes necessary . . . to make a basic investment to raise the standard of all our academic work."[104]

Oldenburg was not mollified. For ten years, he said, the specialists had witnessed Narkompros's "misfortunes" and tolerated its failure

---

[103] See S. F. Oldenburg, "Zadachi sektsii nauchnykh rabotnikov v dele kul'turnoi revoliutsii," *Nauchnyi rabotnik*, 1928 no. 5–6. The idea of such a partnership, implicit in many of Oldenburg's statements, may also be found in the resolution of the First Congress of Scientific Workers calling for "struggle for the creation of a free society built on the *union of science and labor*," *Pravda*, 24 November 1923, p. 4 (my emphasis).

[104] *Izvestiia*, 12 February 1927, p. 2.

to get adequate financing for scholarly institutions. He had expected Lunacharsky to make it clear to the leadership that the situation, on the eve of the industrialization drive, was now critical. He had expected self-criticism from Narkompros. "I am deeply disappointed . . . and it seems to me that we are left to do in an amateur way what our commissar could and should have done with the skilled hand of an expert. *We cannot be silent*, because I think that the commissar will *only thank* us if we point out to him those very large failings that we see in the work of Narkompros."[105]

Marr reinforced this criticism. Narkompros leaders seemed to have no concept of the urgency of the situation, he said. Iosif Khodorovskii (Lunacharsky's deputy) seemed to be speaking from "a place on the moon," and Lunacharsky himself was still worse. "To speak seriously about the state of our professional affairs when responsible Narkompros workers are distributed around points in the galaxy is absolutely impossible."[106]

The academicians were conveying two messages: first, that they expected to get what they wanted because it was in the national interest; and second, that if Narkompros could not look after the interests of higher education and science, the scholarly community could find itself other patrons.[107] But Lunacharsky feared that the specialists had misread the political situation. Perhaps he already had intimations of the forthcoming Shakhty trial, or perhaps simply suspected that the specialists were in touch with the party leadership but not with the mood of the party rank and file or, for that matter, with the worsening situation of some sections of the intelligentsia.[108]

In an article written shortly after the Congress, Lunacharsky warned:

> At the present time we have entered, if not a major crisis in our relations with the intelligentsia, at least a period in which there are some complicating circumstances. . . . The issue is not that the intelligentsia are demanding certain civil rights—they already have them and can use them. No, the point is that the intelligentsia have become the rep-

---

[105] Ibid.

[106] Ibid.

[107] At this time the All-Union Vesenkha was pressing for transfer of various higher educational and scholarly institutions from the Russian Narkompros to Vesenkha. The Academy of Sciences had recently passed from Narkompros's control to that of the Academic Committee (Uchenyi komitet) under TsIK, the Central Executive Committee of the Congress of Soviets. Thus the scientific workers' demand for organizational change in Narkompros's administration of higher education and scientific research, reported by N. I. Lohoda in *Nauchnyi rabotnik*, 1927 no. 2, pp. 16–17, strongly suggested that they might look to Vesenkha or TsIK for support if Narkompros failed to satisfy them.

[108] See below, chap. 5.

resentatives of a general political formation sympathetic to democracy and to a distinctly watered-down version of proletarian dictatorship; the intelligentsia are *waiting for an invitation from Soviet power for the most valuable elements of the aristocracy of the mind to enter the highest organs of government.*

This kind of talk is dangerous, and these tendencies have to be nipped in the bud. . . . There is not the slightest doubt that rightist elements . . . would like to blow a flame out of this spark, would like to create something like a conflict on the question of participation of "chosen intellectuals" in power. It is impossible to refrain from warning our intelligentsia away from this path.

The intelligentsia leaders [*verkhushechnaia intelligentsiia*] may, of course, hope that organs that care for the interests of science, such as Narkompros, will obliquely defend them, and even go out of their way to do so, in order to keep them, as major theoreticians, for the country. But they must not be surprised if the Revolution, which has to defend itself against its enemies meticulously and ruthlessly, has also produced organs that look on such things from a completely different point of view.[109]

(1978)

[109] Lunacharskii, "Intelligentsiia i ee mesto v sotsialisticheskom stroitel'stve," *Revoliutsiia i kul'tura*, 1927 no. 1 (15 November), pp. 32–33, 29 (my emphasis).

CHAPTER 4

Sex and Revolution

Soviet students in the 1920s were a pioneering generation, the first to go through university since the Revolution. Their life, like that of most pioneers, was uncomfortable. Dormitories were overcrowded, and no major maintenance had been done on university buildings since before the war. The newest equipment, library books, and foreign journals had usually been acquired before 1914. The students waited in line to consult textbooks in university reading rooms; and in the social sciences, where Soviet textbooks had yet to be written, they worked from lecture notes supplemented by any prerevolutionary text that came to hand.[1]

A very few institutions, such as the Sverdlov Communist University in Moscow, had been set up since the Revolution specifically to train Communists for leadership positions and had a mainly Communist, or at least Marxist, faculty. The rest were prerevolutionary foundations—universities and former teachers' and technical colleges upgraded to university status[2] since 1917—with their prerevolutionary faculty and an appointed Communist rector. Often the university administration was effectively in the hands not of the rec-

---

[1] The best sources on university life in the 1920s, from which this description is drawn, are the contemporary journals *Krasnaia molodezh'* (1924–1925), its successor, *Krasnoe studenchestvo* (1925–1935); and *Nauchnyi rabotnik* (1925–1930).
[2] That is, the status of VUZ, or higher educational institution.

tor but of the Communist students, who made up about a third of the student body.[3]

Soviet universities in the latter part of the 1920s had a male/female ratio of not quite 3 to 1, with a greater predominance of men in the Communist third of the students.[4] About half of the students came from peasant and working-class families and half from urban white-collar families.[5] Since the original Soviet policy of open admissions had failed to attract the desired proportion of working-class and Communist students, candidates for university entrance were selected on the basis of political and social suitability by local party, soviet, Komsomol, and trade union organizations. Some places were always reserved for free competitive enrollment by examination, and their numbers were increasing in 1926–1927 because of the government's concern about low academic standards. But it was unusual to go straight from school to university. The candidates selected by local organizations were already working, or, in the early years, had been demobilized from the Red Army. Peasants and working-class students without secondary education spent three or four preparatory years at the *rabfak* (workers' faculty), which often put them in their mid-twenties when they finally entered university. Stipends, which were available for about half the students, could scarcely support a student, let alone a spouse or family.

Within the university, there was a gulf between the "bourgeois" students—supported by their families, who would have sent them to university whether or not there had been a revolution—and the "proletarian" students, who were the protégés of the state. The typical proletarian was older, experienced, used to responsibility, poorly educated, and male. The typical bourgeois was young, a secondary-school graduate, inexperienced, and probably still living at home. It was the proletarians who had authority in the university and set the tone of student life.

The students knew that a great deal was expected of them and that great opportunities would be open to them, particularly but not solely to the Communists and proletarians. These students, it was

---

[3] At the beginning of 1928, 15.3% of all university students in the USSR were members or candidate members of the Communist party, and 19.2% were members or candidate members of Komsomol, the Communist youth organization: *Kul'turnoe stroitel'stvo SSSR v tsifrakh (1930–1934 gg.)* (Moscow, 1935), p. 43.

[4] At the beginning of 1928, 28.1% of all students in Soviet universities were women (ibid.).

[5] At the beginning of 1928, the parents of 25.4% of the students in Soviet universities were workers, 23.9% peasants, 41.7% "employees" (white-collar workers), and 9% "other" (merchants, traders, small businessmen, priests, etc.): *Podgotovka kadrov v SSSR, 1927–1931 gg.* (Moscow, 1933), p. 19.

felt, had escaped the corruption of an upbringing under the old regime; they were in the process of mastering the skills of the bourgeoisie in order to outdo them; and they were the chosen of their
generation, marked for future leadership and responsibility. It was
often said in the party that the lineaments of the future socialist society would first be seen in Soviet youth. Students, the elite of youth,
were aware of speaking for the future as well as for the Revolution.

The other side of the coin of expectation is disappointment. The
Communist students disappointed the Central Committee during the
conflict with Trotsky in the winter of 1923–1924, when disproportionately large numbers of university cells voted for the opposition.
Trotsky lost no time in reminding other party leaders of their shared
belief that youth was "the barometer of the party." The Stalinist majority of the Central Committee produced an explanation of what had
gone wrong with the Communist students: they had degenerated
through contact with the essentially bourgeois environment of the
universities and the big cities under NEP.[6]

This was traumatic news for the students. It was peculiarly pain-
ful, having been selected for upward social mobility and experiencing the concomitant discomfort and disorientation, to be accused of
becoming déclassé. It was still worse for the proletarians to have
their class credentials questioned in the pages of Pravda for all, including the bourgeois students, to read. From 1924 to 1928 (when
the First Five-Year Plan policy of massive working-class and Communist recruitment changed the climate of university life) the self-
confidence of Communist and lower-class students was shaken, and
so was the party's confidence in them.[7]

The party accused the students of meshchanstvo. This term was
derived from the old urban estate of meshchane, rendered in Marxist
terminology as "petty bourgeoisie," and it was used in the 1920s to
connote philistinism, the mentality of a small trader or businessman,
unimaginative respectability, slavish adherence to outdated conventions, and inability to comprehend the scope of future tasks. What
the Central Committee meant by this accusation was that the stu-

[6] For the party leadership's debate on youth, see Lev Trotsky's "Novyi kurs,"
Pravda, 11 December 1923, p. 4; 28 December 1923, p. 4; 29 December 1923, p. 4; and
responses by the editors of Pravda, 4 January 1924, p. 5, and G. Zinoviev, 5 February
1924, p. 5.

[7] See the letter of Moscow Communist students quoted by G. Zinoviev in N.
Bukharin, G. Zinoviev, and N. Krupskaia, Partiia i vospitanie smeny (Leningrad,
1924), pp. 13–15. In 1927, after university party cells had partially succumbed to New
Opposition influences, university Komsomols, even if of working-class origin, had
difficulty getting into the party because they were no longer considered true proletarians: L. Milkh, "Partrabota v vuzakh (organizatsionnye voprosy)," Krasnoe studenchestvo no. 1 (1927–1928), pp. 44–45.

dents had capitulated either to the narrow values of academe or to the NEP mores of the city. But to the students, *meshchanstvo* meant following the conventions of the old regime, observing bourgeois courtesies and bourgeois hypocrisies, wearing a tie, preaching the sanctity of the family and chastity before marriage, being bowed to by doormen, not swearing in mixed company.[8]

The difference between the two concepts was greatest in regard to sex. To Old Bolsheviks, *meshchanstvo* in the sexual realm was NEP morality, postwar sexual permissiveness and promiscuity. To Komsomol students, it was conventional bourgeois marriage, sexual coyness, and women talking about love.

The "sex problem" preoccupied students in the 1920s because they were getting contradictory signals on how to behave. One set of signals pointed to sexual liberation. Postwar Russia, especially the cities of Moscow and Petrograd, where most of the students were located, experienced the same relaxation of sexual mores as the rest of Europe. Soldiers demobilized from the Red Army brought back a casual macho attitude toward sex which young brothers worked hard to imitate. Younger sisters absorbed Soviet teaching on the emancipation of women, including emancipation from the bonds of bourgeois marriage and the traditional passive role. The Soviet government legalized divorce and abortion, secularized marriage, gave de facto marriage the same legal status as registered marriage, and tried to remove the social stigma from unmarried mothers and their children.[9] Among the Bolsheviks, Aleksandra Kollontai wrote of free sexual relationships based on love ("winged Eros") in the working commune.[10] Some of the students, especially in the early 1920s, were disciples of Kollontai on sex. Others, ignorant of theory, simply assumed that sexual and political liberation went together and that the Revolution had accomplished both: "Down with the capitalist tyranny of parents! . . . Kiss and embrace! . . . Free love is for free."[11]

[8] On Komsomol and student concepts of *meshchanstvo*, see V. Ermilov, "Komsomol'skaia pechat' i zaprosy molodezhi," *Molodaia gvardiia*, 1926 no. 1, pp. 235ff.; and T. Kostrov, "Kul'tura i meshchanstvo," *Revoliutsiia i kul'tura*, 1927 no. 3–4, pp. 21ff.

[9] For the 1917 decrees on marriage and divorce, the 1920 decree on abortion, excerpts from the 1925 discussion of revision of family law, and the revised Family Code of 1926 recognizing de facto marriage, see Rudolph Schlesinger, *The Family in the USSR* (London, 1949).

[10] On Kollontai, see Beatrice Farnsworth, "Bolshevism, the Woman Question, and Aleksandra Kollontai," *American Historical Review* 81 (April 1976): 292–316; and Barbara Evans Clements, "Emancipation through Communism: The Ideology of A. M. Kollontai," *Slavic Review*, June 1973, pp. 323–38.

[11] From the agitational speech of a self-appointed Komsomol sex instructor in a 1924 short story by Lidia Seifullina, "Instruktor 'Krasnogo molodezha,'" in *Izbrannye proizvedeniia* (Moscow, 1958), 1:385.

The other set of signals pointed to sexual restraint and came in the form of advice from party authorities to Communist youth. The authorities—most of them Old Bolsheviks, who saw the revolutionary cause as a vocation requiring sacrifice—recommended self-discipline, abstinence, fidelity to one partner, and sublimation of sexual energies in work.[12] Theorizing about free love, Lenin said, was an essentially bourgeois occupation typical of intellectuals; and, in practical terms, too much sexual activity distracted Communists from the Revolution.[13] The leadership after Lenin's death held to the same position. In 1926–1927 the party ran a propaganda campaign, directed mainly at Komsomol members and students, against "decadence"—a pose of cynicism and political disillusionment modeled on the poet Sergei Esenin, bohemianism, and the alleged youth ideology of casual sex without responsibility.[14] Students, already suspected of "bourgeois tendencies," now had to answer accusations of sexual degeneracy and promiscuity.

We have two kinds of evidence on how students in the 1920s actually dealt with the sex problem. The first is impressionistic, from contemporary literature and journalism. Here the typical (or at least symbolic) male Soviet student is a materialist in the style of Emmanuel Enchmen, a young and insignificant philosopher *cum* propagandist whom Bukharin attacked in 1923 as representative of an unhealthy tendency among Communist youth.[15] In the typical student of popular literature all thought and emotion are reduced to physiological reflexes. He is conscientiously devoted to promiscuity, offhand and cynical in relations with women, somewhat dissolute and coarse in language, but—at least as Komsomol writers portrayed him—unshakably aware of the primacy of the Revolution and the comparative unimportance of individual human relationships. This student would find *meshchanstvo* in himself if he phrased his proposition to a woman in anything but the crudest terms and in her if she refused, hesitated, or preferred a more traditional approach. He believes that the Revolution has given him an absolute right to sex.

[12] See, for example, writings of N. Bukharin, E. M. Iaroslavskii, A. A. Solts, and others in *Komsomol'skii byt*, ed. I. Razin (Moscow, 1927). The sublimation argument was most strenuously put by the Communist psychologist Aron Zalkind in his *Polovoi vopros v usloviiakh sovetskoi obshchestvennosti* (Leningrad, 1926).

[13] Klara Zetkin, *Recollections of Lenin* (Moscow, 1956), pp. 58–59, 66.

[14] Esenin, noted for his bohemian lifestyle, committed suicide in 1925. *Eseninshchina*—emulation of his lifestyle, degeneracy, expression of political disillusionment, suicide—was the target of the 1926–1927 campaign. In 1928 it was "bohemianism" (*bogema*). On *eseninshchina*, see the Communist Academy volume *Upadochnoe nastroenie sredi molodezhi: Eseninshchina* (Moscow, 1927).

[15] See David Joravsky, *Soviet Marxism and Natural Science, 1917–1932* (London, 1961), p. 94.

He is extremely virile and looks like Mayakovsky.[16] He drinks and can behave riotously when drunk but except in extremis does not go to bed with prostitutes unless he sees them as proletarian comrades. He would never under any circumstances commit a deviant sexual act, particularly a homosexual act. He never reads pornography and regards it with Communist contempt.

"With us there is no love," wrote the heroine of a contemporary novel. "With us there are only sexual relations, because love for us has a suspicious relation to the sphere of 'psychology,' and to our way of thinking only physiology has the right to exist."[17] As one of the female Old Bolsheviks protested, it was assumed that "every Komsomol *rabfak* student and other still beardless boys can and must satisfy their sexual urges. This for some reason is considered an unarguable truth. Sexual restraint is described as *meshchanstvo*."[18]

The literary image of the Komsomol girl and woman student also emphasizes promiscuity, which is often associated with an unfeminine directness and willingness to take the initiative in sex. But the promiscuous woman may also be a victim, suffering humiliation by men, abandonment, abortions, and attempts at suicide, and repenting (in a very conventional literary manner) in the last chapter. The most famous of the heroines, though not the most believable, is Tania Aristarkhova in S. I. Malashkhin's sensationalist novel *Luna s pravoi storony*.[19] Tania, a basically good Komsomol girl of peasant background, is sent to Sverdlov Communist University in Moscow and becomes corrupted by NEP degeneracy and Trotskyist classmates. She has had twenty-two lovers when the novel begins, takes part in orgies, drinks and takes drugs, and is in a state of utter moral confusion. At length she feigns suicide in order to escape to the virgin forest to work, recover her self-respect, and finally return to the party as a pure woman.

Much of the fictional literature on the "sex problem" is better as erotica than as social documentation; the journalism is often partisan, linked either with the antipromiscuity campaign or with its rebuttal by young people. As evidence, it obviously has to be handled with caution. But it can be checked against our second type of evidence, consisting of surveys of the sex lives of students conducted by questionnaires at various higher educational institutions in the 1920s. Four surveys I find useful are I. Gelman's of Sverdlov Com-

---

[16] The avant-garde poet Vladimir Mayakovsky (1893–1930) was a handsome, flamboyant Communist and something of a youth hero.

[17] Panteleimon Romanov, *Bez cheremukhi*, *Molodaia gvardiia*, 1926 no. 6, p. 15.

[18] Sofia Smidovich, "O liubvi," in Razin, *Komsomol'skii byt*, p. 268.

[19] S. I. Malashkin, *Luna s pravoi storony, ili Neobyknovennaia liubov'* (Moscow, 1927); first published in *Molodaia gvardiia*, 1926 no. 9.

munist University (1922),[20] G. A. Batkis's of Moscow medical schools (circa 1924),[21] V. E. Kliachkin's of higher educational institutions in Omsk (1924),[22] and D. I. Lass's of higher educational institutions in Odessa (around 1927).[23] The surveys have technical defects and of course tell us only what the students felt like reporting. But this research at least has the advantage of compensating for a bias in the literary evidence, which comes mainly from outside observers whose preoccupations, as we will see, differ in many respects from those of the students.

The first striking discovery is the comparatively large number of married students. It must be remembered that throughout the 1920s the average age of students, especially male students, was unusually high, and comparatively few came to university straight from school. But contemporaries often commented that students were too poor to marry, and married students are not prominent in fiction. Batkis's remarkable finding that 73.6 percent of his male students (and 43

[20] I. Gelman, *Polovaia zhizn' sovremennoi molodezhi: Opyt sotsial'no-biologicheskogo obsledovaniia* (Moscow, 1923). The questionnaire, which is reproduced, was sent to an unspecified number of students at Sverdlov Communist University in Moscow. There were 1,552 respondents, of whom 1,214 (78%) were men and 338 (22%) women; 37.1% were in the 16–21 age group, 42.4% in the 22–26 age group, and 20.5% were aged 27 or older. No party membership figures are given, but the nature of the school suggests that the majority must have been Communists or Komsomols.

[21] G. A. Batkis, "Opyt podkhoda k izucheniiu problemy pola: Iz rabot Gosudarstvennogo Institute Sotsial'noi Gigieny," *Sotsial'naia gigiena*, 1925 no. 6, pp. 36ff. The questionnaire, which is not reproduced, was distributed to 1,598 medical students of the First and Third Moscow universities and yielded a 40% response. Of 611 respondents, 341 (56%) were men and 270 (44%) women. The age breakdown was as follows: 3% of the men and 14% of the women were under 21; 21% of the men and 37% of the women were aged 21 to 24; 42% of the men and 30% of the women were aged 25 to 28; and 34% of the men and 19% of the women were 29 or older. Of the male respondents, 11.9% were Communists and 1.2% Komsomols; among the women, the proportions were 10% and 2.6%, respectively.

[22] V. E. Kliachkin, "Polovaia anketa sredi Omskogo studenchestva," *Sotsial'naia gigiena*, 1925 no. 6, pp. 124–38. The questionnaire, which is not reproduced, was distributed to an unspecified number of students at the veterinary and medical institutes, the Siberian Academy, the *rabfak*, and the Water-Transport Technical School of Omsk. There were 893 respondents, of whom 619 (69%) were men and 274 (31%) women. No detailed age breakdown is given, but 75.8% of all students (73% of the men and 82% of the women) were in the 19–26 age group. The proportions of Communist or Komsomol men and women were 30.5% and 17.2%, respectively.

[23] D. I. Lass, *Sovremennoe studenchestvo (byt, polovaia zhizn')* (Moscow, 1928). This survey, the most substantial of the four cited, was a project of the hygiene department of the Odessa Medical Institute. The questionnaire, which is not reproduced, was distributed to 3,500 students of the medical, agricultural, polytechnical, pedagogical, economics, chemical-pharmaceutical, music-drama, and art institutes; the Military School; and the Soviet Party School of Odessa, and yielded a 67% response. Of 2,328 respondents, 1,801 (77%) were men and 527 (23%) women. There is no information on party or Komsomol membership. The age breakdown is as follows: 27.6% of the men and 36.3% of the women were aged 16 to 21; 50.2% of the men and 43.4% of the women were 22 to 26; 22.2% of the men and 20.3% of the women were aged 27 or older.

percent of those aged twenty-four or younger) were married may perhaps be discounted, given the low rate of response to his questionnaire and the fact that a full third of his male respondents were aged
twenty-nine or older; but even in the Odessa group 35 percent of the
men and 32 percent of the women were or had been married.[24] The
lowest marriage figure for men (Kliachkin's 23.2 percent, which may
not include the formerly married) is far above the 7 percent reported
in a 1904 survey of Moscow University students.[25] Among women
students, who tended to be younger than men, there seems to have
been a distinct but less dramatic increase in the size of the married
group in comparison with those surveyed in Moscow in 1914.[26] (The
phenomenon of rising marriage rates was not peculiar to students: in
1924 there were 11.4 marriages per thousand of population in European Russia, compared with a rate immediately before the war of 8.3
per thousand.)[27]

These Soviet student marriages were by no means reproductions of
the conventional "philistine" patterns of their parents. In the first
place, a good proportion of them were free or unregistered marriages;
16.5 percent of the married men and 31.7 percent of the married
women in the Odessa group fell in that category. Of the rest of the
married group—both in the Odessa survey and in Batkis's 1924 Moscow survey—about 80 percent had been married in a Soviet registry
office and not in church, with the proportion of church marriages
slightly higher for men than for women.[28]

The marriages were also unusual in that only a small percentage of
couples were able to set up any kind of home of their own. Far more
commonly, the husband or wife went away to study; the couple
lived together, but in a corner of an apartment shared with his or her

[24] Batkis, "Opyt podkhoda," p. 76 (includes formerly married); Lass, *Sovremennoe
studenchestvo*, p. 139, 141. In Gelman's sample, 21% of the men and 31% of the
women were or had been married (*Polovaia zhizn'*, p. 82): these figures may be too
low because, as Gelman points out, respondents were uncertain whether to include
free or unregistered marriage (which is unambiguously included in the Baktis and
Lass surveys).
[25] Kliachkin's figure ("Polovaia anketa," p. 132), like Gelman's, may not include unregistered marriage. The Moscow figure is quoted in Gelman, *Polovaia zhizn'*, p. 82,
from a 1904 survey by M. A. Chlenov.
[26] In the Soviet surveys, the proportion of married and formerly married women
ranges from Batkis's 42.4% ("Opyt podkhoda," p. 76) to Kliachkin's 20.5% ("Polovaia
anketa," p. 132). A 1914 survey of students of the Moscow Higher Women's Courses
by D. Zhbankov found 19% married (cited in Gelman, *Polovaia zhizn'*, p. 82).
[27] *Statisticheskii spravochnik SSSR za 1928* (Moscow, 1929), p. 74.
[28] Lass, *Sovremennoe studenchestvo*, p. 140; Batkis, "Opyt podkhoda," p. 78. Note
that cohabiting partners may have different views on whether or not they are living in
"free marriage." But in Batkis's data, which include a large number of marriages, most
of them "free," women were not reporting more free marriages than men.

parents or with strangers; the couple shared a bed behind a partition
in a student dormitory; or the husband and wife lived separately
in different dormitories. Of the currently married students in the
Odessa survey, only 10 percent of the men and 40 percent of the
women described themselves as "living with spouse."[29] One student
wrote bitterly:

> So what does it matter if I'm in love and married, when three years'
> underground work and then the army and other circumstances pre-
> vented us from living together? Now it's still worse for me. My wife
> and I live in Moscow; I study and live in one dormitory; my wife also
> studies and lives in her own dormitory in another school. We live not
> far from each other and see each other almost every day, but material
> circumstances do not permit us to rent a room so we can live together.
> We are both leading truly monastic lives.[30]

Of course not all spouses were students. Many of the men left
wives in their hometowns or villages when they came to university.
"We live in different towns and are rarely together—four to seven
days every five or six months." "I have to live far from my wife and
don't live a normal life." "I left my wife in L. Now I cannot live
without a sexual relationship. . . . I dream for hours about how to get
a wife in Odessa."[31]

Probably most of the church marriages (more common among men
than among women) were those of students of peasant origin who
were now effectively separated from their wives and might never
return to them. Marital separation was obviously a factor in the high
rates of reported adultery: 62 percent of the married men in Gelman's 1922 Moscow group, 39 percent in the 1924 Omsk survey, 16
percent in the 1927 Odessa survey.[32] But another factor was no doubt
the postwar wave of what Lass calls "disorderly married life," and
the figures seem to bear out his claim that by 1927 this wave was
retreating.[33] In the earlier surveys, a higher proportion of men had
presumably recently come out of the army and kept the habit, or at

[29] Lass, *Sovremennoe studenchestvo*, p. 45. "Living with spouse" evidently means
living together, independently of family, in an apartment. "Living with family" and
"living with comrades" (dormitory or communal living) are separate and nonoverlap-
ping categories.

[30] A 31-year-old working-class Communist respondent quoted in Gelman, *Polovaia
zhizn'*, p. 138.

[31] Quoted in Lass, *Sovremennoe studenchestvo*, pp. 143, 145, 140.

[32] Gelman, *Polovaia zhizn'*, p. 88; Kliachkin, "Polovaia anketa," p. 132; Lass,
Sovremennoe studenchestvo, pp. 148–49. In the 1904 survey of Moscow University
students (see n. 25), only 9% of the married men reported infidelity.

[33] Lass, *Sovremennoe studenchestvo*, pp. 148–49.

least the memory, of casual and promiscuous sex with any available
woman. "During the Civil War I had at least thirty women," wrote
one of Kliachkin's respondents; and another reported that "at one
time I lived with two women at once and sometimes tried it with a
third, but earlier I had at least ten."[34] Both Gelman and Kliachkin
noted the prevalence of infidelity even in the early stages of marriage: one out of three married men in Kliachkin's survey reported
infidelity within the first year of marriage.[35]

Infidelity was less characteristic of the married women, but even
here there were some signs of postwar or postrevolutionary raised
consciousness. Whereas the Omsk men tended to give an apologetic
description of their unfaithfulness as "an abnormal manifestation
[produced] by the long absence of [their] wives during their studies,
weakness of will, and environmental influences," the Omsk women
attributed it, apparently without apology, to "lack of sexual satisfaction from the husband."[36] One technically faithful wife in Odessa
reported:

> Besides having a husband, I'm attracted to other persons who interest
> me. In regard to sex, this takes the form of a desire to kiss and never
> ends with the sex act, since that as such has no particular interest for
> me. My family relations do not suffer from this. Of course, I can't
> speak for my husband here, since all men are great believers in private
> property [sobstvenniki], even the Communists. . . . Men themselves
> can "sow wild oats" but wives, Allah forbid, can't. I am answering in
> kind; I am behaving as men do.[37]

As one might expect, a high marriage rate was accompanied by a
fairly high divorce rate, at least among in the Odessa students.[38] In
this group, sixty-nine men and twenty-six women were divorced;
that is, 4 to 5 percent of all students or 11 and 16 percent, respectively, of all men and women who had ever been married. Even if we
allow for the students' age, however, these figures are hardly spec-
tacular when we consider that the current ratio of marriages to di-

[34] Kliachkin, "Polovaia anketa," p. 129.
[35] Gelman, Polovaia zhizn', p. 88; Kliachkin, "Polovaia anketa," p. 132.
[36] Kliatchkin, "Polovaia anketa," p. 132. In the Odessa survey (1927), only 6 of 142
married women admitted adultery; three had had three or more extramarital affairs, and three only one (Lass, Sovremennoe studenchestvo, pp. 148–49). In the Omsk survey (1924), however, the proportion was higher: 5 out of 50 married women admitted
adultery (Kliachkin, p. 132).
[37] Quoted in Lass, Sovremennoe studenchestvo, p. 148.
[38] Ibid., p. 141. Lass is very confused on this question: he did not discover which, if
any, of his currently married students had been previously married and divorced or if
any students had been divorced more than once. Thus if there was a group of frequent
marriers and divorcers among the Odessa students, Lass's survey missed it. None of
the other surveys provides data on divorce.

vorces was 22 to 10 for the urban population of the European USSR and 13 to 10 in the city of Moscow.[39]

Given the students' living conditions and income, children were a disaster. According to one Odessa respondent, the problems were so enormous that men whose wives gave birth usually ran away. "In my life," wrote a woman student, "I have had affairs with three men and undergone four abortions, for the sole reason that the men had an awful attitude toward my future child."[40] The Omsk women, who evidently were asked whether they thought it possible to combine a career and civic responsibilities with a family, responded relatively optimistically ("We Komsomol women can bring up a child properly no matter what the circumstances"). Most of them, however, were still unmarried.[41]

In the absence of easily available means of contraception, women were dependent on abortion to prevent birth. In theory, legal abortions were not available on demand in the 1920s;[42] in practice, it was normally possible to get an abortion, even if not legally at a hospital or clinic. As a means of preventing conception, Odessa students reported using condoms (308 responses), coitus interruptus (265 responses), and chemical means of contraception (51 responses).[43] But in all the surveys women who responded had to resort to abortion fairly frequently. Approximately 10 percent of all the women students and (with the exception of Gelman's group) between one-quarter and one-half of the sexually experienced ones reported that they had had abortions.[44] There were more abortions than births.[45] Nev-

---

[39] *Statisticheskii spravochnik SSSR za 1928*, pp. 76–79.

[40] Quoted in Lass, *Sovremennoe studenchestvo*, pp. 12, 204.

[41] Kliachkin, "Polovaia anketa," p. 136.

[42] In Smidovich, "O liubvi" (n. 18 above), a member of the Central Control Commission of the Communist party describes an allegedly typical doctor's response to a student's pregnancy: "We permit abortion when giving birth threatens the very life of the mother or when a woman worker is already burdened with too large a family. You don't fit either of these categories" (pp. 268–69).

[43] Lass, *Sovremennoe studenchestvo*, pp. 137, 146 (responses of male and female students; condoms listed separately, as a prophylactic rather than contraceptive).

[44] Despite the formal restrictions on abortion, this was not a particularly delicate subject for the students. The rate and nature of responses to abortion questions suggest no substantial underreporting by the married students, though unmarried students may have been less forthcoming. For calculation of the number of sexually experienced women in each group, see below. In Gelman's group 8% of all women (14% of the sexually experienced) reported an average of 1.2 abortions (*Polovaia zhizn'*, p. 107). This group is taken as atypical because most of the women's pregnancies occurred before they entered the university (which was founded only a year before the survey was conducted) and were carried to term. In Batkis's group 21% of all women (46% of the sexually experienced) reported an average of two abortions ("Opyt podkhoda," pp. 87–88). Among the Omsk students (Kliachkin, "Polovaia anketa," p. 136), 8% of all women (29% of the sexually experienced) had had abortions, an average of 1.3 abortions per woman. Among the Odessa students (Lass, *Sovremennoe stu-*

ertheless, a fair proportion of the married students had children (usually one child). The Sverdlov Communist University students led the way: almost half of the married women had children, most of whom presumably were born before the women entered the university.[46] Among the Moscow medical students surveyed by Batkis, 40 percent of the married men and 23 percent of the married women had children.[47] The proportion was lower in Omsk (15 percent of the married women had children).[48] We cannot, of course, assume that student mothers were living with either their husbands or their children. It seems likely that many of the women in Gelman's group in particular were divorced or separated before they entered the university and that the children were left at home with their grandparents. Other women, formerly married, would have been bringing up their children alone, as in the case of a third-year medical student in Odessa who had become pregnant in her first year at university, had her baby, and left or been left by her husband when the child was six months old.[49]

To put the students' situation in perspective, we need to compare their abortion and birth rates with those of the same age group in the whole urban population. We can do so very roughly on the basis of B. Ts. Urlanis's study of the generation born in 1906. Urlanis calculates that when the urban women of this generation were in their twenties, they were having about 20,000 abortions a year. Thus between the ages of twenty and twenty-four (1926–1930) these urban women had a total of 100,000 abortions. In the same period, the whole 1906 cohort of women gave birth to 2,190,000 children, a figure that yields approximately 300,000 children for the urban women.[50]

---

sexually experienced) had had an average of two abortions each. (In this case, I do not follow Lass's interpretation of his data. Having obtained 142 responses to his abortion/contraception question, he assumes that it was answered only by the 142 currently married women in his survey. In fact, aside from the improbability of a 100% response from any group, the question called for multiple answers; that is, there are more responses than respondents. Therefore I assume that *all* women willing to admit to abortions answered the question.)

[45] Batkis reported 112 abortions to 30 births ("Opyt podkhoda," pp. 87–88); Kliachkin, 29 abortions to 17 births ("Polovaia anketa," p. 136). For the atypical Gelman group, see n. 44.

[46] Gelman, *Polovaia zhizn'*, p. 107. Forty-nine women in this group reported 81 children (as against 31 abortions). If Gelman was not being hoaxed, three women had six, ten, and eleven children, respectively.

[47] Batkis, "Opyt podkhoda," pp. 87, 76.

[48] Kliachkin, "Polovaia anketa," p. 136.

[49] Lass, *Sovremennoe studenchestvo*, p. 209. Lass gives no summary data on births.

[50] B. Ts. Urlanis, *Istoriia odnogo pokoleniia (sotsial'no-demograficheskii ocherk)* (Moscow, 1968), pp. 170, 167. The calculation is based on data in *Statisticheskii spravochnik SSSR za 1928*, pp. 76–79, on urban and rural births in the European part of the

The birth-abortion ratio thus comes to about 300 to 100, whereas the students in Batkis's and Kliachkin's groups had, respectively, 27 and 76 births to 100 abortions.[51] The students, it seems, diverged from the norm of their urban age group less by frequency of abortion than by infrequency of giving birth.[52] In other words, they almost certainly had fewer pregnancies; and this, in the absence of reliable means of contraception, would seem to indicate that the women students were less sexually active than typical urban nonuniversity women of the same age. (This hypothesis is supported to some extent by Batkis's data. The wives of male students in his sample had both more abortions and more children than the married women students.)[53]

Since promiscuity and casual sex figure so prominently in the impressionist literature on student life, we might expect the surveys to show a high rate of sexual activity among the unmarried students—who, except in Batkis's group, form the majority. The men who responded to the 1922 and 1924 surveys do tend to report a highly active sex life, particularly in the past. But the Odessa survey of 1927 gives quite a different picture: the male students' overwhelming preoccupation was with enforced abstinence, lack of sexual opportunity, and apprehension about the damaging consequences of sexual deprivation on their general health and well-being.

For male students, the traditional prerevolutionary pattern of sexual initiation was with a prostitute or a domestic servant. After the Revolution these categories declined somewhat, with a corresponding rise in initiation by "casual acquaintances." But the change, given the social and economic flux of the first years after the Revolution, is probably not very significant. More students reported begin-

---

of the USSR in 1927. Urban births accounted for 13.9% of all births. Unfortunately, we have no way of ascertaining whether this proportion obtains among the mothers in the 20–24 age group.

[51] See n. 45, above.

[52] The Odessa students, with an average age of 22 to 23, were well on the way to achieving the 60 abortions per 100 women that can be calculated for Urlanis's women by the end of their 29th year (Lass, *Sovremennoe studenchestvo*, p. 147; Urlanis, *Istoriia odnogo pokoleniia*, p. 170). The Urlanis rate is calculated from his estimate of 200,000 abortions performed on 360,000 urban women over the ten years from their 20th to 30th birthdays, with a correction of 4 abortions per 100 women to cover abortions before the age of 20. But Urlanis's figures are basically from hospital (that is, legal) abortions only, while the students were reporting both legal and illegal abortions. The student rate may be above the norm, but what is much clearer is that their rate of giving birth was substantially below the norm. Among nonstudents, 20 to 24 was the peak age of childbearing (Urlanis, p. 167).

[53] Of the married men, 54% reported that their wives had had abortions and 11% did not know; 49% of the married women reported abortions. Forty-one percent of the men had children, as against 23% of the married women (Batkis, "Opyt podkhoda," pp. 76, 87–88, 96).

ning their sex lives with girlfriends; comparatively few, however, had their first intercourse with wives, fiancées, or university classmates.[54]

Casual acquaintances continued to play an important part in the sex lives of the unmarried men. No male respondent suggested the possibility of freely satisfying sexual desire by casual comradely arrangements with female fellow students. Had the possibility existed, complaints about sexual deprivation would no doubt have been fewer; but in fact (even if we leave aside the unliberated attitudes of many women students, which will be discussed in due course) the ratio of unmarried male students to potentially available female students in Odessa, for example, was a discouraging 10 to 1, and "casual acquaintances" had clearly to be found outside the university.[55]

As one student put it, "You have no money. But you have to get satisfaction. And you can't go to prostitutes because you might get infected. The only solution is casual acquaintances."[56] Still, the distinction between prostitutes and casual acquaintances was not very clear. In the Omsk survey, which did not use the "casual acquaintance" category, almost half the male students continued to have relations with prostitutes. Working-class students were the most inclined to go to prostitutes, though fewer numbers of this group who were Communists did so. Middle-class male students—of whom there were comparatively few—continued to have intercourse with domestic servants; the exceptions were the middle-class Communists, who absolutely, and no doubt on principle, abstained from relations with servants.[57]

[54] Chlenov's 1904 survey of Moscow University students (n. 25 above) showed that 42% had first intercourse with a prostitute and 36% with a domestic servant (quoted in Lass, *Sovremennoe studenchestvo*, p. 113). Corresponding figures in Gelman's survey were 28% and zero (Gelman, *Polovaia zhizn'*, p. 59); in the Omsk survey, 20% and 14% (Kliachkin, "Polovaia anketa," p. 129); and in the Odessa survey, 14% and 9% (Lass, p. 112). In Batkis's group as a whole, the figures were 17% and 13%, but first intercourse with a prostitute was much more common among those whose sex lives had begun before the Revolution than after ("Opyt podkhoda," pp. 70–71, 81). First intercourse with girlfriends went as high as 38.4% (Batkis, p. 70) and 26% (Kliachkin, p. 129); wives and fiancées accounted for not more than 10% in any of the surveys; the category of "comrades" (which would include university classmates) produced a zero response in Gelman (p. 59), and "girl students" a 1.8% response in Kliachkin (p. 129).

[55] I calculated the numbers of potentially available female students by subtracting the number of virgins and married women (except those who admitted adultery) from the total number of women.

[56] Quoted in Lass, *Sovremennoe studenchestvo*, p. 13.

[57] Kliachkin, "Polovaia anketa," pp. 129–30. For comparative data on employment of prostitutes by working-class men, see the 1924–1925 survey by M. Barash, published in English as "Sex Life of the Workers of Moscow," *Journal of Social Hygiene* 12 (May 1926): 274–88.

The Odessa survey is the only one to provide data on the current frequency of intercourse. Of the male students, 10 percent were virgins, another 10 percent were not but apparently had no current sex life, and 50 percent reported that they had sex "occasionally" (*sluchaino*). The group that reported having sex once a week or more (29 percent of all male students) was slightly smaller than the married group. Not surprisingly, three-quarters of the Odessa men were getting less sex than they wanted.[58]

Frustration was complicated by an unexpectedly high incidence of impotence, which the men seemed to blame on the peculiar strains and privations of student life.[59] In universities, one commentator wrote, "study, intellectual labor, and a great expense of intellectual energy combined with inadequate food considerably soften the acuteness of sexual problems"—so much so, in fact, that 41 percent of the men in the Odessa survey reported impotence, either "complete" (135 respondents) or "relative" (*otnositel'noe bessilie*; 603 respondents).[60] The "half-starved and restless" condition of student life "threatens complete sexual impotence, so that there is very little chance that we Communists will leave descendants," a Gelman respondent wrote in 1922.[61]

The relevant factor here may be less that the students lived in crowded conditions, got too little sleep and too few hot meals, and were unusually liable to anemia and colds—although all these problems are well attested to—than that they were under unusual nervous strain. A survey of Moscow student life contemporary with the Odessa survey reported that 85 percent of the students in a dormitory housing the "academic, party, and trade union *aktiv* of the university" were suffering from "nervous and bronchial disorders."[62] The male student on the edge of nervous breakdown and suffering from anxiety, depression, paranoia, or hysteria is a familiar figure in the literature of the 1920s;[63] and one of the stimuli for the campaign against *eseninshchina* was the mounting rate of suicide among stu-

[58] Lass, *Sovremennoe studenchestvo*, pp. 128, 126. Calculation of the 10% non-virgins who had no current sex life is based on the drop in male response from the question on first intercourse to the question on current frequency of intercourse.

[59] Lass's is the only survey (apart from passing mention by Gelman) to investigate the question of impotence.

[60] E. Troshchenko, "Vuzovskaia molodezh'," *Molodaia gvardiia*, 1927 no. 4, p. 139; Lass, *Sovremennoe studenchestvo*, p. 183.

[61] Quoted in Gelman, *Polovaia zhizn'*, p. 138.

[62] This survey, by the Communist psychologist A. B. Zalkind, was apparently never published, but a summary of his findings appeared in *Pravda*, 9 February 1928, p. 5.

[63] See, for example, S. I. Malashkin's short story "Konapushki na vesne," in *Krasnoe studenchestvo*, 1927–1928 no. 2, pp. 1–18, which depicts madness as an inevitable and almost admirable characteristic of the revolutionary student milieu.

dents. Army veterans were peculiarly vulnerable to neurosis, as were students with social-class problems (the wrong class origin, which had to be hidden or lived down; the problem, particularly acute for working-class Communists, of upward mobility out of the high-prestige working class into the low-prestige intelligentsia) and academic problems.

The kind of academic problem that many male students faced is understandable when we consider their backgrounds. Before entering a university, 29 percent of the Odessa men had been working in agriculture and 25 percent in factories; 41 percent had only primary education, and 20 percent had studied on their own at home or in evening courses.[64] More than half, in other words, were likely to have trouble meeting the demands of university courses; and the effects of this kind of anxiety, as reported by a contemporary medical researcher, were that the student "becomes passive and unsure of himself. He begins to doubt his suitability not only for university study but for work in general and to doubt the value [polnotsennost'] of his own personality."[65]

Anxiety is indicated not only in Odessa man's response on impotence but also in their answers on sexual abstinence and masturbation. Both Lass and Kliachkin found (and deplored) a strongly entrenched belief among male students that abstinence was physically dangerous: "The suggestion that abstinence from sexual relations in student life is harmful to health runs like a red thread through all the questionnaires."[66] A third of all the male students in Lass's survey reported nervous exhaustion, extreme excitement, or "jaded feelings," which they attributed to sexual deprivation. Some also believed that abstinence over a long period produced impotence. One respondent wrote:

> Three years of intensive mental effort and abstinence have had the effect of almost extinguishing the libido. In the Christmas vacation I went on holiday and got to know a woman I could have slept with. In my mind I wanted to, but in practice I couldn't because of impotence. Therefore I think that abstinence kills sexual passion forever. If this impotence continues, then I don't think life is worth living.[67]

All the surveys revealed that some students were driven to what Kliachkin calls "wild opinions": that "until marriage a woman ought

[64] Lass, Sovremennoe studenchestvo, pp. 24–25.

[65] Quoted from a review of S. I. Goldenberg's survey, "Nervnost' studenchestva i ee prichiny," in Krasnoe studenchestvo, 1927–1928 no. 12, p. 78.

[66] Kliachkin, "Polovaia anketa," pp. 137.

[67] Sovremennoe studenchestvo, pp. 194, 193. Both Lass and Kliachkin reported that women felt no ill effects from abstinence.

to give herself [to?] a bachelor two or three times a year," that "women and men of mature age in the universities ought to have relations regardless of whether they love each other"; that as a temporary measure the government should organize brothels "on a free basis for both sexes according to their needs."[68] More commonly (as we shall see) the students thought in terms of another kind of government intervention—measures that would make student marriage and cohabitation in marriage economically viable.

Pending government solution, however, the male students had to live with a situation in which, as they saw it, their health and morale suffered. The dominant attitude toward masturbation among the men made the situation even less tolerable. While a minority of both the Odessa and the Omsk students took the view that masturbation was "not harmful and even useful," the majority of men regarded it with shame and abhorrence.[69] "In regard to myself," one student wrote, "I suspect that the influence of masturbation has been mainly on the memory, which has begun to get noticeably duller. Sometimes when I start to speak, the thought I had in mind to say has got lost somewhere." "When I think about [masturbation]," wrote another, "my hair stands on end. It rises before me like a gigantic monster clutching me in its claws. As a result of ten years of daily masturbation, I myself have turned from a man into a monster."[70]

Perhaps the single most striking feature of male students' sexual behavior (documented in three of the four surveys) is the large proportion of men who denied masturbating in either the present or the past: 43 percent in Batkis's survey, 47 in Gelman's, 49 in Lass's. The comparable figure in Chlenov's 1904 survey was 27 percent.[71] The inference to be drawn, regardless of the accuracy of the responses, is that Soviet students in the 1920s had considerably more inhibitions about masturbation than their prerevolutionary counterparts had had. Lass, who found that "among the persons practicing masturbation there is not one, as our researches show, who had not tried to end his ailment," also reported that despite their fear of the consequences of abstinence, male students suffered so acutely from guilt over masturbation and the frustration of an irregular sex life that 80 percent of them had made at least one attempt to give up sex altogether.[72]

---

[68] Kliachkin, "Polovaia anketa," p. 137; Lass, *Sovremennoe studenchestvo*, p. 198.

[69] Kliachkin, "Polovaia anketa," p. 137.

[70] Lass, *Sovremennoe studenchestvo*, pp. 182, 180–81.

[71] Batkis, "Opyt podkhoda," p. 73; Lass, *Sovremennoe studenchestvo*, p. 166 (quoting Gelman and Chienov). Lass's masturbation report comes under the heading of "sexual deviation," and the strongly negative attitude toward masturbation which it conveys (and the other researchers do not) could have influenced his respondents.

[72] Quoted in Lass, *Sovremennoe studenchestvo*, pp. 183, 192. It is quite possible that

The men's anxieties about abstinence, impotence, and masturbation have no counterpart in the women's responses. As Kliachkin notes, the women tended to feel that problems arose from the existence of sexual relations rather than from their absence.[73] This observation brings us at once to the central fact about female sexual behavior revealed in the surveys: more than half of the women were virgins.[74]

Given that a large proportion of the women were either married or virgins, the remaining group of sexually active but unmarried women is small. Among Gelman's women (older than those of other surveys), 22 percent are in this category; the Odessa figure is 16 percent; the Kliachkin and Batkis surveys produce, respectively, 7 and 3 percent.[75] Ideally, divorced women should be included among the sexually active but unmarried. If they had been added to that group in the Odessa survey (the only one to separate the married from the formerly married), the numbers would increase by 26 and the proportion from 16 to 21 percent.[76]

Taking the women in the four surveys together, we find 55 percent virgins, 32 percent married or formerly married, and 13 percent unmarried but sexually experienced.[77] Thus the great majority appear to fall into quite traditional patterns, giving little support to the suggestion in the impressionistic literature of the time that promiscuity and an ideology of sexual liberation were widespread among women students. The researchers, it must be said, dismiss or ignore this sugges-

---

the sublimation arguments of the official antipromiscuity campaign of 1926–1928 made some headway among the young. I. T. Bobryshev, *Melkoburzhaznye vliianiia sredi molodezhi*, 2d ed. (Moscow, 1928), p. 121, cites the case of a Komsomol commune whose rules "forbade members of the commune, because of their age, to lead a sex life." Zalkind (n. 62 above), who was one of the main champions of sublimation, found that 35% of the students in his Moscow survey were not leading a sex life and that the abstinence of the majority was "motivated by their awareness of "the necessity of diverting sexual energy into creative social activity."

[73] Kliachkin, "Polovaia anketa," p. 132.

[74] Gelman found 108 virgins, or 47% (*Polovaia zhizn'*, p. 106); Batkis, 147 virgins, or 54% ("Opyt podkhoda," p. 76); Kliachkin, 195 virgins, or 71% ("Polovaia anketa," p. 128). Lass did not ask his students if they were virgins, but the largest female response to a question on sexual intercourse was 253, out of a total of 527 women (*Sovremennoe studenchestvo*, p. 98). This finding suggests that 274 women (52%) would have declared themselves virgins if they had been asked.

[75] I obtained these figures by subtracting the number of virgins and married or formerly married women from the total number and expressing the result as a percentage of the total. Absolute numbers in the category are 75 (Gelman), 85 (Lass), 20 (Kliachkin), and 9 (Batkis).

[76] Data from Lass, *Sovremennoe studenchestvo*, pp. 140, 142.

[77] If we apply Lass's figure on divorce (15% of all women who had married) to the women in the other three surveys, we get a total of 55% virgins, 27% currently married, and 18% sexually experienced but not currently married.

tion. Kliachkin (explaining that he had forgotten to ask the women in his survey about their sex partners) brushes the whole question aside: "Of the 79 of our women who have sexual relations," he writes, "59 are married, and the rest dream about love and marriage."[78]

This statement is perhaps a bit sweeping. If we take the question of first intercourse, for example, six out of ten sexually experienced (including married) women reported the partner as husband or fiancé, but of the two surveys that provide the data, one reports three women out of ten whose partner was a "comrade" or "close acquaintance" and one whose partner was a casual acquaintance; the other reports two in each of those categories.[79] The number of Odessa women whose first intercourse was with a comrade or casual acquaintance (90) is close to the number of unmarried women with sexual experience (85) and the number of women reporting that they had sex "occasionally" (97). These women, with the 26 divorcees, give us a group of about one-fifth of all the Odessa women who might be regarded as liberated from traditional norms. One possible inference from the data, however, is that the "liberated" group was less sexually active than the traditionally oriented married group.[80]

Hard evidence of promiscuity is difficult to find. Only one-third of the Omsk women were virgins when they married, but the obvious assumption is that most lost their virginity to their future husbands. Six married women in Odessa admitted adultery, five in Omsk. Seven women in Batkis's survey (6.3 percent of the respondents) reported that they had had simultaneous affairs with more than one man. Two Odessa women were aware of having been infected with venereal disease.[81]

It was widely believed in the 1920s that Communists and Komsomols led the way in sexual liberation. Only two of the surveys give a breakdown by party membership (though most of the Gelman sample must be presumed to be Communist). In Batkis's group—relatively old students, most of them married—12 percent of men and 10 percent of women were Communists, and a small number were Kom-

[78] Kliachkin, "Polovaia anketa," p. 130.

[79] Lass, Sovremennoe studenchestvo, p. 112; Batkis, "Opyt podkhoda," p. 71.

[80] Lass, Sovremennoye studenchestvo, pp. 112, 128. Of Lass's respondents, 110 women—presumably the married group minus those wives separated by long distances from their husbands—said that they had a regular sex life, with intercourse at least once a week (p. 128).

[81] Kliachkin, "Polovaia anketa," pp. 133, 132; Batkis, "Opyt podkhoda," p. 80; Lass, Sovremennoe studenchestvo, p. 152. Ninety percent of all women responded to the question on venereal disease. The male VD rate, according to both Lass and Kliachkin (p. 134), was not high: 24% of the male respondents had had VD at some time in the Odessa group (about the same as those in Chlenov's 1904 survey [n. 25]), 14% in the Omsk group.

somols. In Kliachkin's group, which was younger and mainly unmarried, 31 percent of the men and 17 percent of the women were Communists or Komsomols (with Komsomols presumably predominating).[82] When the two surveys are compared, age rather than party membership seems to explain the differences. The one salient piece of information that emerges (from Batkis) is that virginity was more common among nonparty women (58 percent) than among Communist women (23.5 percent)—but this too may be a product of age if, as seems likely, the Communist women tended to be older than the norm.[83]

Malashkin's fictional picture of student life put great stress on orgies or, as he put it, "Athenian nights." Lass's data suggest some Athenian nights in Odessa, but mainly outside the universities and involving student men and town women. In this survey, 304 men and 13 women reported using alcohol as an accompaniment to sex, and 249 men and 32 women listed drugs among factors that increased sexual excitement. Sixty-eight men and six women reported sexually deviant behavior, mainly "unnatural acts," and all of these women and two-thirds of the men also took drugs.[84]

What is striking in these figures is not the evidence of student debauchery, which seems unremarkable, but the implication that there was a well-established drug culture among Odessa students in the 1920s. Odessa, of course, was an international port not too far from the opium fields of Turkey and not a typical Soviet university town. Still, a total of 697 students—35 percent of all men and 11 percent of all women—said they had taken drugs—almost as many as the 763 students who admitted "use of alcohol."[85]

---

[82] Batkis, "Opyt podkhoda," p. 46; Kliachkin, "Polovaia anketa," p. 125.

[83] Batkis, "Opyt podkhoda," p. 79. For the relationship of age and sexual experience, see ibid., p. 76.

[84] Lass, Sovremennoe studenchestvo, pp. 131–33, 188, 192.

[85] Ibid., pp. 92, 132. Lass's narkomaniia excludes tobacco use. There are other reports on drug use in the 1920s, though they are somewhat fragmentary. Batkis ("Opyt podkhoda," p. 51) found that 15% of his male students and 4% of the females reported drug use, without indication of frequency. The fictional literature of the 1920s portrays drug use among students, the intelligentsia, and the gangs of homeless children (besprizornye) who survived precariously on the streets and railroads and in and out of orphanages at this time. The drugs most commonly used seem to have been opium and cocaine. The Bol'shaia sovetskaia entsiklopediia (Moscow, 1935), 33:266, describes cocaine use as a problem "in the first years of the Revolution, among the remnants of the bourgeoisie, artistic bohemians, and besprizornye." Although, according to the same source, "decisive measures against the cocaine trade" were taken in 1923, it seems that cocaine remained available and in legal use until 1928, when a Soviet government decree forbade the "free circulation" of cocaine, hashish, morphine, and other narcotic drugs (Bol'shaia sovetskaia entsiklopediia, 2d ed. [Moscow, 1954], 29:129). Lass reports on the use of drugs neutrally, but conveys a strong moral disapproval of alcohol. This attitude may explain the students' rather muted response

As we have seen, the reported behavior of Soviet students provides more evidence of the persistence of traditional machismo and
prudent female chastity than of liberating sexual revolution. But
when we come to the students' ideology on sex, love, and marriage,
the situation is somewhat different. Gelman's students—questioned
in 1922; mainly Communists; many of the women probably divorced, separated, or widowed—were radicals on marriage. Only 21
percent of his men and 14 percent of his women described marriage
as the ideal way to arrange one's sex life—and it should be remembered that 31 percent of the women actually were or had been married. About 10 percent of both sexes voted for free love, meaning a
variety of short-term relationships. But this solution was too extreme
for two-thirds of the women and half of the men, whose preference
was for a long-term relationship based on love.[86]

In effect, then, the majority of the Gelman students wanted a relationship similar to marriage but based on love rather than legal obligation or economic interest. Marriage, as many of his respondents
saw it, was an institution deeply corrupted by its bourgeois past. As
Gelman reported:

> Many note the link between marriage and narrow conventionalism [ob
> yvatel'shchina], and therefore reject it. Thus in the women's question
> naires we meet this kind of definition and characterization of marriage:
> "a philistine ritual" [meshchanskii obriad]—"I don't want to link my
> self with philistinism by getting married." One man comments that
> "even among Communist women, it is impossible to find a woman
> who would not bring philistine traditions into marriage." The men of
> ten complain that they do not meet thinking [soznatel'nye] women
> capable of introducing the refreshing element of shared work into mar
> riage. It almost always degenerates into the philistine concept of "a
> quiet anchoring place."[87]

The students of the Omsk survey were younger, less ideologically
sophisticated, and presumably less scarred by the experiences of foreign war, civil war, and unsuccessful marriage. But a significant

---

on the alcohol question. By "alcohol" Lass presumably meant hard liquor, but he does
not specify. He reports no negative response: 763 is apparently the total number of
students who answered Lass's question on the age at which they first drank alcohol.
Batkis, who deals with "alcoholism, [cigarette] smoking, and drug use" in one table
and adds no commentary, found that 332 (of 611) students sometimes drank hard
liquor; 68, including 16 women, drank often; 307 students, including 70 women,
smoked or had smoked; and 60, including 10 women, had taken drugs ("Opyt podkhoda").

[86] Gelman Polovaia zhizn', p. 95.
[87] Ibid., p. 87.

number of them were also radicals on marriage—not in the Kollontai sense of emphasizing love rather than obligation or self-interest but with a more straightforward enthusiasm for revolutionary liberation in the sexual sphere. Less than half the Omsk women chose marriage as an ideal, and a quarter of them opted for "free love" (including a fifth of the married women). The men were less disposed to marriage than the women and more inclined to free love (for which almost half of the married men cast their votes). Despite the clear desire of the researcher to have the students endorse relationships based on love, the students remained indifferent: only 20 percent of the women opted for "long-term relationships based on love" (compared with 67 percent in the Gelman sample), and the proportions of women who explained nonmarriage and chastity in terms of "absence of love" were in the same range.[88]

The great debate in Omsk was clearly marriage versus free love (with "free love" being synonymous with "unrestricted sex"). But the women were also concerned about the possible conflicts of family and professional commitments in the future. Some came down quite sharply on the side of professional and political activism; and a women's independence theme can be seen in a number of the responses: for example, 19 women (9 percent of the unmarried) expressed their unwillingness to marry because they did not wish to be materially dependent on a man.[89]

The Odessa survey (1927) reveals a strong orientation toward marriage among male and female students. The men saw marriage as the solution to their sexual problems and emphasized that married couples ought to be able to live together. The women—a young and middle-class group—showed in general little sign of having broken with their families and family values.[90] Whereas the most common reason given by both men and women in Gelman's group for not being married was "desire not to limit one's freedom," the reason given by the majority of Odessa men (63 percent of respondents) was that they could not afford to marry and by the majority of women (64 percent) that they had not yet found the right man.[91] The radicals—the 6 to 7

[88] Kliachkin, "Polovaia anketa," pp. 133, 132, 131. Thirty-one percent of the men chose marriage as an ideal, and 43% free love. The percentage of men who preferred love was 14, yet only about 5% explained bachelorhood and abstinence by "absence of love" ("too low," Kliachkin comments).

[89] Ibid., p. 132.

[90] According to Lass, Sovremennoe studenchestvo, p. 45, 133 women (of 527) were supported by their parents before they entered the university (p. 24), 207 lived with their families, and 356 retained ties with their parents.

[91] Gelman, Polovaia zhizn', p. 84; Lass, Sovremennoe studenchestvo, p. 143. In Gelman's survey, these reasons were given by 29% of the men and 33% of the women.

percent of both men and women who did not "recognize any kind of relationship" and the 16 percent of the men who recognized "relationships" but preferred them polygamous—were in a minority.[92]

Radicalism is seen clearly in the Odessa students' attitude toward love. For many of them, the question "Does love exist?" (not included in any of the other surveys) acted as a sharp reminder that they were, after all, revolutionary materialists and believers in the primacy of physiology. About 50 percent of the male respondents and 39 percent of the females denied the existence of love, and a third of the students ignored the question, evidently feeling it beneath contempt. "I cannot answer your question about love," wrote one student. "You must know very well that love, as the majority understand it, does not exist." Another, irritated at having to state a self-evident truth, explained that "the basis of love is sexual attraction of two objects to each other."[93] For the sophisticated student of 1927 vintage, it appears, any other definition smacked of petty-bourgeois sentimentality. For this generation, Kollontai's ideas no longer seem influential or even known at all except in distorted form as an encouragement to promiscuity—the notorious "glass of water" theory of sex.[94] If an authority, or at least a representatives spokesman, can be deduced from the students' responses, it is not Kollontai but Enchman, the young iconoclastic advocate of "naked physiologism."

Even on this question, however, the students were more radical in ideology than in practice. Sixty-six percent of the Odessa women affirmed the general proposition that love did not exist. Remarkably, however, 63 percent of the same group reported that they had been in love.[95]

Conclusion

The students were understandably confused about sexual mores. If they behaved as their parents had done, they fell into the trap of *meshchanstvo* by way of "bourgeois marriage." If they behaved like liberated sexual revolutionaries, they fell into the trap of *meshchanstvo* (or so the older generation told them) by way of "bourgeois bohemian irresponsibility." In fact, whatever their inclinations, the "bourgeois-bohemian" lifestyle was not accessible to most students.

---

[92] Lass, *Sovremennoe studenchestvo*, p. 210.

[93] Ibid., pp. 198, 197, 203.

[94] Lass mentions Kollontai only in his introduction (ibid., p. 8). But Gelman, Batkis, and Kliachkin do not mention her at all.

[95] Ibid., pp. 202–3.

Most universities had a heavy preponderance of male students, and among the women students traditional chastity-preserving and marriage-oriented values tended to prevail. But for many students bourgeois marriage was inaccessible. Certainly the students married, but marriage did not give them the bourgeois privilege of setting up a home or even, in many cases, living with their spouses. Not surprisingly, the married students in some of the surveys outnumbered those in favor of marriage.

On the basis of the surveys, it is difficult to argue that the Revolution encouraged students to be promiscuous (though no doubt the aftermath of war and civil war had this effect in the early 1920s). That it was thought to have done so may be explained in part by official Soviet concern about the general boom in the rates of urban marriage, divorce, and abortion—but, as we have seen, the students were apparently not in the vanguard of this trend, and resort to abortion seems to have been more characteristic of the married students than of the promiscuous ones. Another factor that created an image of student promiscuity was the popularity of this subject in contemporary fiction. Malashkin's *Luna s pravoi storony* was a political propaganda piece directed against the Trotskyists; one has the sense that some authors, such as Lev Gumilevskii—whose *Sobachii pereulok* (1927) was essentially a semipornographic popular novel— were trying to evade puritanical Soviet censorship by the quite familiar device of claiming relevance to a contemporary "social problem." The literary sources, in other words, ought to be treated with considerable skepticism.

The students did, in various ways, tend toward a liberated sexual ideology, yet their behavior tended to be fairly traditional—the men interested in establishing their virility but also interested in marriage as a reliable source of sex; the women looking for husbands, prepared to give up their virginity to a fiancé but prudently disinclined to embark on promiscuous premarital sex.

The liberating effects of revolution can be seen in the students' unquestioning acceptance of unregistered marriage, divorce, and abortion. But on other questions they were clearly conservative— unliberated by either modern Western standards or those of the prerevolutionary Russian intelligentsia. Permissive attitudes did not extend to either masturbation, which was a subject of considerable male anxiety, or homosexuality.[96]

---

[96] The reported incidence of homosexuality was very low. Gelman (*Polovaia zhizn'*, pp. 118–19) and Kliachkin ("Polovaia anketa," p. 137) each turned up two cases of homosexuality, three of the four cases being women. Lass (*Sovremennoe studen-*

Granted that anxiety about impotence, masturbation, and the consequences of abstinence is quite normal, the degree of concern evident among male students of the 1920s seems to call for explanation. One explanation can be found in the unusual burden of responsibility and obligation felt by the first postrevolutionary generation of university students. The men tended more than the women to come to university with an inadequate educational background and (if they were Communists) an ingrained suspicion of the bourgeois institutions in which they were to study. They were conscious of having to reject the moral authority of parents, non-Communist teachers, and bourgeois convention. But their own position was unclear because Soviet conventions were not yet established: revolutionary signals for sexual liberation conflicted with authoritative warnings against sexual irresponsibility.

In fact, the surveys suggest that the last thing the students could be accused of was a carefree attitude toward sex, whatever rules of behavior they adopted. Many responded to the questionnaires as if they were being consulted on public policy. The consensus of the men was that sex was a very serious matter and the problems it created were beyond the power of individuals to solve. The government should open free brothels, or oblige female students to satisfy the men's sexual needs, or forbid men with children to desert their wives, or make marriage viable by raising students' stipends. Whatever the solution, "the sexual question in student conditions is extraordinarily complicated, and it must be decided at government level [v obshche-gosudarstvennom masshtabe]."[97]

It is not hard to see these students—the generation of Brezhnev and the post-Stalin leadership—endorsing a return to conservative social policies in the 1930s and, in particular, the principle (unacceptable to the Old Bolshevik leaders of the 1920s) of state intervention in the sphere of private morals. The students had some commitment to an ideology of sexual liberation, but what comes through most strongly is their desire to have norms of sexual behavior firmly

---

chestvo, pp. 188–91) found male homosexuals out of 74 reported cases of sexual deviance. Gelman and Kliachkin display a lively interest in their homosexuals, and there is no note of moral censure (Kliachkin seems disappointed that he found no "hermaphrodites" in his sample). Lass, on the other hand, seems unhappy with sexual deviation—as he is with masturbation and alcohol use—and attempts to link it with poor heredity. Of Lass's deviations, most are "unnatural acts" (apparently for the purpose of preventing conception) or intercourse with animals, reported by about 60 Odessa men (pp. 186, 188) and 24 in Omsk (Kliachkin, p. 129). In each case, about 8% of the total male peasant group in the sample is represented. The students reporting intercourse with animals seem to regard it as a natural part of a peasant childhood.

[97] Quoted from a respondent in Kliachkin, "Polovaia anketa," p. 133.

established. Few students of the 1920s would have advocated the "great retreat" norms of the Stalin period.[98] But even they thought that norms were a government responsibility, and it seems quite possible that a decade later, as solid family men advancing in their careers, they not only approved antiliberation policies but played some part in introducing them.

(1976)

[98] The turn to more traditional family and cultural values in the 1930s is discussed in chap. 9.

CHAPTER 5

The Soft Line on Culture and Its Enemies

The year 1928 was a turning point not only for Soviet cultural policy but for policy in all fields. It was the beginning of a new revolution that overturned everything but the Stalinist leadership, an upheaval so violent that it seemed that the ruling party had revolted simultaneously against the society it governed and its own governing institutions. Among these institutions was Narkompros, the Commissariat of Enlightenment, headed by Lunacharsky and responsible for implementing policy in the sphere of education and the arts. In 1928 Narkompros was accused of softness in its dealings with the intelligentsia, lack of Communist vigilance, and failure to understand the significance of "class war on the cultural front." This softness was not peculiar to Narkompros, except in degree. The "rightist deviation" in the party, it was said, had led a bureaucratized government apparat in retreat from true communism to liberalism; and the essence of this retreat was conciliation of the bourgeois peasantry and intelligentsia.

The soft line, in other words, was the official government and party line before 1928. That line was neither liberal nor non-Communist, as its opponents believed, but the product of a policy of expedient accommodation with the intelligentsia, on nonnegotiable terms laid down by the party leadership and without institutional guarantees.

Cultural policy in the 1920s rested on the premise that the Soviet state needed the services of bourgeois specialists and would have to pay for them. The state's interest was in securing the cooperation of the intelligentsia rather than further antagonizing it. The value of inherited culture and inherited technical skills must be recognized. Those who possessed such skills must be encouraged to work for the Soviet state and rewarded for doing so. Specialists must be supervised but not harassed. Communist conceit (*komchvanstvo*) and specialist baiting (*spetseedstvo*) were repudiated. It was assumed that in the course of time the Soviet state would develop its own intelligentsia, and that to facilitate this process some degree of preferential access to education must be given to "proletarians."[1] Education could not be ideologically neutral; therefore, its ideological content must be Communist. The same applied to art; but in both cases the speed of ideological transformation would be within the limits imposed by a working relationship with the old intelligentsia.

The soft line was not liberal. It operated within a framework of ideological control through censorship, security police, state monopoly of the press, and restriction of private publishing. There was room for difference of opinion among Communists on the proper scope of activity of these institutions; and their conduct could be criticized by Communists. But this license was not extended to the non-Communist intelligentsia, since that was the group to be controlled. According to the conventions of the 1920s, members of the intelligentsia might petition for the redress of individual grievances, but in doing so they were appealing for favors and not invoking rights.

Similarly, the soft line made it possible for the intelligentsia to form associations—but as a matter of privilege, not of right. Some cultural institutions were described as autonomous (the Academy of Sciences, the old imperial theaters), but this was an act of favor that might be revoked, as it was in the cases of Proletkult and the universities. The "autonomous" label was in fact a warning against harassment directed at hard-line Communists, not a legal category. No association was autonomous in the sense that it could exclude Communists or protest against the organization of a Communist fraction within. The soft line might permit non-Communist leadership of an association, but it did not guarantee it.

In the 1920s, official cultural policies were carried out as a rule by

---

[1] In discussions of educational problems the term "proletarian" was often loosely used to cover not only workers and workers' children but Communist Party members, Komsomols, and poor peasants and their children. Statistical breakdowns of social composition (*sotsial'nyi sostav*) in the 1920s, however, usually distinguished between "proletarian" and "poor peasant," sometimes placing children of proletarians and of poor peasants in separate categories, and gave a separate listing for party and Komsomol members.

government agencies, not by the party. The cultural responsibilities of party agitprop and press departments were narrowly interpreted— press departments being concerned largely with the party press and agitprop departments with party schools and recommendation of party members for higher education. Only convention limited the activities of these departments; and the convention could be broken, as it was in 1924 when agitprops supervised the university purge. But it was assumed that a soft line on culture was more appropriate to the Communist government than to the Communist Party, and that party intervention at least threatened suspension of the soft line.

If this situation seems paradoxical, it was part of the general paradox of party and government relations. The party leadership was, on the one hand, formulator of the policies that the government executed. On the other, it was protector of the special party or "proletarian" interest. It was possible—though politically tactless—for Lunacharsky to imagine a situation in which the party leadership would be obliged to dissociate itself from policies that Lunacharsky, a Communist member of the government, would continue to implement. The 1924 party discussion on literature, Lunacharsky thought, might turn up an "overwhelming majority" in favor of a "hard" line on culture. The government was bound to follow a policy of the "utmost neutrality" in art, and not to discriminate in favor of groups representing the Communist or proletarian interest. But a position that was completely inappropriate for the state might be "more or less decent" for the party, Lunacharsky wrote; and in such a case

> it would be natural for party journals and newspapers and party critics to come out in defense of their own trends, to subject persons of other views to severe criticism, and in short to conduct a quite specific cultural line. The party would put its own authority, its talent, and its culture behind [this line], *but of course it could not for a moment expect the state power as such to support it.*[2]

Given that government policy was formulated by the party leadership and that Lunacharsky himself was bound by party discipline, he could only have been assuming that in this situation the party leadership would consciously separate its two roles, and that this separation would be dictated by pressure from the party rank and file for a hard line.

The hard line was the line of class war against internal enemies. It meant militant and repressive policies against the bourgeoisie,

[2] A. V. Lunacharsky, "Khudozhestvennaia politika sovetskogo gosudarstva," *Zhizn' iskusstva* (Leningrad), 1924 no. 10 (March 4), p. 1 (my emphasis).

broadly interpreted to include the great mass of the peasantry and nonparty intelligentsia; and in culture it meant active intervention of the party to protect the "proletarian" interest.

No member of the party leadership consistently advocated a hard line on culture before 1928. Its support appears to have come from the lower ranks of the party, the Komsomol, and Communist vigilante groups such as the Association of Proletarian Writers[3] and the atheists' league, the Union of the Militant Godless. It was the line of radical youth and provincial isolation. Its supporters looked back to the Civil War and talked of politics in military terms, seeing the soft line as a kind of civilian deviation. The hard-liners in the capitals were restless, quarrelsome, jealous, and infatuated with the idea of power and political intrigue. In the provinces they were hard pressed by the hostility of the local population and fearful for their own authority whenever central directives pushed them toward conciliation. "Surely, comrades, you shouldn't forget that all during the Civil War the teachers were hand in glove with the kulaks," protested a delegate to the Thirteenth Party Congress at the suggestion that the local party organization should cooperate with the rural intelligentsia:

> We must never forget that they went hand in hand with the kulaks for the whole revolution and that about 50 percent of our rural teachers are offspring of the clergy. . . . Our rural party forces . . . will be threatened if we invite the teachers into the party, if we begin to draw them in. The teacher will get more authority in the village than our Communists. And, comrades, you know what that means, when the teacher has greater authority and greater trust than our rural Communists.[4]

The hard line on culture—the line of *komchvanstvo* and *spetseedstvo*—was discriminatory and coercive, ignorant or contemptuous of inherited cultural tradition, enthusiastic for "proletarian culture" and especially for the dominance of proletarian cultural institutions, and relatively indifferent to the state's need for the services of technical experts. Its watchword was "vigilance in the face of the class enemy," which to some supporters meant simply *bei intelligentov* (get the intellectuals). Its tactics ranged from local administrative bullying through polemical journalism to backstairs intrigue against vulnerable soft-liners in the leadership.

---

[3] VAPP, later RAPP. In the mid-1920s, the proletarians were often referred to as *napostovtsy*, from the title of their journal, *Na postu* (On guard).

[4] S. Bergavinov (Kiev party organization), in *XIII s"ezd RKP(b): Mai 1924 g.: Stenograficheskii otchet* (Moscow, 1963), pp. 469–70.

Let us look at three areas—university admissions, policy toward
rural teachers, and literature—where we can observe a shifting and
evolving balance between policies of accommodation with the intelligentsia (the soft line) and pressures toward coercion and protection
of the proletarian interest (the hard line).

University admissions

The soft line was at its most illiberal on the issue of university
admissions in the early 1920s. This stance was in part a reaction to
the events of the Civil War years.[5] Narkompros had originally allowed the universities to retain the autonomy they had received
from the Provisional Government; but at the same time it had declared university entrance open to all and created *rabfaks* for adult
workers who lacked the necessary educational qualifications. The
universities resented the *rabfaks*, along with Narkompros and the
Bolshevik government as a whole, and refused to cooperate. At the
end of 1920 they were formally deprived of autonomy, and Communist rectors were appointed by Narkompros. Narkompros's intentions
were still, within the limits of this situation, conciliatory; but the
behavior of some of its officials and appointees was not, and probably accurately reflected the generally belligerent temper of the party
in 1921.

D. P. Bogolepov took up the rectorship of Moscow University with
the uncompromising statement that it was time "to end every kind of
university autonomy and freedom of teaching once and for all, and
not to give the professors any greater rights than other Soviet employees"; it was time to fill the universities with worker-Communists
through the *rabfaks*, since "only Communist *spetsy* can get the country's economy on new tracks and build life anew."[6] Evgenii Preobrazhenskii, appointed to Narkompros as head of the technical education administration (and recent coauthor, with Bukharin, of the
leftist treatise *Azbuka kommunizma*), was another hard-liner. He
wrote in 1921: "At the moment there is a genuine class war at the
doors of the higher school between the worker-peasant majority of
the country, who want to have specialists from among their own
kind in their own state, and the [ex-]governing classes and strata

---

[5] Policy toward universities in the Civil War period is discussed in my book *The
Commissariat of Enlightenment* (New York, 1971) and by James C. McClelland in
"Bolshevik Approaches to Higher Education, 1917–1921," *Slavic Review* 30 (Decem-
ber 1971): 818–31.

[6] D. P. Bogolepov, "Vysshaia shkola i kommunizm," *Pravda*, 27 February 1921, p. 1.

linked with them. The proletarian state openly takes the side of its own people."[7]

But Bogolepov was quickly dismissed, and so was Preobrazhenskii after a wave of university strikes and conciliatory intervention by the Central Committee. When Preobrazhenskii protested that the Central Committee had retreated too far and injured the proletarian cause, he found no supporters in the leadership. Lenin criticized his administrative naiveté and the *komchvanstvo* of the *rabfak* students who supported him.[8] The policy of the Soviet government at this time was to avoid open conflict at all costs short of loss of political control. The old professors kept their jobs, a fair part of their freedom of teaching, and a share in university administration; the appointed rectors were mild. State policy was most assertively Communist with regard to student recruitment. Starting in the early 1920s, only a very small quota of places were left for competitive "free enrollment" to universities. The great majority of places were filled by *komandirovanie*, that is, nomination of politically and socially acceptable candidates by local party, soviet, and trade union organizations.

The system of *komandirovanie* was supposed to fill the universities with reliable proletarian and Communist students without the upheaval and provocation of a major university purge. It had the considerable disadvantage of lowering academic standards and removing the raison d'être of the general secondary schools. But the status of secondary schools was controversial. Many Communists thought of them as irredeemably bourgeois schools that needed to be radically reorganized as technical schools whose graduates would not be admitted to universities. In fact, a rather arbitrarily constituted party meeting on education had passed a resolution to this effect at the beginning of 1921. But Narkompros, with some support from Lenin, ignored the resolution; and only the Komsomol protested.

The party's aim, as stated by Bukharin at the 1924 party congress, was to turn the universities into training schools for a new proletarian and Communist governing class by enrolling workers and Communists as students.[9] But they were to be trained, for the time being, by the old bourgeois professors under soft (in Bukharin's view, excessively soft) supervision by Narkompros. The system of *komandirovanie* turned out to be ill coordinated and the selection

[7] E. A. Preobrazhenskii, "O professional'no-tekhnicheskom obrazovanii," *Pravda*, 10 September 1921, p. 2.

[8] *Odinnadtsatyi s"ezd RKP(b), mart-aprel' 1922 g.: Stenograficheskii otchet* (Moscow, 1961), pp. 85–88, 142.

[9] Resolution on work among youth passed at the Thirteenth Party Congress, in *KPSS v rezoliutsiiakh i resheniiakh s"ezdov, konferentsii i plenumov TsK* (Moscow, 1970), 3:109.

process indiscriminate, even from a sociopolitical point of view. Academic standards dropped sharply. The universities were overcrowded, and their graduates were of such poor quality that employers complained—particularly Vesenkha, the Supreme Council of the National Economy. The last straw came during the leadership struggle of 1923–1924, when the party cells in universities (composed largely of Communist students, since very few professors were party members) came out almost solidly for Trotsky. The party leadership decided to purge the student bodies of all in universities in order to eliminate students who were class enemies ("of alien social origin") or academically unsuccessful, and at the same time to conduct a separate purge of the university party cells to get rid of Trotskyists.[10] The general university purge was conducted in the summer of 1924 by Narkompros and the agitprop departments of the party, under the supervision of Zinoviev for the Politburo.[11]

The purge as an instrument of policy was incompatible with the soft line, for it meant both direct party intervention and revitalization of the concept of class war in cultural and intellectual life. Narkompros was not in a position to resist the purging impulse in the party leadership, but it did its best to defuse it. Not only did it reinstate students expelled by local party agitprop departments and secure the right of later reentry for those expelled;[12] it actually published a denial that "alien" students expelled for their social origin were really alien:

> Owing to oversights on the part of some commissions for the review of the student body, the comment "alien element" was written on the documents of those expelled. . . . It is obvious that in these cases the description "alien element" meant persons who under the present straitened circumstances of higher educational institutions are the least suitable to go through university. . . . The persons expelled from

[10] Zinoviev discussed the general university purge with the collegium of Narkompros at its meeting of 26 March 1924: TsGAOR, f. 2306, op. 1, d. 2945. On Trotskyism, see N. Akimov in *Krasnoe studenchestvo*, 1928–1929 no. 14, p. 4: "Everyone remembers the Trotskyist fever from which the university cells especially suffered in 1923–1924. The partial purge of the party at that time affected primarily the university organizations, more than 25 percent of whose members were purged as decadent and ideologically hostile elements."

[11] About 18,000 students (13–14% of the total) were expelled in the purge, "three-fourths for completely unjustified academic failure and the rest for various other reasons" (*Narodnoe prosveshchenie*, 1925 no. 4, p. 118). But as I. I. Khodorovskii of Narkompros had made clear, academic requirements varied according to the social origin of the student (*Pravda*, 17 May 1924, p. 6).

[12] See, for example, protest from Smolensk gubkom and agitprop to Central Committee agitprop department, 27 September 1924: Smolensk Archive, WKP 518, l. 71.

university are not disgraced, and their expulsion from university does not carry any limitations of their rights.[13]

A side effect of the purge was hard-line resurgence in other areas. When Bukharin's paper was discussed at the Thirteenth Party Congress, the Komsomol seized the opportunity to press its charges against the bourgeois secondary schools, and Narkompros was subsequently obliged to reorganize the secondary schools on a semivocational basis and formally to acknowledge that the *rabfak* had replaced the secondary school as a channel to the university.[14]

In the provinces the purge gained a momentum that not only Narkompros but the party leadership found difficult to control: it was as if local authorities had been only waiting for the moment to settle accounts with universities, schools, teachers, and the whole alien body of the intelligentsia. The experience may have been sobering for the party leadership.[15] It was not, at any rate, repeated during the remaining years of NEP, and the vocabulary of class war tended in those years to drop out of official use.

Other factors encouraged reestablishment of the soft line, notably pressure from the economic ministries for graduates of better quality and soft-line initiatives by Aleksei Rykov, president of the Council of People's Commissars (Sovnarkom). In the summer of 1925, Vesenkha asked the Central Committee to allow some thousands of engineering students to study abroad because of the low standards of Soviet universities. The request was refused, but it provoked Rykov to reexamine the situation in the universities and the training of specialists.[16] As a result, measures were taken to raise academic standards. A revised system of *komandirovanie* was still in force in university admissions, but it was modified in the autumn of 1925 by the addition of two special quotas: one of 2,500 for graduates of secondary and technical schools, another of 1,000 for distribution by trade unions among the "toiling intelligentsia" (otherwise known as "bourgeois specialists"). This was surely a move to conciliate the intelligentsia as well as to raise academic standards, since specialists were unlikely to work with enthusiasm for a government that denied their children access to a university at a time of extremely high unemploy-

[13] Resolution of collegium of Narkompros, 23 September 1924 (TsGAOR, f. 2306, op. 1, d. 3328), published in *Ezhenedel'nik Narkomprosa*, 1924 no. 21 (41), p. 2.

[14] *Narodnoe prosveshchenie*, 1924 no. 8, pp. 5, 51, 73. The secondary school reorganization added a "professional bias" (*profuklon*) to the two senior classes, but the school was still classified as general educational, not technical, to university-entrance level.

[15] See Bukharin's comments in *Partiia i vospitanie smeny* (Moscow, 1926), p. 108.

[16] A. V. Lunacharsky, *Prosveshchenie i revoliutsiia* (Moscow, 1926), pp. 415–16.

ment among young people. When the new quotas were announced in 1925, Lunacharsky's deputy explained that

> the policy and aims of the Soviet government are not at all directed toward closing access to higher school to all except workers and peasants. Each year the government will further widen the paths by which children of the toiling intelligentsia and white-collar workers can go to school. . . . Soviet power is concerned that its social base should become wider, not narrower.[17]

This promise was kept. In 1926 the system of *komandirovanie* was abandoned, and university enrollment was thrown open to free competition. A secondary process of social selection was still operative, but it discriminated against only a part of the intelligentsia, since children of specialists in state employment were declared equal in social status to children of workers.[18] But the main emphasis was on the establishment of academic criteria for university admission. After all, as Lunacharsky cheerfully remarked, it was no good admitting unqualified workers and peasants to be made "martyrs and eyesores [*bel'mo na glazu*], as often happens."[19]

As had been expected, the percentage of workers and party members in the 1926 enrollment dropped, while the numbers of secondary school graduates going directly to university rose sharply. The effect of the new enrollment policy was to reestablish a normal progression from secondary school to university and to cut back adult enrollment. Even the *rabfaks*, which continued to supply from a quarter to a third of the enrollment, were increasingly training adolescents rather than adult workers. In other words, they were evolving into a subsidiary type of secondary school. The proportion of workers' children among the worker enrollees increased in 1927.

Hard-line criticism of the new policy was muted. L. Milkh, a Central Committee official, told Communist students in 1927 that "the new conditions of enrollment in universities are a retreat from the policy of proletarianization"; but his published comments in the Central Committee agitprop journal avoided direct criticism of the policy, while suggesting that Narkompros was giving it an unnecessarily soft interpretation.[20] It was always permissible to attack Narkompros for softness, and particularly so in this context: Vesenkha, which provided powerful backing for academic criteria in en-

---

[17] *Narodnoe prosveshchenie*, 1925 no. 7–8, pp. 102–3.
[18] *Izvestiia*, 26 May 1926, p. 3, and 30 July 1926, p. 5.
[19] *Narodnoe prosveshchenie*, 1927 no. 4, p. 14.
[20] TsGAOR, f. 5574, op. 5, d. 2, l. 9 (conference of Proletstud, January 1927); *Kommunisticheskaia revoliutsiia*, 1927 no. 8, p. 46.

rollment, was at the same time mounting a campaign to have the technical faculties of universities removed from Narkompros's control to its own. But by 1927 the issue of proletarianization and class war had been appropriated by the Party Opposition.

To all appearances the soft line not only was in the ascendant at the Fifteenth Party Congress of December 1927 but was likely to remain so. According to Stalin, "hundreds and thousands of the toiling intelligentsia" and the industrial specialists in particular were eager and willing to cooperate with the Soviet government in achieving the Five-Year Plan. Bukharin congratulated Molotov on his new understanding of the need for educational expansion. Nobody mentioned class war in the universities or took the opportunity to criticize Narkompros (a sure sign that the hard line was under constraint), and the Narkompros journal, for the first and only time, published the relevant debates of a party congress verbatim.[21]

Rural teachers

The status of rural teachers was a question on which Soviet attitudes were straightforward and policy not a matter of controversy in the leadership. The policy was soft. Stalin, concluding his remarks on changing attitudes of the intelligentsia at the Fifteenth Party Congress, said: "I don't even speak of the rural laboring intelligentsia, especially the rural teacher, who has long turned toward Soviet power and cannot fail to welcome the development of education in the countryside."[22] Rural teachers provided no potential political threat as far as the center was concerned, so the soft line encountered no obstacle—except that local authorities persistently ignored it. It is this central/local dichotomy that I want to examine.

The local hard line on teachers was rooted in Civil War memories and Communist isolation in the countryside.[23] In 1918 the anti-Bolshevik teachers' union had gone on strike in the capitals, and local branches had cooperated with the White armies. These actions briefly provoked a hard-line tendency at the center, represented by the Communist splinter group of "teacher-internationalists" who

---

[21] *Narodnoe prosveshchenie*, 1928 no. 1, pp. 1ff.

[22] Ibid., p. 26.

[23] Relations between teachers and the Soviet government in the early years are described in detail in Ronald Hideo Hayashida, "The Third Front: The Politics of Soviet Mass Education, 1917–1918" (Ph.D. diss., Columbia University, 1973), and briefly in Fitzpatrick, *Commissariat of Enlightenment*, pp. 34–43. The major Western work on Soviet schools in the 1920s is Oskar Anweiler, *Geschichte der Schule and Pädagogik in Russland vom Ende des Zarenreiches bis zum Beginn der Stalin-Ära* (Berlin, 1964).

claimed the right of succession to the teachers' union. But neither Narkompros nor the Central Council of Trade Unions would recognize the teacher-internationalists, and the new union that was established in 1919 was a mass professional union with no restrictions on entry and nonmilitant Communist leadership—a typical soft-line conception.[24] The attitude of Narkompros was that teachers, especially rural teachers, were potential allies of the Soviet government and deserved sympathetic treatment, and in 1921 the Central Committee directed that "local party organizations must give up the attitude that they have so far commonly held, that educational workers are saboteurs, for they have long ceased to be so if they ever were."[25]

Old Bolsheviks such as Lenin, Krupskaia, Zinoviev, and Kalinin had an emotional attachment to the rural teacher as a humble and underpaid bearer of enlightenment to the people.[26] But the leadership was also bearing in mind the practical consideration that rural Communists were few and needed support in the countryside. At the Thirteenth Party Congress, in May 1924, Zinoviev sponsored an official welcome to teachers as rural allies of Soviet power; and Krupskaia gave a moving account of the miserable conditions of their lives. The teachers were promised improvement in material conditions, higher wages, considerate treatment from local officials, and even the opportunity to join the party. Some party members saw these steps as capitulation to the class enemy.[27]

In January 1925 an All-Union Teachers' Congress—genuinely representative of the non-Communist teacher, as Narkompros somewhat defensively claimed—was held in Moscow. It was given maximum publicity and was attended by no fewer than six Politburo members and candidates, all of whom endorsed a policy of conciliation and deploring harassment of teachers by local authorities. Rykov promised the teachers protection from arbitrary dismissal and transfer. Zinoviev, "without sinning against the tenets of Marxism," rejected the idea of class war against the rural intelligentsia, since "the majority of teachers are part of the toiling masses led by the proletariat, and must be accepted among us as toilers having equal rights," and

[24] The new organization was the Union of Workers in Education and Socialist Culture (Rabpros). The trade unions objected to Narkompros's choice of the "political" word "socialist" in the title, and it dropped out of use in the early 1920s.

[25] *Direktivy VKP(b) po voprosam prosveshcheniia* (Moscow, 1931), p. 180.

[26] For an impassioned statement on the situation of teachers, their services to the people, and the identity of their cause of popular enlightenment and that of the Communists, see G. Zinoviev, "Proletarskaia revoliutsiia i uchitel'stvo," *Pravda*, 24 April 1924, pp. 2–4.

[27] See V. Kolokolkin, "O derevenskoi intelligentsii (po povodu tezisov kov. Kalinina)," *Pravda*, 20 May 1924, p. 6.

staked the authority of the Central Committee on his claim that local party officials would cooperate.[28]

They did not. Arbitrary dismissals and transfers and (as Narkompros put it) "mockery" of teachers continued to be reported in 1926 and 1927. Cases were cited of local authorities who deprived teachers of the vote as "alien elements," lumping them with Nepmen. A summary of letters from the provinces concluded that party officials treated teachers badly, using "command methods," and Komsomols were even worse. The buoyant mood that had been observed among teachers after the 1925 congress gave way to "dissatisfaction, a feeling of burden, apathy, apprehension, fears, and hopelessness" in the years that followed.[29]

Central party policy was not without responsibility for this situation, despite the prevailing soft line. First, Zinoviev's welcome to teachers had coincided exactly with preparations for the university purge (and may have been intended to prevent a backlash in the schools). Local officials took the purge as an indication that a general hard-line campaign against the intelligentsia had begun, and accordingly undertook to purge the schools of socially alien elements—expelling children, dismissing teachers, often closing secondary schools altogether as "bourgeois."[30] Repeated Narkompros prohibitions, backed up by a "party instruction signed by Comrade Andreev," were ignored or perhaps even misunderstood: a reply received from Tomsk stated reassuringly, "A purge has not been conducted [in the schools], but it is proposed to conduct one before the beginning of the school year."[31] A year later the impact of the purge was still being felt in the provinces.

Second, the teachers were in constant conflict with Pioneer organizations and their Komsomol leaders in the schools. It must not be supposed that the party directed young Communists to attack the teachers; on the contrary, the Central Committee in 1925 decreed that the Komsomol must draw the teachers into Pioneer work, and that "the chief duty of a Pioneer is to be an exemplary pupil in school."[32] The explanation is simply that the teachers, with very few exceptions, were not Communists, and the Pioneers of the 1920s, in

[28] *Narodnoe prosveshchenie,* 1925 no. 2, pp. 39 (Rykov) and 72–73 (Zinoviev).

[29] Ibid., 1927 no. 4, p. 43; 1926 no. 1, p. 34; 1926 no. 9, pp. 85–86; 1929 no. 8–9, p. 103 (of the period 1926–1928).

[30] *Ezhenedel'nik Narkomprosa,* 1924 no. 18 (39), p. 12, and no. 21 (41), pp. 8–9; TsGAOR, f. 2306, op. 1, d. 3328 (presidium of Narkompros collegium, 29 September 1924); Smolensk Archive, WKP 11 (agitprop collegium of Sychevka uezd party committee, 12 August 1924).

[31] *Narodnoe prosveshchenie,* 1924 no. 8, p. 9.

[32] *Direktivy VKP(b) po voprosam prosveshcheniia,* p. 194.

their own understanding, were. Neither the Komsomol nor the Pioneers was a mass movement at this time, and those schoolchildren who joined did so with the purest and most primitive enthusiasm for revolution and class war. Where could they fight the class war but in the schools, against bourgeois *intelligentshchina* (a favorite pejorative word of the 1920s), against their teachers? Party calls for moderation were either unheard or taken as evidence that the party leadership had become "degenerate" and incapable of militant leadership.[33]

It is also true that party calls for moderation were often ambiguous, being addressed to both sides. Bukharin, speaking at the 1925 teachers' congress, said that teachers should defer to Komsomols on political matters, avoid "cultural superciliousness," and acknowledge Komsomol's preeminence in leadership of the Pioneers, while the Komsomol should behave tactfully to the teachers and acknowledge their preeminence as leaders in the school. After the congress there were reports from the provinces that this formulation had not improved the teachers' position: "The Pioneers and their [Komsomol] leaders isolate themselves from school life as a whole, and the teacher is afraid to meddle in their affairs because 'Bukharin did not order it at the teachers' congress'" (though some teachers "were not afraid of Bukharin" and continued to attack the Pioneer leaders for disrupting school life).[34]

Finally, the soft line offered teachers goodwill but no weapons of their own: the teachers' union, at both central and local levels, was neither strong nor professional enough to fight their battles. The branch secretaries recommended by local party organizations were often not teachers by profession but "candidate members of the party or experienced administrators," and their election was a formality to which "ordinary voters are not accustomed to object openly, confining themselves to indignant whispers and ironic smiles." The union had no influence on the appointment or dismissal of teachers, which was conducted by the education department of the local soviet; and victimized teachers rarely appealed to the union for support, because its officials "often act with the administrative organs . . . against the teachers instead of defending them." In cases of arbitrary dismissal or transfer, "the trade union organs remain completely indifferent," and only the *sel'kory* (rural newspaper correspondents) sometimes defended the teachers.[35]

---

[33] See Bukharin's remarks on Komsomol and Pioneer "avant-gardism" in *XIV s″ezd VKP(b), 18–31 dek. 1926 g.: Stenograficheskii otchet* (Moscow, 1926), p. 824.

[34] *Narodnoe prosveshchenie*, 1925 no. 2, p. 140; 1926 no. 9, p. 77.

[35] Ibid., 1926 no. 9, pp. 108–9; 82.

The proletarian literary movement

The conflict of soft and hard lines in literature is remarkable for both its intensity and its apparent triviality—its peripheral relation both to the real concerns of literature and to those of government. It is as an exercise in pure politics that it deserves attention in this discussion.[36]

The main protagonist of the hard line in literature, the proletarian writers' association, VAPP,[37] emerged in the first years of NEP as a product of postwar demobilization and Komsomol activism. It was young, brash, aggressive, self-consciously Communist, and "proletarian" in the sense that it was hostile to the old literary intelligentsia. Its first center—before the founding of the proletarian literary journal *Na postu*—was the editorial office of *Molodaia gvardiia*, a monthly publication of the Komsomol Central Committee, then edited by Leopold Averbakh. Its original members, almost all under twenty-five, had typically joined the party as adolescents just out of (or running away from) gymnasium, fought with the Red Army in the Civil War, briefly held a junior party administrative position, and then drifted into political journalism.[38] Almost all came from families of the intelligentsia; some, such as Averbakh, were well connected in party leadership circles. The young proletarians affected a military style of dress and speech, and felt instinctive antipathy to the "civilian" Communists active in the literary field—A. K. Voronskii, editor of the Communist "thick" journal *Krasnaia nov'*; Lunacharsky at Narkompros; N. L. Meshcheriakov at the State Publishing House, Gosizdat. Their consuming interest was literary politics rather than the actual production of literature. VAPP, nominally an association of proletarian writers (and in the course of time it actually acquired a mass membership of aspiring working-class writers), was originally and essentially a vigilante group of young Communist journalists who proposed to function as the literary arm of the party Central Committee.

[36] Literary policy, unlike its educational counterpart, has been admirably documented by both Western and Soviet research, notably in Robert A. Maguire's *Red Virgin Soil: Soviet Literature in the 1920's* (Princeton, 1968), Edward J. Brown's *Proletarian Episode in Russian Literature, 1928–1932* (New York, 1953), and S. I. Sheshukov's *Neistovye revniteli: Iz istorii literaturnoi bor'by 20–kh godov* (Moscow, 1970). Since literature is only one of the three contexts in which I discuss the opposition of "hard" and "soft" lines, I have not attempted a thorough treatment: I have assumed that the relative familiarity of the material allows me to be more selective here than in the sections dealing with educational problems, on which little has been published.

[37] Vserossiiskaia assotsiatsiia proletarskikh pisatelei. In 1928 the name was changed to Rossiiskaia assotsiatsiia proletarskikh pisatelei (RAPP).

[38] See Sheshukov, *Neistovye revniteli*, p. 114 and passim.

Official literary policy at the beginning of NEP was soft, insofar as it existed at all. Apart from publishers and censorship, Narkompros was the Soviet institution in closest contact with writers, and its policies were invariably conciliatory and, in regard to the cultural heritage, conservationist. Private publishing was permitted, although it existed on a fairly small scale; state publishing was not restricted to the publication of Communist authors. Neither party nor government had chosen to play an active interventionist role on behalf of Communist or proletarian groups: at the end of 1920 the Central Committee had sharply rejected the claims made for special privileges by Proletkult and the Futurists.[39]

The aim of the proletarians was to force the party into active intervention in support of the Communist literary movement; to replace the leadership's soft line with a hard line implemented by their organization on behalf of the party; and to enforce a "proletarian dictatorship" in literature by strict censorship and exclusive Communist control of and access to publishing and the literary press.

One of the most striking facts of VAPP's political career is that at no time did it enjoy the wholehearted support of any member of the party leadership. Trotsky, whom the young proletarians most admired ("loved," Averbakh said) rejected the whole notion of proletarian culture. Lev Kamenev, whose name was listed among the permanent contributors of *Na postu* in its first issues, melted away. Stalin and Zinoviev were simply not interested. The one member of the leadership to show any sympathy with the proletarian cause in culture was Bukharin, who had been an ardent cultural leftist and supporter of Proletkult during the Civil War, despite his later and better-known position as a moderate, and frequently clashed with the tolerant and eclectic Lunacharsky on artistic questions.[40] But Bukharin suffered a change of heart after Lenin's death and became VAPP's most energetic opponent in the leadership.

Nor could it be said that VAPP won favor by toadying to the Central Committee or by demonstrating unswerving loyalty to Stalin. Its early relationship with the Central Committee press department was intensely hostile. In April 1925 the writer Dmitrii Furmanov reported in his diary that his colleagues in VAPP were saying, "Furmanov is a traitor, because he went to the alien (as far as literature goes) and hostile Central Committee, to the enemy of proletarian lit-

---

[39] Letter of the party Central Committee, "O proletkul'takh," *Pravda*, 1 December 1920, p. 1.

[40] See, for example, Bukharin's call to "smash the old theater" in *Pravda* articles of 16 October and 16 December 1919, and Lunacharsky's protest circulated to party leaders (Lunacharsky, *Sobranie sochinenii* [Moscow, 1964], 3:100–105); Bukharin's clash with Lunacharsky at the 1922 Komsomol Congress (*V Vserossiiskii s"ezd RKSM: Stenograficheskii otchet* [Moscow and Leningrad, 1927], pp. 127, 141).

erature Vareikis, and talked to him about our affairs." In general, Furmanov commented, "a tradition has been established that the people in the Central Committee, in the press department, are (except for the late Kanatchikov) beyond hope, and not only should one not maintain or establish any sort of contact with them but one should attack and irritate them continually . . . 'in the interests of literature.'"[41]

As for political reliability, the young proletarians, like the Komsomol, were notoriously susceptible to outbreaks of oppositionism, since as a vigilante group they were constantly on guard against signs of party "degeneration." Of the early leaders, Averbakh and G. Lelevich were Trotskyists until the autumn of 1924. They felt, Averbakh explained, that the Central Committee was following a "degenerate" line and that Trotsky, although also "degenerate" on literary policy, was politically Leninist.[42] Even when Averbakh inherited VAPP leadership in 1926 from the now-Zinovievite Lelevich and his Georgian colleague I. V. Vardin (also an oppositionist), he did not become a devoted Stalinist: in 1929 we find him publicly dissenting from the general condemnation of Lazar Shatskin's "Komsomol" deviation, an exceptionally bold and independent gesture for a Communist at that time.[43] VAPP's sheer political arrogance, its unfailing suspicion of the motives and intentions of the party leadership, astonished contemporaries. What other organization would have "demanded" that the Central Committee forbid *Pravda* and *Bol'shevik* to criticize it, as Averbakh did in 1927?[44] And that was at a time when VAPP's position was dangerously close to the opposition's.

Among the soft-liners, Voronskii of *Krasnaia nov'* was the main target of the proletarians' attack, because, in their view, he denied proletarian writers access to the main Communist literary journal

[41] Dmitrii Furmanov, *Sobranie sochinenii* (Moscow, 1961), 4:352–53. I. M. Vareikis was head of the press department of the party's Central Committee in the mid-1920s, later first secretary of the Central Black Earth obkom during collectivization. S. I. Kanatchikov, editor of the party historical journal *Proletarskaia revoliutsiia*, was not in fact dead, only departed from the press department.

[42] Trotsky expressed his low assessment of the achievement of proletarian writers and his rejection on principle of the possibility that true "proletarian culture" could develop during the transition to socialism in his *Literatura i revoliutsiia*, written in 1923 and published as articles in *Pravda* toward the end of that year. See Leopold Averbakh, *Nashi literaturnye raznoglasiia* (Leningrad, 1927), p. 34.

[43] See *Pravda*, 3 October 1929, for RAPP's condemnation of Shatskin's political deviation and Averbakh's minority opinion on the issue. Shatskin, one of the founders and early leaders of the Komsomol, had criticized party philistinism (that is, careerism, loss of revolutionary dedication). He was expelled from the party in 1930 as an associate of the Syrtsov-Lominadze "right-left bloc."

[44] Sheshukov, *Neistovye revniteli*, p. 207.

and published instead the work of "bourgeois specialists"—the loyal non-Communist writers whom Trotsky described as "fellow travelers." We must assume their campaign provoked some sympathy, or at least attention, in the Central Committee bureaucracy, since Vardin was allowed to put the proletarian case against Voronskii at a special meeting in the press department of the Central Committee in May 1924. But the public response was wholly negative: among the speakers against VAPP were Trotsky, Bukharin, Lunacharsky, N. L. Meshcheriakov, and Ia. A. Iakovlev, representing the Central Committee press department. Only the Old Bolshevik Platon Kerzhentsev, a former Proletkultist, and the poet Demian Bednyi supported the proletarian line.[45]

But with an opponent such as Trotsky, VAPP hardly needed friends; and to its great good fortune Voronskii was both politically associated with Trotskyists and a supporter of Trotsky's literary views.[46] Because of his opposition connections, Voronskii's position on *Krasnaia nov'* was under constant threat from 1924 to 1927, when he was finally ousted. The VAPP leaders—despite former Trotskyist associations of their own—did not neglect this weapon. They made a strong bid "to equate Trotsky's political position with Voronskii's

---

[45] A stenogram of the debate was published in *K voprosu o politike RKP(b) v khudozhestvennoi literature* (Moscow, 1924). For evidence of pre-1923 Central Committee interest in literary politics see A. F. Ermakov in *Obogashchenie metoda sotsialisticheskogo realizma i problema mnogoobraziia sovetskogo iskusstva* (Moscow, 1967), pp. 356–62.

[46] Maguire (*Red Virgin Soil*, pp. 417ff.) concludes that Voronskii's actual participation in the Trotskyist opposition remains unproved, pointing out that the label of "Trotskyism" was often indiscriminately and vindictively applied. The same suggestion has been made by some post-1956 Soviet writers. There is, in fact, no hard evidence of Voronskii's active membership in the post-1923 opposition; but it should be remembered that unfounded accusations of actual opposition membership are characteristic of the late 1930s and not of any period of RAPP's activity. The most scholarly of Voronskii's Soviet rehabilitators—A. G. Dementev in *Kratkaia literaturnaia entsiklopediia* (Moscow, 1962), 1:1046; Sheshukov, *Neistovye revniteli*, p. 43; M. M. Kuznetsov in his article "*Krasnaia nov'*," in *Ocherki istorii russkoi sovetskoi zhurnalistiki, 1917–1932* (Moscow, 1966), p. 229—agree that Voronskii belonged to the 1926–28 opposition and was expelled from the party in 1928 for that reason. Their common (unidentified) source is probably the entry in *Deiateli revoliutsionnogo dvizheniia v Rossii*, 5 vols. (Moscow, 1927–1933): "In 1926–1928 Voronskii belonged to the Trotskyist Opposition and conducted active fractional work, in connection with which he was expelled from the ranks of the VKP(b); later, however, he broke with the opposition and was reinstated as a member of the party. He now works in Moscow as a senior editor of Russian and foreign classics" (vol. 5, pt. 2, p. 1030). My own impression is that this entry is probably accurate. Real opposition membership was clearly embarrassing to Voronskii's post-1956 Soviet rehabilitators, and discomfiture could explain the hinted doubts to which Maguire refers. But if we take it that Voronskii *was* expelled from the party as a Trotskyist in 1928 and readmitted about 1930, what plausible explanation is there except the obvious one—that he had belonged to the 1926–1928 opposition?

line [on literature] and even with the line of all the party comrades who do not support VAPP's point of view."[47] What worried Lunacharsky was that VAPP's smear tactics might finally discredit the soft line on culture altogether. He therefore moved toward quasi-alliance with VAPP, declaring himself a literary "proletarian" prepared to concede to VAPPists everything but organizational control.[48] Voronskii rightly believed that the soft-liners were offering him up as a sacrifice: "Anatolii Vasilevich!" he apostrophized Lunacharsky. "You have entered the *Na postu* realm, and you seem to be quite at home there. . . . But if I am fated to accept the end, then let it not be from the hand of Averbakh."[49]

Voronskii, who had lost control of *Krasnaia nov'* in the autumn of 1924 with the appointment of Fedor Raskolnikov, a VAPP sympathizer, as coeditor, regained it early in 1925;[50] and it was probably because of the controversy surrounding him that the issue of proletarian culture remained on the Central Committee's agenda. A Politburo commission headed by I. M. Vareikis and including Bukharin and Lunacharsky among its members worked through the spring of 1925 on a resolution that was finally passed in June: "On the policy of the party in the field of artistic literature." Why such extended deliberation was necessary is not clear, as no disagreement among members of the commission is recorded; but we do know that Trotsky submitted a written memorandum setting forth his views.[51] It is worth noting that though no influential politician appears to be arguing the case of the proletarians, the official attitude toward them becomes consistently more sympathetic through the resolution of the press department in May 1924, its adoption in slightly edited form in the Thirteenth Party Congress's resolution "On the Press," the reported statements of members of the Politburo commission, and the eventual Central Committee resolution of June 1925, which acknowledged, in direct opposition to Trotsky, the "historical right" of the proletariat to "hegemony" in literature, but proposed that proletarian

[47] Lunacharsky in *Literaturnoe nasledstvo* 64 (1925): 35.

[48] See, for example, his article in *Na postu*, 1925 no. 1 (6) (June). Lunacharsky was not insincere, in that on principle he had always been an advocate of proletarian culture and really did object to Trotsky's views on it. But he disliked VAPP's modus operandi, and the rapprochement was primarily tactical.

[49] A. K. Voronskii, "Mister Britling p'et chashu do dna," *Krasnaia nov'*, 1926 no. 5, pp. 202–3.

[50] F. F. Raskolnikov, a former sailor famous for his activity as a Bolshevik leader at Kronstadt in 1917, later a Soviet diplomat, was close to the literary "proletarians" in the 1920s. At the end of the decade he played a role in the Cultural Revolution as chairman of Glavrepertkom, the government agency in charge of theater censorship, and as RAPP-nominated head of Glaviskusstvo, Narkompros's arts administration.

[51] Ermakov, *Obogashchenie metoda*, pp. 276–77.

writers should earn it for themselves without the "bureaucratic" solution of party intervention on their behalf.[52]

In fact the party bureaucracy was already involving itself deeply in VAPP's affairs, though not altogether in token of approval. One outcome of the 1925 discussion on literature was a decision to create a Federation of Soviet Writers, to include both the proletarian and fellow-traveling groups. The Central Committee press department, which was responsible for organizing the federation, passed the organizational initiative to VAPP, which, under the leadership of Vardin and Lelevich, refused to take it on the grounds that VAPP was not guaranteed "hegemony" in the new organization.[53] For more than a year VAPP and the press department wrestled together with the demons of Zinovievism and "left deviation."[54] As a result, VAPP emerged with a new leader (Averbakh) and a new relationship with the press department—which, from the spring of 1926, was headed by Sergei Gusev, an Old Bolshevik who had formerly headed the Red Army's Political Administration.[55]

The new VAPP was willing to organize the federation of writers, and the new press department was eager to support it in this undertaking. "VAPP is mechanically acquiring—evidently, Comrade Gusev, with your permission—a predominant influence in the federation," protested Voronskii.

> Were there or were there not, Comrade Gusev, attempts to organize the federation in such a way that VAPP and its supporters were in fact handed two-thirds of the votes? . . . I will say frankly that you have unleashed the young VAPP comrades, given them such rights and such privileges that they have lost a sense of proportion, lost humility. . . . You have unleashed them, Comrade Gusev.[56]

On 18 April 1927, Voronskii's editorship of *Krasnaia nov'* was discussed in the Central Committee press department, with reports by Gusev and Voronskii: "The question of *Krasnaia nov'* and the Trotskyist opposition was quite sharply raised. It was said that the journal could not be called oppositionist, but it was noticeable that Vor-

[52] Published in *Pravda*, 1 July 1925.

[53] Sheshukov, *Neistovye revniteli*, p. 197.

[54] See, for example, the speech by Bliakhin of the press department to the VAPP conference, *Biulleten' V.A.P.P.*, no. 1, 10 April 1926, in Smolensk Archive, WKP 257.

[55] Trotsky, writing in 1930 on the occasion of Mayakovsky's suicide, described Gusev as Molotov's right-hand man in the sphere of cultural repression (*Biulleten' Oppozitsii*, 1930 no. 1, p. 40).

[56] A. A. Voronskii, "Ob uzhasnoi krokodile, o federatsii pisatelei i fal'shivykh frazakh (Otkrytoe pis'mo tov. Gusevu)," *Krasnaia nov'*, 1927 no. 6, pp. 241–42.

onskii's membership in the opposition had left its mark."[57] Raskolnikov was once again appointed to the editorial board, and Voronskii left shortly afterward.

With Voronskii gone, the respective strengths of hard and soft lines emerged more clearly. VAPP had brought the Central Committee press department into day-to-day literary politics, but for the specific purpose of uprooting political oppositionism. It had not achieved "hegemony," since the Federation of Soviet Writers simply collapsed as a working institution under the weight of internal bickering; the State Publishing House, Narkompros, and the thick journals *Pechat' i revoliutsiia* and *Novyi mir* remained under "soft" control; and after Voronskii's departure even *Krasnaia nov'* did not function as a VAPP organ. The censoring organs, Glavlit and the theatrical Glavrepertkom, included many hard-liners and always had, but VAPP did not control them. Lunacharsky kept his grip on theatrical affairs, though he was continually subject to hard-line harassment that VAPP did not initiate or lead. Maxim Gorky's return from abroad, rumored at least from the autumn of 1927, represented a potentially powerful reinforcement for the soft line.

But above all, VAPP was embarrassed in 1927 by the virtual identity of its hard line on culture and that of the political opposition. The chief opposition spokesman on culture at this period was Evgenii Preobrazhenskii, a leading Trotskyist whom we have already encountered as a hard-liner on policy toward universities in the early 1920s, supported by the Trotskyist L. S. Sosnovskii (former editor of the peasant newspaper *Bednota*), the Armenian journalist V. Vaganian (former editor of the party's philosophical journal, *Pod znamenem marksizma*), and the former VAPP leaders Vardin and Lelevich, both of whom were Zinovievists.[58] The opposition claimed that the party had degenerated, and this degeneration was reflected

---

[57] Kuznetsov, in *Krasnaia nov'*, p. 229. Since *Krasnaia nov'* was a journal of political and social comment as well as a literary journal, the Stalinist/Bukharinist anxiety over its control by an oppositionist is neither surprising nor misplaced.

[58] The opposition made no reference to cultural policy in its theses to the Fifteenth Party Congress (Averbakh, in *Na literaturnom postu*, 1927 no. 22–23, p. 21). The *locus classicus* is Preobrazhenskii's speech on the phenomenon of *eseninshchina*, or disillusionment and decadence of youth (see chap. 4, n. 14), in the Communist Academy debate in the spring of 1927. Comment on this speech is to be found in V. G. Knorin's article in *Kommunisticheskaia revoliutsiia*, 1927 no. 6, pp. 3ff., and in L. Averbakh, "Oppozitsiia i voprosy kul'turnoi revoliutsii," *Na literaturnom postu*, 1928 no. 8, p. 10; the text is in the stenogram published by the Communist Academy as *Upadochnoe nastroenie sredi molodezhi* (Moscow, 1927). The literary implications are developed by Lelevich, with acknowledgment to Preobrazhenskii, in the Saratov journal *Kommisticheskii put'*, 1927 no. 1 (84), pp. 37ff., and in his contribution to the almanac *Udar*, ed. A. I. Bezymenskii (Moscow, 1927), pp. 94ff.

in its inability to meet the bourgeois challenge in culture. The bourgeoisie remained supreme in literature and the arts, and kept its monopoly of technical expertise and consequent control of higher education. Bukharin had explicitly disclaimed the concept of cultural class war,[59] and the party had adopted a policy of "stabilization" in culture, an indication that it had given up the attempt to raise the cultural level of the proletariat to a point where it could effectively compete with the old intelligentsia. The party had succumbed to "right deviation," with Bukharin offering "a classic image of cultural Struveism."[60] Hence the contemporary "crisis in culture" (Preobrazhenskii's phrase) and the prevalent mood of decadence and disillusionment among Communist youth.

A change of tone can be observed very shortly after Voronskii's condemnation by the press department of the Central Committee in April 1927. In May the Central Committee's agitprop department held a meeting on theatrical affairs at which the main speakers were V. G. Knorin, the Latvian Old Bolshevik who currently headed the department, and Lunacharsky. Knorin (who had joined in the attack on Voronskii) now put his weight strongly behind Lunacharsky and the soft line, which in this context meant repudiation of a belligerent policy of proletarianization directed against the traditional theaters. The hard line had considerable support at the meeting from members of the agitprop departments of the Central and Moscow Committees of the party, the Moscow education department, Glavrepertkom, and other bodies. But, as one speaker noted, the hard-liners were intimidated by Knorin's paper, and did not feel free to attack him as they habitually attacked Lunacharsky. Averbakh tried the smear tactic of associating some minor soft-liners with Trotsky and Voronskii, and delicately raised the question why Knorin and Lunacharsky should perceive the main enemy to the left and not the right. Lunacharsky replied (against interjections from Averbakh and the head of Glavrepertkom) that one hits hard in the direction from which trouble is coming: "We have to strike a blow at you so you don't interfere with us." He also confirmed the assertion of another speaker that the policies of the present VAPP leadership were identical with those of its oppositionist predecessor. Knorin in his concluding speech stated

---

[59] See N. I. Bukharin, "Proletariat i voprosy khodozhestvennoi politiki," *Krasnaia nov'*, 1925 no. 4, p. 266: "Our society has two levels of conflict, internal and external. Externally it stands face to face with the bourgeois world, and there the class war becomes sharper. . . . Inside the country our policy in general does not follow the line of fanning class war but, on the contrary, goes some way to dampen it."

[60] Lelevich, in *Kommunisticheskii put'* (Saratov), 1927 no. 21 (84), p. 40.

firmly that so long as Averbakh put himself with the ultraleft, "we cannot agree with him."[61]

Conclusion

NEP in culture ended abruptly in the spring of 1928, when the trial of the Shakhty engineers put the loyalty of the whole intelligentsia in doubt. Conclusions were drawn by A. I. Krinitskii, the new head of the Central Committee's agitprop department, at a meeting at the end of May.[62] The new line was the hard line of class war against the bourgeois intelligentsia, struggle against "danger from the right" in party and government cultural policy.[63]

In the course of 1928 the soft line was repudiated in all areas. A new policy of massive proletarian and party admissions to the university came into force in the autumn admissions of 1928. Rykov protested unavailingly in the Central Committee that the class issue was irrelevant to the main task of expanding technical education to meet industrial needs.[64] The party press exposed the secondary schools as bourgeois centers of potential juvenile counterrevolution. Local authorities, reacting as they had done in the university purge in 1924, took this criticism as a directive to conduct "social purges" of both pupils and teachers (although no explicit directive was ever issued, and Narkompros and the government continued to condemn the purges).

Komsomol activists harried the teachers; the militant atheists attacked them for their religious beliefs; and even Narkompros was forced to withdraw the tolerance it had previously extended to individual faith. A Voronezh reader wrote sadly to the national teachers' newspaper of the impact at local level:

> My teacher in junior class, meeting me sixteen years after I left school, wept and told me that she is even afraid to live and work at the present time. She has no regrets for the Tsar—he drove her fiancé into the grave and so she is still unmarried at forty. But the icons that they threw out of the school—this was more than she could bear.[65]

RAPP (as VAPP had renamed itself in 1928) received effective powers to scourge and chastise in the name of the party, mounted a

---

[61] S. N. Krylov, ed., *Puti razvitiia teatra* (stenogram of debate of May 1927) ([Moscow], 1927), pp. 202, 220–21, 227ff., 245ff.

[62] Stenogram published in *Zadachi agitatsii, propagandy i kul'turnogo stroitel'stvo*, ed. B. Olkhovyi (Moscow and Leningrad, 1928).

[63] See chap. 6.

[64] *Voprosy istorii KPSS*, 1966 no. 2, p. 33.

[65] Quoted in *Narodnoe prosveshchenie*, 1928 no. 10, p. 140.

successful campaign against "rightism" in Narkompros's arts administration and had Raskolnikov appointed to head it (again!), and began a fierce struggle with a competing group of hard-liners from the Communist Academy for control of the literary press.

Lunacharsky resigned from his position as people's commissar of enlightenment in 1929; Bukharin and Rykov were identified as leaders of a "right opposition" in the party. The soft line on culture was described as right deviationist, and the government institutions that had carried it out were extensively purged.

The victory of the hard line of cultural class war over the soft line of conciliation coincided with Stalin's victory over his opponents in the party leadership. Should we conclude that the policy of class war was Stalin's own? I think not. There is no evidence to suggest that Stalin had any fixed opinions on cultural policy in the 1920s, and his interventions in cultural and educational debates were remarkably few. The story (repeated to me in Moscow) that in 1928 Stalin approached Lunacharsky with an offer of support for the soft line in exchange for Lunacharsky's later denunciation of the Bukharin/Rykov right opposition appears to have at least apocryphal truth as far as Stalin's political tactics are concerned. From 1932, Stalin reverted to policies that in outward form closely resemble those of the 1920s: reestablishment of academic criteria in university admissions, revival of the general secondary school, verbal encouragement and practical neglect of the rural teacher, reinstatement of bourgeois specialists purged as class enemies, dissolution and condemnation of the proletarian writers' association, and formation of a new Union of Soviet Writers under Gorky's leadership, including both Communist and nonparty writers. Of course these policies were *in effect* vastly different from those of the 1920s—not only because, as Stalin said, "cadres decide everything" and the old soft-line Bolshevik administrators had disappeared, but because the proletarian attack had fragmented the intelligentsia and destroyed its old patterns of association.

If Stalin had no interest in class-war policies as such, why did he let the hard-liners win? The answer, in political terms, must be that they were a convenient weapon to use against his opponents in party and government and (if we assume that Stalin had a general concern for the extension of party control) to intimidate the intelligentsia. But this formulation may suggest a wider area of choice than Stalin in fact had. The proletarian hard line was already identified as the political alternative: it was understood by the party and had known support within it. Probably its strength in the party was not so great as to force Stalin, or any party leader in 1928, to accept it (though this notion of overwhelming constituency pressure cannot be discounted, given the incomplete evidence we have on local party opinion and its interpretation by the leadership). But it was strong enough not to be overlooked, and coherent enough to make any selective use—such as the deal that Stalin is reported to have offered Lunacharsky—extremely difficult to carry through.

As I understand the situation, Stalin accepted a predefined opposition platform and support when he moved against his colleagues in the leadership in 1928, just as a hypothetical challenger to Stalin in (say) 1934 would have had to do. Given the platform and its presumptive supporters, his choice was to make the move or not. When he did, the soft line on culture was automatically canceled.

(1973)

CHAPTER 6

Cultural Revolution
as Class War

In the First Five-Year Plan period, the term "cultural revolution" was used in a special sense, different from earlier or later Soviet usages. It described a political confrontation of "proletarian" Communists and the "bourgeois" intelligentsia, in which the Communists sought to overthrow the cultural authorities inherited from the old regime. The aim of the Cultural Revolution was to create a new "proletarian intelligentsia."[1] Its method was class war.

The concept of class war depended on definitions of the old intelligentsia as "bourgeois" and the Communist party as "proletarian." All Communists agreed on these definitions, but not all thought it necessary to make culture a battleground. In the first ten years of Soviet power, the Communist leadership had tended to avoid outright confrontation with the intelligentsia. Lenin had rejected the idea that cultural power, like political power could be seized by revolutionary action. Culture, in his view, had to be patiently acquired and assimilated; Communists must learn from bourgeois specialists, despite their identification with an alien social class; and refusal to learn was a sign of "Communist conceit." During NEP the leadership as a whole had treated harassment of specialists (*spetseedstvo*) as a regrettable by-product of revolutionary zeal rather than as a mark of developed proletarian consciousness.

---

[1] "Cultural Revolution" here refers to the specific episode that is the subject of this chapter.

115

In 1927, on the eve of the industrialization drive, the leadership was still talking in terms of a nonantagonistic relationship with bourgeois specialists. The party's task, Stalin told the Fifteenth Party Congress, was "to strengthen the bond [smychka] of the working class with the toiling Soviet intelligentsia of town and country," and industrialization would only tend to reinforce the alliance, since the technical intelligentsia, "being closely linked with the process of production, cannot fail to see that the Bolsheviks are leading our country forward to better things."[2] On the same occasion, the future "rightist" Rykov and future "Stalinist" Molotov agreed that in the interests of successful industrialization it would be necessary to make a substantially increased investment in culture, particularly in the priority areas of primary education, technical education, and the campaign against illiteracy.[3] Pravda used the term "cultural revolution" in its Leninist sense to describe the nonmilitant development of mass education that industrialization would require:

> Industrialization—our general course—is unthinkable without rationalization. But rationalization in turn is unthinkable without a raising of the cultural level: both the cultural level of "cadres" and the cultural level of the masses. The demand to raise the cultural level of the worker-peasant masses, the demand to carry out a broad and profound "cultural revolution" in the country, is evident: it is now really "in the air."[4]

The switch to a class-war concept of cultural revolution came abruptly a few months after the Fifteenth Party Congress, in an atmosphere of rising political tension. In January 1928 Stalin visited Siberia, where grain procurements had been small despite a good harvest, and decided that the only course was to coerce the peasants and confiscate their hoarded grain. This was the beginning of the policy of class war against prosperous peasants, which later led to the forced collectivization of agriculture. In March 1928 the state prosecutor announced the forthcoming trial of a large group of mining engineers and technicians from the Shakhty area of Donbass on charges of conspiracy and sabotage. The trial, which took place in Moscow in May and June, received maximum publicity and was preceded by highly organized public discussion and condemnation of

[2] Iosif Stalin, political report of the Central Committee, in XV s"ezd Vsesoiuznoi Kommunisticheskoi Partii (b).: Stenograficheskii otchet (Moscow, 1928), pp. 63–64.
[3] A. I. Rykov, report on the Five-Year Plan, in ibid., pp. 778–79; Viacheslav Molotov, report on work in the countryside, in ibid., pp. 1081–83.
[4] Pravda, 30 November 1927, p. 1.

the accused. This was a turning point in Soviet policy toward bourgeois specialists. From this time, the technical intelligentsia ceased to be seen as the party's natural ally in industrialization and became potentially traitors whose real allegiance was to the dispossessed capitalists and their foreign supporters.

The purpose of the Shakhty trial, according to an NKVD official quoted by Roy Medvedev, was "to mobilize the masses," "to arouse their wrath against the imperialists," "to intensify vigilance."[5] This vigilance was directed against the intelligentsia as a class enemy. The necessary condition of successful industrialization was no longer (as Rykov and Molotov had thought in December) more engineers and a more literate population, but more *proletarian* engineers and a population alert for signs of wrecking and sabotage among the bourgeois intelligentsia.

The new concept of cultural revolution was defined by A. I. Krinitskii, head of the agitprop department of the Central Committee, at a special meeting on cultural questions held while the Shakhty trial was in progress. Under present conditions, Krinitskii said, cultural revolution was inconceivable without class war, and the proletariat must fight "against bourgeois elements that are supported by the remnants and survivals of the influence, traditions, and customs of the old society." These bourgeois elements had mounted an attack on the cultural front, "struggling to increase their share, fighting for their own schools, their own art, their own theater and films, trying to use the state apparatus for that purpose." Communist cultural administrators (particularly those in Narkompros, under Lunacharsky's tolerant leadership) had failed to recognize the threat; they had been disarmed by "an antirevolutionary, opportunist conception of cultural revolution as a peaceful, classless raising of cultural standards—a conception that does not distinguish between bourgeois and proletarian elements of culture . . . and does not see the fierce struggle of the proletariat against the class antagonist in everyday life, the school, art, science, and so on."[6]

The period of official sponsorship of class-war cultural revolution

[5] Roy A. Medvedev, *Let History Judge: The Origins and Consequences of Stalinism* (New York, 1971), p. 112.

[6] The meeting was held in Moscow, 30 May–3 June 1928, under the sponsorship of the agitprop department, with other cultural and educational figures as invited guests. The full stenogram is in B. Olkhovyi, ed., *Zadachi agitatsii, propagandy i kul'turnogo stroitel'stva* (Moscow and Leningrad, 1928). Krinitskii's speech was also published separately as *Osnovnye zadachi agitatsii, propagandy i kul'turnogo stroitel'stva* (Moscow and Leningrad, 1928). The quotations here are from pp. 10 and 17, of that work; *Pravda*, 8 June 1928, p. 5; and *Kommunisticheskaia revoliutsiia*, 1928 no. 17–18, p. 166.

in the Soviet Union can be dated from the Shakhty trial (early summer 1928) to Stalin's statement of reconciliation with the old technical intelligentsia three years later (June 1931). Subsequently, from the standpoint of Soviet discussion, the episode was buried—indeed, class-war cultural revolution became a theoretical impossibility, as the Leninist definition of cultural revolution was taken back into Soviet usage from the late 1930s. Western historians, regarding the First Five-Year Plan period in culture as essentially a transition from the relative permissiveness and pluralism of NEP to the regimentation of Stalinism, have usually treated the class-war terminology simply as camouflage for the basic process of Communist intimidation of the intelligentsia.

The Cultural Revolution was not only a more complex phenomenon than this scheme suggests, however, but also one of peculiar importance for an understanding of Soviet political and social development. This was the period in which the social and generational tensions of NEP came to a climax in an onslaught (which the leadership only partly controlled) on privilege and established authority. But these were also the first and formative years of the Stalin era. We are accustomed to the idea that the First Five-Year Plan laid the foundations for Stalinist industrialization, just as collectivization laid the foundations for Stalinist agriculture. It should surely be recognized that the Cultural Revolution was an equally important part of what has been called "the Stalin revolution." The substance behind the rhetoric of class war was large-scale upward mobility of industrial workers and working-class party members into higher education and administrative and managerial jobs. Cultural Revolution was the vehicle for training the future Communist elite and creating the new Soviet intelligentsia.

This feat of social engineering—unprecedented and unrepeated in Soviet experience—was accomplished in the midst of a cultural upheaval, some aspects of which were directly manipulated by the party leadership, others outside the range of leadership vision. The Cultural Revolution had many facets. It was a worker-promotion movement linked to a political campaign to discredit the right opposition within the party. It was an iconoclastic youth movement directed against "bureaucratic" authority. It was a process whereby militant Communist groups in the professions established local dictatorships and attempted to revolutionize their disciplines. It was, finally, a heyday for revolutionary theorists and "harebrained schemers," whose blueprints for the new society not only attracted disciples among the Communist cultural militants but also in many cases gained solid institutional support.

The "rightist danger"

The Cultural Revolution was initiated as a revolution from above. The Shakhty trial and the subsequent show trials of the "Industrial Party" (1930), the Mensheviks (1931), and other groups accused of conspiracy and sabotage can be seen as a mobilization strategy designed to create an atmosphere of crisis and to justify the regime's demands for sacrifice and extraordinary efforts in the cause of industrialization. The trials built on the popular fears aroused by the war scare of 1927, and purported to demonstrate that the "wreckers and saboteurs" of the bourgeois intelligentsia were potential allies of the encircling capitalist powers in the event of a renewed military intervention. The wreckers also served as scapegoats for economic failures, shortages of consumer goods, and a general decline in urban living standards as resources were channeled into the priority area of heavy industry.

In the Cultural Revolution, as in the earlier war scare, the mobilization strategy had the additional purpose of discrediting Stalin's opponents in the Politburo. From the beginning of 1928 Rykov and Bukharin had opposed Stalin on the crucial political issues of the use of force against the peasantry and the tempo of industrialization. Through 1928 a great deal of the energy of the propagandists of class-war Cultural Revolution was devoted to demonstrating that the same party "rightists" who were inclined to conciliate the kulaks were also conciliators of the bourgeois intelligentsia, and thus opponents of the Cultural Revolution.

Contemporaries saw Rykov, head of the Soviet government (chairman of the All-Union Sovnarkom), as the major political figure of the right. Rykov objected to introducing the "class issue" in the discussion on training of engineers that followed the disclosure of the Shakhty wrecking; and, by quoting Lenin's statements on the need to work with bourgeois specialists, he tried to convince the Politburo that persecution of engineers was the wrong policy.[7]

But Rykov's position may not originally have been a factional one. He was the only rightist leader with a background in industry, and it was the "industrialists" (*khoziaistvenniki*) of the party leadership who best knew the value of the bourgeois engineers and were most likely to defend them. Like Rykov, both Valerian Kuibyshev and Sergo Ordzhonikidze, the present and future heads of Vesenkha, reacted to the announcement of the Shakhty trial with public warnings

---

[7] See *Voprosy istorii KPSS*, 1966 no. 2, p. 33, Lazar Kaganovich in *XVI s"ezd VKP(b): Stenograficheskii otchet* (Moscow, 1935), p. 147.

against the danger of *spetseedstvo*.[8] But, since Kuibyshev and Ordzhonikidze were clearly Stalin supporters and committed to rapid
industrialization, their doubts were evidently practical and not ideological or motivated by factional interest.

Mikhail Tomskii, the rightist head of the trade unions, in contrast,
expressed no concern for the bourgeois specialists or opposition to
the principle of class-war Cultural Revolution. Indeed, it was, as natural for the representative of organized labor to support the Cultural
Revolution—a policy that offered workers a chance for upward mobility—as it was for him to oppose the increased power of management over labor which was a concomitant of high-speed industrialization. Throughout 1928 Tomskii behaved more as a trade union
spokesman than as a member of a unified rightist group. The trade
unions, for example, were at odds with Narkompros on the question
of labor training. In mid-1928, when Rykov and Bukharin were making support for Narkompros one of the issues of contention with the
Stalinist group in the Politburo, Tomskii joined the cultural-revolutionary attack on the commissariat.[9]

Bukharin's relation to the new doctrine of Cultural Revolution was
more complicated. His official position as head of the Comintern and
editor of *Pravda* gave him no institutional interest in defending the
bourgeois specialists; and he does not in fact seem to have expressed
early objections to the Shakhty trial. His record on the issue of cultural class war was contradictory. On the one hand, he had opposed
the "proletarian" RAPP and defended the "bourgeois" nonparty
writers in the literary debate of 1924–1925; and in doing so he had
expressed what was then a leadership consensus that "our policy in
general does not follow the line of fanning class war but, on the
contrary, goes some way to damp it."[10] On the other hand, he was the
only member of the party leadership who had been actively involved
in the earlier "proletarian" movement in culture (the Civil War Proletkult), and, unlike Rykov, he was capable of taking at least a rhetorically threatening Communist stance toward the bourgeois intelligentsia (as we saw in Chapter 3).

Stylistic evidence points to Bukharin as the author of *Pravda*'s
first editorial statement on the cultural implications of the Shakhty

[8] *Torgovo-promyshlennaia gazeta*, 11 March 1928, p. 2 (Rykov); *Pravda*, 30 March
1928, p. 3 (Kuibyshev); *Pravda*, 28 March 1928, p. 1 (Ordzhonikidze). I am indebted to
Kendall E. Bailes for the Ordzhonikidze reference.

[9] *Voprosy istorii KPSS*, 1966 no. 2, p. 33; Stalin, speech in XVI s″ezd VKP(b): Stenograficheskii otchet (Moscow, 1931), 1:293. On Tomskii's attack, see Lunacharsky in
Pravda, 2 June 1928, p. 7, and A. K. Gastev in *Pravda*, 7 June 1928, p. 2.

[10] Bukharin, "Proletariat i voprosy khudozhestvennoi politiki," *Krasnaia nov'*, 1925
no. 4, p. 266.

trial, which advocated a militant proletarian isolationism in culture, very much in the spirit of the old Proletkult manifestos. The proletariat and the proletarian party needed an "armor of proletarian culture" to protect themselves from "alien class influences, bourgeois degeneration, petty-bourgeois waverings, dulling of revolutionary vigilance in the face of the more cultured class enemy," *Pravda* stated.[11]

If this was in fact Bukharin's position, it was closer to class-war Cultural Revolution than to conciliation. But it became clear very quickly that whatever Bukharin's opinion of the moment, he was going to be labeled an opponent of the Cultural Revolution. A few days after the *Pravda* editorial, the agitprop department of the Central Committee held a meeting on current cultural tasks. Lunacharsky and other known conciliators of the bourgeois intelligentsia were attacked. Krinitskii, head of the agitprop department, in an unusual omission did not cite the *Pravda* editorial in his keynote speech; instead he went out of his way to suggest that Bukharin opposed the new policy—not mentioning him by name, but referring to his well-known statement of 1925 against "fanning the class war" in culture. "Some comrades," Krinitskii said, "may perhaps reproach me: have I not talked too much about the revival of class war, the attempts at bourgeois counterattack against the triumphant march of the proletariat, the need to give a decisive rebuff to each and every kind of bourgeois maneuver? Isn't this 'fanning the class war'?"[12]

It is doubtful, therefore, that the three Politburo rightists took a united stand on the issue of class-war Cultural Revolution in the spring of 1928. But in political terms this issue was secondary. The important thing was that the rightists disagreed with Stalin on industrialization tempos and the peasant question. For this reason, Stalin no doubt wished to discredit them by any means available; and "softness" on the bourgeois intelligentsia was a position that the working-class majority of rank-and-file party members were likely to condemn.

From the fact that class-war Cultural Revolution was used to discredit Stalin's political opponents, it seems probable that the initiative in introducing the new policy came from Stalin or his supporters. The evidence, however, is largely circumstantial. One source states, evidently on the basis of contemporary party rumors, that the decision to stage the Shakhty trial was made by Stalin over the objections of Rykov, Kuibyshev, and Genrikh Iagoda, the head of the GPU.[13]

[11] "Klassovyi protsess," *Pravda*, 18 May 1928, p. 1.
[12] Krinitskii, *Osnovnye zadachi*, p. 79.
[13] A. Avtorkhanov, *Stalin and the Soviet Communist Party* (London, 1959), p. 29.

In the second half of 1928, during Stalin's battle with the rightists in the Politburo and the Moscow Party Committee, the Cultural Revolution received remarkably detailed coverage in the press, with commentaries that persistently associated the "counterrevolutionary" tendencies of the bourgeois intelligentsia with the "rightist danger" within the party. Since "rightist danger" in effect meant opposition to Stalin, the association was presumably made on Stalin's behalf, if not on his personal initiative.

The press coverage of 1928 was heavy with innuendo, since the exact location of the political "rightist danger" had not yet been disclosed. Only one cultural rightist was clearly identified, and that was A. I. Sviderskii, who was removed from the Russian Commissariat of Agriculture because of policy disagreements in the spring of 1928. From that time he headed the Narkompros arts administration; and there Sviderskii had no real line because he had no expertise: he was convicted in advance of cultural "rightism" because he had been a rightist in agriculture.[14]

Lunacharsky and his colleagues at Narkompros were also accused of cultural "rightism," although, with the important exception of Nadezhda Krupskaia, they were not in fact politically associated with Stalin's opponents in the Politburo.[15] Between April and July 1928, however, the Central Committee was discussing the transfer of control of higher technical schools from Narkompros to Vesenkha; and on this issue Rykov and Bukharin apparently supported Narkompros, while Stalin and Molotov supported Vesenkha.[16] In the summer of 1928 Iosif Khodorovskii was dismissed as head of Narkompros's technical education administration and Andrei Vyshinsky (later notorious for his prominent prosecutorial role during the Great Purges) was appointed in his place.[17] Since Vyshinsky had just served as presiding judge at the Shakhty trial, there was the disturbing possibility that his Narkompros assignment was in the same line of duty—and in fact the second of the show trials (the "Industrial Party" trial of 1930) featured Vyshinsky as prosecutor, charging a number of experts formerly sympathetic to Narkompros's position on

[14] The campaign against Sviderskii is described in detail in Sheila Fitzpatrick, "The Emergence of Glaviskusstvo: Class War on the Cultural Front, Moscow, 1928–29," *Soviet Studies*, October 1971.

[15] Krupskaia, Lenin's widow, was one of Lunacharsky's deputies and head of Glavpolitprosvet, Narkompros's political education administration, Glavpolitprosvet, throughout the 1920s.

[16] F. Vaganov, *Pravyi uklon v VKP(b) i ego razgrom (1928–30 gg.)* (Moscow, 1970), p. 102.

[17] The exact date of Vyshinsky's appointment is not known, but he apparently began work in Narkompros in September (interview with Vyshinsky in *Pravda*, 25 September 1928, p. 6).

engineering training with "wrecking," and citing a volume edited for Narkompros by Khodorovskii as one of the basic documents on which the prosecution had built its case.[18]

These links were enough to connect the cultural "rightism" of Narkompros with the political "rightism" of Rykov and Bukharin and the wrecking activities of the bourgeois specialists. Stalin's supporters did not neglect to point this out. What was the "rightist danger in art"? Krinitskii offered two answers. On the one hand, it was the danger of bourgeois influence, or of excessive Communist susceptibility to such influence. On the other, it was "the rightist danger in the ranks of the Party transferred into the language of art."[19]

As the Cultural Revolution gathered momentum, it became clear that Bukharin was to be its exemplary victim among the political rightists. Because Bukharin, unlike Rykov or Tomsky, really was an intellectual with literary and artistic interests and some bourgeois literary friends, he could plausibly be included in the category of "Communist literati" of whom Stalin spoke contemptuously both before and after the Cultural Revolution—those who "sat for years in [European] cafés, drank beer, and were nevertheless unable to learn Europe or to understand it," and who, on returning to Russia, lacked the stamina to remain in the leadership during successive periods of crisis.[20] Bukharin, moreover, was on bad terms with the leading vigilantes of the Cultural Revolution: both the RAPP leadership and the Komsomol Central Committee had taken the brunt of his sarcasm and no doubt had personal scores to settle.[21]

As Communist scholars in the professions established ascendancy over the local bourgeoisie, their tendency was to fall into warring

[18] The volume edited by Khodorovskii, *Kakogo inzhenera nuzhny gotovit' nashi VTUZy*, was a marshaling of specialist opinion in support of Narkompros's policy, which was currently under attack from Vesenkha. Khodorovskii's co-editor, P. S. Osadchii, was a witness and unindicted co-conspirator in the Industrial Party trial, and several other contributors were accused or named during the Shakhty or Industrial Party trial. Vyshinsky described *Kakogo inzhenera* as one of "those historic documents on which investigation and subsequent prosecution in the affair of the Shakhty wreckers and the Industrial Party affair were based" (*Nauchnyi rabotnik*, 1930 no. 11–12, p. 25).

[19] *Komsomol'skaia pravda*, 15 November 1928, p. 4.

[20] Conversation with Emil Ludwig on 13 December 1931, in I. V. Stalin, *Sochineniia*, 13 vols. (Moscow, 1947–1952), 13:121. and comment on Communist literati (1925) in ibid., 7:42–43.

[21] For much of the NEP period, Bukharin was the Politburo's liaison with the Komsomol and spokesman for youth. His lack of rapport with the Komsomol, however, may be judged from his description of the typical Komsomol leader as an ignorant, manipulative little apparatchik (speech to Moscow Party conference, 1927, in *Krasnoe studenchestvo*, 1927–1928 no. 11, p. 32). As for the RAPP leaders, Bukharin had not openly disagreed with them, but he had ridiculed them (see his "Proletariat i voprosy khudozhestvennoi politiki," *Krasnaia nov'*, 1925 no. 4).

factions that exchanged accusations of political deviation. The deviations most frequently mentioned were "Trotskyist-Menshevist" and "Bukharinist." The scholarly attacks on Bukharin began in the Communist Academy's Institute of World Economy and Institute of Philosophy in 1929.[22] A few months earlier, Bukharin had been appointed head of the Vesenkha administration of scientific and technical research institutes. This post was not only politically unrewarding but compromised: Bukharin replaced an earlier opposition leader, Lev Kamenev; Kamenev moved to the still less desirable position of head of the Chief (Foreign) Concessions Committee, formerly held by Trotsky; and Trotsky had just been expelled from the Soviet Union altogether.[23] These appointments provided an apt illustration—and, given Stalin's cast of mind, probably not an accidental one—of the downward path: oppositionism led to association with the bourgeois intelligentsia, then to dealings with international capitalism, and finally to disgrace and exclusion from Communist society.

The leadership struggles of the 1920s had developed the politics of rumor, smear, and guilt by association into a fine art. These techiques were fully in evidence in the cultural-revolutionary campaign against the right. The anti-right propaganda created the image of a continuum running from the rightists in the Politburo through Narkompros and the bourgeois intelligentsia to the Shakhty wreckers. As scientific research chief at Vesenkha, Bukharin was virtually bound to associate himself in some way with a "technocratic interest," thus discrediting himself further.[24] Lunacharsky, who left Narkompros in the autumn of 1929, became the victim of rumors that portrayed him as a kind of Communist cultural Nepman, corrupted by privilege, foreign travel, and the good life.[25] Both Bukharin and

[22] Vestnik Kommunisticheskoi Akademii, 1929 no. 35–36, pp. 227ff., 297ff.

[23] The new appointments of Bukharin and Kamenev were announced in Komsomol'skaia pravda, 1 June 1929, p. 4.

[24] For evidence of Bukharin's development of tendencies toward "technocratic thinking" in his new job, see Kendall E. Bailes, "The Politics of Technology: Stalin and Technocratic Thinking among Soviet Engineers," American Historical Review, April 1974.

[25] Such rumors are, by their nature, difficult to reconstruct. At the agitprop meeting in May 1928, Krinitskii suggested that Lunacharsky's interest in commercial profit for the Soviet film industry was "a mistaken transfer of NEP principles into the field of ideology" (Krinitskii, Osnovnye zadachi, p. 23). At a teachers' congress in 1929, Lunacharsky was obliged to give a long self-justification in answer to a question on his charging "fantastic" fees for public lectures (TsGAOR, f. 5462, op. 11, d. 12, ll. 45–46). He was reprimanded by the Central Control Commission of the party for holding up the Leningrad-Moscow express train to suit his convenience (Pravda, 22 June 1929, p. 3). Other rumors concerned his wife (a stage and film actress), his contacts with the acting and literary world, his frequent trips abroad, and an unelucidated diamond-smuggling scandal involving one of his wife's acquaintances.

Lunacharsky were elected to the Academy of Sciences (under party pressure) at a time when their political fortunes were at their lowest ebb and the academy itself was being pilloried in the press as the last refuge of aristocratic internal émigrés.[26]

The Cultural Revolution carried the message that conciliators of the peasantry, conciliators of the intelligentsia, bureaucrats (the press represented Narkompros as the archetypal "bureaucratic" commissariat), Nepmen, kulaks, café-haunting *literati*, wreckers, expropriated capitalists, and foreign spies were all on the same side in the political struggle and collectively represented the "rightist danger" to the party. Stalin's political opponents were not yet accused of direct communication with foreign espionage agents, as they were to be in the show trials of the late 1930s. But for a potential Communist leader, the suggestion of association with the privileged and anti-Communist bourgeois intelligentsia was damaging enough.

The class-war motif

Our discussion so far has dealt with an aspect of the Cultural Revolution that appears to have been directed and manipulated from above. But this is only one part of the picture. The Cultural Revolution also involved a response on the part of the leadership to pressures within the Communist movement and the society as a whole. The class-war concept of confrontation between proletariat and bourgeoisie reflected real social tensions between the materially disadvantaged and the privileged. The antibureaucratic drive of the Cultural Revolution—often verging on an attack on established authority per se—reflected real grievances of the younger generation. Within the professions, Communists and non-Communists tended to gather in potentially antagonistic camps: the appeal for "proletarian hegemony" in scholarship and the arts did not originally come from the party leadership, but came from groups within the professions and scholarly institutions. The specific forms the Cultural Revolution took in different areas were determined largely by existing tensions and conflicts. From this perspective, the Cultural Revolution was not only an attempt to resolve the contradictions of NEP but a product of those contradictions.

The class-war component of the Cultural Revolution was built on a solid foundation of working-class and Communist tradition. In this

[26] See Loren R. Graham, *The Soviet Academy of Sciences and the Communist Party, 1927–1932* (Princeton, 1967), pp. 114–15. Bukharin was elected to the academy in February 1929, Lunacharsky in January 1930.

connection, it is important to remember that in the period after Lenin's death both the Communist Party and Komsomol took in large new enrollments of workers. By the First Five-Year Plan period, they were mass organizations with predominantly working-class membership: in 1930, 56.3 percent of Communist Party members were of working-class origin and 46.3 percent were workers by current occupation.[27] This affiliation may have made them more amenable to manipulation by politically sophisticated leaders, as Western analysts often suggest, but it surely also made the leaders more sensitive to the opinions and grievances expressed by their working-class constituents.

A militant class-war tradition in the party, however, predated the mass recruitment of workers after Lenin's death. It developed during the Civil War—another big period of lower-class recruitment—when the party became a fighting organization that identified its enemies in class terms. Besides the foreign interventionists, the "class enemies" of the Bolsheviks during the Civil War were the capitalists, the kulaks, the clergy, and the intelligentsia.

Despite the revolutionary tradition of the Russian intelligentsia, almost none of its members supported the Bolsheviks in the first months after October. Even students were overwhelmingly opposed to the October Revolution; teachers in Petrograd and Moscow went on strike; professional associations refused to recognize Soviet power. During the Civil War, the provincial intelligentsia largely supported the Whites, and many followed the retreating White armies. Large numbers of prominent cultural figures drifted south from the capitals: some later left the Crimea with the evacuation of Baron Wrangel's army, while others, still doubtful and suspicious of the new regime, returned to Moscow or Petrograd.

The Old Bolsheviks were surprised and indignant at the solid hostility of the intelligentsia, but remained cautious about classifying them as outright enemies of the Revolution. This was not the attitude of the Civil War recruits to the party, however, and probably was not that of the post–Civil War party as a whole. Rank-and-file Communists continued to regard the intelligentsia as class enemies, despite the leadership's policy of conciliation of the bourgeois specialists, introduced at the beginning of NEP.

Throughout NEP, many Communists regarded the toleration of bourgeois specialists as a limited and revocable tactic, similar to the tactics that governed the party's relations with kulaks, Nepmen, and

[27] T. H. Rigby, Communist Party Membership in the U.S.S.R., 1917–1967 (Princeton, 1968), p. 116.

priests. The ambivalent attitude of the Old Bolshevik leaders was indeed difficult to communicate to Communists of the post-October generation. The intelligentsia was described as "bourgeois," yet its members—unlike Nepmen, kulaks, and priests—had the vote, and were supposed to be respected for their skills. In the mid-1920s, the party leaders sometimes went to considerable lengths to assure the intelligentsia of their goodwill.[28] But they did not repudiate the idea of class war. The NEP policy, in Bukharin's words, was not to fan the flames.

One of the reasons that members of the intelligentsia were officially referred to as "bourgeois specialists" was that in Communist usage the term "intelligentsia" was pejorative. Proletarian and Communist students in Soviet universities during NEP were warned against succumbing to *intelligentshchina*. The Communists students who voted for Trotsky in 1923–1924 were held to be corrupted by *intelligentshchina* and the "petty-bourgeois environment" of NEP. The youth cult of the poet Sergei Esenin after his suicide in 1925 was condemned in similar terms.[29]

NEP provided further grounds for resentment, since in social terms it meant an acceptance of privilege and inequality. The Civil War had acted as a leveler by temporarily reducing the entire urban population to near subsistence conditions. The effect of NEP was to make at least some sections of the population more prosperous. But at the same time there was widespread unemployment in the towns, affecting primarily unskilled workers and the young, but also intermittently touching skilled workers, trade unionists, and party members.

With some exceptions, the intelligentsia rose quickly from the poverty of the Civil War years. By the mid-1920s, the old intelligentsia of the capitals were clearly a privileged group—in material terms, part of an emerging "Soviet bourgeoisie." Specialists employed by government agencies earned very high salaries. As we have seen, professors, despite their vociferous complaints of ill treatment, had high salaries and special privileges in such areas as housing and access to higher education for their children. White-collar workers as a group earned more than industrial workers, were less liable to unemployment, and were better housed.[30]

To many Communists, especially those whose standards of living

[28] For examples, see the discussion in chap. 5 of the conflict between leadership policy toward the bourgeois specialists and Communist rank-and-file attitudes.

[29] See chap. 4, n. 14.

[30] The average monthly salary of employees in the central administration of the RSFSR in the first quarter of 1926–1927 was 150.95 rubles, as against 60.02 for workers in census industry (*Itogi desiatiletiia sovetskoi vlasti v tsifrakh 1917–1927* [Moscow, 1927], p. 342).

had not risen with those of the professionals and "bureaucrats," the cafés and cabarets of the NEP city symbolized a shameful retreat from revolutionary ideals. The clientele of these cafés—Nepmen, Soviet bureaucrats, members of the literary and artistic intelligentsia—combined those apparently disparate categories of the urban population that came under heaviest attack during the Cultural Revolution.[31]

In discussing the Cultural Revolution as a response to social grievances, one must also consider the cultural revolutionaries' claim that in 1927–1928 the Soviet system was threatened by an actual "bourgeois attack" (nastuplenie). To some extent, of course, this fear can be related to the supposed external threat that provoked the war scare of 1927. But there were other specific causes of concern. In 1927–1928 there was an outburst of anti-Communist organization by schoolchildren, sometimes overtly political, sometimes aggressively apolitical, as in the case of the Esenin cult.[32] The schools most affected were the "bourgeois" urban secondary schools. Contemporary Soviet sources reported, too, that the religious organizations were making an unprecedented number of converts among peasant youth. Two million young people were said to be enrolled in religious youth organizations in 1928, and the Baptist "Bapsomol" and Mennonite "Mensomol" supposedly had more members together than the Soviet Komsomol.[33]

The Shakhty trial represented a response to an alleged bourgeois threat. Soviet historians in the post-Stalin period have produced no evidence to support the concrete allegations of sabotage and conspiracy, and some Soviet accounts come close to saying outright that the trial was fraudulent. Nevertheless, the possibility remains that rank-and-file Communists were inclined to believe that the non-Communist intelligentsia posed a political threat to the new regime, and even perhaps to suspect the party leadership of falling dangerously under the influence of its bourgeois specialists.

There are also a few tantalizing intimations that a proposal to establish a closer alliance with the intelligentsia may have been floated in the party leadership by persons unknown: in 1927 Lunacharsky

[31] The café milieu is portrayed disapprovingly but with fascination obviously based on personal observation in V. Kirshon and A. Uspenskii's topical play Konstantin Terekhin (Rzhavchina) (Moscow, 1927).

[32] For information on anti-Communist and other organizations in the schools, see E. Strogova in Komsomol'skaia pravda, 1 April 1928, p. 2; I. Chernia in Kommunisticheskaia revoliutsiia, 1928 no. 17–18; Narodnoe prosveshchenie, 1928 no. 5, pp. 25, 32, 39. On the Esenin cult, see Upadochnoe nastroenie sredi molodezhi: Eseninshchina (Moscow: Communist Academy, 1927), and M. Koriakov, " 'Eseninshchina' i sovetskaia molodezh'," Vozrozhdenie (Paris) 15 (1951).

[33] M. Gorev in Izvestiia, 13 June 1929, p. 4; F. Oleshchuk in Revoliutsiia i kul'tura, 1928 no. 10 (31 May), p. 21.

warned leaders of the non-Communist intelligentsia against over-reaching themselves, noting that, while the intelligentsia were confidently "awaiting a call from Soviet power to bring the most valuable elements of the aristocracy of the mind into the highest organs of the government," some people (presumably members of the party leadership) "would like to create a conflict on the issue of the participation of 'chosen intellectuals' in power."[34]

Social purging

Perhaps genuine fears of an emerging and politically ambitious intelligentsia lobby were in part responsible for the arrests and prison sentences that were one aspect of the Cultural Revolution. If so, the party leadership's fears evidently centered on the engineering profession and, to a lesser extent, the Academy of Sciences. More than one hundred of the academy's workers—among them a few academicians, some historians, and Secretary Oldenburg's assistant—were arrested in 1929 and 1930, and many of them spent the remainder of the Cultural Revolution period in exile or imprisonment.[35] The engineers suffered *en masse*. The Smolensk Archive contains a report, dated June 1928, that the GPU suspected twenty of forty local engineers of subversive activities, together with a request that "if possible, specialists should not be pulled out in bunches but gradually, so as not to denude industry."[36] Kendall Bailes quoted contemporary estimates of arrests of engineers ranging from two thousand to seven thousand—most of them presumably coming from the group of university-trained engineers currently working in large-scale industry and numbering somewhat over ten thousand.[37] Arrest, of course, was not necessarily followed by imprisonment. But a report of April 1929 from the engineers' association, VMBIT, stated that "after the Shakhty affair the number of engineers in production jobs declined by 17 percent," evidently through imprisonment and the flight of engineers who feared arrest.[38]

[34] A. Lunacharsky, "Intelligentsiia i ee mesto v sotsialisticheskom stroitel'stve," *Revoliutsiia i kul'tura*, 1927 no. 1, p. 32. The context of this warning is described in chap. 3; chap. 10 (p. 253) quotes a later report on similar lines.

[35] Graham, *Soviet Academy of Sciences*, pp. 120–30.

[36] Smolensk Archive, WKP 33: gubkom bureau, 11 June 1928.

[37] Bailes, "Politics of Technology," p. 446.

[38] *Rabochaia gazeta*, 17 April 1929, p. 8. For other reports of intensified *spetseedstvo* and flight of engineers after the Shakhty trial, see S. A. Fediukin, *Velikii Oktiabr' i intelligentsiia* (Moscow, 1972), pp. 386–87. VMBIT = Vsesoiuznoe mezhsektsionnoe biuro inzhenerov i tekhnikov.

Another kind of purge was going on at the same time. Its victims were "bureaucrats" and "social aliens," and for a number of reasons it deserves to be considered as a phenomenon distinct from the police purging, despite an area of overlap. The main differences between the two were that the victims were fired from their jobs or expelled from school but not arrested, and that their purging was to a large extent a product of local initiative and an expression of strongly felt grievances against privilege and the "bureaucratic degeneration" of the Revolution.

One could, of course, point to the existence of such grievances against the "bourgeois engineer" in the factory: workers commonly resented the privileges offered to persons associated with the old regime, and Communist directors often clashed with nonparty chief engineers. But the post-Shakhty arrests of engineers were not in any direct sense products of these grievances. Local authorities took action against the engineers under instructions from the center. If they did not take action, they were rebuked, and in uncovering "wrecking and sabotage" they were expected to follow the Shakhty model quite closely.[39]

The pattern of antibureaucratic and social purging was different. Here central initiative and instructions *followed* widespread local practice, and sometimes contradicted it. There was no original central model for local authorities to imitate. The decisions of the leadership that did most to stimulate social purging—for example, the high "proletarian percentages" recommended to universities and to technical schools after the July 1928 plenum of the Central Committee, and the tightening of franchise qualifications for the Soviet elections of 1929—were framed with other policy considerations in mind, and at most could only imply a tolerance of social purging of institutions.

But social purging seems to have been an activity that required only absence of discouragement from the center to flourish, for good Communists had always been suspicious of "bureaucrats" and "class aliens." The Cultural Revolution produced an upsurge of a condition that had been chronic since 1917 and remained so through the 1930s. Like most chronic conditions, this one had a tendency to flare

[39] The Vakhitov soap factory in Kazan presents an interesting case, because its Communist director *had* in 1926 exercised local initiative against a group of engineers and been rebuked for "harassment." As a result, the Kazan party organization was slow to draw implications from the Shakhty trial, despite the fact that the local GPU had unmasked a plot closely modeled on the Shakhty scenario, and had to be rebuked for its failure to harass the engineers. Data from *Deiatel'nost' partiinoi organizatsii Tatarii po osushchestvleniiu leninskikh idei stroitel'stva sotsialisticheskogo obshchestva* (Kazan, 1971), pp. 201–2.

up under stress. A society undergoing rapid industrialization, faced with food-procurement problems, and aware of the possibility of foreign intervention, war, and internal collaboration with the enemy was under a high degree of stress. The result was that the activists of the society turned on those whom they had traditionally suspected, using the familiar method of the institutional purge.

The Komsomol initiated the antibureaucratic movement with its "light cavalry" raids on the government apparat during the rationalization campaign of 1927. These attacks were directed mainly against corrupt and incompetent bureaucrats, but the offense was naturally judged more harshly if the offender were an old *chinovnik* (tsarist official) of doubtful social origins. From 1928, purges of the local state bureaucracy were conducted locally by any organization—Komsomol, party, soviet, or worker-peasant inspectorate—that considered itself particularly vigilant. Soviet historians have described these purges as "spontaneous" and conducted essentially on the basis of social criteria. They report that in the Irkutsk okrug, for example, "800 persons—former officers, policemen, and *chinovniki*— were driven out of government institutions. In their places 130 persons, mainly Communists and workers from industry, came to work."[40]

Local party committees conducted extensive purges of the universities, expelling sons and daughers of kulaks, priests, merchants, tsarist officers, and (less frequently) intellectuals and state employees. These purges come into a special and rather peculiar category, in terms of the source of initiative: they were more or less secretly sponsored by the party Central Committee and more or less openly opposed by the republic education commissariats.[41]

Spontaneous local purging of the secondary schools followed. Government condemnations of social purging were published in the central press, including Pravda, but had little effect. In early 1929, however, the situation became extremely complicated when *Pravda* published an editorial that, in somewhat Aesopian language, ap-

---

[40] K. V. Gusev and V. Z. Drobizhev, eds., *Rabochii klass v upravlenii gosudarstvom (1926–1937 gg.)* (Moscow, 1968), pp. 144–45.

[41] The Central Committee published no instructions on purging, but in July 1928 the Smolensk gubkom obviously received verbal encouragement from the Central Committee rapporteur (V. V. Lominadze) to do so (Smolensk Archive, WKP 33, meeting of plenum of Smolensk gubkom, 16 July 1928). Narkompros RSFSR tried to discourage purging or, when its efforts proved unsuccessful, to restrict it according to guidelines published in *Ezhenedel'nik Komissariata Prosveshcheniia RSFSR*, 1929 no. 15, pp. 18–19. There was open conflict on the question between the Ukrainian Narkompros and Ukrainian Party Central Committee (see *Kul'turnaia revoliutsiia v SSSR 1917– 1965* [Moscow, 1965], p. 325).

peared to sanction school purging.[42] This support heartened local Komsomol groups, which were in the forefront of the school purging movement, and discouraged local officials of the education departments who were trying to follow Narkompros's instructions. In Smolensk, for example, the education department had just succeeded in persuading the local party committee not to purge the schools when the *Pravda* editorial appeared. Soon after, "a group of young people turned up in the education department and announced that we had to start a purge."[43]

There was a functional explanation for the school purges, in that local authorities were under pressure to improve the "proletarian percentage" in the schools, and it was easier to expel or refuse to admit "socially alien" children than to recruit children of workers. But local authorities were subjected to various and conflicting pressures, and the actions of local Communists were often determined by their own assumption that only workers had an absolute right to education, whereas the rights of other groups—such as their right to vote—were conditional and subject to instant withdrawal. The Russian Narkompros took a principled stand against social purging, but in doing so felt that it opposed the will of the working-class and Communist majority. As V. N. Iakovleva, the deputy commissar of education, remarked with unusual frankness,

> If we educational leaders are going to say yes to all these decisions that the masses demand, and are not going to stand up for our point of view energetically, . . . then the masses will not even learn from their mistakes. . . . It is a question of cultural leadership, and our country is uncultured.[44]

The campaign against bureaucracy

The most lively antibureaucratic campaign was conducted by the Komsomol, whose activities resembled those reported of the Red Guards in the Chinese Cultural Revolution of the late 1960s—a movement whose many similarities with its Soviet precursor still remain to be investigated by scholars. The Komsomol was a traditional enemy of bureaucracy, but for most of the NEP period its antibureaucratic enthusiasm was regarded with some suspicion by the party leadership, since it was associated with a tendency to support

---

[42] "Boevye zadachi kul'turnoi revoliutsii," *Pravda*, 5 February 1929, p. 1.
[43] *Narodnoe prosveshchenie*, 1929 no. 3–4, p. 20.
[44] Ibid., p. 51.

party oppositions and to accuse the leadership of "bureaucratic degeneracy." Stalin, it is true, encouraged the Komsomol attacks on the bureaucracy in 1928, probably because the campaign against the "bureaucratic" trade union leadership in particular was serving a useful purpose from his point of view.[45] But it would be a considerable oversimplification to see the Komsomol simply as Stalin's tool when it undertook this campaign. *Komsomol'skaia pravda* was firing in every direction, but its main targets make sense in terms of the Komsomol's priorities, not Stalin's: the newspaper devoted more space in 1928 to denunciations of the (presumably "Stalinist") bureaucrats of Vesenkha for their stand on the employment and training of young people than it did to attacks on the "rightist" bureaucrats of the trade unions; and its favorite rightist target was the politically insignificant N. S. Golovanov, the "bourgeois specialist" who conducted the Bolshoi Theater orchestra and who was later to be awarded a Stalin Prize.[46]

The Komsomols were enthusiasts of cultural revolution, which they understood in the most iconoclastic sense as an overturning of "reactionary" and "bureaucratic" authority. They treated the Cultural Revolution as a replay of the October Revolution and Civil War, in which many of them had been too young to participate. It sometimes seemed that they were engaged not so much in class war as in a class war game: "fortresses" such as the tradionalist Bolshoi Theater and the Academy of Sciences had to be "stormed"; cultural "fronts" had to be defended against bourgeois counterattacks; illiteracy had to be "liquidated" by a "cultural army" with the aid of "cultural ambushes" (*kul'tzasady*), "cultural bombs" (*kul'tbomby*), and "cultural espionage" (*kul'trazvedka*).[47]

It was characteristic of the Komsomol that its chief cultural-revolutionary initiative, the "cultural campaign" or *kul'tpokhod* against illiteracy, should have been conducted in quasi-military style and been directed not only against illiteracy but also against the educational bureaucracy that had so far failed to cope with the problem.[48] Adult education, including instruction in reading and writing, came under the jurisdiction of local education departments. Komsomol re-

---

[45] Stalin, *Sochineniia*, 11:72, 78–79, 127–36.

[46] The story of the Komsomol's farcical attempt to fight the class war on the stage of the Bolshoi Opera is told in Fitzpatrick, "Emergence of Glaviskusstvo," pp. 244–45.

[47] On the war games of the Komsomol Cultural Army, see L. S. Frid, *Ocherki po istorii razvitiia politiko-prosvetitel'noi raboty v RSFSR (1917–1929 gg.)* (Leningrad, 1941), p. 141.

[48] The *kul'tpokhod* movement was announced at the Eighth All-Union Congress of the Komsomol in May 1928. The best source is V. A. Kumanev, *Sotsializm i vsenarodnaia gramotnost'* (Moscow, 1967).

garded these departments, which were part of the local state apparatus and had appointed officials, as quintessentially bureaucratic
organizations. As an alternative organizational form, the Komsomol
Central Committee first proposed to revive the popularly elected
"educational soviet" with which Narkompros had briefly experi-
mented in 1918.[49]

The 1928–1929 *kul'tpokhod* against illiteracy produced its own
organizational form, however. The "cultural general staff" or *kul't-
shtab*, was established on an ad hoc basis, if possible under the patronage of the local party committee, to recruit volunteers to teach
reading and writing and to raise funds for the purpose by eliciting
voluntary contributions from the population and subsidies from local organizations such as trade unions, cooperatives, and industrial
enterprises.

The *kul'tshtaby* had no paid officials and no budget. But in certain
areas, such as Saratov, their achievements in the literacy campaign
of 1928–1929 were considerable, and the party leadership praised
them for their energy, enthusiasm, and low-cost results.[50] The party
leadership clearly had no thought of dismantling the existing education departments and replacing them with improved *kul'tshtaby*. But
this was the objective of the *kul'tpokhod* enthusiasts. As the Saratov
organizer put it, "we began [our] work outside the education system.
. . . And that work was in fact an attack on the education authorities
and an attempt to reorganize the education system on new bases."[51]

The education departments were subordinate to both the local soviets and the central Narkompros. Narkompros might have been expected to react very negatively to demands for the abolition of local
departments, but in fact the reaction was relatively sympathetic,
partly because the departments were not very effectively subordinated to Narkompros, partly because the Narkompros leadership itself was susceptible to arguments against bureaucracy and in favor of
revolutionary popular participation in government.

A popular mass movement for a cultural revolution had developed
outside the educational bureaucracy, Narkompros informed its local
departments in an excited and somewhat incoherent document in
mid-1929.

> Like every revolution, it proceeds spontaneously [*stikhiino*] to a con-
> siderable extent. Many of us did not understand, and some of us to this

[49] *Komsomol'skaia pravda*, 14 December 1928, p. 4.

[50] See Central Committee resolution "O Saratovskom *kul'tpokhode*," cited in
Kumanev, *Sotsializm i vsenarodnaia gramotnost'*, p. 191, from *Pravda*, 13 October
1929; Kaganovich and Bubnov, in *XVI s"ezd*.

[51] *Na putiakh k novoi shkole*, 1930 no. 1, p. 57.

day do not understand, that the very cultural revolution we urged and talked about so much is already developing before our eyes. Many people imagined cultural revolution as a process coming from above. . . . [But] in fact the cultural revolution, like all revolutions, arose and is developing as a mass movement, a movement that is continually changing form.[52]

Shortly afterward *Pravda* called for mass initiative in the rooting out of "bureaucratic methods," and the party leadership approved the creation of educational soviets to advise the education departments.[53] By these moves the leadership essentially was not taking the initiative but responding to what was already going on. Narkompros's response went even further. Early in 1930 it was considering abandoning its departments altogether in favor of soviets with partly elected, partly delegated membership.[54]

With official sponsorship, however, the spontaneous and potentially anarchic elements of antibureaucratic cultural revolution tended to disappear. The *kul'tpokhod* was warmly praised for its achievements in literacy at the Sixteenth Party Congress in the summer of 1930, but meanwhile the Central Committee had found a fine bureaucratic solution to the question of local forms of educational organization: the departments, or "divisions of public education," were to remain, but they were now to be called "organs of public education," to indicate repudiation of their past bureaucratic tendencies.[55]

The same waning of spontaneity can be observed in the movement of social purging. After a year of sporadic and disorganized social purging of institutions, the Sixteenth Party Conference (held in the spring of 1929) decided to authorize a formal purge of the entire government bureaucracy. The central commissariats were purged in the winter of 1929–1930 by commissions of Rabkrin (the Commissariat of Workers' and Peasants' Inspection), backed up by brigades of workers from Moscow factories. Throughout the country about a million and a half Soviet employees went through the purge, and 164,000 were fired.[56] The purge was described as part of the general

---

[52] *Novye formy i metody prosvetitel'noi raboty* (Moscow, 1929), pp. 13–14.

[53] "Boevye zadachi narodnogo obrazovaniia," *Pravda*, 30 August 1929, p. 1; Orgburo resolution of 5 August 1929, "O rukovodiashchikh kadrakh rabotnikov narodnogo obrazovaniia," *Narodnoe prosveshchenie*, 1929 no. 12, p. 12.

[54] *Biulleten' Narodnogo Komissariata po Prosveshcheniiu RSFSR*, 1930 no. 19, pp. 21ff.

[55] Central Committee resolution, "Ob ocherednykh zadachakh kul'turnogo stroitel'stva v sviazi s itogami II Vsesoiuznogo partsoveshchaniia po narodnomu obrazovaniiu," 25 July 1930, in ibid., no. 23, p. 5.

[56] I. Trifonov, *Ocherki istorii klassovoi bor'by v gody NEPa, 1921–1937* (Moscow, 1960), p. 174.

campaign against rightism, exemplifying the militant proletarian class line. But it was in fact a bureaucratic purge of bureaucracy, quite efficiently conducted by Rabkrin in a spirit of organizational rationality.[57] The theme of class enemies was comparatively little emphasized, at least in the center, and voluntary participation and initiative were almost completely absent.

Radicalism in the professions

The nature of the Cultural Revolution within the professions was complex. "Class war" in this area was conducted by and on behalf of groups that claimed to be proletarian but in fact consisted of Communist intellectuals of overwhelmingly white-collar or intelligentsia background. The Communist intellectuals were often extremely aggressive but at the same time unsure of their credentials. They tended to question their own value to society, to suggest that factory workers could do their jobs better, and to waver on the brink of demanding liquidation of the intelligentsia as a class. What one observer called "the disease of self-flagellation in a collective of intellectuals" became epidemic during the Cultural Revolution.[58]

In essence, the Cultural Revolution in the professions meant that Communists were encouraged to go for all-out victory in existing professional conflicts. To some extent, these conflicts were already perceived in class-war terms—particularly in the universities, where the so-called proletarian nucleus of students really was predominantly working class, and the professors often emphasized their own bourgeois or prerevolutionary orientation.

During NEP, from the standpoint of Communists in the professions, there was a confrontation of the new Communist culture and the "establishment" culture of the old intelligentsia. The old intelligentsia, however, saw no such cultural confrontation, but only a political threat to culture per se. (The threat, as the old intelligentsia saw it, came from the regime rather than from the Communist professionals, most of whom were young, former students, and not to be taken seriously.) Thus, paradoxically, both Communist and bourgeois intellectuals regarded themselves as underdogs during NEP, each group considering that the other had special and undeserved advantages.

The most striking instance of an existing and already politicized

---

[57] Day-by-day reports on the purge of Narkompros appeared in *Vecherniaia Moskva* in December 1929 and January 1930.

[58] *Narodnoe prosveshchenie*, 1929 no. 10–11, p. 144.

professional conflict is seen in the field of literature—probably the only profession where it could be claimed that Communists achieved power during the Cultural Revolution almost entirely as a result of their own efforts. The Communist militants' group was RAPP (earlier, VAPP), an association founded by young intellectuals in the early 1920s to promote proletarian literature. By 1924 VAPP was already clamoring for a mandate from the Central Committee to establish the hegemony of "proletarian" Communists over "bourgeois fellow travelers," and the Central Committee's decree of 1925 declaring that the proletarians must earn their hegemony in literature was in effect a refusal of such a mandate.

VAPP's original base was the Komsomol, and in particular the Komsomol journal, *Molodaia gvardiia*. This connection is important, for in many respects VAPP's literary development in the 1920s is best understood in the context not of literary debate but of generational conflict within the Communist movement. Both VAPP and the Komsomol leadership were chronic sufferers from the disease that Bukharin called "revolutionary avant-gardism." They tended to suspect the older generation of succumbing to the temptations of power, losing revolutionary momentum, and falling into bureaucratic lethargy. They were potential supporters of any "revolutionary" opposition (and, by the same token, enemies of any moderate opposition to a revolutionary leadership). Even after thorough purging of Trotskyists and Zinovievists, the VAPP and Komsomol Central Committee positions on social and cultural questions were hard to distinguish from the platform of the 1926–1927 opposition in their criticism of social privileges and inequality, emphasis on the grievances of working-class youth, contempt for "bourgeois" literature and "bourgeois" schools, and calls for Communist vigilance and class war.[59]

Nevertheless, the VAPP leaders commended themselves to the party leadership by repenting their former oppositionism and savagely attacking oppositionist tendencies (real or imagined) in other literary groups. By 1928 RAPP, renamed but still lacking a formal mandate, had assumed leadership in the campaign to unmask the "rightist danger" in the arts and scholarship. Between 1928 and 1932 the RAPP leaders exercised a repressive and cliquish dictatorship over literary publication and criticism. This dictatorship, supposedly

[59] Compare, for example, the opposition line on problems of working-class youth described in *Molodaia gvardiia*, 1926 no. 9, pp. 99–100, with opinions expressed by Aleksandr Milchakov (one of the minority of anti-opposition members of the Komsomol Central Committee in 1926) in ibid., 1926 no. 4, p. 83; and note the similarity of the expressed opinions of the RAPP leader Averbakh with the opposition line on literature, which he is attacking, in *Na literaturnom postu*, 1928 no. 8, p. 10.

in the name of the proletarian party, was in fact not under effective Central Committee control.[60]

The Cultural Revolution was a time of intense competition between the RAPP leaders and the Communist radicals of the Communist Academy and Institute of Red Professors ("schoolboys playing professors" [professorstvuiushchie shkol'niki], as a RAPP leader unkindly described them).[61] Protagonists on both sides had political ambitions within the party and attempted to discredit each other by accusations of political deviation. This tendency was widespread among Communist intellectuals, and was, of course, encouraged by the use of cultural revolution as a weapon against the right opposition in the party. (The accusations of "left deviation," made in 1930 and 1931 against those who had been too extreme in attacking the "rightist danger" or who had former Trotskyist connections, reflected a rather heavy-handed attempt by the party leadership to subdue the militant cultural revolutionaries and normalize the atmosphere in the professions.)

The relation of the party leadership to the cultural revolutionaries has puzzled both Western and Soviet historians. The activists usually claimed to have a party mandate, but it was rare that anything resembling a mandate was actually published or even written down. A more exact metaphor for the relationship was provided by A. K. Voronskii, the embattled editor of Krasnaia nov', when he complained indignantly that the Central Committee press department had "unleashed" the young VAPPists who were his noisiest and most immoderate critics.[62]

The image of "unleashing" can be applied to groups other than the young Communist militants. The Cultural Revolution also unleashed the "visionaries" (as Frederick Starr describes them) and "cranks" (David Joravsky's term) of the NEP period, many of whom are memorably described in René Fülop-Miller's Mind and Face of Bolshevism.[63] Most of these characters were outsiders in their professions,

---

[60] Examples of RAPP's insubordination include its attacks on Gorky; Averbakh's repeated refusal to accept a Central Committee posting outside Moscow during the Cultural Revolution (S. Sheshukov, Neistovye revniteli: Iz istorii literaturnoi bor'by 20–kh godov [Moscow, 1970], pp. 223, 322–25, 355); his support of the Shatskin-Sten criticism of bureaucratic attitudes in the party; and his failure as editor of the RAPP journal Na literaturnom postu to publish, or even for some months to comment upon, the Central Committee resolution of April 1932 dissolving RAPP.

[61] Averbakh, in L. Averbakh et al., S kem i pochemu my boremsia (Moscow and Leningrad, 1930), p. 4.

[62] Krasnaia nov', 1927 no. 6, p. 242.

[63] See S. Frederick Starr, "Visionary Town Planning during the Cultural Revolution," in Cultural Revolution in Russia, 1928–1931, ed. Sheila Fitzpatrick, pp. 207–40

excited by the Revolution but not necessarily Communists, with a radically innovative theory and a small group of committed disciples.

In the 1920s all Communists shared to some degree a vision of a society transformed by collective spirit, rational scientific organization, and technology. In the Civil War period and again during the Cultural Revolution this vision tended to become intensified and at the same time divorced from reality.

Communist visions of Utopia and peasant visions of the coming of Antichrist (frequently reported during the First Five-Year Plan and the collectivization period) arose from the same perception that the familiar world was being destroyed. Until Stalin explicitly denied it in the middle of 1930, many Communist intellectuals thought—as they had thought during the Civil War—that Engels's prophecy of the withering away of the state was already being realized.[64] Evgenii Pashukanis's theory of the withering away of law and V. N. Shulgin's theory of the withering away of the school gained great impetus from the Cultural Revolution simply because legal and educational institutions seemed to have begun a spontaneous process of self-liquidation. It was observation, not authority or theoretical argument, that gave such ideas currency.

Because the Cultural Revolution was, among other things, an attack on accepted ideas, most of the ideas that flourished under its auspices were radical, and some were distinctly eccentric. Every Communist with a private blueprint, scheme or invention felt that the Cultural Revolution spoke directly to him. So did every non-Communist intellectual whose project had previously been ridiculed

---

(Bloomington, Ind., 1978); David Joravsky, "The Construction of the Stalinist Psyche," in ibid., p. 108; René Fülop-Miller, *The Mind and Face of Bolshevism* (London and New York, 1927). Fülop-Miller describes virtually every Communist visionary who could be met in Moscow around 1924. He vastly overestimates their importance at that time, but many of the men and ideas he mentions really did become influential later, during the Cultural Revolution.

[64] Stalin, Political Report of the Central Committee to the Sixteenth Party Congress, in his *Sochineniia*, 12:369–70: "We are for the withering away of the state. And at the same time we stand for the strengthening of the dictatorship of the proletariat, which is the mightiest and most powerful of all state powers that have existed up to the present time. The highest development of state power for the purpose of preparing conditions for the withering away of state power—that is the Marxist formula. Is that 'contradictory'? Yes, it is contradictory. But it is a contradiction of life itself, and it wholly reflects Marx's dialectic." Even after Stalin's statement, ideas about the withering away of the state and of social classes and about the distinctions between mental and physical labor and town and countryside continued to circulate. Two years later Molotov had to explain again that no such radical transformation could be expected during the Second Five-Year Plan period: *XVII konferentsiia Vseoiuznoi Kommunisticheskoi Partii (b): Stenograficheskii otchet* (Moscow, 1932), pp. 145–48.

or ignored. Even government institutions, urged to throw off habits of bureaucratic conservatism, responded to the Cultural Revolution by subsidizing the innovators.

Radical plans for the Socialist City were devised by architects and accepted by planning organizations and building trusts.[65] A government commission considered plans for calendar reform, and some enthusiasts counted 1917 as Year One of the new era. The Institute of Labor, run by a working-class poet, contracted with Vesenkha to train a new labor force on the principles of conditioned reflex. Ia. F. Kagan-Shabshai, a private entrepreneur in the field of engineering training with a grudge against what he called "engineering intellectuals," made very profitable contracts with the industrial trusts to train engineers at "shockwork" tempo. Professor Nikolai Marr's unorthodox Japhetic theory of language was exalted. Professor B. L. Iavorskii's theory of "melodic rhythm," ignored by the reactionary professors of the Moscow Conservatory, was championed by Komsomol music students. The "pedologists," who had been struggling to establish a new discipline on the borders of pedagogy and psychology, finally broke down the barriers to their professional establishment in the schools.[66]

Communist intellectuals had tended to have an uneasy relationship with their own disciplines, as was natural both for the Old Bolshevik generation, whose first profession was revolution, and for the young Communists, who felt themselves to be professional outsiders. They might tend toward intellectual abolitionism in their own discipline, like Pokrovsky in history; they might become reductionists, like the literary "sociologists" or the reflexologists in psychology; they might recommend the transformation of literature into journalism or theater into "biomechanics." The Cultural Revolution brought these transformational and abolitionist tendencies to a climax. Communist intellectuals began to predict the imminent merging of town and countryside, education and industrial production, art and life. These predictions were a kind of running commentary on contemporary processes of institutional disintegration and social flux. They were predictions in which hope and fear were mingled: the cultural revolutionaries' favorite concept of "withering away" (otmiranie), however optimistic in Marxist terms, was still in Russian translation a way of dying.

[65] See Starr, "Visionary Town Planning."
[66] See the comment by A. S. Bubnov in his Stat'i i rechi (Moscow, 1959), pp. 358–59. The relevant legislation is in Biulleten' Narodnogo Komissariata po Prosveshcheniiu RSFSR, 1931 no. 12, pp. 2–3; 1931 no. 14–15, pp. 21–26; 1933 no. 11, p. 7; 1933 no. 13, p. 6.

Proletarian promotion

We come finally to the movement for "proletarian promotion" (*vydvizhenie*), which was the positive corollary of the campaign against the bourgeois intelligentsia and the social purging of the bureaucracy. This theme, very much emphasized in the Soviet literature on "the forming of the Soviet intelligentsia," has been almost ignored in the Western literature. One of the reasons, undoubtedly, is that a great deal of Western research has concentrated on the cultural professions, in which the attack on bourgeois authorities was carried out by Communist intellectuals whose only claim to be proletarian was their party membership.

The Cultural Revolution had, indeed, both pseudoproletarian and genuinely proletarian aspects. In the sphere of pseudoproletarianism, Communist intellectuals sought to make contacts with industrial workers in order to establish their own legitimacy, and Soviet institutions put themselves under the patronage of local factories in order to avoid accusations of bureaucracy. In the rhetoric of the Cultural Revolution, working-class opinion was the touchstone of good and evil, and working-class participation was essential to the success of any undertaking. Thus writers began to read their latest works before factory audiences and worked as consultants on collective histories of industrial enterprises. Universities invited workers to participate in the reelection of professors. Factory brigades were organized to assist the Rabkrin purge of government commissariats. After receiving delegations of Moscow workers (organized by the Komsomol) protesting against its policy of "class neutrality" in education, the collegium of Narkompros began holding its meetings in factories to hear proletarian criticism of its decisions.[67]

The substantive proletarian aspect of the Cultural Revolution was the promotion of workers into responsible white-collar and administrative jobs and their recruitment to higher education (described in detail in Chapter 7). This was a period of enormous expansion of high-status professional and administrative jobs. Between the end of 1928 and the end of 1932, the numbers of engineers employed in the civilian sector of the Soviet economy rose from 18,000 to 74,000, while the number of professionals employed in administration, government, and exchange rose from 63,000 to 119,000.[68] The policy of

[67] A report on the workers' delegation to Narkompros is in *Komsomol'skaia pravda*, 6 February 1929, and of the Narkompros collegium meeting at the Geofizika factory in *Izvestiia*, 26 February 1929.

[68] N. de Witt, *Education and Professional Employment in the USSR* (Washington, D.C., 1961), p. 783.

the Soviet leadership was to promote industrial workers and Communists of working-class origins into these jobs. The process of promotion usually involved training at a technical school or college and was often accompanied by entrance into the party. The radical reorganization of Soviet higher education in the First Five-Year Plan years was determined in large part by the worker promotion policy and the new emphasis on technical training. The scope of worker promotion through education cannot be judged with complete accuracy because forged documents of social origin were plentiful, and children of white-collar and peasant families could become "proletarian" by working for a few years in a factory after leaving school. But, even allowing for exaggeration, the figures are impressive: over 120,000 university students in 1931 were classified as workers or children of workers, as against 40,000 in 1928.[69]

By the beginning of the Second Five-Year Plan (1933), half of the directors of industrial enterprises and their deputies were former workers.[70] But this was only the top stratum of upwardly mobile workers within industry. As the number of jobs at all levels increased, the plants organized their own training schemes and promoted from within. Unskilled workers moved into skilled jobs; skilled workers became foremen, masters, and technicians; technicians became engineers.

The school system was also reorganized in a way that maximized access to secondary and higher education for the working-class. For a few years during the First Five-Year Plan, the "bourgeois" general secondary school virtually ceased to exist, while the working-class factory apprenticeship (FZU) schools expanded their enrollment from 1.8 million in 1928 to 3.3. million in 1931.[71] The FZU schools, established in the early 1920s to train adolescents entering industry, were supposed to be serving the same purpose during the First Five-Year Plan. In practice, however, the majority of apprentices took the opportunities offered to them as working-class students with secondary education, and went on to technical schools and universities.[72]

The worker promotion policy was clearly part of the "revolution from above." But at least a prima facie case can be made for a view of the policy as to some extent a leadership response to working-class grievances of the NEP period. According to Narkompros reports of

[69] Calculated from *Sotsialisticheskoe stroitel'stvo SSSR: Statisticheskii ezhegodnik* (Moscow, 1934), pp. 406, 410.

[70] Gusev and Drobizhev, *Rabochii klass*, p. 157.

[71] *Sotsialisticheskoe stroitel'stvo SSSR* (Moscow, 1934), p. 410.

[72] *Za promyshlennye kadry*, 1933 no. 8–9, p. 76; Vsesoiuznyi komitet po vysshemu tekhnicheskomu obrazovaniiu pri TsIK SSSR, *Biulleten'*, 1933 no. 9–10, p. 7; A. N. Veselov, *Professional'no-tekhnicheskoe obrazovanie v SSSR* (Moscow, 1961), p. 285.

the 1920s (based on substantial though unsystematic sampling of public opinion), workers viewed university education as a right won for the working class by the Revolution. When workers' access to university was limited, as it was during NEP, they considered themselves betrayed. But working-class families were unwilling to keep their children in the upper grades of the bourgeois general secondary school. Young adult workers should have the opportunity to go to university through the *rabfak* and receive a stipend. The preferred school for working-class adolescents was the FZU, which taught a trade, paid students an industrial wage, and was free of bourgeois influence.[73]

The education system that emerged during the First Five-Year Plan—highly irrational from many points of view, including that of industry—corresponded closely to this pattern. But its most striking feature was the emphasis on recruiting adults without a full secondary education to university. This requirement was dictated by the decisions of the leadership to send the Communist Party to school. The typical party member in 1928 was a former worker with primary education.[74] Earlier in the 1920s it had been assumed that the future Communist elite should be trained in Marxist social science. But the First Five-Year Plan decision was to train Communists—especially former workers, and including future administrators—in the engineering schools. The imperative in this situation was an education system that allowed adults with primary education to enter higher technical schools and gave priority in enrollment to working-class Communists.

The end of the Cultural Revolution

Stalin's rehabilitation of the bourgeois engineers (in June 1931) and his condemnation of the fruitless theorizing of Communist intellectuals (in a letter to the editors of *Proletarskaia revoliutsiia* published a few months later) marked the end of official sponsorship of the Cultural Revolution.[75] In some areas, this intervention brought ongoing developments to a jarring halt. In others, the revolutionary impulse had already exhausted itself and combatants were locked in

[73] See, for example, comments by Iakovleva, Pokrovsky, and Krupskaia in *Narodnoe prosveshchenie*, 1929 no. 3–4, pp. 30, 43, 51.

[74] *Sotsial'nyi i natsional'nyi sostav VKP(b): Itogi vsesoiuznoi partiinoi perepisi 1927 goda* (Moscow, 1928), pp. 41, 25.

[75] Speech of 23 June 1931, in I. Stalin, *Sochineniia*, 13:69–73; "On some questions of the history of Bolshevism," *Proletarskaia revoliutsiia*, 1931 no. 6; also in Stalin, *Sochineniia*, 13:84–102.

bitter scholastic disputes and mutual denunciation. With or without intervention, there was a natural time limit on the Cultural Revolution as an enthusiastic dismantling of the institutions and conventions of NEP. The pressures for a restoration of order and rebuilding of institutions were, even in the comparatively short run, irresistible.

The finite limits on the Cultural Revolution are particularly evident in the sphere of worker promotion—not the promotion of working-class Communists, which continued at a high level for some years, but the promotion of workers from the factory bench.[76] By 1931, when the factories took the first steps to tighten labor discipline and pull workers back from outside activities, schools and universities were already finding it difficult to meet their proletarian quotas. Recruitment at the factory encountered increasing resistance from the enterprises, which were experiencing an acute shortage of skilled labor. The young workers willing and able to go on to higher education had already volunteered. The traditional working class (whose members were now called kadrovye or potomstvennye rabochie [cadre or hereditary workers]) was depleted by promotion and assignment to the new construction sites, and was swamped by the vast influx of peasants into the industrial labor force.

There were not only practical but also conceptual problems in fighting cultural class war on behalf of a proletariat whose members were to a large extent peasants recently uprooted by collectivization. The imagery of the early 1930s was not of battle but of passing on the torch. The Komsomol no longer spoke of kul'tpokhod but of kul'testafeta, or cultural relay race. In the factories and new construction sites, experienced workers became exemplars and teachers (shefy) to the new arrivals, verbally transmitting the necessary skills and traditions of the industrial working class.

Social discrimination was gradually dropped in educational admissions. The education system was reorganized along lines that were conservative and traditionalist even in comparison with NEP, let alone the ultraradicalism of the Cultural Revolution. In literature, predictably, the militant proletarians proved difficult to displace, but in 1932 RAPP was dissolved, and by 1934 a new Union of Soviet Writers incorporating all Communist and "bourgeois" groups had been created. In scholarship, the Communist Academy—center of

[76] Central Committee resolution of 25 March 1931, "O polnom prekrashchenii mobilizatsii rabochikh ot stanka na nuzhdy tekushchikh kampanii mestnymi partiinymi, sovetskimi, and drugimi organizatsiiami," Partiinoe stroitel'stvo, 1931 no. 7, p. 63. The resolution also forbade reduction of the workday for factory workers engaged in part-time study or any public or social activities.

cultural-revolutionary activity—gradually conceded authority to the old Academy of Sciences and the reconstituted universities. Disgraced bourgeois scholars were rehabilitated. Arrested bourgeois engineers were released, usually to occupy positions comparable with those they had involuntarily left.

The fate of three groups after the Cultural Revolution is of particular interest to us: the Communist intellectuals who had carried out the Cultural Revolution, the nonparty intellectuals who had suffered from it, and the promoted workers and worker-Communists who formed the core of the new "Soviet intelligentsia."

The Communist intellectuals, suffering the proverbial fate of those who go for a ride on a tiger, turned out to be the ultimate victims of the Cultural Revolution. The general assumption during the Cultural Revolution had been that the militant radicals had the endorsement of the Stalinist leadership: when, for example, Andrei Bubnov replaced the conciliatory Lunacharsky as head of Narkompros in 1929, he found it natural to turn to V. N. Shulgin, theorist of the withering away of the school, not because he knew anything about his ideas but because of the Communist "fighting spirit" he sensed in him.[77] Yet it has already been pointed out that Stalin's endorsement of militance in the arts, if he endorsed it at all, was really very cautious. On a few occasions Stalin encouraged belligerent activity against rightists and bourgeois intellectuals, but he also took occasional action to protect bourgeois victims such as the writer Mikhail Bulgakov, and in a private letter expressed the opinion (which at the time nobody else could possibly have expressed) that the whole campaign against "rightism" in art was based on an absurd premise.[78]

In many fields the Communist factional fighting during the Cultural Revolution discredited and demoralized the participants, distracted them from their real work, and ended some promising profes-

[77] A. S. Bubnov, speech of 23 April 1931, in *Kommunisticheskoe prosveshchenie*, 1931 no. 12, p. 18.

[78] He supported militance in his speech to the conference of Marxist rural scholars, 27 December 1929, for example (in Stalin, *Sochineniia*, 12:141ff.), and in his verbal encouragement to the young Communist Academy radicals Pavel Iudin and Mark Mitin to attack the former Menshevik philosopher A. M. Deborin (see David Joravsky, *Soviet Marxism and Natural Science, 1917–1932* [London, 1961], p. 262). Yet Stalin wrote in a letter to the proletarian dramatist Bill-Belotserkovskii on 2 February 1929: "I consider the very posing of the question of 'rightists' and 'leftists' in our literature . . . incorrect. The concept of 'right' and 'left' in our country is a party concept or, more exactly, an inner-party concept. 'Rightists' and 'leftists' are people deviating to one side or the other of the pure party line. Therefore it would be strange to apply these concepts to such a nonparty and incomparably wider field as literature" (*Sochineniia*, 11:326).

sional developments of the NEP period. The Communist intelligentsia was far too deeply involved in ideological and factional politics to respond to the leadership's demands for practically useful work. In fact, it was "politicized" to the point of being virtually useless to the Soviet regime, except in the fields of journalism and agitprop.

In the aftermath of the Cultural Revolution, those of the Communist intellectuals who were not permanently excommunicated as left or right deviationists were left to make the best of professional careers among presumably hostile ex-bourgeois colleagues and *vydvizhentsy* of completely different life experience and outlook. A few former cultural revolutionaries—the philosophers Pavel Iudin and Mark Mitin of the Communist Academy, the writer Aleksandr Fadeev of RAPP—held prominent positions through the Stalin period, but many more suffered premature eclipse in the purges of the late 1930s. In general, the young Communists trained for leadership during NEP in such institutions as the Sverdlov Communist University and the Institute of Red Professors turned into something of a lost generation. What was required of a future Communist leader in the Stalin period was not Marxist social science and polemical skill but technical training and experience in industrial administration.

The old intelligentsia came out of the Cultural Revolution in better shape than its members had probably expected or than Western historians have generally recognized. A very large number of bourgeois engineers served time in prison or at work under GPU supervision; some distinguished historians died in exile; and many more intellectuals suffered psychologically as a result of the cultural revolutionaries' attacks. As a whole, however, the old intelligentsia had not been subject to mass arrest, like priests, or mass deportation, like peasants. Its members (except for the relatively small number of engineers working as convict specialists) were not sent out of the capitals to the new construction sites or to the countryside to teach in rural schools, as apparently happened in the Chinese Cultural Revolution. No form of labor conscription was ever proposed, even for such socially useful specialists as doctors, teachers, and agronomists. Despite the social purging of scholarly institutions, the shortage of specialists in all fields was so acute that only in exceptional circumstances was a purged specialist left without professional employment.

The result was that, when the Cultural Revolution ended and the regime was ready to offer compensation, the old intelligentsia was in a position to receive it. The immediate improvement—not only in comparison with the Cultural Revolution but also in comparison with NEP—was that the bourgeois nonparty intellectuals were no longer subject to attack within their professions by organized Communist groups or to harassment on grounds of social origin. In many fields, the old professional establishment won back its previous authority. Arrested and exiled specialists returned to responsible jobs (sometimes even the same jobs they had held at the time they were arrested). Scientific leadership returned to the Academy of Sciences. Such traditional artistic institutions as the Bolshoi Theater recovered preeminence.

But the class war of the Cultural Revolution was waged on behalf of the proletariat, and it was surely the proletarian *vydvizhentsy* (and to a lesser extent *vydvizhentsy* from the peasantry) who emerged as its chief beneficiaries. During the Cultural Revolution, hundreds of thousands of workers from the factory and Communists of working-class origin were promoted into technical jobs, management, and administration, or recruited to higher education.[79] This was a unique cohort in Soviet history—a group whose upward mobility was the result of a conscious policy of the party leaders in the period of the Cultural Revolution to create a new "workers' and peasants'" elite, and, moreover, one that was to be the primary beneficiary of a second social upheaval, the Great Purges of 1937.

It is appropriate to speculate on the influence the experience of the Cultural Revolution may have had on this generation's attitudes toward culture and social control. The *vydvizhentsy* were a very different group from the Communist intelligentsia formed during NEP, which provided the militant activists of the Cultural Revolution. Those sent to university during the First Five-Year Plan were in a position to observe the cultural revolutionaries' activities at firsthand, and it seems likely that many of their observations were unfavorable. The *vydvizhentsy*, by all accounts, were a highly motivated and practical-minded group, interested in acquiring useful knowledge as efficiently as possible. Their studies were undoubtedly made more difficult by the methodological experimentation and organizational chaos produced in the universities by the Cultural Revolution.

The militants of the Cultural Revolution were not only experimenters on a grand scale but also ideological hairsplitters and obsessive faction fighters. It would not be surprising if many *vydvizhentsy* came to the conclusion—reinforced by the post-1931 decisions of the party leadership—that intellectuals of the cultural-revolutionary

[79] According to one source, between January 1930 and October 1933, 666,000 worker Communists were promoted to administrative or managerial positions or sent to higher education: I. F. Petrov, ed., *Kommunisticheskaia partiia—um, chest' i sovest' nashei epokhi* (Moscow, 1969), pp. 221–22. I am indebted to Jerry Hough for this reference.

type were a dangerous breed: factious, vicious, anarchic, and totally lacking in common sense. Certainly the party leadership of the 1930s and 1940s, of which the *vydvizhentsy* cohort formed an increasingly important part, seemed inclined to such an opinion and determined to avoid any repetition of the chaotic "unleashing" of the Cultural Revolution.

(1974)

CHAPTER 7

Stalin and the Making of a New Elite

"Cadres decide everything," Stalin proclaimed in 1935.[1] The slogan is familiar, as is the image of Stalin as a politician skilled in the selection and deployment of personnel. But who *were* his cadres? The literature on the prewar Stalin period tells us little even about his closest political associates, let alone those one step down the political hierarchy—Central Committee members, people's commissars and their deputies, obkom secretaries—and in key industrial posts. Only the Old Bolsheviks and the military leaders seem to emerge as individuals. The rest are relegated to that servile and faceless bureaucracy about which Trotsky wrote from afar.[2] Their very anonymity (which might also be described as our—and Trotsky's—ignorance) has become part of a sociological generalization.

The same generalization has often governed discussion of Stalin's criteria in the selection of cadres. Virtually the only criteria suggested in the literature are unconditional loyalty to Stalin and lack of individual distinction.[3] Because these qualities are attributed to cadres both before the Great Purges (except the Old Bolsheviks and the military) and after them, the unhappy fate of the first group is difficult to explain. Paranoia and permanent purge are two possi-

---

[1] I. V. Stalin, "Rech' na vypuske akademikov Krasnoi Armii" (4 May 1935), in his *Sochineniia*, ed. Robert H. McNeal, 3 vols. (Stanford, 1967), 1:61.

[2] Leon Trotsky, *The Revolution Betrayed* (London, 1937), chap. 5.

[3] See, for example, Tucker's discussion of the new "serving class" in Robert C. Tucker, ed., *Stalinism* (New York, 1977), pp. 99–100.

bilities, but historians are likely to be somewhat dissatisfied with both explanations.[4] The question has been frequently discussed, and the focus of attention has always been on the victims of the purge rather than on its beneficiaries. The assumption has been that Stalin had an overpowering desire to get rid of the old cadres but no special interest in the new ones.

I am convinced that Stalin did have a special interest in the new cadres. He believed them to have specific qualifications that were essential for Soviet leadership, and he also believed that the old cadres' lack of such qualifications exposed the regime to manipulation by its present and potential enemies. During the Cultural Revolution, Stalin initiated a program through which over 100,000 workers and Communists from the factories and apparats were mobilized and sent to higher technical schools. As a result of the Great Purges, this group received dramatic promotions into positions of industrial, government, and party leadership. It remained a core group in the Soviet political leadership up to the end of the Brezhnev period.

Reds and experts

My starting point, like Stalin's, is the dichotomy between "Red" and "expert" which existed in the Soviet Union on the eve of the industrialization drive under the First Five-Year Plan. In 1917 the Bolsheviks had little expertise of their own to drawn on, and ten years later the situation remained basically unchanged. In 1927 less than 1 percent (8,396) of Communists had completed higher education, and even this small group was of limited practical use in providing technical expertise.[5] Almost half of its members were working in the spheres of health, education, and welfare (mainly as administrators), and only 7 to 8 percent had received their degrees from technical schools.[6] According to Molotov, a grand total of 138 Communist engineers worked in Soviet industrial enterprises in 1928.[7] Thus the overwhelming majority of experts—from plant engineers and chief accountants to consultants and senior officials in government

[4] On the concept of permanent purge, see Zbigniew K. Brzezinski, *The Permanent Purge: Politics in Soviet Totalitarianism* (Cambridge, Mass., 1956).

[5] *Sotsial'nyi i natsional'nyi sostav VKP(b): Itogi vsesoiuznoi partiinoi perepisi 1927 g.* (Moscow, 1928), p. 41.

[6] *Partiinaia zhizn'*, 1977 no. 21, p. 30. Data for 32 gubernias of the RSFSR can be found in *Kommunisty v sostave apparata gosuchrezhdenii i obshchestvennykh organizatsii: Itogi vsesoiuznoi partiinoi perepisi 1927 g.* (Moscow, 1929), p. 15.

[7] V. Molotov, "Podgotovka novykh spetsialistov," *Krasnoe studenchestvo*, 1928–1929 no. 1 (1 October 1928), p. 21.

commissariats—were non-Communists and, in Soviet terminology, "bourgeois." Most were subordinate to Communist directors, often former workers with little education and no knowledge of the field they had been sent to administer.

This arrangement sometimes produced friction, but it was equally likely to lead to a comfortable working relationship in which the experts made the decisions and the Communists signed the papers and attended the meetings. Vesenkha, the state's industrial ministry, had a non-Communist expert as a member of its presidium, and its key agency in charge of the metallurgical industry was effectively run by another expert who had been director and shareholder in two of the biggest plants before the Revolution.[8] Experts of this status attended meetings of the highest government bodies—Sovnarkom and STO, the Council of Labor and Defense—and occasionally were even invited to Politburo meetings. But they were employed only in the government sector, not in that of the party. The Central Committee Secretariat, small in the 1920s, had no nonparty experts and did not normally intervene in policy decisions requiring technical expertise.

There was little reason in 1927 to expect a basic change in the dichotomy between Reds and experts. The low educational level of Communist Party members reflected the working-class and peasant origins of the majority of party members (in 1927, 56 percent of Communists had been workers by occupation when they entered the party).[9] But the leadership showed no intention of changing the recruitment pattern established with the "Lenin levy" of workers in 1924, and indeed continued to place more and more emphasis on the working-class nature of the party. The cadres—that is, Communists in responsible administrative positions—did not differ substantially in class origin and education from the party membership as a whole. About 20,000 Communists left the factory bench each year for white-collar and administrative positions, further education, and the army, and in 1927, 44 percent of cadres were former workers. The cadres as a whole averaged four to five years of schooling, or not much more than primary education.[10]

Under prevailing recruitment rules, bourgeois experts had little chance of joining the Communist Party even if they wanted to. In

---

[8] The non-Communist expert on the presidium was A. N. Dolgov; the dominant expert in the metallurgical-industry agency was S. A. Khrennikov.

[9] *Sotsial'nyi i natsional'nyi sostav VKP(b)*, p. 41.

[10] I. N. Iudin, *Sotsial'naia baza rosta KPSS* (Moscow, 1973), p. 129; *Kommunisty v sostave apparata*, pp. 25, 12. The figure of 44% relates to Communists "on leading work" in 32 gubernias of the RSFSR.

institutes of higher education—the training ground for future experts—working-class and Communist students remained a minority, despite admissions discrimination in their favor.[11] Only 10,000 Communists graduated from higher educational institutes during the first decade of Soviet power, and almost all of them came from white-collar and professional families, a fact that made them somewhat suspect in the eyes of the lower-class majority of party members.[12] The indications were that the next generation of experts would be as bourgeois as the present one, although the impending industrialization drive was likely to increase reliance on their expertise.

The party leadership as a whole seemed unperturbed by the situation (in fact, Lenin had said that it was unavoidable for the foreseeable future), and the government commissariats had clearly accepted it completely and could imagine no other way of functioning. During NEP, the institution that had shown the most uneasiness over the Red/expert dichotomy was the Central Committee Secretariat, and this concern must have increased when its statistical department (one of the few functioning centers of Communist expertise) analyzed the results of the 1927 Party Census and saw how little expertise and education party members possessed. Of the party leaders, Stalin and Molotov were the most closely associated with the Secretariat and questions of cadres.

A radical change of policy toward the bourgeois experts was signaled by the state prosecutor's announcement early in 1928 that a large group of mining engineers from the Shakhty region of the Donbass was to be tried in Moscow for sabotage and conspiracy with foreign powers.[13] The announcement was quickly followed by public discussion of the broader implications of the trial, indicating that the bourgeois intelligentsia as a group was now under suspicion. But senior government and industrial spokesmen were simultaneously trying to reassure the experts (and perhaps also themselves). Reading the news during a business trip in Europe, two experts in high positions in the agency of Vesenkha in charge of coal mining in the Donbass concluded that the storm would not touch them and returned to Moscow, whereupon they were arrested as members of a "Moscow Center" of the conspiracy. At the trial, held in Moscow in May and

[11] In 1927–1928, 26.5% of students in Soviet higher schools (excluding party and military schools) were classified as working class, while 17.1% were full or candidate members of the Communist Party (see *Bol'shaia sovetskaia entsiklopediia* [Moscow, 1929], 16:34).

[12] The total figure for graduations is from Iudin, *Sotsial'naia baza rosta KPSS*, p. 181. Of the 8,396 Communists with higher education in January 1927, 91% had entered the party as white-collar workers (see *Sotsial'nyi i natsional'nyi sostav*, p. 41).

[13] *Pravda*, 10 March 1928, p. 1.

June 1928, testimony on Vesenkha and its coal administration was heard in closed session.[14] The new policy, it appeared, threatened not only bourgeois experts but also the Communist administrators who had worked with them.

Stalin is reported to have taken the initiative in staging the Shakhty trial, possibly without consultation with other members of the leadership.[15] He certainly took the initiative in explaining the political significance of the Shakhty affair, and unlike other leadership spokesmen, he did not limit his discussion to the bourgeois experts. In Stalin's account, the incompetence of Communist administrators was scarcely less disturbing than the experts' treachery. The threat from the experts was grave, Stalin said. By virtue of their class position, they were potential pawns in the unremitting struggle of the capitalist powers to overthrow the Soviet regime. Hitherto the capitalists had put their faith in military intervention. With the inauguration of the First Five-Year Plan, however, their efforts would be concentrated on sabotaging the Soviet industrialization drive. But, according to Stalin, the experts had been able to commit acts of sabotage because they, not the Communist administrators, were effectively in charge. Lacking education and technical expertise, the Communists had allowed themselves to be dominated and hoodwinked by their nominal subordinates. Thus there was only one solution: Communists must acquire technical expertise, and the old dichotomy between Red and expert must be abolished.[16]

Obviously it was no simple matter for Communist cadres—men perhaps in their late thirties, ill educated, and burdened with administrative responsibilities—to acquire technical expertise. Stalin expressed his confidence that they could do so:

People say that it is impossible for Communists, especially for working-class Communist industrial administrators [*khoziaistvenniki*], to master chemical formulaes and technical knowledge in general. That is not true, comrades. There are no fortresses in the world that the toilers, the Bolsheviks, cannot storm.[17]

---

[14] *Ekonomicheskaia kontrrevoliutsiia v Donbasse (Itogi Shakhtinskogo dela)* (Moscow, 1928), p. 209. The officials were S. P. Bratanovskii and N. I. Skorutto. Bratanovskii's confession is quoted in ibid., pp. 268– 69.

[15] See the account in A. Avtorkhanov, *Stalin and the Soviet Communist Party* (London, 1959), p. 29.

[16] I. V. Stalin, "O rabotakh aprel'skogo ob"edinennogo plenuma TsK i TsKK" (April 13, 1928), in his *Sochineniia*, 13 vols. (Moscow, 1948–1952), 11:53–54, 57–59.

[17] Ibid., p. 58.

But his exhortations were often combined with reproaches for past
failings or implicit threats of demotion for those who refused to educate themselves.

> Bolsheviks must master technology. It is time for Bolsheviks them-
> selves to become specialists. In the reconstruction period, technology
> decides everything. And the industrial administrator who does not
> want to study technology, who does not want to master technology, is
> a joke and not an administrator.[18]

To the younger generation of Communists, Komsomols, and workers
Stalin presented the mastery of technology as a challenge. In 1928 he
told the Eighth Komsomol Congress:

> In order to build, you need knowledge, you need to master science.
> And to get that knowledge, you need to study. To study patiently and
> stubbornly. To learn from everybody—from enemies and friends, espe-
> cially from enemies. To learn with clenched teeth, not fearing that our
> enemies will laugh at us, at our ignorance and backwardness.

But for those who met the challenge, Stalin seemed to promise great
rewards and future leadership. Educated youth could become "a
builder of the new life, . . . a real replacement of the old guard."[19]

Stalin's statements certainly contain a hint of the possibility of
premature retirement for the old cadres, but we should be careful not
to exaggerate its significance. Mastery of technology was only one of
the characteristics that Stalin demanded of cadres. An even more
important characteristic, judging both by Stalin's statements and by
the actual policies of the First Five-Year Plan period, was working-
class background. And the old cadres in key administrative spheres
could hardly be criticized on this criterion. Almost two-thirds of the
cadres in industry and just under half of those working in the party
apparat in 1927 were former workers. Moreover, the Communist in
the top position was more likely to be a former worker than the Communists immediately subordinate to him.[20]

In emphasizing the criterion of working-class background, Stalin
was following a Bolshevik practice established during the first years
of Soviet power. The practice had never been given a real theoretical
justification, probably because it simply seemed obvious that the
proletarian dictatorship should draw cadres from the proletariat. But

---

[18] I. V. Stalin, "O zadachakh khoziaistvennikov" (4 February 1931), in ibid., 13:41.
[19] I. V. Stalin, "Rech' na VIII s"ezde VLKSM (16 May 1928)," in ibid., 11:76–77.
[20] *Kommunisty v sostave apparata*, pp. 25, 12 (where educational levels are shown).

the Bolsheviks also had some inhibitions about discussing cadres in terms of general principle, because their principles did not really admit the possibility of a permanent and professional Soviet administrative elite. The cadres, of course, already constituted such an elite in the 1920s, but the Bolsheviks had not found an acceptable way of admitting it.

Stalin made two changes in the established practice of recruiting cadres from the working class. In the first place, he dramatized that practice by calling on the proletariat to repel the counterrevolutionary threat from the bourgeois specialists. In the second place, he greatly increased the rate of recruitment. But perhaps the most interesting change was in the realm of theory. By using the word "intelligentsia" for the administrative and specialist elite, Stalin was able to articulate a principle that had long guided Bolshevik practice— that the Soviet regime, like any other, needed its own elite, and that this elite should be recruited primarily from the working class:

> Not a single ruling class has managed without its own intelligentsia. . . . We do not need just any kind of commanding and engineering-technical cadres. We need commanding and engineering-technical cadres capable of understanding the policies of the working class of our country, capable of mastering those policies and prepared to carry them out conscientiously. What does that mean? It means that our country has entered the phase of development when the working class must create its own productive-technical intelligentsia, capable of standing up for its own interests in production as the interests of the working class.[21]

Training proletarian experts

The outlines of a new cadres policy began to emerge at the Central Committee plenums of April and July 1928, though in rather confused form that reflected disagreements within the leadership. First, the bourgeois specialists as a group were under suspicion and would be subject to harassment. Second, Communist administrators working with bourgeois specialists had shown insufficient vigilance and competence. They needed technical training, which would be supplied either by part-time courses or by study in the new industrial academies created for the specific purpose of retraining cadres who

---

[21] I. V. Stalin, "Novaia obstanovka—novye zadachi khoziaistvennogo stroitel'stva" (23 June 1931), in his *Sochineniia* (Moscow), 13:66– 67.

already held responsible jobs.[22] Third, the state bureaucracies had to be purged of unreliable "bourgeois elements" and strengthened by the promotion of workers from the bench.[23] Fourth, it was imperative to begin training a new generation of cadres who would be both Red and expert. The normal higher education system, especially the engineering schools, would provide the training. This meant curriculum changes and a new admissions policy that would discriminate strongly in favor of working-class and Communist applicants, even if their educational preparation was poor.[24]

Despite the fact that Stalin was the chief advocate of the new policy, it provoked sharp controversy within the leadership. This in fact may have been Stalin's intention, since it would certainly have been possible to avoid controversy over the new training programs had they not been explicitly linked with the Shakhty trial. But Stalin was already in conflict with the emerging right opposition in the Politburo over the handling of the grain-procurement crisis, and more trouble was brewing in regard to the targets of the First Five-Year Plan's industrialization drive. His new cadres policy—essentially anti-intelligentsia and pro-worker—was likely to be popular with the Communist rank and file. Politically, he could only profit from putting his opponents in the position of being pro-expert—that is, soft on the bourgeoisie.

The right attempted to circumvent this danger by basing its argument on Leninist principles. At the April 1928 plenum of the Central Committee and Central Control Commission, Rykov quoted Lenin's statements that the party had no alternative to cooperation with bourgeois experts, since it could not replace them in the foreseeable future, and therefore should avoid harassing them or showing "Communist conceit." He also produced documentation to demonstrate that the experts were still irreplaceable and that the industrialization drive would fail without their support, and suggested that "the class issue" (increased recruitment of workers and Communists) be kept

[22] On the industrial academies, see P. M. Mikhailov, "Iz istorii deiatel'nosti Kommunisticheskoi partii po podgotovke rukovodiashchikh kadrov promyshlennosti v period sotsialisticheskoi rekonstruktsii narodnogo khoziaistva," *Voprosy istorii KPSS*, 1976 no. 10, pp. 79–86.

[23] See Central Committee resolution of November 1928, "O verbovke rabochikh i regulirovanii rosta partii," in *KPSS v rezoliutsiiakh i resheniiakh s"ezdov, konferentsii i plenumov Tsk* (Moscow, 1970): 4:143. A weaker statement is contained in the Central Committee and Central Control Commission resolution of April 1928, "Shakhtinskoe delo i prakticheskie zadachi v dele bor'by s nedostatkami khoziaistvennogo stroitel'stva," in *ibid.*, p. 91.

[24] Central Committee resolution of July 1928, "Ob uluchshenii podgotovki novykh spetsialistov," in *ibid.*, pp. 111–18. The April plenum's resolution contained a weaker and somewhat contradictory recommendation (see "Shakhtinskoe delo," pp. 88–90).

out of the discussion of the training of specialists.[25] The last two arguments brought Rykov onto delicate ground as far as the public debate was concerned, though many leaders not linked with the right may have silently agreed with him.[26] Any Communist who had run a large bureaucracy was likely to feel that a good expert was worth his weight in gold, that young Communist graduates were generally inexperienced, cocky, and quarrelsome, and that workers promoted from the bench to white-collar jobs were often simply a nuisance. Stalin's new policy was obviously bound to cause trouble for industry (which stood to lose engineers to the GPU, and skilled workers to the engineering schools and bureaucracies), and it could destroy the educational system. Besides, it would cost money when the budget was already strained to capacity by the industrialization drive.

But the political atmosphere of 1928 made it extremely difficult to oppose a pro-worker and anti-expert policy on practical grounds, let alone on the "bureaucratic" grounds of administrative and financial rationality. Nikolai Uglanov, a future rightist, discovered this as early as January 1928, when his remarks to the Moscow party committee on orderly administrative procedures were interrupted by a shout from the floor: "What about *vydvizhenchestvo* [worker promotion into the apparat]?" Having briefly characterized worker promotion as a way of swelling the bureaucracy and probably "holding back the tempo of our construction effort by 30 percent," Uglanov recommended the promotion of persons with real qualifications, such as college graduates. This suggestion provoked another interjection: "But the graduates we ought to take are those from the factory, from the worker's bench!"[27]

By July, when the crucial decision on training of Red experts was made at the Central Committee plenum, the right had evidently come to the conclusion that it was useless to fight on the central issue of large-scale recruitment of workers and Communists into higher education. But it was not an outright victory for Stalin and Molotov. The right fought on a relatively peripheral issue (whether the educational or industrial authorities should control the higher

[25] Reported by Ordzhonikidze in *XVI s"ezd Vsesoiuznoi Kommunisticheskoi partii: Stenograficheskii otchet*, pt. 1 (Moscow, 1931), p. 568; quoted in *Voprosy istorii KPSS*, 1966 no. 2, p. 33.

[26] The entire controversy was kept out of the press, but it was known to all attentive Communists because of the practice (apparently discontinued in the early 1930s) of circulating verbatim reports of Central Committee meetings to local party organizations.

[27] *Vtoroi plenum MK VKP(b), 31 ianvaria–2 fevralia 1928: Doklady i rezoliutsii* (Moscow, 1928), p. 43.

technical schools) and forced a compromise resolution.[28] The implication is that even Stalin's supporters may have been lukewarm about the cadres policy, and the impression is reinforced by the absence of enthusiastic advocacy of any part of the policy by any leader other than Stalin, Molotov, and Kaganovich.[29]

The most important plank of the new policy—large-scale recruitment of adult workers and Communists into the engineering schools to "master technology"—was also, on the face of it, the most difficult. Narkompros was uncooperative, even after Vyshinsky, the presiding judge in the Shakhty trial, was sent to strengthen its resolve.[30] It took more than a year to prod the trade union leadership into real acceptance of the unions' new role in selecting workers for higher education and putting them through preparatory courses.[31] The unions argued with industry about who should pay the worker-students while they were in college, and the industrial and educational authorities argued about who should run the engineering schools. In the colleges themselves the professors were resentful, the new students had trouble adjusting to the classroom again, and work was repeatedly disrupted by administrative reorganizations and changes in curriculum. Local party organizations often misdirected their energies into purging "bourgeois" students, who then simply transferred to another college.

[28] For a detailed discussion of this episode, see Sheila Fitzpatrick, *Education and Social Mobility in the Soviet Union, 1921–1934* (London and New York, 1979), pp. 127–29.

[29] The Central Committee's resolution "Ob uluchshenii podgotovki novykh spetsialistov" (July 1928) was based on a report by Molotov (see M. Savelev and A. Poskrebyshev, *Direktivy VKP(b) po khoziaistvennym voprosam* [Moscow and Leningrad, 1931], p. 466). Its later resolution, "O kadrakh narodnogo khoziaistva" (November 1929), calling for further expansion of higher and technical education and increased educational recruitment of Communists and workers, was based on a report by Kaganovich (see text of resolution in *KPSS v rezoliutsiiakh*, 4:334–45; identification of the rapporteur is found in *Ezhenedel'nik Narodnogo komissariata prosveshcheniiia RSFSR* no. 50 [1929], p. 3). For other statements by Molotov and Kaganovich, see nn. 39 and 40 below.

[30] Vyshinsky was appointed head of Narkompros's administration of technical education in the summer or early fall of 1928 (see *Pravda*, 25 September 1928, p. 6).

[31] In early 1929 the Central Council of Trade Unions (VTsSPS) responded quite skeptically to Vyshinsky's report on recruitment of workers into higher education: speakers said the mobilization of the first trade union "Thousand" had been a chaotic last-minute effort, and some feared massive dropouts of worker-students. By December 1930 the unionists' attitude had changed completely. They now referred to the *vydvizhentsy* as the cream of the working class, abused Vesenkha for delaying college admission of some thousands of graduates of trade union preparatory courses and other faults of educational administration, and in general expressed an officiously proprietorial attitude toward the higher technical schools. [See TsGAOR, f. 5451, op. 13, d. 14, ll. 188–92, and f. 5451, op. 13, d. 15, ll. 125–34 (stenographic reports of meetings of VTsSPS, 11 January 1929 and 8 December 1930).

Despite these difficulties, the party mobilized almost 10,000 Communists to engineering and other colleges in the years 1928–1931, and an additional 8,000 to higher military schools in 1931–1932.[32] The trade unions mobilized another 5,000 to 6,000 Communist workers and almost 4,000 workers who were not party members.[33] These students—the "Thousanders"—were the most highly publicized of the Cultural Revolution *vydvizhentsy,* but the success of Stalin's policy did not depend on them alone. The real question was whether Communists and workers who were *not* selected as Thousanders would decide to answer the call to higher education. Education promised advancement in the future, no doubt, but in the short term it required one to enter a strange and in some respects hostile environment, survive on a student stipend, live in an overcrowded dormitory away from one's family, and struggle with unfamiliar bookwork. Sheer administrative pressure could not make the policy succeed, if only because of the possibility that the new students would drop out en masse. Communists and working-class adults had to see college as their salvation; every ambitious young person in the country had to wonder if he or she could afford to be left out.

The winter of 1929–1930 seems to have been the turning point, the beginning of a mass influx into technical education. Part of the reason was that new colleges opened and more places became available. But for young adult workers—the majority of the new students—other factors were probably equally important: college may suddenly have seemed a more desirable option when the alternative might be mobilization to the countryside for collectivization or pressure to transfer to a new industrial plant in distant Magnitogorsk. In any case, whatever the reasons for their choices, young Communists and working-class adults streamed into higher and secondary technical schools during the years 1930–1932. By the beginning of 1933, 233,000 Communists—the equivalent of almost a quarter of the party's total membership at the end of 1927—were full-time students in some type of educational institution, and 166,000 of them were in institutes of higher education (exclusive of higher party and military schools and industrial academies). Almost two-thirds of this group were studying engineering.[34]

The number of former workers among college students at the end

[32] Data from S. Fediukin, *Sovetskaia vlast' i burzhuaznye spetsialisty* (Moscow, 1965), p. 243; and B. S. Telpukhovskii in *Voprosy istorii KPSS,* 1976 no. 8, p. 93.

[33] TsGAOR, f. 5451, op. 15, d. 785, l. 65 (VTsSPS Sector of Industrial Cadres).

[34] Data from Iudin, *Sotsial'naia baza rosta KPSS,* p. 180; *Sotsialisticheskoe stroitel'stvo SSSR: Statisticheskii ezhegodnik* (Moscow, 1934), p. 410; and Nicholas de Witt, *Education and Professional Employment in the USSR* (Washington, D.C., 1961), pp. 638–39.

of the first Five-Year Plan cannot be ascertained exactly because of deficiencies in the statistics; it was probably in the vicinity of 90,000 to 100,000, somewhat over half of whom were Communists.[35] This estimate gives a total group of about 150,000 Communist and worker *vydvizhentsy*. But perhaps a clearer sense of the phenomenon can emerge if we consider a few individual biographies. The following people—all men who later rose to very high positions in the party and government leadership—are the cream of the group and tend to have a more solid precollege education than the average:

Brezhnev, Leonid Il'ich, born 1906 in Kamenskoe (Dneprodzerzhinsk), Ukraine. Father a factory worker. Graduated from agricultural school and worked as land surveyor in 1920s, rising to deputy head of Urals Department of Agriculture. Candidate member of party 1929, full member 1931. In 1930 entered Timiriazev Agricultural Academy in Moscow, but left the same year and returned home with wife and child to take a job as worker at Dneprodzerzhinsk Metallurgical Plant. Simultaneously enrolled as student in local metallurgical institute, from which he graduated in 1935.

Kosygin, Aleksei Nikolaevich, born 1904 in St. Petersburg. Father a worker. Fought in Civil War, then graduated from technical school and worked in Siberian consumer-cooperative network. Party member from 1927. Entered Leningrad Textile Institute in 1930.

Ustinov, Dmitrii Fedorovich, born 1908 in Samara. Father a worker. Trained and worked as fitter and machinist before entering Moscow Military-Mechanical Institute around 1930. Party member from 1927.

Malyshev, Viacheslav Aleksandrovich, born 1902 to family of provincial teacher. Graduated from railroad technical school, worked on railroads, and rose to locomotive driver. Party member from 1926. Entered Bauman Mechanical-Mathematical Institute, Moscow, as party Thousander in 1930.

Patolichev, Nikolai Semenovich, born 1908 to peasant family. (Father, who had remained in Imperial Army after conscription in 1902, died fighting with Red Army in Civil War.) Incomplete primary education in village school. From age sixteen, worked at Chernorech'e Chemical Plant and studied at its apprentice school. Became secretary of plant's Komsomol organization. Mobilized for collectivization in 1930. Party member from 1928. In 1931 entered Mendeleev Chemical-Technological Institute in Moscow (which was quickly split into several schools,

---

[35] For the calculation on which this estimate is based, see Fitzpatrick, *Education and Social Mobility*, p. 187.

one of which was the Military-Chemical Academy from which Patolichev later graduated).

Chuianov, Aleksei Semenovich, born 1905. Both parents laborers at grain-collection point in southern Russia. Completed seven-year general school, then worked in Komsomol apparat. Joined party in 1925. After unsuccessful effort to enter a *rabfak* in 1927, selected in 1929 as a party Thousander and sent to Lomonosov Mechanical Institute in Moscow. (This institute was also split up in the early 1930s. The school from which Chuianov later graduated was the Moscow Chemical-Technological Institute of the Meat Industry.)[36]

The sending of 150,000 Communist and worker *vydvizhentsy* into higher education—most of them scheduled to graduate only from 1935 to 1937—constituted a very large investment in future cadres. Immediate needs were met to a large extent by direct promotion of persons without educational qualifications but untainted by bourgeois origins or service under the old regime. From 1928 to 1933 some 140,638 workers were promoted from the factory bench to responsible administrative and specialist positions, the majority being trained on the job as plant technicians, engineers, and managers in industry. Over half of this group did not belong to the party.[37] A much larger group moved upward from manual to white-collar occupations of all types. According to one Soviet source, from 1930 to 1933 alone 666,000 Communist workers left the factory for white-collar employment or full-time study.[38] No similar figures are available for nonparty workers, but if we assume that Communists were at least as likely as non-Communists to be promoted into responsible positions (a classification covering about one-tenth of all white-collar jobs in 1933), 666,000 appears to be a minimum estimate of the nonparty workers directly promoted. The total number of workers

[36] Biographical data from Borys Levytsky, *The Soviet Political Elite* (Munich, 1969), and *Ezhegodnik Bol'shoi sovetskoi entsiklopedii, 1971* (Moscow, 1971). Additional data on Brezhnev from John Dornberg, *Brezhnev: The Masks of Power* (New York, 1974), pp. 54–55; and *Leonid I. Brezhnev: Pages from His Life* (New York, 1978), pp. 26–32; data on Malyshev from *Pravda*, 22 November 1937, p. 2; on Patolichev from N. S. Patolichev, *Ispytanie na zrelost'* (Moscow, 1977), passim; and on Chuianov from A. S. Chuianov, *Na stremnine veka: Zapiski sekretaria obkoma* (Moscow, 1976), passim.

[37] *Sostav rukovodiashchikh rabotnikov i spetsialistov Soiuza SSR* (Moscow, 1936), pp. 8–11. The figures are based on a survey of leading cadres taken in November 1933. The group numbered over 800,000 and constituted about one-tenth of all white-collar workers at that time. Cadres working in the military, security, and party apparats were excluded.

[38] *Kommunisticheskaia partiia—um, chest' i sovest' nashei epokhi* (Moscow, 1969), pp. 221–22.

who moved out of manual occupations into white-collar and administrative positions and full-time study in this period was probably at
least 1.5 million.

The "wreckers'" testimony

Neither direct promotion of new cadres nor the training of qualified cadres for the future solved the immediate problem that Stalin
had noted in 1928: the existing Red cadres still lacked technical expertise. This fundamental point was sometimes overlooked in the
enthusiastic reports of proletarian promotion characteristic of the
First Five-Year Plan period. Yet the frequent announcements of new
conspiracies and wrecking by the bourgeois specialists implied that
the old cadres were still being hoodwinked by their subordinates.
This theme dropped out of public view after Stalin's first commentaries on the Shakhty affair, so it is all the more striking to find it
emphasized in leadership discussions conducted in camera.

Speaking to a closed party audience in 1929, Molotov warned that
the Shakhty trial "was an enormous lesson for all of us, but especially for the Communists in the industrial leadership; yet by no
means all of our comrades have pondered the lesson seriously to this
day."[39] Kaganovich spoke more bluntly in his private meetings with
trade union leaders, whose obsession with the old struggle of labor
and management, he thought, blinded them to real political dangers:

> You reduce everything to the khoziaistvenniki [Soviet industrial man-
> agers], but the fact is that it's not the khoziaistvenniki who make the
> decisions. Take the director of some plant, say the Tomskii or Rykov
> plant in the Donbass—he's a pawn, he's powerless on his own, he runs
> around and rushes from place to place, but he himself can do nothing.
> The technical personnel make the decisions.

And again, a few weeks later, Kaganovich warned: "You are wrong
in thinking that it's the Presidium of Vesenkha that matters, that it
controls the economy. It's not the Presidium or Vesenkha that will be
doing that. When it comes to firing heads of departments, the majority of people who will be doing that are nonparty."[40]

At the Sixteenth Party Congress in mid-1930, Sergo Ordzhonikidze,

---

[39] V. Molotov, report to Pervaia Moskovskaia oblastnaia konferentsiia Vsesoiuznoi
Kommunisticheskoi partii (bol'shevikov): Stenograficheskii otchet (Moscow, 1929), 1:42.
[40] TsGAOR, f. 5451, op. 13, d. 14, ll. 23, 51 (stenographic reports of meetings of
VTsSPS, 2 and 25 January 1929).

then head of the party's Central Control Commission, presented a
report highly critical of Vesenkha's direction of industry. But the real
sting was not in Ordzhonikidze's report (at least in its published
form) but in the supporting materials circulated in numbered copies
to Congress delegates. These materials contained extracts from the
interrogations of experts formerly employed in the industrial and
transport administrations and currently under arrest for wrecking.
The experts said almost nothing about the bizarre conspiracies to
which some of them later confessed in such show trials as that of the
"Industrial Party" late in 1930. They mainly described how the industrial bureaucracies really functioned and what they thought of
their own Communist bosses. One may, of course, doubt testimony
given under duress (though one of the remarkable features of the
confessions is the passion with which many experts defended their
positions on old policy conflicts, often explaining that they had been
"too timid" to engage in blatant sabotage of those experts who had
taken the opposing side). But the very fact that such materials were
circulated at the Congress indicates that Ordzhonikidze, and presumably also Stalin, thought that the experts were saying something
of value, and the message could hardly have brought joy to the
khoziaistvenniki.

Though often sympathetic to their Communist directors, the experts strongly emphasized their bosses' lack of technical expertise.
According to S. A. Khrennikov (formerly a powerful figure in Vesenkha), "the man in charge of metallurgy [in 1925–1926]—Comrade
Berezin, a Communist—was completely unacquainted with the field,
and any wrecking act could be got past him," and I. V. Kosior found
it "hard to get a grasp of things" when he was transferred from the
oil industry to Ukrainian steel. The former chief engineer of Vesenkha's Rifle and Machine Gun Trust testified that G. I. Bruno, chairman of the trust, "could not understand technical matters at all (he
was a railroad technician, never worked in defense plants, and
didn't know the field)," and that I. A. Mirzakhanov, another Communist leader of the trust, performed better but could still be fooled by
the experts.[41]

I. N. Strizhev, formerly a senior official in Vesenkha's fuel administration and earlier a manager of the Nobel company's Dagestan oil
fields, explained why the Communists were less effective than prerevolutionary managers:

[41] *Material k otchetu TsKK VKP(b) XVI s"ezdu VKP(b): Sostavlennyi OGPU (k do-
kladu t. Ordzhonikidze)* (Moscow, 1930), pp. 50, 44–45.

The Communist industrialists mainly didn't know how to do the work
and were only learning. . . . When I was a manager of oil enterprises
before the Revolution, I went round the works every day, . . . I knew
each worker and each employee. . . . The present administrators of the
oil fields don't go that far. They were surrounded by papers and red-
tape, bureaucratism, and millions of meetings. They had no time to do
the work.[42]

But in some cases, according to the experts, Communists actually
saw it as their function to cope with bureaucratic and political im-
pediments, while the experts handled the business. According to the
confession of V. A. Domenov, former technical director of the trust,
when G. I. Lomov, who had the misfortune to head the Donbass coal
administration in 1928, was in charge of the Urals Platinum Trust in
the early 1920s, he "was busy with the Urals soviet, and actually I
had all the responsibility." This statement was confirmed by the
trust's former chief mechanic, who added that Lomov "described
himself as a battering ram, making a breach in the wall so that in the
future the path would be smooth, without big obstructions."[43]

Many of the experts said that they had had a close relationship
with their Communist bosses—so close that the bosses would not
hesitate to defend them against outside criticism, and seemed to put
institutional interest above their duty as party members to observe
the confidentiality of communications from higher party and security organs. When M. S. Mikhailov, the Old Bolshevik chairman of
the Leningrad Machine Building Trust, received a "completely secret
memorandum" from the GPU criticizing the trust's policy of cutting
back defense production in certain Leningrad plants, he handed it
over to a nonparty engineer, Dukelskii, who was one of the main
targets of GPU criticism. On Mikhailov's instructions, Dukelskii
drafted the trust's reply "in an obviously improper manner, dragging
in facts that were meant to justify the Machine Trust's actions and
my own."[44]

An even more distressing report came from G. I. Khabarov, formerly chief engineer in one of the electrotechnical trusts and a
strong supporter of the Erikson automatic telephone system, which
the trust had decided to install in several cities. On receiving an
objection from the GPU to the choice of the Erikson system over the
competing system of the German Siemens firm, the trust's Communist chairman, I. P. Zhukov, handed it over to Khabarov and (using

---

[42] Ibid., p. 49.
[43] Ibid., pp. 39, 40.
[44] Ibid., p. 53.

the familiar form of address) asked if he had enemies who might have taken a complaint to the GPU. Khabarov suggested a few experts in the field, evidently supporters of the Siemens system, but Zhukov quickly rejected one of them: "It can hardly be Vilner, because he's getting a going over himself." Khabarov, of course, composed the trust's answer to the GPU, but he still felt the need to consolidate the pro-Erikson position against attack from the Siemens supporters (both firms were foreign, but there was no apparent suggestion that they had been involved in any sinister way, or that there was more to the conflict than a difference of professional judgment). Therefore, he mentioned the problem to his friend V. A. Sergievskii, another future "wrecker," who published the technical case for the Erikson system in the journal of the Commissariat of Posts and Telegraph, in the hope of disposing of the professional opposition, despite its aggressive tactics in enlisting the GPU's support.[45]

The entire document must have caused quite a stir at the Sixteenth Party Congress, because some of the Communist names mentioned were highly respected, including those of two of Kuibyshev's deputy commissars at Vesenkha, V. I. Mezhlauk and I. V. Kosior. It is not surprising that Kuibyshev, Vesenkha's chairman and a Politburo member, returned from this session of the Congress in a state of deep shock.[46] A few months later he was replaced as chairman of Vesenkha by Ordzhonikidze, who was to remain at the head of Soviet industry—first as chairman of Vesenkha, then from 1932 as commissar of heavy industry—until February 1937, when he committed suicide a few weeks after his deputy, G. L. Piatakov, was sentenced to death.

Ordzhonikidze in charge

Sergo Ordzhonikidze entered Vesenkha as its new chairman in mid-November 1930 with a mandate to purge and raise the quality of the industrial cadres. With the trial of the Industrial Party experts in progress, among his first actions were the appointment of a commission "for liquidation of the consequences of wrecking" (headed by an official who was probably seconded from the OGPU)[47] and a

[45] Ibid., pp. 54–55.

[46] A. F. Khavin, *U rulia industrii* (Moscow, 1968), p. 82.

[47] The official was G. E. Prokofev, probably the same G. E. Prokofev who attended the Seventeenth Party Congress in 1934 as an OGPU delegate. He was appointed head of the temporary group for the liquidation of the consequences of wrecking in November 1930, moved to head of Vesenkha's control (*proverka ispolneniia*) section in Janu-

thunderous denunciation of "traitors and enemies of Soviet power"
formerly associated with Vesenkha and now implicated in the Industrial Party affair.[48] But punitive purging was not Ordzhonikidze's
style. Even as Central Control Commission chairman he had seemed
skeptical of Molotov's accusations against the bourgeois experts and
maintained cordial personal relations with party oppositionists even
at the height of the struggle against them.[49] Within a few months of
his arrival at Vesenkha, he was expressing confidence in the future
loyalty of the experts and, according to one report, recommending
the release of those who had been arrested.[50] His dealings with major
party oppositionists in the Vesenkha apparat were similarly conciliatory. Bukharin's authority in the scientific-technical sector was reinforced, and the left oppositionist Piatakov was restored to his pre-
1928 position as deputy commissar.[51]

Stalin, in his famous "six conditions" speech of June 1931, announced major policy changes, including the rehabilitation of the
bourgeois experts, which the industrialists had been advocating for
the past six months.[52] His speech also foreshadowed the end of large-
scale *vydvizhenie* of workers and Communists into full-time higher
education, although it was not until the college reorganization of
1933 (in which Ordzhonikidze's commissariat played a leading part)

---

ary, and was released from the Vesenkha presidium in August 1931. [See Tsentral'nyi
gosudarstvennyi arkhiv narodnogo khoziaistva SSSR (TsGANKh), f. 3429, op. 1, d.
5233, l. 150; d. 5251, l. 31; and d. 5259, l. 227 (Prikazy Vesenkha SSSR).

[48] Order no. 6 (4 January 1931), signed by Ordzhonikidze, expelling from Vesenkha
the "wreckers" A. M. Ginzburg, L. B. Kafengauz, L. K. Ramzin, A. L. Sokolovskii, S. D.
Shein, and S. A. Khrennikov (TsGANKh, f. 3421, op. 1, d. 5251, l. 12).

[49] Ordzhonikidze, making a later appearance at the conference at which Molotov
had reported (see n. 39 above), said that he considered the Gosplan "wrecker" V. G.
Groman to be "a man who could not be bought," although his ideology made him
dangerous. *Pervaia Moskovskaia oblastnaia konferentsiia*, p. 181. At a mid-1927
meeting of the Central Control Commission, the oppositionist Nikolai Muralov had
difficulty getting a hearing in an extremely tense atmosphere, but he made a friendly
reference to Ordzhonikidze, who later responded in a bantering and distinctly non-
hostile manner. See *VI Plenum TsKK sostava XIV s"ezda VKP(b), 26–27 iiulia 1927 g.*
(stenographic report for limited circulation) (Moscow, 1927), pp. 99, 102.

[50] Speech to Conference of Industrialists, in *Za industrializatsiiu*, 2 February 1931,
p. 2; memoir by I. S. Peskin, in *Byli industrial'nye: Ocherki i vospominaniia* (Moscow, 1970), p. 183.

[51] In May 1931 Ordzhonikidze gave warm approval to Bukharin's proposal for a
conference on scientific planning, which turned out to be a big step forward on
Bukharin's road to political rehabilitation. In October he entrusted the reorganization
of Vesenkha's planning sector—an important task, which might well have been as-
signed to one of the trusted colleagues Ordzhonikidze had brought with him from
TsKK—to G. L. Piatakov. See TsGANKh, f. 3429, op. 1, d. 5244, p. 243 (file of the
Ukrainian Vesenkha containing central instructions for 1931), and d. 5262, p. 26 (order of Vesenkha USSR, no. 705).

[52] Stalin, "Novaia obstanovka," pp. 51–80.

that the policy came into full operation. It is possible that Stalin felt that he had suffered a defeat with these policy changes,[53] or at least that Ordzhonikidze had preempted the initiative. But the educational *vydvizhenie* had earlier been described as a short-term measure, and for practical reasons it could hardly have been otherwise. Stalin took full credit for the "six conditions"—in fact, the publicity surrounding them pushed the Stalin cult to new heights—and the new policies he announced remained in force for the rest of the Stalin era. Ordzhonikidze was no less concerned about the quality of industrial cadres. Appointments and transfers came under Ordzhonikidze's personal control at Vesenkha, and the Central Committee Secretariat, whose confirmation was required for all appointments of Communists, apparently simply rubber-stamped Ordzhonikidze's orders.[54]

Ordzhonikidze's cadres, as they emerged in the early 1930s, were essentially a different group from the Red directors of the 1920s.[55] Although many of the old Red directors were reduced to relatively minor positions (the former defense industry leader G. I. Bruno, for example, was appointed head of the Fifth Construction Trust in 1931),[56] Ordzhonikidze vastly enhanced the authority of plant directors and appointed new cadres to these positions. Many of these cadres had previously held high positions in the central apparat, and a few were recent graduates of the engineering schools, having entered higher education during NEP. But there was no single or predominant recruiting ground for Ordzhonikidze's cadres. His strategy

[53] Kendall E. Bailes makes this argument in *Techology and Society under Lenin and Stalin* (Princeton, 1978), chap. 7. A somewhat different view is presented in Fitzpatrick, *Education and Social Mobility*, chap. 10.

[54] See Chuianov, *Na stremnine veka*, p. 41. Soon after his appointment to the industrial section of the Central Committee department of leading party organs, Chuianov unintentionally caused confusion by flouting this unwritten rule. Virtually all orders on appointments and personnel matters in Vesenkha and later in the Commissariat of Heavy Industry were signed personally by Ordzhonikidze as well as by the head of his cadres sector, I. M. Moskvin (the majority of orders on other types of questions were signed by one of the deputy commissars). Breaking with the practice of his predecessor, Valerian Kuibyshev, on 3 December 1930 Ordzhonikidze ordered that the cadres sector be directly subordinated to the Vesenkha chairman (TsGANKh, f. 3429, op. 1, d. 5233, l. 250 [order no. 1,373]).

[55] On the various generations of *khoziaistvenniki*, see the firsthand account in A. F. Khavin, "Kapitany sovetskoi industrii, 1926–1940 gody," *Voprosy istorii*, 1966 no. 5, pp. 3–14.

[56] TsGANKh, f. 3429, op. 1, d. 5251, l. 15. Not all the industrialists named with Bruno in the document circulated at the Sixteenth Party Conference were demoted by Ordzhonikidze. Of those mentioned earlier, Lomov was transferred to Gosplan in 1931, but Zhukov and Mirzakhanov prospered in their respective fields, and Ordzhonikidze restored Mezhlauk and Kosior to the status of deputy commissar shortly after his arrival at Vesenkha.

was bold promotion and lavish reward for anyone with a good performance record or, in the case of the young, signs of practical initiative and energy.

Most contemporaries admired Ordzhonikidze's achievements with regard to the industrial cadres. But the problem of technical expertise remained, since, no matter how he juggled cadres, too few of them were qualified for the jobs that had to be filled. The annual output of the engineering schools was increasing rapidly during the first half of the 1930s, but Ordzhonikidze did not consider the majority of new graduates ready for immediate promotion to responsible positions.[57] A few thousand cadres emerged each year from the industrial academies, and Ordzhonikidze sent quite large numbers of his industrialists on trips to the capitalist West, especially to the United States, to study modern technology in action. These measures, however, had relatively little impact on the lower level of cadres, whose training remained a preoccupation of the leading party organs.

In 1932 the Central Committee noted the poor results and "extraordinarily slow tempo" of the campaign to educate industrial cadres, and in 1934 the Seventeenth Party Congress decreed that all industrial cadres should be required to pass a "technical minimum" examination.[58] In heavy industry, 2,386 cadres passed this examination the following year, and by mid-1935 a total of 6,320 were enrolled in the courses. It is difficult to judge how much real effect this kind of training had. Many cadres must have been in the position of the shop head promoted from the bench in 1930 whose formal education had ended in primary school thirty-four years earlier. After taking the technical minimum course, they could follow technical discussions at the plant, but they were still far from the level of specialists or even technicians.[59]

[57] In his speech to the Central Committee plenum of January 1933, Ordzhonikidze warned against overly rapid promotion for the more than 20,000 engineers who had graduated from higher schools between 1929 and 1932: "At all costs, we must make sure that the engineer graduating from higher technical school does not immediately become a big boss [bol'shim nachal'stvom] at the plant. Let him go and work for awhile as an assistant foreman and he can begin to move up from there" (*Materialy ob"edinennogo plenuma TsK i TsKK VKP(b), 7–12 ianvaria 1933 g.* [Moscow, 1933], p. 127).

[58] "O tekhnicheskom obuchenii khoziaistvennikov, professional'nykh i partiinykh kadrov" (17 January 1932), in *Resheniia partii i pravitel'stva po khoziaistvennym voprosam* (Moscow, 1967), 2:371–73; resolution of the Seventeenth Party Congress on organizational questions (February 1934) and resolution of TsK and Sovnarkom USSR, "Ob organizatsionnykh meropriiatiiakh v oblasti sovetskogo i khoziaistvennogo stroitel'stva" (15 March 1934), in *ibid.*, pp. 466–68.

[59] S. Ia. Andelman, ed., *God ucheby khoziaistvennikov* (Moscow and Leningrad, 1935), pp. 9, 14, 40–42.

In the spring of 1935 Stalin indicated that he remained dissatisfied with the speed at which the cadres were mastering technology. The Soviet Union, he said, had acquired technology but lacked the trained personnel to make full use of it. The old slogan "Technology [*tekhnika*] decides everything" must be replaced by a new slogan: "Cadres decide everything":

> Technology without the people who have mastered that technology is dead. Technology directed by people who have mastered that technology can and must produce miracles. If there were enough cadres capable of installing that technology in our best plants and factories, in our state farms and collective farms, and in the Red Army, the country would get two or three times the benefit that it gets now. That is why we must put the stress on people, on cadres, on personnel with a mastery of technology.[60]

This speech, addressed to graduates of the Red Army Academy, was clearly an appeal to the whole cohort of rising young specialists and First Five-Year Plan *vydvizhentsy* to challenge their elders and lead the country forward. But one young Stakhanovite worker, Ivan Gudov, believed that Stalin was talking about people like him—workers who challenged the plant managers and engineers by showing that the current production norms underestimated the real capacity of the plants.[61] This may not have been a correct analysis, but it was a good forecast. By the end of the year, Stalin was using the Stakhanovite movement to launch a new attack on the industrial cadres.

The Stakhanovites, Stalin told the first Stakhanovite meeting in November 1935,

> are free from the conservatism and inertia of some engineers, technicians, and industrialists. They go boldly forward, breaking outmoded technical norms and creating new and higher ones. They introduce corrections into the projected capacity and economic plans composed by the leaders of our industry; they often supplement and correct the engineers and technicians; frequently they teach them and give them a push forward.[62]

Stalin suspected that plant managers and engineers were intentionally keeping the norms low so that they could show high figures

[60] Stalin, "Rech' na vypuske akademikov Krasnoi Armii," p. 61.

[61] Ivan Gudov, *Sud'ba rabochego*, 2d ed. (Moscow, 1974), p. 60.

[62] I. V. Stalin, "Rech' na pervom vsesoiuznom soveshchanii stakhanovtsev" (17 November 1935), in his *Sochineniia*, ed. McNeal, 1 (14):84–85.

of plan fulfillment. From his standpoint, the merits of the Stakhanovites lay not only in their ability to break production records but also in their tendency to cause trouble at the plants and shake up the bosses' cozy mutual protection arrangements. (The early Stakhanovites were not quite the ideal Soviet citizens represented in the literature: those who risked the hostility of fellow workers as well as management by vastly overfulfilling norms were often natural loners of quarrelsome disposition.)

When trouble broke out between plant managers and would-be Stakhanovites in 1936, local press and party organizations were encouraged to take the side of the Stakhanovites. In the spring of that year a number of plant and mine directors were fired, and some were arrested for sabotage as a result of such conflicts. Although Ordzhonikidze made every effort to demonstrate his commissariat's support for the Stakhanovites, the campaign for higher norms was politically damaging to him. After the summer of 1936, when Piatakov was arrested as a Trotskyite wrecker, it was clear that worse was to come.[63]

The Great Purges

For the Soviet public and the outside world, the unfolding of the Great Purge was closely linked with three dramatic show trials of Old Bolsheviks: the Zinoviev-Kamenev trial in the summer of 1936, the Piatakov-Radek trial at the beginning of 1937, and the Bukharin trial early in 1938. The Piatakov trial, involving no former party leader of the first rank, may at first sight seem the least interesting. Nevertheless, it was the Piatakov trial, together with Stalin's and Molotov's commentaries on it at the February–March plenum of the Central Committee in 1937, that gave the signal for mass demotions and arrests of the Soviet political and managerial elite. The timing suggests that it was not merely one of the Great Purge trials but the crucial one.

Piatakov and the group of Old Bolsheviks and industrialists on trial with him were described as saboteurs who had conspired both with the exiled Trotsky and with intelligence agents of foreign powers. The scenario was obviously quite similar to those used in the show trials of bourgeois experts during the First Five-Year Plan.

---

[63] *Sovet pri Narodnom komissare tiazheloi promyshlennosti SSSR, 25–29 iiunia 1936 g.: Stenograficheskii otchet* (Moscow, 1936), pp. 38, 92–93, 390. On the arrest and the reaction of industrialists, including Ordzhonikidze, see Gudov, *Sud'ba rabochego*, pp. 102–4.

But what is more interesting is that Stalin and Molotov insisted that there was a continuity in policy between the Shakhty trial of 1928 and the Piatakov trial of 1937. In 1928, they said, the state had been threatened by the sabotage of a group of technical experts who were not Communists, whereas in 1937 the threat came from Communists who were not technical experts (according to Stalin, Piatakov and his like were "simply loudmouths and improvisers from the point of view of technical training").[64] Stalin and Molotov reminded the Central Committee that the Shakhty wreckers had unwittingly provided the stimulus for a major training program for cadres during the First Five-Year Plan. As a result, "during the time between the Shakhty period and the present we have produced tens of thousands of Bolshevik cadres who are genuinely tempered in a technical sense. . . . In technical respects, our people are better qualified than the Trotskyists, the present wreckers."[65]

Stalin made it clear that the reason for the continuity of this policy was the party leadership's concern that Bolshevik cadres had not yet mastered technology. Ignoring the substantial personnel changes that had taken place under Ordzhonikidze, he equated the industrial cadres of 1937 with those who had been content with "the role of inept commissars under the bourgeois specialists" in 1928. He claimed that they had refused or been unable to acquire technical expertise:

> You must remember how unwillingly our industrial cadres then recognized their mistakes, how unwillingly they acknowledged their technical backwardness, and how sluggishly they grasped the slogan "Master technology." And what happened? The facts showed that the slogan "Master technology" had its effect and gave good results. Now we have tens and hundreds of thousands of marvelous industrial cadres who have already mastered technology and are moving our industry forward. But we would not have those cadres now if the party had yielded to the stubbornness of the industrialists who did not wish to confess their technical backwardness, if the party had not recognized their mistakes and corrected them in time.[66]

Nobody could have doubted that this was an indictment of a whole group rather than of individual Trotskyist wreckers. This impression was reinforced by the press campaign of the first months of

[64] I. V. Stalin, "O nedostatkakh partiinoi raboty i merakh likvidatsii trotskistkikh i inykh dvurushnikov" (speech to Central Committee plenum, 3 March 1937), in his *Sochineniia*, ed. McNeal, 1 (14):203.

[65] V. M. Molotov, "Uroki vreditel'stva, diversii i shpionazha iapono-nemetsko-trotskistskikh agentov" (edited version of speech to Central Committee plenum), *Bol'shevik*, 1937 no. 8 (15 April 1937), pp. 24–26.

[66] Stalin, "O nedostatkakh," p. 203.

1937, which criticized the industrialists for a series of faults that had nothing to do with Trotskyist conspiracy, including conservative resistance to innovation, unwillingness to promote promising young engineers and workers, mutual protection arrangements, self-aggrandizement, and alienation from the masses.[67]

Yet Stalin had referred to "tens and hundreds of thousands of marvelous industrial cadres" at the nation's disposal. Who were they? A group of prominent Donbass industrialists, undoubtedly hoping that an engineering degree would guarantee membership in the favored group, hastened to complete their part-time studies in mid-1937 and announced their achievement to the press,[68] but, as it turned out, their diligence did not save them from being purged. Others concluded that the prime characteristic of "marvelous industrial cadres" was youth. When Mirzakhanov, an Old Bolshevik director of a big defense industry plant, accompanied one of his junior engineers to Moscow (knowing that the younger man was to replace him as director), he broke his morose silence during the journey only once:

"How old are you?"
"I will soon be thirty-three."
"A good age," he remarked.[69]

But distinctions were to be made even among the young and technically trained. In the spring of 1937 the industrial newspaper carried an article criticizing a group of young engineers, probably graduates of the late 1920s, who had been sent abroad to study American technology in the early 1930s and had held high positions in an important plant since their return. Despite their youth, the paper charged that these men had become conservative opponents of change: "Although in the past they boldly defended new technology, they have succumbed to slavish veneration of ten-year-old blueprints and tracings, for the sole reason that they come from abroad."[70] The writer

[67] See, for example, *Za industrializatsiiu*, 9 March 1937, p. 3, and 22 March 1937, p. 2; and editorial in *Pravda*, 14 February 1937, p. 1.

[68] *Za industrializatsiiu*, 5 July 1937, p. 4. Included in the group were N. V. Radin, director of the Il'ich plant at Mariupol, and Ia. S. Gugel, director of the Ordzhonikidze metallurgical combine (Azovstal').

[69] Memoir by N. E. Nosovskii (Mirzakhanov's replacement) in *Byli industrial'nye*, p. 124.

[70] S. Koff, "O tekhnicheskom progresse i chesti inzhenerskogo mundira," *Za industrializatsiiu*, 9 March 1937, p. 3. Koff, an experienced industrial journalist with considerable technical expertise, may well have been flying his own trial balloon with this article. It would not have been read as an authoritative political statement, although it almost certainly led to trouble for the Moscow transformer plant, which was the butt of the article's criticism.

seemed to suggest that, in addition to the dubious American connection, they were disqualified by having already achieved the status of leading cadres. In the plant, they were holding back the promotion of real innovators—engineers of almost their own age, but who had graduated more recently, men who had "been around" and had good rapport with the workers; in short, *vydvizhentsy* sent to college during the Cultural Revolution. The leader of the group challenging the "young graybeards" in charge of the plant was a former party Thousander.

The article's conclusions, however, were unusual for the time in which it was written. The speeches of Stalin and Molotov at the February–March plenum had not been published immediately, and even when they appeared, the press seemed uncertain about what commentary to offer. For Central Committee members, the drama of the plenum lay in Stalin's and Molotov's attacks on obkom secretaries and the attempts by a few members of the leadership to force a thorough purge of party organizations.[71] These attempts had failed, the campaign to broaden the base of party democracy had been approved by the plenum, and all party committees and officers were up for reelection by secret ballot.[72] The elections were designed to bring new leaders up from the ranks. The rhetoric of this period was strongly anti-elitist and, in many instances, pro-worker.

Reinforcing this theme, in October Stalin appealed to the "humble people" to help get rid of the bosses as a group: "The people's trust is a big thing, comrades. Leaders come and go, but the people [*narod*] remain. Only the people are eternal. All the rest is transient."[73] Again he referred specifically to the industrial cadres, but this time without touching on the issue of technical qualifications. The press concluded that as far as industry was concerned, the right note to strike was good workers versus corrupt management, and obliged with many exhortations to promote Stakhanovite workers into managerial positions.[74]

But by the early months of 1938, the quasi-populist aspect of the Great Purges was already receding. Official spokesmen began to em-

[71] See Khrushchev's secret speech to the Twentieth Party Congress, in N. S. Khrushchev, *Khrushchev Remembers*, trans. Strobe Talbott (Boston and Toronto, 1970), p. 577.

[72] See Central Committee resolution, "Podgotovka partiinykh organizatsii k vyboram v Verkhovnyi Sovet SSSR po novoi izbiratel'noi sisteme i sootvetstvuiushchaia perestroika partiino-politicheskoi raboty," in *KPSS v rezoliutsiiakh*, 5:286–89.

[73] I. V. Stalin, "Rech' na prieme rukovodiashchikh rabotnikov i stakhanovtsev metallurgicheskoi i ugol'noi promyshlennosti rukovoditeliami partii i pravitel'stva" (29 October 1937), in his *Sochineniia*, ed. McNeal, 1 (14):254.

[74] See, for example, editorial in *Pravda*, 9 June 1937, p. 1.

phasize the need for *qualified* cadres and to call for a realization of the huge investment put into higher and secondary technical education since 1928. Even in the midst of the Bukharin trial, the allocation of the most recent group of graduates (12,520 students who received their degrees in the last quarter of 1937, 57 percent of whom were engineers) appeared on the front pages of newspapers: in an unprecedented act, the party Central Committee and government had chosen to decide this question at the highest level.[75] Over 2,000 graduates, almost all engineers, were appointed directly to extremely responsible positions in the industrial, government, party, and educational apparats.[76]

The graduates in question had entered higher education in 1931 and 1932 and thus were part of the last large class of Cultural Revolution *vydvizhentsy*. By the beginning of 1938, *vydvizhentsy* of earlier classes were already experiencing rapid promotion, in common with other qualified and unqualified persons in industry and the lower ranks of the apparats. But it was not until the resolution of the Central Committee and government that this cohort became widely identified as a group peculiarly suitable for leadership, or that large numbers of engineer *vydvizhentsy* began to move out of the plants into purely administrative positions. Although Stalin had earlier said that *Bolsheviks*—not just Bolshevik *khoziaistvenniki*—should master technology, his slogan had often been given a narrower definition. From the spring of 1938, however, a new theme appeared in the press coverage of the rebuilding of the apparats. Young engineering graduates, it turned out, were particularly successful in bringing a new style of practical leadership to party organizations.[77]

This was a time of extraordinary opportunities for the *vydvizhentsy*, and there is no shortage of success stories. Of the six whose precollege careers were outlined earlier, Brezhnev was the least outstanding, though in any other context his promotions would have

[75] Resolution of Sovnarkom USSR and the party Central Committee, "O raspredelenii okonchivshikh vysshie uchebnye zavedeniia v IV kvartale 1937 g.," published in *Pravda*, 6 March 1938, p. 1; also in *Industriia*, 6 March 1938, p. 1, and elsewhere.

[76] Of the total, 482 graduates were to be appointed directors, chief engineers, and deputy chief engineers in industrial enterprises; 507 were to go to the central government commissariats as heads and deputy heads of departments and as inspectors; 116 were to become directors and deputy directors of educational institutions; and 131 were to be sent to leading work (that is, as chairmen, secretaries, or department heads) in the regional and republican soviets and party committees.

[77] See, for example, *Industriia*, 8 April 1938, p. 3, and 21 April 1938, p. 3 (about G. I. Khabarov's experience in a Stalingrad raikom), and *Pravda*, 10 May 1938, p. 3 (regarding A. Aksenov's work in the Stalinsk gorkom).

been remarkable. Graduating in 1935, he worked briefly as an engineer and put in a year's military service before becoming deputy chairman of the Dneprodzerzhinsk soviet in 1937. Two years later, at the age of thirty-three, he was appointed second or third obkom secretary in Dnepropetrovsk, a major industrial center. Two other members of the group reached even higher positions in the party apparat. Patolichev, who graduated only in 1937, worked as an engineer for a few months, then moved to the Central Committee Secretariat as an instructor, and in August 1938 he was sent as party organizer for the Central Committee to the Iaroslavl rubber combine, which had been completely disrupted by a succession of purges. He took the risk of protesting the continuation of the local purges, and it paid off. In 1939, not yet thirty-one years old, he was appointed first secretary of the Iaroslavl obkom. Chuianov, a 1934 graduate, had time to do some research work on refrigeration problems before receiving an appointment to the Central Committee Secretariat. For him, as for Patolichev and many other younger Communists working there, this position was a stepping-stone to higher things. In 1938, when he was thirty-three, he was appointed first secretary of the Stalingrad obkom, and departed the same day to a city he had never seen, in a new suit supplied by Central Committee Secretary Andrei Andreev. (Two of his colleagues and fellow *vydvizhentsy* left the Secretariat about the same time—P. K. Ponomarenko as first secretary of the Belorussian Communist Party and S. V. Kaftanov as head of the all-Union administration of higher education.

In the space of a few years, Kosygin, Ustinov, and Malyshev all rose from plant engineer to government minister (people's commissar). Two years after his graduation in 1935, Kosygin was made director of a major texile plant, and in 1939, at the age of thirty-five, he was appointed commissar of the textile industry of the USSR. Ustinov similarly headed a major plant in the defense industry before his appointment in 1941, when he was only thirty-three years old, as commissar of armaments of the USSR. Malyshev's rise, unlike that of the other five, was accompanied by a great deal of press publicity, many public speeches, and election to the Supreme Soviet. Chief engineer at the big Kolomna Machine Building Plant in 1937 and director of the plant in 1938, he became commissar of heavy machine building of the USSR in 1939, at the age of thirty-seven.[78]

But these, of course, are the success stories. Not all of the Cultural

[78] Biographical data from Levytsky, *Soviet Political Elite*; *Leonid I. Brezhnev: Pages from His Life*; Chuianov, *Na stremnine veka*; Patolichev, *Ispytanie na zrelost'*.

Revolution *vydvizhentsy* were able to rise so fast or so far, and it might be assumed that the cohort provided its share of victims as well as beneficiaries of the Great Purges. This does not seem to have been the case, however. In January 1941 Gosplan made a survey of "leading cadres and specialists" in the Soviet Union which included data on the number of college graduates and their year of graduation. From 1928 to 1932, 152,000 leading cadres had graduated, and 266,000 had graduated from 1933 to 1937.[79] Other sources (published before the 1941 survey, which was purely for internal government use) provide the total number of graduates from all higher educational institutions, except military ones, over the same periods. For 1928–1932, the total number of graduates was 170,000, and for 1933–1937, 370,000.[80] Thus 89 percent of all First Five-Year Plan graduates were leading cadres in 1941, and because the survey did not include the military, security, and party apparats, one must assume that the percentage surviving and holding responsible jobs was actually much higher. Of the Second Five-Year Plan graduates, 72 percent were leading cadres in 1941. But this figure must reflect a substantial rate of army call-up and continuation in graduate school, as well as the simple fact that even in this generation not all graduates could expect jobs in the "leading cadres" category within four or five years of graduation.

Undoubtedly there were purge victims among the graduates of 1928–1937, especially among the relatively small group in leading positions before the Great Purges, and there could have been any number of short-term arrests followed by release and promotion. But the conclusion that must be drawn from these data is that the great majority of the group survived the purges and in fact benefited from them through rapid promotion.

---

[79] The survey was first published (in abbreviated form) from the material in Soviet archives in *Industrializatsiia SSSR, 1938–1941 gg.: Dokumenty i materialy* (Moscow, 1973), pp. 269–76 ("Iz dokladnoi zapiski TsSU SSSR v Prezidium Gosplan SSSR ob itogakh ucheta rukovodiashchikh kadrov i spetsialistov na 1 ianvaria 1941 g.," 29 March 1941). Conceivably the report was inaccurate or incomplete, but there seems to be no other reason to question a document produced not for publication but for internal government use.

[80] Data taken from the statistical handbook *Kul'turnoe stroitel'stvo SSSR* (Moscow, 1940), p. 112. This is among the most professional of the compilations of educational statistics published in the prewar period: in some areas, the statisticians have checked and lowered exaggerated figures published in earlier handbooks, and they are unusually scrupulous in defining categories. Because the educational authorities had some interest in overstating graduation figures, however, it is still possible that those figures are too high. In that case, a lower proportion of 1928–1937 graduates was missing from the 1941 cadres survey.

Beneficiaries of the purges

At the Eighteenth Party Congress, held early in 1939, Andrei Zhdanov said that the party's method of mass purging had produced "excesses" and would not be used in the future.[81] For many of those present, this was undoubtedly the most important statement made at the congress, for it implied a repudiation of the mass arrests that took place in 1937–1938 and of the mass purging of the party (through membership reviews and reregistration) from 1933 to 1936. But Stalin, who scarcely mentioned the excesses, had different priorities. One of the great achievements of the past five years, he said, was the creation of a new intelligentsia (that is, a new administrative and specialist elite):

> Hundreds of thousands of young people, offspring of the working class, the peasantry, and the toiling intelligentsia, went to colleges and technical schools, and returned from the schools to fill the depleted ranks of the intelligentsia. They poured new blood into the intelligentsia and revitalized it in a new Soviet way. They radically changed the contours of the intelligentsia, remaking it in their own image. The remnants of the old intelligentsia were dissolved in the body of a new, Soviet, people's [*narodnaia*] intelligentsia, firmly linked with the people and ready en masse to give them true and faithful service.[82]

If the new intelligentsia or elite were, in Zhdanov's words, "yesterday's workers and peasants and sons of workers and peasants promoted to command positions," it was clearly inappropriate to continue past practices of discrimination against the intelligentsia and in favor of the working class.[83] Many discriminatory policies had already been dropped, but the rules governing admission to the party still gave preference to workers by occupation over former workers promoted to white-collar jobs, causing "confusion and bitterness among comrades whose only 'fault' is that they moved up the ladder."[84] Henceforth the party would not give preference to any one social group in Soviet society, but would try to recruit "the best people." This phrase may have been, as many scholars have suggested, a

---

[81] *XVIII s"ezd Vsesoiuznoi Kommunisticheskoi partii (b): Stenograficheskii otchet* (Moscow, 1939), pp. 519–24.

[82] I. V. Stalin, "Otchetnyi doklad na XVIII syezde partii" (10 March 1939), in his *Sochineniia*, ed. McNeal, 1 (14):398.

[83] Zhdanov first used the phrase in a speech to a Komsomol audience on 29 October 1938 (see *Partiinoe stroitel'stvo*, 1938 no. 21 (1 November 1938), p. 18). It was later incorporated in a resolution of the Eighteenth Party Congress, "Izmeneniia v ustave VKP(b)" (20 March 1939), based on Zhdanov's report (see *XVIII s"ezd*, p. 667).

[84] Zhdanov in *XVIII s"ezd*, p. 515.

euphemism for "intelligentsia," but it does not seem that the old (formerly bourgeois) intelligentsia was the group the party most desired to attract. Judging by speeches at the Eighteenth Party Congress, the very best people were those who had recently risen from the lower classes into the elite.

The creation of a new Soviet intelligentsia, merging the separate administrative and specialist elites of the 1920s, had been described by Stalin as the chief aim of the cadres policy of the Cultural Revolution period. Once the result was achieved—as he clearly believed it had been by 1939—Stalin's attitude toward the working class changed. Workers (the majority of whom were in fact yesterday's peasants) were no longer the regime's main source of social support, and their anti-intellectual and anti-elite feelings were no longer politically useful. Stalin told the congress that the party would ultimately make all workers and peasants "cultured and educated." Until that time came, however, they should respect those who had already received culture and education. The new elite had not betrayed their class origins (as some unenlightened working-class Communists believed), but had shown how to rise above them.[85]

The second objective of Stalin's Cultural Revolution cadres policy had been to educate the party and, in particular, the cadres. According to spokesmen at the congress, dramatic gains had been made. Of the 333 regional and republican party secretaries, 96 now had higher education. Almost all of this group had graduated from engineering and other higher schools between 1934 and 1938, and one-third of them had been appointed to their positions directly after graduation. Almost 6,000 Communists with higher education were working as secretaries in the party organization as a whole. Among voting delegates to the congress—close to 40 percent of whom had risen to the status of leading cadres since the Seventeenth Party Congress in 1934—26.5 percent (418 delegates) had completed higher education, as opposed to 10 percent of Seventeenth Party Congress delegates.[86]

These figures certainly indicate a substantial increase in the number of party cadres with higher education, although they also suggest that the process of educating the cadres still had some way to go. Probably more significant in respect to Stalin's original objectives was the entry of the Cultural Revolution cohort into the top political leadership. In the new Central Committee elected by the Eighteenth Party Congress in 1939, at least 20 of the 138 full and candidate members were *vydvizhentsy*, sent to higher education as adults dur-

[85] Stalin, "Otchetnyi doklad," p. 399.

[86] Data from speeches of Andreev, Zhdanov, and Malenkov in XVIII s"ezd, pp. 106, 529. 148.

ing the Cultural Revolution.[87] In the next Central Committee, elected by the Nineteenth Party Congress in 1952, the proportion of *vydvizhentsy* was substantially higher—36 percent of full members on whom educational data are available.[88]

The primary reason for the prominence of Cultural Revolution *vydvizhentsy* in the Soviet government of 1952 was that engineering graduates of this cohort tended to dominate the large number of industrial ministries represented in the Council of Ministers of the USSR. Of 115 ministers and deputy ministers for whom educational data are available, 50 percent had entered institutes of higher education as adults during the Cultural Revolution. Of this group (a total of 57), 65 percent either were of working-class origin or had at some time been workers by occupation, and 74 percent had been trained as engineers. About half had been workers by occupation immediately before entering higher education, and about a quarter had been employed in apparat jobs (these proportions were almost exactly reversed in the 1952 Central Committee membership). The majority of the engineering graduates had worked for a few years after graduation as plant engineers before being promoted to managerial or government positions in the late 1930s or at the beginning of the 1940s.[89]

Both Khrushchev and Brezhnev, the two leaders who dominated the first three decades of the post-Stalin period, were members of the Cultural Revolution cohort, Khrushchev a 1931 graduate of the Stalin Industrial Academy in Moscow. In the 1979 Soviet Politburo, exactly half of the full members (Brezhnev, Aleksei Kosygin, Andrei Kirilenko, Dmitrii Ustinov, Andrei Gromyko, D. A. Kunaev, and Ar-

[87] Of these *vydvizhentsy*, the full members were V. M. Andrianov, A. G. Zverev, N. S. Khrushchev, A. N. Kosygin, V. A. Malyshev, I. K. Sedin, and P. K. Ponomarenko; the candidate members were A. I. Samokhvalov, A. F. Gorkin, V. G. Zhavoronkov, N. S. Patolichev, A. S. Chuianov, P. S. Popkov, G. M. Popov, V. P. Pronin, S. V. Kaftanov, I. S. Khokhlov, I. G. Makarov, I. I. Maslennikov, and L. A. Sosnin. This list is based on biographical data on Central Committee members and candidates collected from a variety of biographical sources, memoirs, and contemporary press accounts, and supplemented by information provided by Jerry F. Hough (Duke University) and Seweryn Bialer (Columbia University). I have included those who were sent to industrial academies as well as regular higher educational institutions in the years 1928–1932, but excluded those who were sent to trade union higher school (Z. T. Serdiuk) and Marxism-Leninism courses under the Central Committee (D. S. Korotchenko). Also excluded are those such as N. M. Pegov and F. A. Merkulov, who entered higher education after 1932.

[88] I am indebted to Jerry F. Hough for the biographical card files on the party and government leadership of 1952 on which these figures and the following analysis are based.

[89] Biographical data from Levytsky, *Soviet Political Elite; Ezhegodnik Bol'shoi sovetskoi entsiklopedii, 1971;* and *Deputaty Verkhovnogo Soveta SSSR* (Moscow, 1966).

vid Pelshe) were *vydvizhentsy* who had entered higher education as adults during the First Five-Year Plan. All but Gromyko and Pelshe were trained as engineers, and all but Kunaev (a Kazakh from a white-collar family) came from working-class or peasant backgrounds.

Conclusion

This chapter could, no doubt, have been called "The Training of the Brezhnev Generation," since a particular interest attaches to the cohort of Cultural Revolution *vydvizhentsy* that rose so abruptly to prominence at the end of the 1930s and dominated Soviet government and political culture for almost half a century. But for historians, the phenomenon of proletarian "promotion" during the Cultural Revolution has other important implications as well. In the first place, it requires examination of the Great Purges from a rather unfamiliar angle. The purges had beneficiaries, and among the foremost of them were men whom Stalin had sent to be trained as future leaders during the Cultural Revolution. We cannot suppose that Stalin was inexorably carrying out a master plan conceived in 1928, since no politician can have total control over events or foresee the future. We may reasonably suspect, however, that one of the contingencies envisaged by Stalin in 1928 was a future radical turnover of elite personnel.

Moreover, the successful implementation of Stalin's Cultural Revolution policy of proletarian promotion had implications of its own. The fact that the *vydvizhentsy* were becoming available for cadre positions in the second half of the 1930s made mass purging of the elite a much more viable policy than it would have been, say, five years earlier. At the same time, the emergence of the *vydvizhentsy* from institutes of higher education created a potential problem: the *vydvizhentsy*, better qualified than the old cadres, were on the average only about ten years younger. In the natural course of things, they would probably have had to wait a very long time for top jobs.

Judgment of competence and even of qualifications tends to be subjective, and we need not necessarily accept Stalin's opinion on the relative merits of the pre-purges cadres and their successors. The performance of the successors during World War II and the postwar reconstruction period, however, does suggest a much higher degree of competence than many observers would have predicted in 1938. The Cultural Revolution *vydvizhentsy* supplied only a part of the post-purges elite, but they may have provided a much larger portion of its competence.

The second important point that emerges is that Stalin made the decision to train future leading cadres *as engineers.* There was no precedent for such a decision, and it went against the traditional Bolshevik assumption that future leaders should be trained in Marxist social science. In terms of political recruitment, it pushed the Soviet Union in a direction quite different from that of most Western countries (and also from that of such developing nations as India), where the basic path into political life has been through training and practice in law. Stalin represented this decision as flowing from Soviet commitment to modernization and rapid industrialization. Because Stalin's Russia is seen more often as a police state than as a modernizing one, this explanation may not be readily accepted. But it is certainly arguable that Soviet politics of the 1930s should be viewed as a conflict between policemen (those like Molotov, whose primary concern was internal security and control) and industrializers (the Ordzhonikidze type), with Stalin normally standing above the conflict but combining the characteristics of both groups. If we accept this dual image of Stalin, we may see Stalin the industrializer training cadres during the First Five-Year Plan, and Stalin the policeman solving the problem of their promotion in the Great Purges.

Finally, the story of Stalin and the making of a new elite brings us back to an old problem: the relation of the Bolsheviks' "proletarian dictatorship" to the proletariat. It was Stalin who, from 1936 to 1939, abandoned the concept of proletarian dictatorship and revised the formal status of the intelligentsia (or elite). But it was also Stalin who, during the first Five-Year Plan period, seemed to be trying to give substance to the dictatorship of the proletariat through his policies of proletarian promotion. This shift is less contradictory than it seems. Stalin used Marxist language, but his real interest was in a process that is almost completely ignored in Marxist theory: social mobility. As he said in 1931, the Soviet regime did not need "just any kind" of elite, and he might have added that he was not interested in "just any kind" of worker. The elite that he wanted had to be created through upward mobility from the working class and peasantry, and the workers he was interested in were those with the potential for promotion.

The industrialization of the 1930s would inevitably have produced large-scale upward mobility, with or without Stalin's encouragement. But Stalin's proletarian promotion policies dramatized the phenomenon and, in effect, took credit for it in advance. It seems likely that in Stalin's Russia, as in the United States at an earlier period, many citizens linked their own individual upward mobility with their country's form of government. Such a perception might well be a major factor in the legitimization of the regime. Among the members of the new elite, the pride of self-made men must surely have been combined with a sense of indebtedness. For, as they saw it, it was the Revolution (or Stalin) that had given them the opportunity to rise.

(1978)

CHAPTER 8

The Lady Macbeth Affair: Shostakovich and the Soviet Puritans

The New Year was celebrated enthusiastically in Moscow in 1936, to judge by reports in the Soviet press. University students held a masked ball. There were goods in the stores, and many Muscovites had new clothes. Dance halls had recently opened up; foreign jazz groups were touring the country.[1] A new note of lightness, almost frivolity, had appeared in Soviet public discourse since Stalin's pronouncement in 1935 that "life has become better, life has become more joyful."

After the tribulations of the Cultural Revolution, the intelligentsia was breathing more freely. The distinguished engineering professor Leonid Ramzin and other alleged counterrevolutionaries convicted in the 1930 Industrial Party trial were amnestied.[2] Sergei Prokofiev and the writer Maxim Gorky had returned from emigration to live in the Soviet Union. The militant Communist organizations that had terrorized "bourgeois" artists and writers—RAPM (the Russian Association of Proletarian Musicians) in music, RAPP in literature—had been dissolved, and the oppressive censorship they had imposed had been eased.

[1] See reports of New Year celebrations in *Vecherniaia Moskva*, 23 January 1936, p. 1; *Trud*, 3 January 1936, pp. 1 and 4. An advertisement in Leningrad's *Vecherniaia krasnaia gazeta*, 9 February 1936, p. 4, announced that the dance hall at 8 Vosstaniia Street had reopened for evenings of ballroom and contemporary dance, and *Vecherniaia Moskva*, 20 January 1936, p. 6, announced the coming tour of Weintraub's Syncopators.

[2] *Pravda*, 5 February 1936, p. 1.

A new slogan, "socialist realism," had replaced RAPP's threatening demand for proletarian hegemony in culture. But socialist realism was not a dogmatic orthodoxy and would not be used punitively or for the purposes of exclusion, musicians were assured by the new head of the Moscow Composers' Union.[3] It was intended rather as an umbrella large enough to cover a variety of schools and trends.

Soviet performing artists were winning international competitions, and *Pravda* and other newspapers celebrated their achievements. Theater and opera seemed to be flourishing in the new climate, benefiting from the patronage of a number of leading political figures and the cessation of RAPP's pressure for politically correct repertoire and librettos rewritten in the right revolutionary spirit.

Dmitrii Shostakovich, not yet thirty years old, was one of the rising young stars of Soviet music. True, some of his early work had aroused controversy during RAPM's heyday. His first opera, *The Nose*, which premiered at Leningrad's Malyi Theater in 1930, was harshly treated by RAPM critics,[4] and a ballet, *Bolt*, had been taken out of the repertoire in 1931. All the same, Soviets took pride in his achievements and his growing reputation in the West. Unlike Prokofiev, who had first made his reputation before the Revolution and lived outside Russia during the 1920s, Shostakovich had been trained in the Soviet period at Petrograd Conservatory and shared the revolutionary experiences of his generation and, indeed, many revolutionary values. His Second Symphony was dedicated to the October Revolution and used a text by the proletarian poet A. I. Bezymenskii;[5] his Third Symphony was titled *May Day*. Shostakovich, in short, was regarded as "ours"—a real Soviet composer, and one the West took seriously.

Shostakovich's second opera, *Lady Macbeth of the Mtsensk District*, with a text based on a story by the nineteenth-century realist writer Nikolai Leskov, was begun in 1930 and completed in 1932. In the two years between its completion and its first performance, the musical press praised it to the skies, calling it "the best Soviet work, the chef-d'oeuvre of Soviet creativity."[6] It was anticipated that this would become the first truly Soviet work in the national and interna-

---

[3] N. Cheliapov, "Marksistsko-leninskoe muzykovedenie na novuiu stupen'," *Sovetskaia muzyka*, 1933 no. 4.

[4] See Laurel E. Fay, "The Punch in Shostakovich's Nose," *Russian and Soviet Music: Essays for Boris Schwarz*, ed. Malcolm Hamrick Brown, pp. 229–43 (Ann Arbor, 1984).

[5] In 1927, when the symphony was composed, this choice was likely to be a gesture of commitment rather than the result of coercion.

[6] Comment by the composer Ivan Dzerzhinskii in *Sovetskaia muzyka*, 1936 no. 5, p. 33.

tional repertoires. A poem published in one of the daily newspapers noted that the combined age of three brilliant young opera composers—Shostakovich, Ivan Dzerzhinskii (*The Quiet Don*, after Mikhail Sholokhov's novel), and Valerii Zhelobinskii (*Komarinskii muzhik*)—was a mere eighty years, and concluded complacently that

> There is no other country
> With such a flowering of talents.[7]

Lady Macbeth premiered at the beginning of 1934 with almost simultaneous productions in the two capitals—by the Malyi Opera Theater in Leningrad and (as *Katerina Izmailova*, after the story's heroine) the Nemirovich-Danchenko Musical Theater in Moscow.[8] It was immediately hailed as a major event in Soviet music—"A triumph of musical theater" was the heading in the newspaper *Sovetskoe iskusstvo*, which devoted a whole page to the opera[9]—and the musical press continued to publish analyses and commentaries on it for a whole year after its premiere.

By the end of 1935 the opera had already chalked up ninety-four performances at the Nemirovich-Danchenko Theater and more than eighty by the Malyi Opera in Leningrad.[10] On 26 December 1935 the Bolshoi Theater's Second Company in Moscow launched a new production of the opera under the baton of Melik-Pashaev. A few weeks later, Leningrad's Malyi Opera took its own *Lady Macbeth* production on tour to Moscow, giving the first Moscow performance on 8 January 1936.[11] The Bolshoi production was not widely reviewed in the press, and some recollections of it are unfavorable: the style and idiom of Shostakovich's opera may not have suited the traditionalist Bolshoi troupe.[12] But the tour of Leningrad's Malyi Opera seems to

---

[7] *Vecherniaia Moskva*, 17 January 1936, p. 2, poem by A. Flit.

[8] A. Gozenpud, *Russkii sovetskii opernyi teatr (1917–1941): Ocherk istorii* (Leningrad, 1963), p. 277.

[9] S. M. Khentova, *Shostakovich v Moskve* (Moscow, 1986), p. 79.

[10] Ibid., p. 278.

[11] The occurrence of two separate Moscow premieres of the same opera within a two-week period has caused a great deal of confusion among historians, especially as both took place on the same stage (Bolshoi II) and were staged by the same man (N. V. Smolich). I am very grateful to Laurel E. Fay, an expert on Shostakovich's music, for alerting me to this complexity and supplying copies of the programs of the two productions.

[12] Gozenpud, *Russkii sovetskii opernyi teatr*, p. 291, says the attempt to convert the Leningrad Malyi production into "the magnificent spectacle characteristic of Bolshoi Theater productions of those years" was unsuccessful, and some of the performers "did not overcome the usual operatic clichés." Osap Litovskii (then an official at Glavrepertkom, the theatrical censorship agency) thought it was done "very badly" by

have been a great hit in Moscow. In addition to *Lady Macbeth*, the Malyi's repertoire for the tour included two other operas by young Soviet composers, Ivan Dzerzhinskii's *Quiet Don* and Valerii Zhelobinskii's *Komarinskii muzhik*, as well as a new production of Tchaikovsky's *Queen of Spades*.[13] The Leningraders' premieres in Moscow were triumphant events, with the French ambassador in attendance, along with assorted other "public figures and masters of culture." The opening night of *Lady Macbeth* was reported in Leningrad as a great success, and Moscow's evening paper reviewed it enthusiastically, saying it was even better than the original Leningrad production, though with the same director (Nikolai Smolich) and conductor (Samuil Samosud).[14] Dzerzhinskii's *Quiet Don*, another new opera by a Leningrader having its Moscow premiere, was also very favorably received.

The ultimate accolade for the Leningrad tour came when Stalin and Molotov decided to attend a performance of *The Quiet Don* on 17 January. After the third act, Stalin, Molotov, and other leading political figures, including Andrei Bubnov, Lunacharsky's successor as the head of Narkompros, conversed with the young composer and others associated with the production.[15] It was assumed that the opera's "Soviet" libretto—based on the Sholokhov Civil War novel—was one reason for this great mark of favor.[16] In addition, at least one participant in the discussion—the conductor, Samosud—took it that Stalin was putting his imprimatur on the Leningrad Malyi's efforts to promote a new, specifically Soviet opera:

> I raised the question whether the theater had taken the right course, since our path has not been all that smooth, and it has been a big struggle to get a Soviet opera produced. There was a time when people attacked us a lot for our position on that. Comrade Stalin asked: "Who attacked you?" and answered his own question with a jocular remark:

---

the Bolshoi, "staged extremely naturalistically," so that "the physiologism of the music was only strengthened." Moreover, "the Bolshoi Theater, as if intentionally, made every effort to emphasize and bring to the fore all that was ugly and atonal in the opera" (*Tak i bylo* [Moscow, 1958], p. 236). Litovskii may mean that "intentionally" literally, as he was no fan of the traditionalists at the Bolshoi, and the Bolshoi singers were reported to have complained that the score was too hard to sing and lay awkwardly for the voice.

[13] *Pravda*, back-page advertisements for Bolshoi Theater II, tour of Leningrad Malyi Opera, 6, 13, 15 and 16 January 1936.

[14] *Vecherniaia krasnaia gazeta* (Leningrad), 9 January 1936, p. 2; *Vecherniaia Moskva*, 9 January 1936, p. 3.

[15] The director, Tereshkovich, and the conductor, Samuil Samosud, also took part in the conversation.

[16] "Stalin and Molotov . . . noted the significant political-ideological value of the production of the opera *The Quiet Don*": *Vecherniaia Moskva*, 20 January 1936, p. 1.

"The old folk, I suppose." Then he made a very important comment to the effect that of course the classics of the operatic repertoire are very important, but it's about time we had our own classic operas as well.[17]

A few dissonant notes could be discerned in Stalin's generally positive reaction. Evidently Stalin and Molotov liked Dzerzhinskii's music, which was simple, tuneful, and readily accessible, but did not so much care for the staging and decor, which were more modernist than the music. Among other critical remarks, Stalin "commented unfavorably on constructivist elements in the staging of the opera and expressed a wish for the creation of Soviet classics," which he obviously thought required a more traditional artistic language.[18]

On 26 January, Stalin and Molotov attended a performance of *Lady Macbeth*—not the production of the Leningrad Malyi Opera, which had already left town, but the less successful production of the Bolshoi Theater's Second Company.[19] Shostakovich, who was in Moscow, was told to stand by in case the party leaders wanted to meet him.[20] But he was not in fact summoned into their presence, although Stalin, Molotov, and other party leaders attended the performance as scheduled. Two days later, disaster struck in the form of an editorial in *Pravda* attacking Shostakovich's opera root and branch.

The unsigned editorial in the central party newspaper, reputedly written by Andrei Zhdanov, a Politburo member and close associate of Stalin's, was forthrightly headed "A Mess [*sumbur*] Instead of Music," with the subhead "On the Opera *Lady Macbeth of the Mtsensk District*." This opera, the editorial noted, had been highly praised, but it turned out to be an avant-garde monstrosity—a musical version of "the most negative traits of 'Meyerholdism,' multiplied to the nth degree." Like Meyerhold's theatrical productions and other "leftist" art, Shostakovich's opera constituted an *intentional* repudiation

---

[17] S. Samosud, "Rabotniki Leningradskogo Malogo opernogo teatra o besede s avtorami opernogo spektaklia 'Tikhii Don,'" *Pravda*, 21 January 1936, p. 3. Note that while Samosud's remarks about critics almost certainly referred to RAPM, which had been skeptical of the value of opera as a genre, Stalin evidently took him to be referring the conservative musical establishment ("*stariki*"), which was in favor of classical opera but skeptical of modern Soviet works.

[18] *Kul'turnaia zhizn' v SSSR, 1928–1941: Khronika* (Moscow, 1976), pp. 490–91; *Vecherniaia Moskva*, 20 January 1936, p. 1.

[19] Because of the well-publicized meeting of Stalin and Molotov with Dzerzhinskii, composer of the other new opera presented by the Leningrad Malyi, it is often wrongly assumed that it was the Leningrad production of Shostakovich's opera that the party leaders attended. In fact, the Leningrad Malyi's Moscow tour, which began on 5 January, had ended on 17 January. (Information from Laurel E. Fay.)

[20] Shostakovich to Ivan Sollertinskii, in *Sovetskaia muzyka*, 1987 no. 9, pp. 78–79.

of classical principles, such as "simplicity, realism, comprehensibility of image, and the natural sound of the word."

> From the first moment, listeners are flabbergasted by the intentionally dissonant, confused stream of sounds in the opera. Snatches of melody, embryos of musical phrase, drown, burst forth, once again disappear in the din, the grinding noises, the squeals. It is hard to follow this "music," and to remember it is impossible.

The style was primitive and vulgar, "the crudest naturalism,"

> copying its nervy, convulsive, epileptic music from jazz so as to give "passion" to its heroes. The music shouts, quacks, explodes, pants, and sighs, so as to convey the love scenes in the most naturalistic manner. And "love" is smeared all over the opera in the must vulgar form. The merchant's double bed occupies the central place in the stage design.

Noting that the opera had been well received by bourgeois audiences abroad, *Pravda*'s editorial attributed this success to the fact that, in addition to being absolutely apolitical, it suited "the perverted tastes of the bourgeois audience." It represented a dangerous trend in Soviet music, and indeed in Soviet art as a whole. "Leftist grotesquerie [*urodstvo*] in opera springs from the same source as leftist grotesquerie in painting, poetry, pedagogy, and science"; that is, the urge for novelty and sensation, which "leads to alienation from genuine art, from genuine science, from genuine literature."[21]

To many people, including Shostakovich himself, the denunciation of *Lady Macbeth of the Mtsensk Distrist* seemed to come "like a bolt from the blue."[22] Yet the antimodernist, implicitly anti-Western attitudes expressed in *Pravda*'s editorial were already familiar in Soviet musical life, most notably in connection with the Russian Association of Proletarian Musicians (RAPM), which had exercised oppressive control over Soviet music in the period of the militant Communist Cultural Revolution from 1928 to 1932. No doubt RAPM's abrupt dissolution by order of the Communist Party's Central Committee in 1932[23] had led Shostakovich and others in the artistic

---

[21] *Pravda*, 28 January 1936, p. 3.

[22] Lebedinskii quotes the phrase from N. I. Cheliapov's opening speech at the discussion of the *Pravda* articles on Shostakovich at the Moscow Composers' Union: *Sovetskaia muzyka*, 1936 no. 3, p. 21.

[23] "O perestroike literaturno-khodozhestvennykh organizatsii" (23 April 1932), in *Kommunisticheskaia partiia Sovetskogo Soiuza v rezoliutsiiakh i resheniiakh s"ezdov, konferentsii i plenumov TsK* (Moscow, 1971): 5:44–45.

world to hope that the young Communist leaders of RAPM and its sister organizations had been definitively crushed by the party leadership and that their narrow, censorious meddling would not disturb Soviet cultural life again.

But this hope was clearly overoptimistic. A spirit of puritan vigilantism, directed primarily against Western-influenced "formalism" in art, was deeply embedded in Soviet revolutionary and Communist culture. Although there are intriguing similarities between the Soviet antiformalist campaign inaugurated with the 1936 attack on Shostakovich and the Nazis' almost contemporaneous onslaught on "degenerate" art in Germany,[24] the Soviet rejection of "bourgeois decadence" had its own historical roots and a lifespan that extended over many decades.

The attack on Shostakovich's *Lady Macbeth* must be seen in the context of Soviet "antiformalism," stretching from the RAPM episode at the end of the 1920s to the *zhdanovshchina*—Zhdanov's disciplining of the arts for excessive Western influence and avant-gardism—in the late 1940s. The RAPM episode is the least known of the three, and the only one in which the main impetus for the drive against avant-garde music was clearly *not* coming from the party leadership. This is what makes it particularly relevant to the argument that the repeated attacks on decadent, "bourgeois" modernism in the Soviet Union reflected attitudes that were widely held by Communists and other groups in Soviet society.

The proletarian episode in Soviet music

The Russian Association of Proletarian Musicians, RAPM, was home to the Young Turks of the musical world in the 1920s. Their aim was to politicize the musical world by identifying "bourgeois" and "proletarian" trends and groups in music and promoting "class struggle" between the two.[25] Although the leading RAPMists and RAPPists were Communists, the party leadership gave them little encouragement in their early efforts to upset the cultural establishment, which remained essentially "bourgeois," in the RAPMists' view, despite the Revolution.

Before 1929, RAPM can best be understood as a fringe group of

---

[24] Note, however, that the Soviet campaign has no overt anti-Semitic element.

[25] "It must be understood . . . that struggle between groups of musicians, reflecting the ideology of different social groups, is unavoidable": L. Lebedinskii, speech at a meeting on music held by the agitprop department of the party Central Committee, June 1929, in *Proletarskii muzykant*, 1930 no. 2, p. 5.

aspiring young musicians and music journalists, many of them still students and none with any serious professional reputation, who had the zeal and militancy of revolutionary activists. They were capable of making a considerable uproar in the musical press, and could sometimes intimidate their bourgeois opponents by invoking the name of the party and the Revolution (though, unlike their literary counterparts in RAPP, none of the RAPM leaders seem to have had pull with the party leadership). They had great difficulty even establishing a journal of their own, and complained that for many years they were ignored by the state music publishing house, the state radio, the philharmonics, and other key institutions of musical life.[26] Their main impact in the mid-1920s was in the Leningrad and Moscow Conservatories, where they attacked the professors for trying to teach them such "bourgeois" and "aristocratic" music as Tchaikovsky's, and "preached the pointlessness of professional training, arguing that it spoils original talents and makes them hackneyed."[27]

RAPM was a polemical association above all, defined as much by what it was against as by what it was for. In principle, it was against anything bourgeois in music. In practice, this stance translated into a constant battle on two fronts: with "formalism" (modernism) on the one hand and "light music" on the other.

On the formalist front, RAPM's main target was the Association for Contemporary Music (ASM), an affiliate of the International Society for Contemporary Music (ISCM), in which the critic Boris Asafev (Igor Glebov) and the avant-garde composer Aleksandr Mosolov were prominent. Although musical modernism had its home-grown advocates in Russia inside and outside ASM, it was regarded in the 1920s as an international or Western phenomenon. ASM was proud of its international connections and of the fact the works of Russian composers such as Mosolov—as well as the famous Russian émigrés Igor Stravinsky and Sergei Prokofiev—were performed at ISCM concerts. Such ASM critics as Sollertinskii often chided the Soviet musical world for being insufficiently in touch with the exciting developments in the West. The RAPMists and other opponents considered that the modernists' international orientation was evidence that they were spiritually in bondage to the capitalist West, and thus out of step with the Revolution. To them atonalism was a sign of the decadence of postwar art in the West.

[26] L. Kaltat and D. Rabinovich, "Na dva fronta," *Sovetskaia muzyka*, 1933 no. 2.

[27] B. I. Zagurskii, "Moi konservatorskie gody," in *Leningradskaia konservatoriia v vospominaniiakh* (Leningrad, 1962), pp. 117–18. See also Iu. Elagin, *Ukroshchenie iskusstv* (New York, 1952), pp. 247–50.

RAPM's second main target was "light music" (*legkii zhanr*), a genre that included the whole range of what was later called variety (*estradnaia*) music: "gypsy" music, music hall songs, syncopated dance music ("foxtrot"), and salon romances.[28] To RAPM this sort of thing was the music of the urban petty bourgeoisie and Nepmen, imbued with Philistine petty-bourgeois values and ideologically harmful to the proletariat.[29]

Such attitudes were by no means peculiar to RAPM. Jazz, in particular, was often identified by Soviet writers of the 1920s with the decadent eroticism of the Western bourgeoisie in the last stages of capitalism.[30] This association enabled theater directors such as Meyerhold to enliven their productions of contemporary plays by playing jazz whenever Western capitalist villains appeared onstage, in contrast to the revolutionary marches that accompanied the Soviet proletarian heroes of the dramas.[31] Shostakovich used a similar device in his ballet *Golden Age* when he called upon Vincent Youmans's syncopated "Tea for Two," renamed "Tahiti Trot," to point up the decadence of the capitalist world.[32] But the ploy got him into trouble with RAPM critics, who not unreasonably suspected the motives of composers who made such excursions into jazz idiom.[33]

RAPM's sudden rise to power and visibility in 1928–1929 was part of the broader phenomenon of the Cultural Revolution.[34] The

[28] For a case study of the campaign against the popular song "Kirpichiki" (Little bricks) in the 1920s, see Robert Rothstein, "The Quiet Rehabilitation of the Brick Factory: Early Soviet Popular Music and Its Critics," *Slavic Review* 39, no. 3 (1980): 381–88.

[29] Resolution on light music, published in *Nash muzykal'nyi front: Materialy vserossiiskoi muzykal'noi konferentsii (iiun' 1929 g.)*, ed. S. Korev (Moscow, 1930), pp. 250–52. The linkage of variety music with the private entrepreneurs of NEP ("Nepmen"), in addition to some financial scandals associated with private publishers of popular songs, contributed greatly to the success of RAPM's campaign against the genre.

[30] See, for example, Maxim Gorky's diatribe "O muzyke tolstykh" (1928), in *Gor'kii ob iskusstve: Sbornik statei i otryvkov* (Moscow and Leningrad, 1940), pp. 208–9; and Lunacharsky's more reflective analysis of the sociology of the foxtrot and tango in "Sotsial'nye istoki muzykal'nogo iskusstva" (1929), in A. V. Lunacharskii, *V mire muzyki: Stat'i i rechi*, ed. I. A. Sats, 2d ed. (Moscow, 1971), pp. 374–76.

[31] For example, in Meyerhold's 1924 production of *Trust D. E.*, based on Ilia Ehrenburg's novel about American capitalists and their Soviet antagonists: S. Frederick Starr, *Red and Hot: The Fate of Jazz in the Soviet Union, 1917–1980* (New York, 1983), pp. 50– 52.

[32] See Solomon Volkov, "Dmitri Shostakovich and 'Tea for Two,'" *Musical Quarterly*, April 1978.

[33] Shostakovich felt obliged to write a letter to the RAPM journal explaining that he used the jazz motifs in *Golden Age* purely in a spirit of caricature, without intending to convey any approval of jazz as an artistic genre: *Proletarskii muzykant*, 1930 no. 3 (11), p. 25.

[34] On RAPP's part in this process, see Sheila Fitzpatrick, "Cultural Revolution as

party's leading organs encouraged groups of militant young Communist "proletarians" of the RAPM type to challenge, intimidate, and humiliate their bourgeois elders and competitors in various spheres of culture, and for the first time they got control of key cultural institutions—the literary and theatrical censorship, publishing houses, the specialized press, and so on. In this process RAPM was the junior partner of a much more flamboyant and ambitious proletarian organization, RAPP, which (unlike RAPM) had a large mass membership by 1928 as well as a well-connected and politically savvy leadership. When the party Central Committee's agitation and propaganda department finally threw its weight behind RAPP's demand for "hegemony" in literature and theater, RAPM found itself the beneficiary in music.

RAPM's achievement of a dominant position in the organization of musical life was evident at the national conference on musical affairs called by the newly radicalized Arts Administration of Narkompros in mid-1929.[35] For the next two and a half years, nobody in the musical world could ignore RAPM's militant and interventionist presence. For RAPM, hegemony in music meant, above all, the opportunity to repress and censor musical trends it deemed bourgeois.

One of its first goals was control of the opera repertoire, especially the operas presented by the major houses of Moscow and Leningrad. RAPM was eager to remove ideologically unsuitable works (such as, Tchaikovsky's *Eugene Onegin* and *Queen of Spades* and Wagner's *Parsifal*) from the classical repertoire and prevent productions of new works by contemporary European composers that "directly or indirectly reflect the degenerate tendency of contemporary bourgeois culture, . . . particularly [works by Russian] émigrés or composers affiliated with the Association for Contemporary Music."[36]

RAPM also got control of music publishing, managing to impose a total ban on sheet-music publication of "light" (variety) music and making it very difficult for serious composers who wrote in a modernist idiom (particularly those associated with ASM) to publish their works.[37] Performances and productions of new works by com-

Class War," and Katerina Clark, "Little Heroes and Big Deeds: Literature Responds to the First Five-Year Plan," both in *Cultural Revolution in Russia, 1928–1931,* ed. Fitzpatrick (Bloomington, Ind., 1978).

[35] The proceedings of the conference were published under the title *Nash muzykal'-nyi front* (1930). On the radicalization of the Arts Administration, see Sheila Fitzpatrick, "The Emergence of Glaviskusstvo: Class War on the Cultural Front, Moscow, 1928–29," *Soviet Studies* 23, no. 2 (1971).

[36] *Nash muzykal'nyi front,* pp. 152–53.

[37] *Proletarskii muzykant,* 1930 no. 1 (9), pp. 31–32 (letter of Viktor Belyi et al.); The

posers on RAPM's blacklist—notably Shostakovich—were very harshly reviewed by RAPM critics in the regular and musical press, and sometimes had to close as a result. Shostakovich's first opera, as we have seen, and his ballet *Bolt* were among the casualties.

RAPMists were critical of jazz, particularly in combination with the avant-garde "serious" music with which such European composers as Ernst Křenek, Darius Milhaud, and Kurt Weill were experimenting in the 1920s and early 1930s. They succeeded in closing down the production of Křenek's jazz operetta *Jonny spielt auf* at the Nemirovich-Danchenko Theater in 1929, and then "launched a campaign to ban the saxophone from the Soviet Union."[38]

Like other Communist militant organizations in the arts, RAPM was clearer about what it was against than what it was for. It did have one positive cause, however: the promotion of revolutionary mass songs, generally marches, written by RAPM composers such as Aleksandr Davidenko and Viktor Belyi. When a group of RAPM supporters became influential in Soviet radio programming around 1930, a handful of these songs—Belyi's "Proletarii vsekh stran" (Workers of the world), Davidenko's "Pod'em vagona" (The hoisting of the wagon) and "Nas pobit', pobit' khoteli" (They wanted to beat, to beat us), and Shekhter's "Pesnia frantsuzskogo revoliutsii" (Song of the French Revolution)—began to be broadcast almost daily, sometimes three or four times a day. According to one later report, this practice "called forth the just protests of radio listeners and did not so much propagandize the works of RAPM composers as push listeners away from them."[39]

The endless repetition of Davidenko's "Nas pobit', pobit' khoteli," which celebrated Soviet victory over the Japanese on the Chinese Eastern Railway in 1929, particularly infuriated Shostakovich. In 1931 he parodied the song in his music for a production of *Hamlet* at the Vakhtangov Theater.[40] The memoir edited by Solomon Volkov also reflects, this irritation, together with an accurate general assessment of RAPM's impact on morale in many musical circles:

> Once [RAPM] began to control music, it seemed that Davidenko's "Nas pobit', pobit' khoteli" was going to replace all available music. This worthless song was performed by soloists and choirs, violinists and

---

composer Lev Knipper later remarked that during RAPM's heyday, "I wrote, but put what I wrote in the drawer—because Muzgiz [the State Music Publishing House] wouldn't publish me": *Sovetskaia muzyka*, 1933 no. 3.

[38] Starr, *Red And Hot*, p. 85.
[39] *Sovetskaia muzyka*, 1933 no. 4, p. 66.
[40] Elagin, *Ukroshchenie iskusstv*, p. 40.

pianists, even string quartets did it. . . . You can see there was plenty of reason to despair. It looked as though neither orchestral music nor the opera had any prospects at all. And most musicians were in a terrible mood. One after another, with bowed heads, they joined the ranks of RAPM.[41]

Shostakovich and RAPM

Although Shostakovich portrayed himself as RAPM's chief victim and a sympathetic contemporary described him in the same terms, he in fact had quite a lot in common with RAPM and its young revolutionary iconoclasts.[42] Like the theater director Vsevolod Meyerhold and his fellow composer Lev Knipper, Shostakovich related to the militants of the proletarian organizations more like an intimate sparring partner than a distant antagonist.[43] He evidently shared many of their revolutionary values in the 1920s (though this was something he and most other people conveniently forgot in later life); and they in turn shared much of his ambivalent fascination with light music and jazz (for all that they denounced it) and even with the modernism of the international contemporary music movement.

As Lev Knipper pointed out in the 1936 discussions of *Lady Macbeth*, Western modernism inevitably had an influence on a composer who came of age in Leningrad during the 1920s, when such works as Stravinsky's *Petrushka* and *Pulcinella*, Alban Berg's *Wozzek*, Křenek's *Jonny spielt auf* and *Der Sprung über den Schatten*, and Franz Schreker's *Der ferne Klang* were premiered to great excitement in the musical world, Paul Hindemith visited, and so on.[44] Shostakovich was affected by the furor, of course; and though he was never an

[41] Dmitri Shostakovich, *Testimony: The Memoirs of Dmitri Shostakovich*, as related to and edited by Solomon Volkov, trans. Antonina W. Bouis (New York, 1980), p. 112. There has been much dispute about the exact provenance of this work and its status as a memoir. But whether the book was written by Shostakovich, by Shostakovich and Volkov, or by Volkov alone on the basis of his conversations with Shostakovich, it provides a vivid and useful commentary on Shostakovich's life and times from a perspective that is often recognizably and always plausibly Shostakovich's. I have therefore used it here, though relatively sparingly and with the caution appropriate to all memoir and quasi-memoir sources.

[42] Ibid.; Knipper, in *Sovetskaia muzyka*, 1936 no. 3, p. 24.

[43] RAPM critics mocked Knipper for his opera *North Wind*, yet it was based on a play by the RAPP leader Vladimir Kirshon, and Knipper said (after his fall from grace) that he "agreed with RAPM on many things," but RAPMists rebuffed his overtures (*Sovetskaia muzyka*, 1933 no. 3). As for Meyerhold, the "proletarians" sometimes criticized him, along with Mayakovsky, as a leftist, but in other circumstances defended him vigorously as a revolutionary. For a case study, see Fitzpatrick, "Emergence of Glaviskusstvo," pp. 246–50.

[44] *Sovetskaia muzyka*, 1936 no. 3, p. 24.

ASM member or even a close associate, his work had clear stylistic affiliations with Western contemporary music, particularly the Germans. But the leading RAPMists—young composers such as Marian Koval, Boris Shekhter, and Viktor Belyi—had been exposed to the same influences and had also, in their time, come under the influence of avant-garde Western culture.[45]

"RAPM regarded Shostakovich as a 'fellow traveler,' talented but reluctant to subordinate himself to the genre regulations," writes a Soviet musicologist. "More than once the association tried to direct his themes and style, alternating praise with abuse. He returned the compliment, mocking the limitations of the dogmatists."[46]

To be sure, relations between Shostakovich and RAPM deteriorated sharply during the period of RAPM's "hegemony," especially in connection with RAPM's attacks on *Bolt* and *The Nose*. "At that time [1931–1932] I was going through a serious [professional and personal] crisis," we read in the Shostakovich memoir. "I was in terrible shape. Everything was collapsing and crumbling. I was eaten up inside. . . . I was being pulled in all directions. I was being bothered." To lessen his vulnerability to RAPM's attacks, "I protected myself by working at TRAM [the Theater of Worker Youth in Leningrad]."[47]

Whether out of conviction or expediency, Shostakovich was vociferous in his opposition to light music (except when it was used, as in some of his works, in a spirit of parody). When the RAPM journal *Proletarskii muzykant* polled various prominent people in the music world on its campaign to ban the publication of light music, no response was so stern and irreconcilable as Shostakovich's: he was the only respondent to refer to the work of composers who wrote such music as "wrecking activity," and the only one to specify and endorse practical punitive measures: an absolute ban on the publication and performance of light music and the expulsion of its composers from authors' societies (in effect preventing them from collecting royalties on their work). For good measure, Shostakovich added the warning: "Be on guard against gypsy and foxtrot music under disguise—they will put a '100% ideologically reliable' text to a gypsy romance."[48]

When RAPM was dissolved by order of the party Central Commit-

---

[45] Kaltat and Rabinovich, "Na dva fronta."
[46] *Aleksandr Davidenko: Vospominaniia, Stat'i, Materialy* (Leningrad, 1968), p. 16 (editor's introduction).
[47] Shostakovich, *Testimony*, pp. 85–86, 112.
[48] *Proletarskii muzykant*, 1930 no. 3 (11), p. 25.

tee in April 1932, many musicians openly rejoiced.[49] But Shostakovich was not one of them: he was too much a radical iconoclast himself to want to see the old, conservative, bourgeois musical establishment triumph. At a meeting in 1933 to celebrate the first anniversary of the Central Committee's resolution, he sarcastically recalled the behavior of old-guard conservatives of the music world who "met each other with joyful embraces [after the publication of the resolution], like philistines of the city of Glupov receiving the news of the fall of a city boss,[50] and said: 'Now we'll show them!'" Using a very RAPM-like turn of phrase, Shostakovich warned that "the class war continues in the country, and it also continues in musical art."[51]

The antiformalism campaign

The decision to dissolve the proletarian cultural organizations was quickly followed by the creation of new umbrella professional unions, the Union of Soviet Composers and the Union of Soviet Writers, which were intended to be more accommodating to artistic pluralism than the old proletarian associations and their modernist competitors such as ASM.[52] The Writers' Union was established in a blaze of publicity under Maxim Gorky's leadership and Politburo supervision, with the new slogan "socialist realism." The Composers' Union came into existence obscurely around 1933, under the leadership of a little-known Communist lawyer,[53] and on the evidence of its first few years it proved capable of accommodating traditionalists, former proletarians, and even (especially in its Leningrad branch, to which Shostakovich belonged) modernists.

Although the Central Committee had dissolved the proletarian artistic organizations, proletarian attitudes were far from alien to the

[49] "O perestroike literaturno-khudozhestvennykh organizatsii" (23 April 1932), in *Kommunisticheskaia partiia Sovetskogo Soiuza v rezoliutsiiakh s"ezdov, konferentsii i plenumov TsK* (Moscow, 1971), 5:44–45.

[50] Glupov is the subject of Saltykov-Shchedrin's nineteenth-century satire on provincial life, *Istoriia odnogo goroda* (The history of one town).

[51] Report in *Rabochii i teatr*, 1933 no. 11, p. 10, cited in *Aleksandr Davidenko*, p. 19.

[52] The proletarian writers' association, RAPP, was the real target of the party leader's dissatisfaction, partly because of its hostility to the distinguished writer Maxim Gorky, whose return from quasi-emigration the Soviet government was in process of negotiating, and partly because the RAPP leaders had been playing high politics and in general behaving obstreperously. See S. Sheshukov, *Neistovye revniteli: Iz istorii literaturnoi bor'by 20–kh godov* (Moscow, 1970).

[53] On Nikolai Ivanovich Cheliapov and his work in the Composers' Union from 1933 to 1937 (when he disappeared in the Great Purges), see M. Grinberg, "V puti," *Sovetskaia muzyka*, 1966 no. 12, pp. 5–6.

party leaders. The belief that modernism was decadent and that artistic decadence was a product of the last stages of capitalism was shared by most Soviet Communists, including the party leaders and the proletarians in RAPM and RAPP, and constituted an important aspect of Soviet political culture. But the proletarian organizations parted company with the party leaders when they vigorously opposed *all* bourgeois culture, both modernist and traditional. It became clear in the 1930s, when the party leadership for the first time formulated a distinct policy on questions of artistic style, that to the party leaders, the nineteenth-century classics (and their twentieth-century descendants) that RAPM dismissed as "bourgeois" and "aristocratic" were the quintessence of real culture.

The sociologist Nicholas Timasheff discerned signs of a "great retreat" from revolutionary values in the cultural and social policy of the 1930s.[54] The retreat was exemplified by the return to the classics in literature, the reevaluation of the Russian national heritage and history, and the repudiation of progressive methods in education. A similar return to traditional values could be observed in the sphere of morals, sex, and family life, most notably with the outlawing of abortion in 1936. Of particular relevance to the *Lady Macbeth* affair, perhaps, was the new, tougher line against pornography introduced in 1935.[55] This new puritanism was frequently justified by reference to the decadence of the capitalist West, in contrast to the healthy, life-affirming values natural to a socialist society.

The *Lady Macbeth* affair and the broader antiformalist campaign of 1936 were surely related to Timasheff's "great retreat" syndrome. But other, more specific factors can also be cited to explain this dramatic intervention of the party leadership in cultural matters. Some of the old leaders associated with policies of cultural restraint—such men as A. V. Lunacharsky and A. S. Enukidze—were gone.[56] The general political climate had deteriorated markedly in the aftermath of Sergei Kirov's murder at the end of 1934, and a particular shadow had fallen over Leningrad, the site of the murder. (It was probably not

[54] See Nicholas S. Timasheff, *The Great Retreat: The Growth and Decline of Communism in Russia* (New York, 1946).

[55] This law of 17 October 1935 made the authors and artists of works deemed pornographic, as well as their manufacturers and distributors, liable to a minimum term of five years' imprisonment: *Sovetskaia iustitsiia*, 1936 no. 2, p. 23.

[56] Lunacharsky, who headed the People's Commissariat (Ministry) of Enlightenment for the first twelve years of Soviet power, had died at the beginning of 1934. Enukidze, the long-time secretary of the All-Union Central Executive Committee (TsIK), who was known as a connoisseur of the arts and patron and protector of the theatrical world, was first removed from his job and then expelled from the Communist Party and its Central Committee "for political and moral degeneration" in 1935. See *Za industrializatsiiu*, 8 June 1935, p. 2.

accidental that Shostakovich, the first victim of the antiformalist campaign of 1936, was a Leningrader, or that Zhdanov, one of the initiators of the campaign, was head of the Leningrad party organization as well as the Politburo's point man on culture.) At the beginning of 1936, just before the *Lady Macbeth* affair, a new All-Union Committee for the Arts was established under the leadership of an Old Bolshevik, Platon Kerzhentsev, who had a long association with the militant proletarian approach to culture.[57]

The *Pravda* editorial of 28 January on *Lady Macbeth* was the first of a series of signals that announced the new antiformalist campaign. The "formalist" label was applied to art that was stylized, modernist, and pessimistic, and took its inspiration from the West. The antithesis of formalism—that is, the art that *Pravda* endorsed and sought to encourage—was realistic, traditional, and optimistic, and took its inspiration from folk art.

Within ten days of the editorial on *Lady Macbeth*, *Pravda* came out with a second attack on a Shostakovich work, this time his ballet *Limpid Stream*, staged by the Bolshoi Theater.[58] *Limpid Stream* was a collective-farm ballet celebrating the bringing in of the harvest at a kolkhoz in the Kuban, in the fertile south of Russia. According to the anonymous *Pravda* reviewer, however, the ballet failed utterly to give a real picture of kolkhoz life. It was artificial; its characters were puppet-like. The music was not so offensive as that of *Lady Macbeth*, but there was nothing specifically regional or rural about it: apparently it never occurred to Shostakovich or his librettist to investigate the folk culture of the area. "The composer is as contemptuous toward the folk songs of the Kuban as the librettists and the directors are toward folk dances. As a result, the music has no character; it jingles along but expresses nothing." Shostakovich lifted some of the music from his earlier "industrial" ballet, *Bolt*, the reviewer noted, so it was scarcely surprising that it did not fit the kolkhoz theme.

A week later, *Pravda* published a sharp critique of the film *Prometheus*, directed by I. P. Kavaleridze for Ukrainian State Film. In this case, the criticism was both artistic and historical. The main artistic criticism—very similar to that of Shostakovich's *Limpid Stream*—was that the characters in the film were "wooden invented figures, masks, and not living people"—that is, it was a formalist

---

[57] For the government resolution of 17 January 1936 establishing the new committee, see *Sobranie zakonov SSSR*, 1936 no. 5, art. 40. For Kerzhentsev's appointment, see ibid., 1936, pt. II, no. 2, art. 21. On Kerzhentsev's background in "proletarian" cultural movements during the Civil War and Cultural Revolution, see Sheila Fitzpatrick, *The Commissariat of Enlightenment* (New York, 1971), pp. 146–47, 158–59, and "Emergence of Glaviskusstvo," pp. 250–51.

[58] "Baletnaia fal'sh'," *Pravda*, 6 February 1936, p. 3.

production. The critic objected to the great amount of naturalistic detail (blood, gruesome deaths, and so on), and found the music "naturalistic" and too noisy, successful only in those rare scenes where it used snatches of folk tunes.[59]

On 1 March Pravda extended the campaign to the visual arts with an article headed "Artist-daubers," attacking formalist, nonrealist illustrations of children's books by such artists as V. V. Lebedev.[60]

The criticism was summed up early in April when *Pravda* published for the first time Maxim Gorky's article "On Formalism," written the previous year. Gorky argued that "formalism as a 'manner,' as a 'literary technique,' most often serves to cover up emptiness or poverty of the soul." As anyone can see by comparing such formalists as Marcel Proust and James Joyce with Shakespeare, Pushkin, and Tolstoy, straightforward realism and simplicity are best, and "unnecessary ornamentation and elaboration" only diminishes the impact of a work. Healthy people have a "biological need" for harmonious forms; they "love melodically organized sounds and bright colors"; they want art to make their life happier and more beautiful, not complex and depressing.[61]

Discussion of the *Pravda* editorial

Pravda's editorial on *Lady Macbeth* was addressed to a broader public than musicians. It was one of those policy pronouncements from which practitioners in *all* fields of culture and scholarship were meant to draw conclusions for their own future activity, as Kerzhentsev (head of the new Committee on the Arts) made clear at a meeting of leading cultural figures, specially summoned to consider the implications of the *Pravda* editorial, on 14 March. The articles

[59] *Pravda*, 13 February 1936, p. 4. The film dealt with the fight of Shamil and the Caucasus mountain people against Russian imperialism, and the reviewer objected in particular to the implication that the resistance depended on British money rather than the mountaineers' own heroic efforts.

[60] *Pravda*, 1 March 1936, p. 3. Vladimir Vasilevich Lebedev (1891–1967), former suprematist, well known for his cubist-influenced posters in the 1920s, illustrated several of Marshak's books for children in the late 1920s and 1930s: *Sovetskii reklamnyi plakat* (Moscow, 1972), pp. 121–22. Andrei Andreev, the Central Committee secretary, had made some of the same points as the *Pravda* critic when he spoke to the First All-Union Meeting on Children's Literature, called by the Komsomol on 19 January: *Pravda*, 29 January 1936, p. 3.

[61] *Pravda*, 9 April 1936, p. 2. The article was evidently written around August 1935 as a summary comment on the discussion of formalism that had been running in the press in recent weeks, and was one of the ailing writer's last publications (he died in June 1936). See the editorial note in M. Gor'kii, *O literature: Literaturno-kriticheskie stat'i* (Moscow, 1953).

on Shostakovich, he emphasized, "apply to all fields of art without exception."[62] In practical terms, the message was that meetings should be held in each field to determine how—and above all to whom—the new policy should be applied. The assumption was that formalists in all artistic fields should be named, criticized, and made to change their ways.

The general policy directive to be extracted from the *Pravda* editorial was against "formalism" (Western-influenced modernism) and "naturalism" (vulgarity, pornography, tastelessness) in art. The term "Meyerholdism" (*meierkhol'dovshchina*) was sometimes used to express this particular combination; and indeed Vsevolod Meyerhold, the famous theater director who had close professional and personal relations with the much younger Shostakovich, was in some respects probably the hidden target in the *Lady Macbeth* affair. Since shortly after the October Revolution, the gifted and flamboyant Meyerhold had epitomized the combination of left art and revolutionary politics. Often at the center of controversies and scandals, Meyerhold also enjoyed an enviable international reputation as a theatrical innovator. Within the Soviet Union, he counted many members of the party elite as his patrons, protectors, and social acquaintances.

Although Meyerhold's radical revision of Tchaikovsky's opera *The Queen of Spades* was one of the Smolich/Samosud productions that the Leningrad Malyi Theater brought to Moscow along with *Lady Macbeth* and *The Quiet Don*, Meyerhold was not attacked by name in any of the *Pravda* articles, with the exception of the guarded but telling phrase in "A Mess Instead of Music" describing *Lady Macbeth* as a musical version of "the most negative traits of 'Meyerholdism,'" multiplied to the nth degree." But *The Queen of Spades* was dropped from the repertoire along with *Lady Macbeth*, despite its earlier success with public and critics; and Kerzhentsev singled out Meyerhold as the "big boss [*vozhd'*] of formalism" in his speech at the Committee on the Arts on 14 March (which was not reported in the press).[63]

Neither Meyerhold nor Shostakovich, however, was present at the Moscow meeting of 14 March when Kerzhentsev spoke. Both were in Leningrad, attending one of a series of meetings on the *Pravda* editorial.[64] This was the occasion when Meyerhold delivered the speech that became famous as "Meyerhold against Meyerholdism," in which

---

[62] Reported in Iu. Elagin, *Temnyi genii (Vsevolod Meierkhol'd)* (New York, 1955), p. 363. Elagin, then active in Moscow theatrical and musical circles, says he was present at the meeting.

[63] Ibid., p. 365.

[64] *Vecherniaia krasnaia gazeta*, 7 February 1936, p. 2, reported that several meetings of Leningrad writers and literary and theater critics had already been held to discuss the *Pravda* editorial.

he made some general criticisms of formalism but praised Shostakovich—an act of daring that first stunned the hall and then provoked an outburst of applause. All eyes turned toward the composer, who sat sweating in the audience, nervously wiping his forehead with a handkerchief.[65]

On 23 March Meyerhold was once again at center stage in the anti-formalist campaign. He was the main target of attack at a meeting on the formalist heresy addressed not only by Kerzhentsev but also by Aleksei Angarov, deputy head of the cultural department of the Central Committee. Reportedly Meyerhold essentially repeated his Leningrad speech, despite pressure to recant his sins more seriously and thoroughly and to join in the attack on Shostakovich.[66]

The national daily press gave little if any coverage to Meyerhold's defiance, or to similar outbursts in other arts (if any took place). But it dutifully reported that meetings on the *Lady Macbeth* editorial had been held by filmmakers in February and March and by artists of the variety stage (*estrada*) in April.[67]

The literary world was a little slow to react seriously to the new signal, perhaps hoping that its impact could be confined to arts connected with the stage. The question was not on the agenda of a plenary meeting of the Union of Soviet Writers in Minsk in mid-February; it was raised only when a delegation from the Bolshoi Theater showed up unexpectedly and one member made an unscheduled statement about the importance of the *Pravda* articles, noting Stalin's personal involvement (that is, his backstage conversation with the leaders of the Malyi Theater after the Dzerzhinskii performance) and the recent establishment of the All-Union Committee on the Arts.[68]

It was not until 5 March that *Literaturnaia gazeta* first mentioned the *Pravda* articles, and on 10 March it reported an extraordinary meeting of writers held in Moscow to consider "questions of the struggle with formalism, leftist eccentricities, and naturalism in literature."[69] Despite the writers' initial reluctance, formalist scapegoats were found in this field also, including the poet Boris Pasternak, the literary critic Viktor Shklovskii, and the novelist Boris Pilniak.[70]

In the music world, discussions of the *Pravda* editorial began

---

[65] Khentova, *Shostakovich v Moskve*, pp. 61–63.
[66] Elagin, *Temnyi genii*, p. 367.
[67] *Kul'turnaia zhizn'*, pp. 498, 506.
[68] See *Pravda*'s report from Minsk on the plenum, 14 February 1936, p. 3.
[69] *Literaturnaia gazeta*, 1936 no. 14 (5 March), p. 1, and no. 15 (10 March), p. 1.
[70] Other prominent victims were Semen Kirsanov and Kornelii Zelinskii: see *Literaturnaia gazeta*, 1936 nos. 16 (15 March), pp. 1 and 3, and 17 (20 March), p. 1. It may be noted that Shklovskii (unlike the others) could accurately be called at least a former formalist, since he had belonged to the (self-described) formalist school of literary criticism in the 1920s.

early—on 5 February in Leningrad and 10 February in Moscow—
and the Composers' Union journal carried extensive reports of the
discussions in its March and April issues.[71] Even before the discussions got under way, however, "organizational conclusions" were being drawn by theater and concert-hall managers and performers: you
didn't have to be a Kremlinologist to see that association with Shostakovich was bad news. The Leningrad Malyi Opera Theater canceled a performance of *Lady Macbeth* scheduled for 13 February and
replaced it with *Carmen*. A pianist removed Shostakovich's concerto
from the program of his forthcoming concert. A musicologist who
had been specializing in the study of Shostakovich's opera and had
earlier published a long and favorable review of the *Lady Macbeth*
score hastened to request reassignment from the treacherous waters
of Shostakovich to Dzerzhinskii's *Quiet Don*.[72]

Musicians in Leningrad, who were more closely in touch with
Western modernism than the Muscovites and also felt a special local
pride in Shostakovich, reacted badly to the *Pravda* editorial. The
first discussion (at a regularly scheduled meeting of the music critics'
section of the Leningrad Composers' Union) was a fiasco. Critics associated with the cause of contemporary music, such as Ivan Sollertinskii and A. S. Rabinovich, argued with "the helpless rapporteur"
(one G. Orlov) and defended Shostakovich and *Lady Macbeth*.[73] Rabinovich openly disagreed with the *Pravda* article and said defiantly
"that he will remain a militant formalist . . . because he is a small
man, not ambitious, for whom 'a crust of bread' is sufficient."[74] At a
meeting of the youth section of the Leningrad Composers' Union, a
young composer named Pustylnik directly criticized the *Pravda* article, saying it reminded him of the stone-throwing practiced against
composers by RAPM in the past. Other speakers called the article
"harsh" and "tendentious."[75]

Such defiance was much admired, at least in some circles. Sollertinskii was still sticking to his modernist guns at the plenary meeting
of Leningrad composers at the end of March, and his disciples "put

[71] *Sovetskaia muzyka*, 1936 nos. 3 and 4. See the reports of the meetings of members
of the Leningrad branch of the Composers' Union on 5 and 7 February in *Vecherniaia
krasnaia gazeta* (Leningrad), 7 February 1936, p. 2, and *Pravda*, 10 February 1936, p.
5; and of meetings on 10, 13, and 15 February in *Vecherniaia Moskva*, 11 February
1936, p. 1; 14 February 1936, p. 3; 16 February 1936, p. 2.
[72] *Vecherniaia krasnaia gazeta*, 7 February 1936, p. 4; *Sovetskaia muzyka*, 1936 no.
3, p. 37.
[73] *Vecherniaia krasnaia gazeta*, 7 February 1936, p. 2.
[74] According to a speech by V. Iokhelson, head of the Leningrad branch of the
Leningrad Composers' Union, during discussions in late February or early March:
Sovetskaia muzyka, 1936 no. 4, p. 10.
[75] *Vecherniaia krasnaia gazeta*, 16 February 1936, p. 2.

him on a pedestal because of his alleged 'consistency and principled stand' in the discussions"; and even Dzerzhinskii, composer of the tuneful *Quiet Don*, praised him for not recanting.[76] Although the Leningrad branch of the Composers' Union was in fact divided about contemporary music and had had sharp disagreements on this issue in the past, its leaders were collectively on the defensive after the *Pravda* article, and felt obliged to rebut accusations that they had been asleep at the wheel and failed to recognize the formalist danger.[77]

In Moscow the discussion took a somewhat different course. There former RAPM leaders such as Belyi were quick to take up a cause that was close to their hearts. They took a prominent part in the criticism of formalism, and charged that Shostakovich had been led astray by his admiration for "the decadent music of the contemporary bourgeois West" and his love of the grotesque.[78]

The RAPM group took the *Pravda* articles as an encouraging sign that the policies of the past few years had been reversed and that RAPM—or at least the RAPM program—had an opportunity to make a comeback. *Pravda*'s editorial was "like a searchlight shining into the formalist fog," the former RAPMist L. N. Lebedinskii said gratefully. It was now clear that Shostakovich did not belong to the mainstream of socialist realism, Lebedinskii argued. The mainstream composer was Dzerzhinskii—and surely his simple, tuneful work was squarely in the fine tradition of the late Davidenko, composer of songs for the masses (and, incidentally, former leader of RAPM). Indeed, but for the pernicious influence of the formalists, Lebedinskii remarked, Davidenko's music would never have been slighted and forgotten.[79]

The critic Boris Shteinpress, also a former RAPMist, went so far as to claim that *Pravda* (and by implication the party leadership) had gone over to the RAPM's side. But this remark provoked such an uproar that he was unable to finish his speech.[80] His view was also firmly repudiated by *Pravda* a few days later, when it rebuked Shteinpress and criticized Lebedinskii for trying to substitute a new cult of Davidenko for the old cult of Shostakovich.[81]

The Moscow discussions also disclosed considerable envy and re-

[76] *Kul'turnaia zhizn'*, pp. 502, 11; *Sovetskaia muzyka*, 1936 no. 5, p. 33.

[77] See *Sovetskaia muzyka*, 1936 no. 4, pp. 6–7, for details of these disagreements, and statement by V. Iokhelson in *Sovetskaia muzyka*, 1936 no. 4, pp. 6–7.

[78] *Pravda*, 17 February 1936, p. 3.

[79] *Sovetskaia muzyka*, 1936 no. 4, pp. 21–22. Davidenko died prematurely in 1934. For a similar statement of advocacy for RAPM by Viktor Belyi, see ibid., no. 3, pp. 30–34.

[80] Ibid., no. 4, p. 35.

[81] *Pravda*, 17 February 1936, p. 3.

sentment of the praise heaped on Shostakovich over the past few years. The whole younger generation felt obliged to become "little Shostakoviches," one composer complained.[82] A student at the Moscow Conservatory—probably the young Vano Muradeli, who was to find himself at the center of a similar row twelve years later—said that those who disliked modernism had been intimidated by Shostakovich's great prestige and afraid to criticize it.[83] Tikhon Khrennikov (future head of the Composers' Union) and other speakers in the Moscow discussions were particularly bitter about earlier comments that Shostakovich was virtually the sole exception to the general "provincialism" of Soviet music, the only home-grown composer whose work had won real acceptance in the West.[84] The accusation of provincialism was particularly resented in Moscow because it was associated with Leningrad's claim to cultural superiority and greater sophistication.[85]

Yet despite these partial signs of positive response to *Pravda*'s signal and the absence of any outright defense of Shostakovich in the Moscow discussions, the Moscow composers' and critics' reaction was still relatively lukewarm. The head of the Composers' Union, Nikolai Cheliapov, sounded no more than dutiful in his criticism of Shostakovich.[86] Formalist music critics in Moscow who might have been expected to engage in public self-criticism failed to do so.[87]

Several major figures on the Moscow musical scene either failed to show up at the meetings or failed to speak. Prokofiev, who had just resettled permanently in the USSR and was no less vulnerable than Shostakovich to charges of Westernism and modernism, had the

[82] *Sovetskaia muzyka*, 1936 no. 3, p. 21.

[83] *Pravda*, 17 February 1936, p. 3. Muradeli's opera *Velikaia druzhba* (The great friendship) provided the occasion for Zhdanov's attacks on Soviet music in 1948. For his comments in the *Lady Macbeth* discussions, see *Sovetskaia muzyka*, 1936 no. 3, pp. 52–53.

[84] See reports of Khrennikov's speech in *Pravda*, 17 February 1936, p. 3, and *Sovetskaia muzyka*, 1936 no. 3, p. 45. The comments were attributed particularly to Prokofiev and Ivan Sollertinskii.

[85] The composer Lev Knipper recalled with irritation that Sollertinskii and other trend-setting Leningraders had "shouted that Miaskovsky and 'Miaskovskyism' were the basis of the vile provincialism that reigned in Moscow": *Sovetskaia muzyka*, 1936 no. 3, p. 24.

[86] *Sovetskaia muzyka*, 1936 no. 3, pp. 8, 16–19. Note that at the time of his appointment to the Composers' Union in 1933, Cheliapov had objected to the notion that the slogan "socialist realism" should be used to distinguish "pure" and "impure" composers (ibid., 1933 no. 4, editorial). He seems to have had a personal commitment to cultural tolerance and to have disliked punitive political labeling, so the new militant line against formalism was likely to sit poorly with him.

[87] Ibid., p. 6; *Pravda*, 17 February 1936, p. 3. The critics named by *Pravda* were Markov, of the journal *Sovetskoe iskusstvo*, and Osip Beskin, of the daily *Vecherniaia Moskva*.

good fortune to be out of the country on tour when the *Lady Macbeth* scandal broke.[88] His old friend Nikolai Miaskovsky, the distinguished and honorable Moscow composer whose work was not particularly formalist, stayed away from the discussions anyway. The modernist composer Vissarion Shebalin reportedly put in an appearance at the first meeting, promised to speak later, and never came back.[89]

For a life-affirming, classical art

One aspect of the 1936 antiformalist line clearly had resonance among musicians, not to mention the concertgoing public: Stalin's call for new Soviet classics after the *Quiet Don* performance. The term "Soviet classics" could mean various things. In the first place, it suggested works that grew out of the classical tradition in music. The basic models were the great Russian composers of the nineteenth century (Rimsky-Korsakov, Tchaikovsky, Borodin, Mussorgsky), plus Beethoven.[90] For many musical traditionalists, this was undoubtedly a cheering message, all the more welcome after the dismissive attitude toward the classics shown by RAPM and earlier revolutionary setters of the musical agenda.

In the second place, "Soviet classics" signified music that was "life-affirming"—full of high seriousness and celebration of life's beauty. This idea was most often articulated by Maxim Gorky and by Romain Rolland, the French writer and Soviet fellow traveler of the 1930s, but it was by no means theirs alone. Many people in the music world were completely apolitical on most levels, but nevertheless felt that Soviet composers ought to be writing music along the lines of Beethoven's Ninth Symphony and its "Ode to Joy" rather than Shostakovich's *Lady Macbeth*.[91]

Most musicians were probably upset and dismayed by *Pravda's* and Stalin's intervention in musical life, yet the message that Soviet music needed more high seriousness and uplifting harmony and less modernist flippancy and dissonance was in a completely different

---

[88] Harlow Robinson, *Sergei Prokofiev: A Biography* (New York, 1987), pp. 309–10, 317.

[89] *Sovetskaia muzyka*, 1936 no. 3, pp. 58–59.

[90] See Cheliapov's comments in the Moscow discussions and Iokhelson's in Leningrad: *Sovetskaia muzyka*, 1936 no. 3, p. 19, and no. 4, pp. 13–14. Iokhelson added Bach to the list. Cheliapov specifically rejected Sollertinskii's suggestion that Gustav Mahler be regarded as one of the classical wellsprings of Soviet music.

[91] Beethoven's Ninth had a special place in Soviet mythology of the 1920s and 1930s, as it did in Nazi Germany. Tengiz Abuladze used the "Ode to Joy" as a trope for Stalinism in his film *Repentance*.

category from RAPM's message of the early 1930s that it needed more "mass songs" in 4/4 time with foursquare revolutionary lyrics. The 1936 message made sense to virtually all performers and many composers, though it was less popular with music critics (whose prominent place in the Composers' Union, however, was probably resented by other musicians). The RAPM message had offended performers, composers, and most critics alike; in practical terms, it offered little to anybody except bandleaders and the most amateur choral groups.

Genrikh Neigauz, the pianist and friend of Pasternak who was director of the Moscow Conservatory, was the most articulate spokesman for the new classicism. Neigauz hailed the *Pravda* article on *Lady Macbeth*, though he emphasized that the criticism should be taken to heart by everyone, not just Shostakovich, who was a gifted composer with a bright future. Despite this encomium, however, Neigauz admitted that he had found *Lady Macbeth* so boring that he left after the second act.[92]

Neigauz, influenced by Gorky's and Romain Rolland's concept that the Revolution deserved an art of high seriousness, something beyond even Beethoven's Ninth Symphony, deplored Shostakovich's "skepticism, . . . even cynicism." "Cynicism in music in impermissible," he said.[93] In an emotional speech, "imbued with deep and genuine feeling," Neigauz

> called the *Pravda* articles a joyous event. . . . "We are going to the Himalayas of art," said Professor Neigauz. "How petty, insignificant seem those feelings and passions that are depicted in music like *Lady Macbeth*. That music is crude and cynical. Its eccentricities astonish us the first time, but then—and very quickly—they simply become boring.[94]

Neigauz's commitment to high seriousness in music had led him at the beginning of the 1930s to approve RAPM's proposed ban on the publication of light music because "the light genre in music . . . [is], in the overwhelming majority of cases, the same thing as pornography." He was not the only classical musician who felt that way: the Beethoven specialist B. S. Psibyshevskii compared light music to pornography and alcohol.[95]

To the *New York Sun*, Shostakovich's *Lady Macbeth* was also a

[92] *Sovetskaia muzyka*, 1936 no. 3, p. 16.
[93] Ibid., p. 27.
[94] *Pravda*, 17 February 1936, p. 3.
[95] *Proletarskii muzykant*, 1930 no. 3 (11), pp. 22, 24.

pornographic work.[96] The *Pravda* editorial, arguing along similar lines, condemned it for vulgarity and "the crudest naturalism"; the explicitness of the bedroom scene and its musical accompaniment caused particular distress. The journalist Alexander Werth quoted Khrennikov, a dozen years later, recalling the sexual content of Shostakovich's *Lady Macbeth* with disgust: it was "even more naturalistic, even more horrible" than Wagner's *Tristan*, he said.[97]

The sense that formalist art was *morally* unacceptable had broad currency in the Soviet Union, as it did elsewhere in the world in the interwar period. Around the same time as the *Lady Macbeth* scandal, the most notorious Russian avant-garde composer of the 1920s, Aleksandr Mosolov, was expelled from the Composers' Union for drunken brawling, and *Pravda* commented darkly that his "moral disintegration . . . was no accident."[98] According to the emerging norms of the Stalin era, formalist art denied natural beauty and harmony; classical and socialist art affirmed them.

The aftermath of the *Lady Macbeth* affair

Reading the annals of the *Lady Macbeth* scandal, one might guess that the affair was to destroy Shostakovich's reputation permanently, totally discredit Western modernism, devastate jazz and all light music, and impose a rigid socialist-realist orthodoxy in which caricature and parody were forbidden and high seriousness was de rigueur. In fact, some of these things happened and others did not. Even in Stalin's Russia, policy instructions should never be confused with outcomes.

The biggest casualty was contact with the West, especially with the international contemporary music movement. Contemporary Western music was no longer performed in public in the Soviet Union, and Soviet composers could no longer write in a contemporary idiom if they wanted their works to be published and performed. Soviet musicians' contact with Western counterparts dropped to a minimal level. With the exception (for a few years) of Prokofiev, only performers traveled to foreign countries, and then mainly to play in competitions. Soviet music entered a period of isolation from the West.

Shostakovich was a casualty, but only to some degree and for a

[96] William Henderson, quoted in Boris Schwarz, *Music and Musical Life in Soviet Russia*, rev. ed. (Bloomington, Ind., 1983), pp. 120–21.

[97] Alexander Werth, *Musical Uproar in Moscow* (London, 1949), pp. 90–91.

[98] *Pravda*, 17 February 1936, p. 3. See also Schwarz, *Music and Musical Life*, p. 86.

relatively short time. The 1936 criticism was, of course, a great psychological blow to him. He wrote no more operas, and Lady Macbeth was not performed again until the 1960s (as Katerina Izmailova). Both he and Prokofiev toned down their Western modernism and flippancy, and he took no more risks with "vulgarity" in large-scale works. But Shostakovich's film music was a success, and he was back in official favor by the beginning of 1938.[99] His reputation soared with the wartime Seventh Symphony, which was acclaimed as a work of high seriousness and tragic heroism.

Vsevolod Meyerhold—the theater director who was "the big boss of formalism"—was less fortunate. His creative career effectively ended with the withdrawal of The Queen of Spades in 1936, when he was in his early sixties, and his theater was closed down by order of Kerzhentsev's Committee on the Arts at the beginning of 1938.[100] He himself survived the worst years of the Great Purges, however, only to be arrested in mid-1939, a few days after delivering a bold speech at a conference of theater directors calling for loosening of controls over theatrical repertoire and productions.[101] He died in prison or labor camp a few years later.

As far as music was concerned, it turned out that the dramatic intervention of 1936 was not the beginning of a new era of stifling repression. On the contrary, one émigré commentator labeled the decade 1938–1948 a new NEP in music; that is, a return to the relative tolerance and cultural pluralism of the mid-1920s.[102] Music was more fortunate than literature and painting because its nonrepresentational nature made it more difficult to censor effectively. In the new musical NEP, composers were wise to avoid modernism and dissonance and cultivate melody—many took to using folk tunes as motifs in large-scale works, like their nineteenth-century Russian predecessors—but they were not subjected to any more detailed tutelage. Indeed, the constraints on them were not dissimilar to those imposed by the market and concertgoing public on composers and performers in the West. The main difference was that professional musicians in the Soviet Union did not have the option of writing or performing for the small, highbrow audience that supported contemporary music in the West.

[99] The popular film Podrugi, directed by L. Arnshtam with music by Shostakovich, was released on 19 February 1936, just a few weeks after Pravda's editorial on Lady Macbeth. Another Arnshtam film with music by Shostakovich, Druz'ia, was released in 1938. See Ocherki istorii sovetskogo kino, vol. 2: 1935–1945 (Moscow, 1959), pp. 749–50.

[100] Izvestiia, 8 January 1938, p. 4.

[101] See Elagin, Temnyi genii, pp. 389–91, 406–10.

[102] Elagin, Ukroshchenie iskusstv, pp. 406–8.

Perhaps the most surprising aspect of the decade after the *Lady Macbeth* affair was the popularity of jazz and variety music. Despite *Pravda*'s distaste for the "nervy, convulsive, epileptic music [copied] from jazz" in Shostakovich's opera, jazz flourished in this period as never before or since. The leading jazzmen were not only immensely popular and visible, they were also immensely well paid by the state. The only real restriction in this field was that the jazz was home-grown: after the Great Purges, foreign jazz groups did not tour the Soviet Union.[103]

Light music of the type that had been assailed as petty-bourgeois in the 1920s flourished as well. Such songwriters as Isaak Dunaevskii, who wrote the music for the enormously successful films *Veselye rebiata* (Happy guys) (1934), *Circus* (1936), and *Volga-Volga* (1938), received honors, serious analysis from musicologists, and handsome material rewards. Dunaevskii himself was awarded the Order of the Red Flag and elected a deputy to the Supreme Soviet. In 1937 he became chairman of the Leningrad branch of the Union of Composers, one of whose members was, of course, Shostakovich.[104]

No *Pravda* editorial had ever recommended that light music and comedy should become major genres in Soviet cultural life, or that socialist realism was best projected through the medium of Hollywood-style musicals. Yet something of this sort did happen in the 1930s, and this development strongly suggests that the preferences and tastes of the Soviet public played a role at least as significant as the Politburo's in the shaping of cultural values. In the mid-1930s, with Stanislavsky-style realism becoming jaded and Meyerholdian modernism in eclipse, comedy assumed the dominant position in the theater.[105] Films won a mass audience in the 1930s, and several of the most popular were set in idealized and wildly unrealistic collective farms (the "boy meets girl meets tractor" genre).[106] More to the point from the public's standpoint, however, these films were mainly light, bouncy comedies, generously supplied with tuneful, rhythmic music that was as often performed by jazz ensembles as in folk style with harmonicas and balalaikas.[107]

---

[103] On jazz in the 1930s, see ibid., pp. 339–65, and Starr, *Red and Hot*, chaps. 7–8.
[104] Elagin, *Ukroshchenie iskusstv*, pp. 368– 73.
[105] See *Ocherki istorii russkoi sovetskoi dramaturgii, 1934–1945* (Leningrad and Moscow, 1966), pp. 15–23.
[106] Epitomized by the film *Traktoristki* (Girl tractor drivers) (1939; dir. E. Pomeshchikov, music by the Pokrass brothers).
[107] Successful films in this genre include *Veselye rebiata* (Happy guys) (1934; dir. G. Aleksandrov, music by I. Dunaevskii, performed by Leonid Utesov's jazz ensemble); *Circus* (1936; dir. G. Aleksandrov, music by I. Dunaevskii, with jazzman Aleksandr Tsfasman); *Podruzhki* (Girlfriends) (1936; dir. L. Arnstam, music by Shostakovich);

The *zhdanovshchina* of the late 1940s

Thus antiformalist and puritan themes in Soviet discourse about music can be seen to persist from the activism of RAPM at the end of the 1920s to the uproar about *Lady Macbeth* in 1936. An equally striking continuity can be seen between the events of 1936 and those of 1948, when Muradeli's opera *Velikaia druzhba* (The great friendship) was denounced in a special resolution of the party's Central committee, Zhdanov publicly raked Shostakovich and Prokofiev over the coals for writing music that was corrupted by formalism and inaccessible to the broad public, and leading musicologists were pilloried for overestimating Western influences in the development of Soviet music.[108] Boris Schwarz and other scholars of Soviet music have recognized the relationship between these events and the *Lady Macbeth* brouhaha, but it has not always been obvious to Sovietologists outside the music field, who tend to assume that the anti-Westernism characteristic of the *zhdanovshchina* of the late 1940s was a new phenomenon in Soviet cultural policy.

Zhdanov himself emphasized the continuity between 1936 and 1948. Looking back on the party's stand against modern art in the 1930s, he said:

> Bourgeois influences were strong in our painting at one time, and these influences used to fly all kinds of leftist banners—futurism, cubism, modernism. "Down with the rotten academic canons!" they cried. It was a madhouse. They would paint a girl with one head and forty legs. . . . It all ended in a complete fiasco.[109]

Zhdanov quoted extensively from the 1936 *Pravda* editorial on *Lady Macbeth*, and noted that "the faults of Muradeli's opera are very like the mistakes that earlier marked Comrade Shostakovich's opera *Lady Macbeth of Mtsensk*. What was then [in 1936] con-

---

Volga-Volga (1938; dir. G. Aleksandrov, music by I. Dunaevskii); and *Bogataia nevesta* (The rich fiancée) (1938; dir. E. Pomeshchikov, music by I. Dunaevskii).

[108] The text of the Central Committee resolution "On the opera *Velikaia druzhba* by V. Muradeli," dated 10 February 1948, is in *Sovetskaia muzyka*, 1948 no. 1, pp. 3–6. The proceedings of the composers' meeting with Zhdanov at the Central Committee in January were published as *Soveshchanie deiatelei sovetskoi muzyki v TsK VKP(b): Stenogrammy rechei* (Moscow, 1948) and partially translated with commentary in Werth, *Musical Uproar*. On the fate of Soviet musicology in the late 1940s, see Schwarz, *Music and Musical Life*, chap. 10.

[109] Speech at a meeting on Soviet music in the Central Committee of the Communist Party, January 1948, *Sovetskaia muzyka*, 1948 no. 1, p. 21.

demned is still alive," he concluded, "and not only alive, but setting the tone for Soviet music."[110]

Although Shostakovich had recovered his reputation with the Fifth and particularly the Seventh ("Leningrad") symphonies, and the large-scale works of Shostakovich and Prokofiev had been lauded as triumphs of Soviet life-affirming art in the interval, Shostakovich and Prokofiev were major targets in 1948, along with the other leading Soviet symphonists, Aram Khachaturian, Dmitrii Kabalevsky, and Nikolai Miaskovsky. Their music was reminiscent of contemporary Western modernism, a trend that reflected the decadence of bourgeois culture, Zhdanov said.[111] A few months earlier, rebuking Soviet philosophers for their excessive dependence on the European intellectual tradition, Zhdanov cited Jean Genet's *Diary of a Thief* (publicized and praised by one of the Soviet Union's most famous foreign sympathizers, Jean-Paul Sartre) as a symptom of "the whole depth, baseness, and loathesomeness of the decay of the bourgeoisie" in the West.[112]

As in 1936, some leading figures in the music world added their own variations on the "Who wants to listen to this awful modern music?" theme in 1948. The aged professor Aleksandr Goldenveizer of the Moscow Conservatory lamented the decline of music in the West since the death of "the last two German geniuses, Brahms and Wagner." The modernists had taken over in the West, but there was no need for the Soviet Union to take the same path.

> I am tired of false notes. . . . When I hear the clatter of false chords in some contemporary symphonies and sonatas, I feel with horror—it is a terrible thing to say—that these sounds are more appropriate as an expression of the ideology of the decadent culture of the West, up to and including fascism, than to the healthy nature of a Russian, Soviet man. Unfortunately, people can get used to anything. In China, they say, they use castor oil for cooking. All the same, we ought to break the habit of harmonic muddle and false notes in music as quickly as possible.[113]

Again, there were notes of genuine-sounding resentment at the acclaim and rewards heaped on the top Soviet composers, especially Shostakovich and Prokofiev. According to Khrennikov, soon to become head of the Composers' Union, the "Big Four" (Shostakovich,

---

[110] *Sovetskaia muzyka*, 1948 no. 1, pp. 12–13.

[111] Ibid., p. 25.

[112] A. Zhdanov, "Vystuplenie na diskussiiu po knige G. F. Aleksandrova 'Istoriia zapadnoevropeiskoi filosofii' (24 iiunia 1947 g.)," *Bol'shevik*, 1947 no. 16, p. 22.

[113] *Soveshchanie deiatelei*, p. 55.

Prokofiev, Khachaturian, and Kabalevsky) "found themselves in a sort of privileged position: they were immune to criticism and isolated from public opinion. They became musical state bureaucrats [sanovniki]." Deferential critics praised everything they wrote as a work of genius, and young composers felt obliged to imitate them."[114]

"Vulgar" light music and jazz also came under heavy attack in the late 1940s. The story of jazz, told by S. Frederick Starr in his fascinating Red and Hot, is particularly striking. Jazz had become enormously popular during the war years. But large-scale arrests of jazz musicians (many of whom were Jewish or from Poland and the Baltic states) began immediately after the war; and a few years later a major public campaign was launched against jazz as a tool of American imperialism and a degenerate art form with close ties to pornography. Jazz tunes were purged from the repertoire of variety ensembles, and in 1949 saxophones were banned and musicians whose workbooks described them as "saxophonists" transformed themselves into oboists and bassoonists by a stroke of the pen.[115]

The old concern—once so strongly articulated by RAPM—about the morally corrupting effect of "cheap" music had been partially resurrected in 1946, when the party's Central Committee, in condemning the movie The Great Life for excessive "naturalism" in its depiction of the lives of Donbass workers, noted that the songs in Bogoslovskii's score were "pervaded with drunken melancholy and . . . alien to the Soviet people."[116] This criticism was duly recalled at the congress of the Union of Soviet Composers in April 1948, and one speaker even switched back into the idiom of the 1920s for an instant and called Bogoslovskii's music "petty-bourgeois" (meshchanskaia).[117]

In the 1948 discussions, writers of light music as well as symphonists were encouraged to turn to the folk songs of the peoples of the Soviet Union as a source of inspiration and moral regeneration, and warned against the dangers of seduction by the corrupt, cosmopolitan allure of Tin Pan Alley. Nevertheless, the consensus in these dis-

[114] Ibid., p. 28. Khachaturian, Shostakovich, and Kabalevsky, along with R. M. Glière, Iurii Shaporin, and Viktor Belyi, were members of the committee that had led the Union of Soviet Composers since 1939. For an expression of similar sentiments at the congress of Soviet composers that was held in April 1948, see the speech of the songwriter Vladimir Zakharov in Pervyi vsesoiuznyi s"ezd sovetskikh kompozitorov: Stenograficheskii otchet (Moscow, 1948), p. 359.

[115] Starr, Red and Hot, p. 216.

[116] Cited by Tikhon Khrennikov in his report as general secretary of the Union of Soviet Composers, Pervyi vsesoiuznyi s"ezd, p. 47.

[117] Ibid., p. 23. The speaker was Vladimir Zakharov, himself a composer of popular songs. But he quickly pushed the focus of critical attention away from light music and back to the elitist symphonists such as Shostakovich and Prokofiev.

cussions was that the light-music composers as a group were in good shape in comparison with the symphonists, since many of their songs had achieved enormous popularity with the Soviet masses and were sufficiently vivid, simple, and tuneful to satisfy even such a connoisseur of folk melody as Comrade Zhdanov.[118]

Conclusion

A virulent strain of puritanism, combining antimodernism and anti-Westernism with concern about pornography and the debasement of public morals through art, was endemic in Soviet political culture from the early years after the Revolution until the end of the Stalin era and beyond. Shostakovich—like Meyerhold, Kurt Weill, and other European artists of the left in the 1920s and 1930s—could be accused of both formalism and fascination with jazz and other popular music. This interest got him into trouble at the beginning of the 1930s (the era of RAPM hegemony), in 1936, and again in 1948, though his disgrace on each occasion proved temporary and his stature as an acknowledged "great Soviet composer" survived these debacles.

"Formalist" was the code word for a composer who strayed in the direction of the modern, wicked West. The antithesis of formalism was socialist realism, an aesthetic concept of vague and shifting meaning, whose sometimes contradictory characteristics in music included tunefulness (as long as the melodies were not "vulgar," "tasteless," or "sentimental"), folk-music influences, romantic harmony, "classical" (generally nineteenth-century) form, grandeur of conception, profundity, simplicity, and accessibility. Beethoven's Ninth Symphony, notably the "Ode to Joy," was probably the ideal socialist-realist work in the minds of many Soviet opponents of formalism.

Soviet puritanism and objections to modern art had much in common with similar public attitudes in many other parts of the world in the twentieth century. What made it distinctive was that it specifically identified "the bourgeois West"—later "the imperialist, capitalist West"—as the source of the corruption and decadence. In Nazi Germany, similarly, the source of artistic corruption was specifically identified as the Jews. In both the Soviet and the German cases, strenuous efforts were made to eliminate the source of corruption

[118] On Zhdanov's alleged extraordinary expertise in the field of folk song, see Zakharov, speaking at the February 1948 meeting of composers and musicologists in Moscow, *Sovetskaia muzyka,* 1948 no. 1, p. 99.

and punish its carriers. The Soviet solution was to close the frontiers to foreign modernist art and attempt to impose a cultural quarantine on the country.

It proved difficult to eradicate artistic formalism and decadence in all its manifestations in Soviet culture. The "deviant" artistic works that were easiest to deal with were those that lacked a broad constituency. Thus the avant-garde composers associated with the Society for Contemporary Music in the 1920s vanished swiftly from the scene. Shostakovich, whose work had more public appeal, was repeatedly attacked and repeatedly returned to favor. "Light" or "cheap" music was essentially impossible to stamp out, and its most popular producers won exceptionally high status and material rewards in the Soviet Union, even though at times it was prudent for them to write a few good marches or folk-song-like melodies and eschew syncopated rhythms. The crackdown on jazz in the postwar 1940s had a dramatic impact, but this move came in a climate of virulent anti-Americanism; and it should be noted that an attempted crackdown in the Great Purge period of the late 1930s misfired completely.

It would be an oversimplification to treat Soviet antiformalism purely as the policy of Stalin and his Politburo. As the RAPM case makes clear, militant puritan initiatives did not necessarily come from above; they also came from within the profession and were supported at least tacitly by the musical and concertgoing public. Such initiatives had no obvious connection to Marxist ideology. The input from Stalin and the Politburo was intermittent and often inconsistent, as in the well-known case of Mayakovsky, who would surely have been posthumously listed with the formalists in the 1930s if Stalin had not pronounced him to be the greatest Soviet poet. Antiformalism in music was less a Soviet policy than a Soviet mentality shared by much of the musical profession, the concertgoing public, and members of the Communist Party alike.

Nevertheless, the puritan mentality alone would not have produced such dramatic episodes as the scandal that enveloped Shostakovich's opera and disrupted Soviet musical life after *Pravda*'s editorial on *Lady Macbeth* in 1936. Those episodes were the results of the politicization of Soviet cultural life and the understandably nervous reactions of the musical profession to any political signal coming from above. Under Soviet conditions, composers and critics knew that the penalties for nonconformity could be high, and that artistic categories often could not be separated from political ones. Yet the rules of the game were not fixed; they were constantly evolving. Despite his earlier experience with RAPM, Shostakovich was stunned

by *Pravda*'s attacks on his music and could barely manage a coherent response in the long, acrimonious discussions that followed.
Those less immediately concerned reacted variously, some attempt-
ing cautious defiance or seeking to interpret the political signal in
the most limited and innocuous manner, others taking the opportunity to further sectarian interests and settle personal scores, and
still others sitting quietly and waiting until the storm passed.

(1988/1991)

CHAPTER 9

Becoming Cultured: Socialist Realism and the Representation of Privilege and Taste

To outsiders, especially Marxists disappointed by the Soviet regime, there was a glaring contradiction between the egalitarian, ascetic socialist ideals associated with the Bolshevik Revolution and the emergence in the 1930s of a privileged new elite whose values would have been labeled "bourgeois" a decade earlier. Trotsky spoke of a betrayal of the revolution, and the thrust of Milovan Djilas's later description of the "New Class" and its privileges was on the same lines. Outside the Marxist camp, the émigré sociologist Nicholas Timasheff wrote of a "great retreat" from revolutionary values in the 1930s, and Vera Dunham characterized the culture of the Stalin period as a triumph of "middle-class values."[1]

Did insiders—in particular, the newly risen Communist elite whose Biedermeier tastes seem to be especially associated with embourgeoisement—have the same perceptions? Evidently they did not, since then they would have had to be cynics, accepting their own role as betrayers of the Revolution, and there are no signs of such blatant demoralization among the Soviet elite in the prewar period. But if they did not see things in the same way as Trotsky and Djilas, how did they see them? Assuming that the social phenomena that

[1] Leon Trotsky, The Revolution Betrayed (London, 1967) (first published 1937); Milovan Djilas, The New Class: An Analysis of the Communist System (New York, 1957); Nicholas S. Timasheff, The Great Retreat: The Growth and Decline of Communism in Russia (New York, 1946); Vera S. Dunham, In Stalin's Time: Middle-Class Values in Soviet Fiction (Cambridge, 1976).

outsiders associated with embourgeoisement really existed in Soviet society, how did insiders explain and justify them?

The members of the new Soviet elite of the 1930s strove for a "cultured" way of life, were attentive to domestic comfort and consumer goods, and were concerned about social protocol and propriety. Since this Stalinist way of thinking arose from their tendency to view the present through the prism of an imagined future, I call it "the discourse of socialist realism."

Socialist realism may be regarded as a literary theory, a blueprint for literary production that the regime handed to Soviet writers, or the organizing principle of a particular body of literature.[2] But here I am approaching it from a different angle. What I mean by "socialist realism" is a method of representation characteristic of the Stalin period and the Stalinist *mentalité*.[3] Its most notable impact, from my perspective, lay outside the field of literature proper. It was ubiquitous in Soviet journalism of the 1930s, and its traces can also be found in every bureaucratic report and statistical compilation of the period. In the socialist-realist view of the world, a dry, half-dug ditch signified a future canal full of loaded barges, a ruined church was a potential kolkhoz clubhouse, and the inscription of a project in the Five-Year Plan was a magical act of creation that might almost obviate the need for more concrete exertions.

An English children's book written in the 1930s, describing the adventures of two American teenagers on their first visit to the Soviet Union, caught the spirit of socialist realism perfectly. Shortly after their arrival, as they rode in a taxi through Moscow, their guide pointed out a row of ramshackle wooden houses:

> "The old houses are coming down soon. . . . We'll have a park here."
> She waved to the old houses as if they were sprouting trees and flowers. Peter whispered to Judy when they got out:
> "She's got it too. She sounds like the Russian on the train."
> "*Soon and now are all mixed up here*," whispered Judy.[4]

---

[2] For a range of approaches to socialist realism in literature, see C. V. James, *Soviet Socialist Realism: Origin and Theory* (London, 1973); Rufus W. Mathewson, Jr., *The Positive Hero in Russian Literature*, 2d ed. (Stanford, 1975); Katerina Clark, *The Soviet Novel: History as Ritual* (Chicago, 1981); and Régine Robin, *Le Réalisme socialiste: Une Esthétique impossible* (Paris, 1986).

[3] This approach has much in common with that of Abram Tertz (Sinyavsky), *On Socialist Realism*, trans. George Dennis (New York, 1960), though I identify the central trope of socialist realism somewhat differently.

[4] Marjorie Fischer, *Palaces on Monday* (Harmondsworth, 1947) (first published 1937), p. 55; my emphasis. The title—another socialist-realist reference—is explained in the epigraph: "An Eastern juggler . . . / Planted plum pips on Sunday, / Which came up palaces on Monday."

The socialist-realist method of representation was particularly valuable in providing a way of handling such awkward topics as privilege, social hierarchy, and acquisitive consumerism—areas in which a New Class sense of entitlement had emerged but the old revolutionary condemnation had not completely disappeared from consciousness.

A key word in the discourse of socialist realism was *kul'turnost'*, the attribute of being cultured, which was implicitly contrasted with being uncultured, uncivilized, "dark," and "backward" like a peasant. Vera Dunham, who was the first scholar to draw attention to the importance of this concept in the Stalinist system of values, defined *kul'turnost'* as an ersatz, derivative version of *kul'tura*, the best that the new Stalinist *meshchanstvo* could do to reproduce the "higher culture" that was the prerogative of the old Russian intelligentsia.[5] That is a rather loaded definition, but in one respect it sheds useful light on the concept of *kul'turnost'* and its relation to *kul'tura* in the usage of the Stalin period. *Kul'tura* was something that one naturally possessed; *kul'turnost'* was something that one purposefully acquired. A sense of becoming, striving, and taking possession was associated with *kul'turnost'*: it was the attribute of one who had recognized that *kul'tura* was a scarce and essential commodity and set out to get some.

One of the great advantages of the concept of *kul'turnost'* in a post-revolutionary society burdened by hangovers of revolutionary puritanism was that it offered a way of legitimizing what had once been thought of as "bourgeois" concerns about possessions and status: one treated them as an aspect of *kul'tura*. Becoming cultured had always been a proper and necessary individual goal in Bolshevik terms. In the 1930s the concept was simply expanded to include acquisition of the means and manners of a lifestyle appropriate to the new masters of the Soviet state.

Another key word in the discourse of socialist realism was "intelligentsia," used as a euphemism for "elite" or "upper class" from the mid-1930s. In the 1920s this word had applied to the old bourgeois Russian intelligentsia, and was often pejorative in use; but in the aftermath of the Cultural Revolution the concept of a "Soviet intelligentsia" emerged. This composite social entity included the old (formerly bourgeois) intelligentsia, the new intelligentsia of proletarian and peasant *vydvizhentsy*, and, in addition, all Communist administrators and officeholders regardless of educational level.[6] In

[5] See Dunham, *In Stalin's Time*, pp. 22–23.
[6] See chap. 7. For statistical purposes, the "intelligentsia" category also included

his remarks on the new constitution in 1936, Stalin identified the intelligentsia as one of the three basic components of Soviet society, the others being the working class and the collectivized peasantry. This tripartite arrangement conveyed a clear sense of a social hierarchy in which the intelligentsia was the upper class.

I treat the term "intelligentsia" here as the nonpejorative equivalent in Stalinist discourse of Trotsky's "bureaucracy," Djilas's "New Class," and Dunham's "middle class."[7] Its function within the discourse was to provide a way of conceptualizing hierarchy and privilege in terms of the only kind of superiority that could be freely acknowledged—that of cultural level and education.

Soviet provincial newspapers of the 1930s are among the best available sources on questions of taste, propriety, commodities, and consumerism, and they show very clearly how present and future were represented in a true socialist-realist projection. On the one hand, provincial newspapers often did a surprisingly thorough job of reporting on the actual problems of everyday life, when socialism was only in the process of construction and culture and consumer goods were both in short supply. On the other hand, mindful of their obligation to give an upbeat view of Soviet life to their readers, the newspapers reported eagerly and in detail on every portent of the abundance of commodities and culture that would appear when the building of socialism was completed.

Life as it is

Life was dominated by shortages in the early 1930s. The shortages of food, clothing, and housing were the most basic; but from the consumer's point of view, almost everything was in short supply. Women suffered particularly from the shortages, because they were the main family shoppers and organizers of domestic life. Rationing was in force from 1929 to 1935, and some groups (both blue- and white-collar, in this transitional period of Soviet values) had higher ration priority than others. The newspapers gave detailed information on the rationing system and the various categories of ration cards, since these matters were of vital importance to their urban readers. They also provided extensive coverage on the availability and nonavailability of consumer goods—perhaps, since the journal-

---

low-level white-collar workers. In practice, however, *sluzhashchie* continued to be regarded as a separate group with lower status than the intelligentsia.

[7] See Dunham, *In Stalin's Time*, pp. 4–5, 16–17.

ists were men, slightly overemphasizing consumer items of special interest to men, such as the harsh cigarettes known as *makhorka*—and dealt intermittently with the black market.

In the Voronezh newspaper we find a characteristic report of shortages in the countryside in the summer of 1933. The general store attached to the Red Partisan kolkhoz had had no sugar for a year, and it also lacked such household items as cups and glasses. Kerosene and soap, if available at all, were in extremely short supply. But at the end of the sowing, tobacco and matches were sent; salt arrived a month or so later.[8]

The towns were generally better supplied than the countryside, but they too experienced acute shortages. A week before the opening of the 1935–1936 school year, none of the stores in Iaroslavl had any children's shoes at all. Although bread rationing had been lifted by this time, this industrial town far from the main grain-growing regions still went short, and prices were higher there than in other areas. The newspaper addressed local dissatisfaction with a short explanation of Soviet pricing policy.[9] An outraged worker reported his efforts to buy bread in Iaroslavl on one particularly bad day:

> On 6 July I sent my wife, son, and daughter in search of bread, and went looking for it myself. We went round the shops and stalls of our ORS for three hours.[10] We were unable to buy any bread. In store no. 10, I stood in line for three hours and reached the front of the queue. I was already getting out my money to pay for two kilograms when the shop assistant said: "We're out of bread, citizen." My wife went into town. She left at one in the afternoon and returned at five, having finally bought two kilograms of black bread.[11]

The newspapers often attributed the shortages to distribution problems. They were at least partly right, for at the end of the 1920s the state had abolished private trade without putting an adequate system in its place; the cooperative and state trading networks functioned very poorly, especially at the beginning of the 1930s. A recurring difficulty was the shortage of packing and wrapping materials. Tobacco lay in warehouses because there were no boxes to ship it in, although this consumer item was of particular importance to the working masses; bottled beer disappeared from the market in the

[8] *Kommuna* (Voronezh), 6 July 1933, p. 3.

[9] *Severnyi rabochii* (Iaroslavl), 26 August 1935, p. 4; 2 January 1935, p. 4.

[10] The Department of Worker Supply (Otdel rabochego snabzheniia) in an industrial plant was part of the closed distribution system set up under rationing, but many of these departments continued to function after rationing was lifted in 1935.

[11] *Severnyi rabochii*, 9 July 1935, p. 4.

Caucasus town of Ordzhonikidze because the brewery had no bottles.[12]

But theft was an even larger part of the problem. At every point in the state distribution chain, employees were funneling off the goods for their own use or for resale on the black market. Ordzhonikidze's beer-bottle crisis, for example, was the result of systematic theft over a long period by one of the plant warehousemen, who stole a total of 24,000 bottles.[13] In Moscow, "deficit" goods such as suits, woolen cloth, and phonographs disappeared from the regular stores and turned up in commission (secondhand) stores at vastly inflated prices.[14] Goods that were received in the state stores were often unavailable to ordinary customers. When galoshes appeared in Kazan's main department store, "speculators crowded honest buyers from the counters." When forty bicycles came in, the store manager kept them in the warehouse and sold them quietly (for a consideration) to friends and black-market operators.[15] Thus "honest buyers" often had no choice but to buy on the black market. An inquiry among unmarried workers of the Cheliabinsk Tractor Plant in 1935 revealed that 72 percent bought their last pair of shoes on the black market. (The percentage of married workers was considerably lower: they had wives to wait in line.)[16]

When goods were available, the quality was often appalling. This problem was particularly acute in regard to clothes and shoes, because private tailors, dressmakers, and bootmakers had been forced out of business during the First Five-Year Plan.[17] The shoe question was extremely sensitive because the shortage of leather was related to mass slaughter of livestock during the first years of collectivization, and the newspapers handled it with caution. But poor-quality tailoring by the state-sponsored tailors' cooperatives was a subject dear to the hearts of Soviet journalists. "You often see lopsided passers-by on the streets," wrote a reporter for Moscow's evening newspaper in jocular vein. "Who are they? Invalids? No, customers of [the Moscow Sewing Cooperative]. Unwittingly, they are playing the role of living mannequins, advertising botched-up suits and overcoats."[18]

[12] *Kommuna*, 6 May 1933, p. 3; *Sotsialisticheskaia Osetiia* (Ordzhonikidze), 24 December 1937, p. 3.

[13] *Sotsialisticheskaia Osetiia*, p. 3.

[14] *Za industrializatsiiu*, 29 May 1935, p. 2.

[15] *Krasnaia Tatariia* (Kazan), 4 April 1938, p. 4; 9 April 1938, p. 4.

[16] *Za industrializatsiiu*, 27 May 1935, p. 3.

[17] Private tailoring and dressmaking (but not bootmaking) became legal again in 1935, but garments could be made only for a specific customer, and the customer had to provide the materials.

[18] *Vecherniaia Moskva*, 10 February 1937, p. 3.

In a more serious vein, the Leningrad newspaper reported various abuses in the local garment industry, including the fact that finished products were likely to lack sleeves, collars, or linings because someone at the plant had cut them out for resale. The old private tailor would never have dared offer such low-quality goods as were routinely sold by state industry and the cooperatives, the newspaper commented.[19] If things were bad in Leningrad, they were bound to be worse in far-off, provincial Ufa. In 1938 three local party and Soviet leaders were so incensed by the grotesquely ill-fitting suits delivered to them by the Sixteenth Party Congress tailoring artel that they paraded them before a meeting of the Bashkir soviet, provoking general hilarity and public censure of the tailors.[20]

The housing problem was reflected in many sad stories of overcrowding and substandard living conditions and reports of lawsuits related to contested living space. Flies and bedbugs were so bad in one Iaroslavl hostel that "workers are obliged to take their beds out to the street at night and sleep in the open."[21] Urban living space was at such a premium that a government resolution on the care of homeless children included a special warning against foster parents "who use their guardianship for profit (occupying living space and using property remaining after the death of parents, and so on)."[22]

Homeless children (besprizornye) were not only potential victims of exploitation but also actual disturbers of the peace. The problem appeared to be worse in the outlying regions than in central Russia. The schools in the Siberian town of Tomsk were plagued by gangs of besprizornye who would hang around for days on end, using foul language, fighting, and harassing pupils and teachers (one day they "lassoed passing girls with a rope"); and the local newspaper put part of the blame on state stores that "freely sell tobacco products and liquor to children, even those who are too small to be seen over the counter."[23]

Education was a growth industry in the Soviet Union, and the newspapers gave extensive coverage to the problems of school overcrowding (many urban schools were operating on two or three shifts) and shortages of textbooks, as well as to the positive achievements of workers who passed their technical minimum and peasants who learned to read. The back page of all newspapers, provincial as well

[19] Leningradskaia pravda, 8 April 1937, p. 3.
[20] Krasnaia Bashkiriia (Ufa), 29 May 1938, p. 4.
[21] Severnyi rabochii, 28 August 1935, p. 3.
[22] Za industrializatsiiu, 1 June 1935, p. 1.
[23] Krasnoe znamia (Tomsk), 29 December 1936, p. 3.

as national, carried announcements that local teachers' training colleges and engineering schools welcomed applications.

As for cultural opportunities, few provincial centers could match the sophistication of Moscow, where the Hotel Metropol advertised not only dancing and *dzhaz* but also (in English) "FIVE O'CLOCK TEA."[24] Movies, however, were widely advertised and shown, even some foreign films. A survey of young workers revealed that in the last quarter of 1935, 90 percent went to the movies at least once, and 70 percent went to theaters or concerts.[25] Kolkhoz youth could not quite match this record, according to a similar survey a few years later, but 90 percent went to the movies at least once in 1937, and 37 percent of the young *kolkhozniki* said they owned a clock and 24 percent a radio.[26]

A poignant picture of the struggle for *kul'turnost'* comes from Khabarovsk in the Far East, a city notable for its high crime rate and shortage of women. On 12 May 1937 Khabarovsk held the grand opening of its new Park of Culture and Rest:

> Orchestras played, flags blew in the wind, jazz summoned young people to the dance floor. City dwellers went to the park hoping to relax and have a good time.
> While it was light, everything went perfectly. But when evening came, the park began to be flooded by hooligans appearing from nowhere. Taking advantage of the fact that the park is poorly lit and completely dark in some alleys, the hooligans began "doing the rounds." . . . [They] bumped women unceremoniously from behind, knocked off their hats, used foul language, and started fights on the dance floor and in the alleys.[27]

While the park gave Khabarovsk citizens a glimpse of life as it was becoming, the hooligans served as a depressing reminder that in life as it was, *kul'turnost'* was still a goal to be pursued.

Life as it is becoming

The newspapers pointed out the deficiencies of the present, but they were also diligent in drawing public attention to portents of a

[24] *Vecherniuiu Moskva*, 29 January 1936, p. 4.

[25] *Sotsial'nyi oblik rabochei molodezhi po materialam sotsiologicheskikh obsledovanii, 1936 i 1972 gg.* (Moscow, 1980), p. 38.

[26] *Sotsial'nyi oblik kolkhoznoi molodezhi po materialam sotsiologicheskikh obsledovanii, 1938 i 1969 gg.* (Moscow, 1976), pp. 23–24.

[27] *Tikhookeanskaia zvezda* (Khabarovsk), 14 May 1937, p. 4.

future when goods would be abundant and cultured behavior the norm. In Moscow a luxury food store opened on Gorky Street in 1934 (it was the old Eliseev store, now called Grocery No. 1), and the evening paper detailed its wonders:

> The new store will sell more than 1,200 foodstuffs. . . . In the grocery department there are 38 kinds of sausage, including 20 new kinds that have not been sold anywhere before. This department will also sell three kinds of cheese—Camembert, Brie, and Limburger—made for the store by special order. In the confectionery department there are 200 kinds of candies and pastries. . . . The bread department has up to 50 kinds of bread. . . .
> Meat is kept in refrigerated glass cases. In the fish department there are tanks with live carp, mirror carp, bream, and pike. When the customers choose their fish, they are scooped out of the tank with nets. . . .[28]

The next day, 75,000 people visited the store, but it was reported that there were no lines "since there are a lot of cash registers." High prices were another possible reason for cautious buying. A few years later the same store was selling hothouse strawberries from the old Marfino estate (now a state farm) at 100 rubles a kilo.[29]

As better-quality goods appeared (for a price) in Moscow stores in the mid-1930s, a new type of discerning customer appeared:

> This morning reporter Avdeev bought a present for his wife in Mostorg [department store]—teaspoons. He spent a long time at the counter choosing them, comparing shape, luster, and design. Recently he has been particularly drawn to simple, attractive, and well-made things. Earlier he somehow did not notice crude spoons and bowls in the dining rooms, torn or dirty jackets, ugly ties.[30]

Reporter Avdeev was clearly a model that others were expected to emulate. It was fortunate that he lived in Moscow, however, because the opportunities for discerning consumerism remained rather limited elsewhere. It is true that even in Tomsk he could have bought an artificial palm tree to decorate the office, and there was a new women's magazine to tell his wife how to knit (if she could find the wool) and make lampshades that were "useful, attractive and rational, and give a soft light to the room."[31] But in the provinces, luxury goods were generally available only by mail order, to judge from

[28] *Vecherniaia Moskva*, 4 October 1934, p. 2.
[29] Ibid., 7 October 1934, p. 2; 9 May 1937, p. 1.
[30] *Za industrializatsiiu*, 26 September 1935, p. 4.
[31] *Krasnoe znamia*, 15 December 1936, p. 4; *Obshchestvennitsa*, 1937 no. 6, p. 31.

the newspaper advertisements. In 1937 the Irkutsk branch of the state mail-order company offered phonographs at 367 rubles and re-conditioned wristwatches at prices ranging from 280 to 500 rubles.[32]

Nevertheless, in the second half of the 1930s, even provincial stores could be relied on to stock one kind of seasonal luxury mer-chandise—decorations for the New Year *elka* (fir tree). "Elka" was officially designated a children's festival for the winter holidays.[33] Decorations and toys began to arrive at the stores in late December, and the newspapers gave the event big coverage. In Tomsk, for exam-ple, "Unusual excitement reigned yesterday in the Children's World section of the department store. Dozens of childish hands stretched toward the counter with its alluring display of New Year [*elochnye*] toys—beautiful, shining balls, fish, popguns, little baskets, artificial candy, ribbons, candles, and so on." The Siberian Trading Company (Sibtorg) had already sold more than 130,000 rubles' worth of New Year decorations in Tomsk, and was expecting another consignment of toys and decorations from Moscow. One New Year specialty—artificial fruit made out of cotton wool glazed with paraffin—was even made locally at the Tomsk Cultural Goods Plant.[34]

Culture in the narrower sense was also available to the population. Large editions of the nineteenth-century Russian literary classics were published: in 1935, 1.2 million copies of works by Pushkin were issued, 695,000 by Saltykov-Shchedrin, 550,000 by Tolstoy, 515,000 by Nekrasov.[35]

Cultural milestones such as the Pushkin centenary in February 1937 were celebrated in the daily newspapers as well as the literary journals; David Oistrakh was front-page news when he won first prize at the International Competition for Violinists in Brussels.[36] Asked to name their ideal man or woman, young workers at the Sta-lin Auto Plant in Moscow listed Leonardo da Vinci, Maxim Gorky, and the actor Ivan Moskvin along with Stalin and Stakhanov.[37]

Education was an even more pervasive theme than artistic culture. "To study" and "to build" were the ubiquitous verbs of the 1930s: they indicated the means by which life was becoming what it would and must be. *Kolkhozniki* were learning to be tractor drivers. Workers were studying to go to technical school. Teachers were raising their qualifications by taking courses. Even factory directors went to eve-

---

[32] *Tikhookeanskaia zvezda*, 15 October 1937, p. 4.
[33] *Komsomol'skaia pravda*, 14 December 1937, p. 4.
[34] *Krasnoe znamia*, 23 December 1936, p. 4.
[35] *Izvestiia*, 5 May 1936, p. 3.
[36] *Pravda*, 2 April 1937, p. 1.
[37] *Komsomol'skaia pravda*, 7 November 1937, p. 4.

ning classes. Out of 865 young Stalin Auto workers, 405 stated that "continuing my education" was their main personal objective in the next two or three years.[38] Education was a challenge, an opportunity, and a reward for achievement. Maria Demchenko, Stakhanovite field-team leader on a Ukrainian sugar-beet kolkhoz, received her mission to study from Stalin himself:

> I said: "Comrade Stalin, I have done what I undertook to do. I want you to give me some new task."
> He thought for a moment, and said: "Do you want to study?"
> "I want that more than I can tell you."
> He turned to his companions and said: "Do you know what, Comrade Demchenko is going to study. She will become an agronomist."[39]

But Russia was still a backward country: there was not yet enough culture to go round, just as there were not enough consumer goods. Inevitably, in a world of shortages, some people had priority access to the supply of material and cultural goods. There were different kinds of priority access, some highly publicized, others discreetly ignored in the newspapers. The most publicized priority was that given to ordinary people—individual high achievers (udarniki and Stakhanovites) in the factories and collective farms—as a reward for outstanding achievement. The newspapers reported these awards frequently, often in the same stories that described severe shortages for the public as a whole. At the Red Partisan kolkhoz, whose store lacked many of the basic necessities of life in 1933, F. Ia. Samsonov, who had earned credit for 104 workdays was rewarded by June 1, with a peasant blouse (tolstovka), 3 meters of sateen for a shirt, and a pair of galoshes, all issued specially for him.[40]

The theme of material rewards loomed very large at the widely publicized national meetings of Stakhanovites in the mid-1930s. Stakhanovite workers and peasants reported their achievements, plans, and prizes, and government and party leaders applauded and made jocular interjections. Peasant women in particular were encouraged to gloat over their prizes.

> Everything I'm wearing I got as a prize for good work in the kolkhoz. Besides the dress and shoes, I got a sewing machine in Nalchik.
>
> For the harvest I got a prize of a silk dress worth 250 rubles (Applause.)

---

[38] Ibid.
[39] *Geroini sotsialisticheskogo truda* (Moscow, 1936), pp. 37–38.
[40] *Kommuna*, 6 July 1933, p. 3.

> I got 500 rubles from the Ukrainian Commissariat of Agriculture, and a certificate and pass to a health resort from the regional agriculture department. From the Food Industry Commissariat I got 1,000 rubles, and the kolkhoz gave me a horse and a cow.[41]

Sometimes Politburo members pressed for further details, as in this exchange between Mikoyan and the Stakhanovite worker Slavnikova, who operated as a team with her friend Makarova and earned 886 rubles in one month.

> MIKOYAN: And how much did your friend earn?
> SLAVNIKOVA: My friend earned 1,336 rubles in October.
> MIKOYAN: What does she do with the money?
> SLAVNIKOVA: I wondered what she'd do with the money, too. I asked my friend: "Marusia, what are you going to do with the money?" She said: "I'm buying myself ivory-colored shoes for 180 rubles, a crêpe-de-chine dress for 200 rubles, and a coat for 700 rubles."[42]

At the simplest level, this exchange signified that lavish material rewards were available for those who worked hard. But another message—the superimposition of a better "soon" on a still imperfect "now" that was the basic trope of socialist realism—was also being transmitted. It can be summarized as follows: Material rewards, like culture, are as yet available only to the few. But they can be won by hard work; and one day, when the building of socialism is completed, there will be abundance for all to share.

Reticence about privileges and material rewards

In the real world, of course, not all the crêpe-de-chine dresses went to Stakhanovites. A system of priority access to consumer goods also developed for the new middle class of administrators, professionals, military officers, NKVD personnel, and members of the creative intelligentsia. This group had a disproportionate share of the society's culture and education, since these advantages were concomitants of elite jobs, as well as a disproportionate share of its material goods. But they were rewarded discreetly for their achievements. The privileges of the elite—high salaries, good apartments, exclusive resorts, servants, access to chauffered limousines and special stores—were only dimly reflected in the newspapers.

[41] *Geroini*, pp. 71, 54–55, 102.
[42] Ibid., pp. 6–7.

Take the network of closed or restricted stores that came into exist-ence along with rationing during the First Five-Year Plan and lasted until the mid-1930s.[43] They were of various types: some catered to workers in factories, some to white-collar employees in government offices, and a third category served the specialists and administrators attached to various government bureaucracies. The workers' stores (ORSy), though closed to the general public, were often discussed in the newspapers. But the stores for white-collar personnel were invis-ible (that is, invisible to newspaper readers) as long as they remained part of the closed distribution network.[44] They reappeared only after their conversion into commercial stores such as Grocery No. 1, which used the price mechanism to restrict access.

There was less reticence about the Torgsin stores, which sold goods unavailable elsewhere for gold and foreign currency in the years 1930–1936.

> The Voronezh Torgsin announces to the public that it has opened a department store at 197 Bolshaia Petrovskaia (B. Chizhevka) Street. For sale without restriction [of quantity] for gold, silver, jewelry, coin (old mint coins), and coupons are these goods: textiles, knit goods, perfume and haberdashery, shoes, ready-made dresses, furs, FOOD AND BREAD.[45]

Unlike the Soviet hard-currency stores of a later period, the Torgsins had display windows in which scarce goods were temptingly ar-rayed. Malcolm Muggeridge was offended by the unfairness of the displays, when much of the population was going hungry, and even a Soviet memoirist recalled his distress when he looked from the sidewalk at "oranges, lemons, and mandarins arranged in a big pyra-mid" and knew that "for me they were absolutely inaccessible."[46] But the Torgsins were not intended to drive home a point about elite privilege, even though they did serve elite members who received coupons as part of their salaries. Their visibility was meant to en-courage ordinary, couponless Soviet citizens to bring out the gold watches and family silver hidden under the bed, so that the state could buy foreign machinery and pay foreign specialists in hard cur-rency.

[43] See Leonard E. Hubbard, *Soviet Trade and Distribution* (London, 1938), pp. 36–40, 239–40.

[44] A partial exception was the OGPU Cooperative on Kuznetskii Most in Moscow, serving OGPU employees and members of the OGPU armed forces. The cooperative did not advertise in the newspaper, but for some reason it listed itself in the 1930 Moscow City Directory, *Vsia Moskva: Adresno-spravochnaia kniga za 1930 g.* (under "Torgovye predpriiatiia," trading enterprises).

[45] *Kommuna*, 8 May 1933, p. 4.

[46] Malcolm Muggeridge, *Winter in Moscow* (London, 1934), p. 146; Iu. Emelianov, *O vremeni, o tovarishchakh, o sebe*, 2d ed. (Moscow, 1974), p. 240.

From time to time the newspapers reported construction of special housing for engineers and other professional groups,[47] but they were generally silent about similar housing provided for high officials. Another topic on which reticence was considered appropriate was the employment of domestic servants. Servants had been a permissible topic and recognized occupational category as long as there was a capitalist bourgeoisie to employ them; that is, until the end of NEP. In the 1930s they disappeared from the occupational statistics and, as a general rule, from public discussion. But the ban was not complete: local newspapers still carried small advertisements on the back page, and they included notices inserted by job seekers as well as by potential employers. Thus in Iaroslavl in 1935, "middle-aged housekeeper [*domrabotnitsa*]" seeks work; in Tomsk, "nanny, housekeeper seeks position"; and in Moscow's evening newspaper, "experienced housekeeper, able to cook, required."[48]

Mixed signals about the New Class

The newspapers' reticence about the privileges accorded the elite indicates that the subject was still awkward in the era of *kul'turnost'*, when a taste for crêpe-de-chine dresses went hand in hand with appreciation of Pushkin, and that earlier revolutionary discourses about class war and equality were not wholly forgotten. Few Soviet citizens but Stalin himself were able to read Trotsky's *Revolution Betrayed* when it came out in the West.[49] But the terms in which Trotsky condemned the privileges of the Soviet "bureaucracy" (which he identified as a new Soviet bourgeoisie and source of corruption) would have been both familiar and plausible to many a Soviet reader:

> Limousines for the "activists", fine perfumes for "our women" [that is, the highly placed wives who, according to Mikoyan, "demand" such goods], margarine for the workers, stores "de luxe" for the gentry, a look at delicacies through the store windows for the plebs—such socialism cannot but seem to the masses a new re-facing of capitalism, and they are not far wrong.[50]

[47] See, for example, *Za industrializatsiiu*, 26 March 1932, p. 1.
[48] *Severnyi rabochii*, 2 January 1935, p. 4; *Krasnoe znamia*, 9 December 1936, p. 4; *Vecherniaia Moskva*, 8 January 1936, p. 4.
[49] Stalin read it at one sitting at the beginning of 1937, according to his Soviet biographer: Dmitrii Volkogonov, *Triumf i tragediia: Politicheskii portret I. V. Stalina* (Moscow, 1989), bk 1, pt. 2, p. 174.
[50] Leon Trotsky, *Revolution Betrayed*, p. 120. The Mikoyan reference is on p. 118.

Though it was far beyond the limits of acceptable Soviet discourse to indict the system as Trotsky did, it was by no means out of bounds to attack individual officeholders for having developed "aristocratic" pretensions and a taste for luxury. Indeed, such attacks became commonplace during the Great Purge, when the newspapers reported the downfall of former bosses in a distinctly anti-elitist, populist vein. The tone of 1937 reporting was not new; but it was half a dozen years since the Cultural Revolution, when it was last in vogue, and this was the first detailed exposé of *Communist* (as opposed to professional) elite privileges that had ever been offered to the general Soviet public. Of course, the "enemies of the people" were accused of treason, sabotage, and spying, not the possession or even the abuse of privilege. They had privilege, nevertheless; and the Purge commentaries offered a lot of incidental information, usually presented with lively malice, about the luxurious lifestyle of enemies of the people. The director of the publishing house *Molodaia gvardiia*, for example, not only had connections with spies and traitors, according to newspaper reports, but "also became degenerate in terms of his everyday life—he ripped off the state shamelessly. In a resthouse that the publishing firm is building, a luxurious apartment has been equipped for Leshchintser [the director]. Furniture of Karelian birch has been bought for that apartment. He is a bourgeois degenerate."[51]

At Makeevka Metallurgical Plant, the top brass—now found to be enemies of the people—flaunted their power and privilege in a totally unacceptable way: "There was the notorious occasion at the plant when Ivanov [the deputy director] called in a responsible executive, the head of the administrative-economic department, and said: 'Call a doctor to my home—the dog has fallen ill.'"[52]

In Kazan, the former heads of the city soviet allegedly wasted 225,000 rubles of the state's money maintaining dachas where they entertained their families, friends, and various "suspicious characters" in style: "Here, beneath the canopy of firs and pines, nobody bothered about accounts and accountability. . . . Lunches, dinners, suppers, snacks and drinks, bed linen—everything was given out free; and the generous hosts, hospitable at the state's expense, paid not the slightest attention to material considerations."[53]

Bosses were also criticized for their eagerness to get their hands on private cars, a major status symbol in the 1930s: "There is an experimental shop in the Stalin Auto Plant. More than twenty foreign cars

[51] *Pravda*, 25 July 1937, p. 3.
[52] *Za industrializatsiiu*, 8 April 1937, p. 2.
[53] *Krasnaia Tatariia*, 21 April 1938, p. 4.

were bought for experimental purposes. But many of those cars have been missing from the experimental shop for a long time. Plant administrators and officials from various People's Commissariats are riding round in them."[54]

As the old bosses disappeared, a new generation made its debut. The newspapers published an extraordinarily large number of biographical sketches of the New Men in late 1937 and 1938, and they almost invariably emphasized two factors: the educational qualifications of these people and their humble origins. The typical New Man was from a poor working-class or peasant family—though some, of unknown social origin, were orphans brought up in state children's homes—and embarked early on a laboring career, only later and by dint of struggle acquiring an education and moving up in the world to their present eminence.[55] It was clearly implied that the New Men were a different breed from the old bosses. How could "sons of the working class" succumb to bourgeois degeneracy and abuse of power as their predecessors had done?

This was not a period when the reporter Avdeev's appreciation of the finer things in life was likely to receive favorable mention in the press. Kul'turnost' was still an approved value, however, and a similar story might well have been published in 1937 if Avdeeva had been substituted for Avdeev as a connoisseur of teaspoons. Even in 1935, it was something of an anomaly for a man to be interested in the consumer aspect of kul'turnost'; this was more properly the woman's sphere. The difference in the rules for New Man and New Woman became more marked during the Great Purges. Education was an advantage for both sexes, though more important for men because they were given responsible jobs. A man who rode around in a foreign car and entertained lavishly at a dacha, however, might always be a target of criticism, while a woman who kept a comfortable home and had a good tailor to make her husband's blue serge suits was just doing her duty as the wife of a Soviet executive.

It was generally acknowledged in the 1930s that women had a right and even an obligation to value material possessions, because they were the keepers of the family hearth. They should be shrewd bargainers at the market and connoisseurs at the department store, whereas men should normally be innocent of commercial instincts. Women, moreover, were depicted as the natural bearers of culture within the family. A successful man might be something of a rough diamond, as befitted his proletarian origins, but his wife should ex-

[54] *Pravda*, 19 May 1937, p. 4.
[55] The national newspapers carried particularly large numbers of these biographies during Supreme Soviet elections in November–December 1937 and June 1938.

ert a civilizing influence and make him accompany her from time to time to the ballet.

These womanly qualities were discussed not only in the newspapers but also in the women's journal *Obshchestvennitsa* (an almost untranslatable title that means roughly "The civic-minded woman"), which began publication in 1936 and continued until the war. *Obshchestvennitsa* was not really aimed at all women, since journals for working-class and peasant women already existed.[56] It was aimed at middle-class urban women, and specifically the wives of Soviet executives (*otvetrabotniki*) and professionals. The *obshchestvennitsa* who was the putative reader of the journal was a public-spirited Soviet woman who was married to a successful man in the administrative-professional class. He was undoubtedly a member of the Communist Party; she was probably not. She did not hold a paid job, but had the time (and, by virtue of her husband's position, the moral obligation) to take on voluntary work that enabled her to use her cultural and practical skills for the public benefit. The role of the Soviet *obshchestvennitsa*, in short, was conceived on very much the same lines as that of the woman who did volunteer work for charities in capitalist societies.

The *obshchestvennitsa* (women's volunteer) movement received great publicity in the press in May 1936, when an All-Union Meeting of Wives of Industrialists and Engineering-Technical Personnel in Heavy Industry was held in the Kremlin, with Stalin and other Politburo members in attendance.[57] A similar meeting of wives of military officers was held the following year. The volunteers' role was to improve living conditions and bring culture to their husbands' factories and regiments. At the 1936 meeting the industrialists' wives described how they supervised cooks in the factory kitchens so that the food would be edible and hygienically prepared, put up curtains and arranged for the installation of bathtubs in the workers' hostels, advised young girls on morals and personal hygiene, planted trees, and organized day-care centers, drama groups, and study circles.

The women's volunteer movement can be seen, in one light, as a revival of the old tradition whereby upper-class wives saved themselves from boredom by doing voluntary charitable work. Its "bourgeois" character disturbed Krupskaia, Lenin's widow, though her objections sounded anachronistic in 1936.[58] The movement also had

---

[56] The journals were *Rabotnitsa*, for working-class women, and *Krest'ianka*, for peasant women.

[57] See *Izvestiia*, 11 May 1936, p. 1; 12 May 1936, pp. 1–2; 14 May 1936, pp. 1–3.

[58] *Vsesoiuznoe soveshchanie zhen khoziaistvennikov i inzhenerno-tekhnicheskikh*

considerable practical utility, however, as Sergo Ordzhonikidze recognized. The down-to-earth commissar for heavy industry saw it as a
way of circumventing his managers' natural tendency to use the
funds allocated for social and cultural needs for purposes more directly related to production. The boss's wife, Ordzhonikidze rea-
soned, could break the bottleneck because she had special leverage,
not only over her husband but also over his subordinates.[59]

Gender, class, and values

The volunteer movement was notable as the first occasion since
the Revolution when wives (as distinct from women) were treated as
a category worthy of respect and capable of performing a useful function. Housewives had previously had very low status in Soviet eyes:
they were held to be both unemancipated and unproductive. The
change in the Soviet attitude toward wives is part of the broader
readjustment of values that Timasheff identified as "the great retreat." Nevertheless, the process was more complicated than Timasheff suggested. The new "great retreat" values did not apply equally
to all sections of society. They were values that were associated primarily with and recommended to the elite, and their relevance diminished sharply as one descended the social scale.

The traditional family values whose reemergence Timasheff noted
were values that only an elite could maintain in this society.[60] For
leisure-class women, obligations to husband and family clearly had
first priority. Volunteer work did not take precedence over family
obligations. The model to emulate was Professor Iakunin's wife, who
joined the volunteers during a boring stint in the provinces and later
became a prominent organizer of the movement in Moscow:

> Neither the bulging briefcase nor the innumerable telephone calls [as-
> sociated with Iakunina's volunteer work] give Professor Iakunin occa-
> sion to complain that his wife neglects the home. In her room there is
> exemplary order and warm, feminine comfort. As before, she herself
> does all the housework without [domestic] help. As before, when her
> husband comes home he finds a welcoming, attentive wife.[61]

---

rabotnikov tiazheloi promyshlennosti: Stenograficheskii otchet (Moscow, 1936), p.
130.
[59] See Ordzhonikidze's interjection when Poberezhskaia, wife of the director of the
Stalin Plant in Perm, complained of a shortage of funds: "Put the squeeze on Comrade
Poberezhskii!" (Vsesoiuznoe soveshchanie, p. 194).
[60] Timasheff, Great Retreat, pp. 192–203.
[61] Obshchestvennitsa, 1939 no. 6, p. 46, and no. 9, pp. 25–26.

Volunteers might be encouraged by their successful emergence into the public world to further their education or take paid professional jobs. But in the opinion of *Obshchestvennitsa* and its readers, the wife of a responsible professional man or administrator should not take paid employment if her husband disapproved, despite the high value generally put on women's employment in the 1930s.[62]

Working-class women, by contrast, were expected to work for wages. It was important to draw them into the labor force, and their husbands had no right to forbid their participation. Nevertheless, the husband's work was probably more important than the wife's, and she should help him to do it well. When a brigade of middle-class women volunteers visited the homes of skilled railroad workers who were performing poorly on the job, they found cases where "the wife was also responsible to some degree for the poor work [of the husband]" because she nagged him or made scenes. "In such cases, the brigades gently but insistently tried to convince the wife how important it is for an engine driver to be in a calm and harmonious frame of mind. 'What about him?' responds the wife. 'Is he allowed to abuse me?'"[63]

The middle-class volunteers "delicately unraveled these complex issues"; but actually the question exposed a contradiction in their own and society's attitudes. For all the "family" values they espoused in their own lives, they were still very sympathetic to lower-class women whose husbands abused them.[64] Engine drivers, to be sure, were in the upper working class, and ought to be capable of rising to middle-class norms. But it would clearly have been unreasonable to apply those norms to the lower working class, culturally so close to the peasantry.

The norms for peasant women in the 1930s provided a striking contrast to those for the middle class. It was assumed that peasant women, like those of "backward" non-Russian nationalities, still needed to be liberated from the oppression of the patriarchal family. Nobody suggested that their first obligation was to husband and children. They should see themselves as producers, persons of importance in their own right; they were full-fledged members of the kolkhoz *as individuals*, not just subordinate members of households, as they had been in the old village community. The modern *kolkhoznitsa* should strive to be a Stakhanovite, even if her husband disapproved. The message of women's liberation was strongly em-

---

[62] See discussion in ibid., 1937 no. 3, p. 27, and 1937 no. 9–10, p. 28.

[63] *Obshchestvennitsa*, 1939 no. 4, p. 10.

[64] See, for example, case histories in ibid., 1937 no. 3, p. 27, and 1939 no. 9–10, p. 28.

phasized in the speeches of peasant women at the Stakhanovite meetings of the 1930s. An Armenian woman who had become a kolkhoz brigade leader reported:

> Comrade Stalin very correctly said that woman was oppressed earlier. That was particularly clear in our Armenian village, where a woman was a real slave. Now our kolkhoz women have become free, now they sometimes earn more than their husbands. And when you earn more than your husband, how can he oppress you? That makes him curb his tongue.[65]

If peasant husbands stood in the path of their wives' progress, the wives were justified in divorcing them, though divorce in higher strata of Soviet society was already frowned upon. Peasant women Stakhanovites could refer proudly to a divorce as an episode in their emancipation: "They married me off [at sixteen]. I was married against my will, according to the old custom that still survived then [in Bashkiria]. After living with my husband for a year and a half, I separated from him and began to work independently in the kolkhoz. There I got the opportunity for a good life." They might also speak patronizingly of their husbands in public, if the husbands' consciousness lagged behind their own: "When I joined the kolkhoz in 1929, I had to struggle not only with backward *kolkhozniki* but also with someone very close to me—my husband. But I overcame him. My husband has now joined the kolkhoz and is already doing pretty well. In 1935 he became a shock worker, won several awards, and received good prizes."[66]

These same Stakhanovite peasant women eagerly embraced other bourgeois values, such as acquisitive consumerism and *kulturnost'*, and they were applauded for doing so. But the family was one realm in which Stalinist discourse continued to differentiate by class; the proper balance between women's emancipation and work, on the one hand, and women's responsibility to husbands and children, on the other, was not the same for the peasantry as it was for the New Class. The new family values were appropriate only for the upper strata of society—the cultural vanguard that had long ago cast off backwardness and stood ready, in the formula of the time, to march forward into socialism. For the lower strata, tradition-bound and culturally backward, the emancipation values of the 1920s remained relevant even in the generally conservative, postrevolutionary climate of the 1930s.

[65] *Geroini*, p. 59.
[66] Ibid., pp. 87, 92–93.

Conclusion

In the discourse of socialist realism, a true representation of a society that was in the process of building socialism involved the depiction not only of "life as it is" but also of "life as it is becoming." If life as it was in the 1930s lacked culture and consumer goods, the socialist future promised both to all Soviet citizens. In the meantime, the new Soviet intelligentsia had priority of access, since it was the most cultured group in a still-backward society. Within the context of Stalinist discourse, therefore, Soviet society did not have a new surreptitiously privileged "elite"; rather, it had a new justly rewarded "intelligentsia," a vanguard in the march to socialism, who proudly displayed their cultural and material acquisitions.

The idea of a vanguard (related, undoubtedly, to the revolutionary idea of the vanguard party) was important in the discourse of socialist realism. Stakhanovite workers and peasants also played a vanguard role vis-à-vis their respective classes; and the Stakhanovites, unlike the intelligentsia, were privileged persons whose social position was outside the elite. The fact that Stakhanovite workers and peasants were admitted to the circle of privilege underlined the message that *in principle* (a good socialist-realist phrase) all were eligible, and in the long run all would be admitted.

The *vydvizhentsy* played the role of a vanguard as well, for they were the cream of the lower classes, selected for immediate transfer to the socialist condition of material and cultural abundance that all would one day reach. Still regarding themselves as "sons of the working class," connected in some basic way with the masses, the *vydvizhentsy* could be represented as the spearhead of a much larger process of raising up the masses and making them cultured. "We want to make all workers and all peasants cultured and educated, and we will do it in time," Stalin told the Eighteenth Party Congress in 1939. But meanwhile, he reminded his audience with some impatience, at least a segment of the working class—the *vydvizhentsy*—had been promoted and civilized, and that was already a major achievement.[67]

The vanguard image broke down, however, with regard to women. On the one hand, women were indisputably more closely linked to *kul'turnost'* than men were. On the other hand, it was scarcely possible to conceive of women as a vanguard in the march to socialism. A

---

[67] I. V. Stalin, "Otchetnyi doklad na XVIII s″ezde partii—19.III.1939," in his *Sochineniia*, ed. Robert H. McNeal (Stanford, 1967), 1(14):398–400. Stalin was rebutting the view that workers at the bench were superior in Marxist terms to upwardly mobile *former* workers.

female vanguard would have relegated men to the status of rear guard (or perhaps passive freight?), which was completely incompatible with the spirit of revolutionary vanguardism, not to mention traditional social norms.

This was one of the instances where the discourse of socialist realism showed its fragility. Revolutionary vanguardism had always been a male prerogative. The image of the revolutionary proletarian had strongly marked male characteristics in Bolshevik mythology. In the 1920s, working-class women were rarely credited with "proletarian consciousness"; often, indeed, they were seen as having distinctly nonproletarian ("peasant" or "petty-bourgeois") attitudes, especially attachment to property and preoccupation with hearth and home.[68] Zealous young (male) Komsomols tended to suspect that there was something intrinsically bourgeois about the female sex. Communists were warned against marrying bourgeois women, and the "degeneration" of revolutionary cadres was often attributed to the corrupting influence of their wives.[69]

Thus the question of women and culture set up some uneasy notes in the discourse of socialist realism. To the degree that women were the culture-bearers in Soviet society, there was always the possibility—at least in the 1930s, when revolutionary memories were still alive—that a sudden switch of discourses would show *kul'turnost'* to be not the culture of socialism but the culture of *meshchanstvo*.

(1988/1991)

[68] For elaboration of this point, see Sheila Fitzpatrick, "New Perspectives on the Civil War," in *Party, State, and Society in the Russian Civil War: Explorations in Social History*, ed. Diane P. Koenker, William G. Rosenberg, and Ronald Grigor Suny (Bloomington, Ind., 1989), pp. 12–14.

[69] See, for example, I. Razin, ed., *Komsomol'skii byt: Sbornik* (Moscow, 1927), pp. 65–66, 278–81.

CHAPTER 10

Cultural Orthodoxies under Stalin

Much is known about Soviet cultural life under Stalin. It has been described in a large memoir literature that basically, whether it is published in the Soviet Union or the West, expresses the viewpoint of the old Russian intelligentsia and tends to be a literature of moral protest, either against the Soviet regime as such or against the abuses of the Stalin period. An equally impressive body of Western scholarly literature analyzes the syndrome of "totalitarian control" of culture, with its arbitrary repression, destruction of traditional associations, enforced conformity, censorship, political controls, and injunctions to writers and artists to act as "engineers of the human soul" in the Communist transformation of society. The element of moral condemnation in the concept of totalitarianism—developed in the postwar years, which were also the formative years of American Soviet studies—makes the scholarly literature strikingly similar in tone to the memoir literature of the intelligentsia.[1]

Scholars have offered various explanations for developments in

---

[1] The categories of scholarly and memoir literature overlap in a number of works that have influenced Western thinking about Soviet culture under Stalin; for example, Max Eastman, *Artists in Uniform* (New York, 1934); Andrey V. Olkhovsky, *Music under the Soviet: The Agony of an Art* (New York, 1955); Iu. Elagin (J. Jelagin), *Ukroshchenie iskusstv* (New York, 1952); Konstantin F. Shteppa, *Russian Historians and the Soviet State* (New Brunswick, N.J., 1962).

the culture/politics relationship in the Stalin period, but all of them have emphasized the party's drive for total control and Stalin's personal drive for total power and absolute authority. The party controlled culture and Stalin controlled the party. Involved in this interpretation are some specific propositions and assumptions, among which are (1) that the party assumed responsibility for guiding, and if necessary forcing, scholarship and the arts in certain directions, generally directions suggested by ideology; (2) that Stalin required an identifiable "party line" on all cultural questions, and thereby excluded the possibility of fundamental debate within the cultural professions; (3) that the Stalinist party rejected even the limited concepts of professional autonomy and academic and artistic freedom which had been accepted under NEP, and by imposing total control deprived cultural institutions and professional organizations of all powers of initiative and negotiation; (4) that, as a consequence, there was a "we–they" relationship between the cultural intelligentsia and the party, with the party striving—usually successfully—to infuse its values into the intelligentsia.

Yet in all periods the relationship between the party and culture was far more complex than a "we–they" image suggests. Stalinist cultural policy is not adequately explained by a chronicle of Stalin's personal interventions, or even by descriptions of the broad "conclusions" drawn when Stalin intervened in specific cases. The data here are fragmentary, inconsistent, and above all slight. For satisfactory explanations we have to look further and cast a net wide enough to include input from social and professional groups and government institutions, as well as from the Politburo and Stalin himself.

If final authority was vested in the party, the party nevertheless delegated, bestowed, or countenanced other types of cultural authority that resided in individuals or cultural institutions. Indeed, the legitimization of cultural policy was often developed *not* by reference to party doctrine or the pronouncements of party leaders but by reference to non-Communist authority figures with status in their own professions, such as Gorky, Stanislavsky, and Pavlov, or nonparty *praktiki* such as Trofim Lysenko and Anton Makarenko. Certainly the political leadership was determined to prevent the arts from posing a political or philosophical challenge, or from depicting reality so starkly that a challenge might be provoked. Yet at the same time, the leadership's attitude toward many established cultural values was more often deferential than destructive. As party values penetrated culture, the cultural values of the old intelligentsia were penetrating the party.

From Cultural Revolution to Great Retreat

As we have seen, the Cultural Revolution of the First Five-Year
Plan period was an attack by young Communist militants on the hegemony of the bourgeois intelligentsia in culture. Though the signal
may have come from Stalin, the zest and the specific lines of attack
came from the militants themselves, as did the notion that "hegemony" in culture was something that had to be seized on behalf of the
Revolution. The militants of RAPP and similar organizations knew
exactly and concretely what they meant by "seizing hegemony." It
was what they (and their equally aggressive avant-garde competitors,
such as Mayakovsky's Left Front in Art) had been trying to do all
through the NEP period: to convince higher party and government
organs—the party Central Committee, Narkompros, the State Publishing House, and so on—that their group should be given monopo-
listic powers in a given area (say, literature). Once these powers had
been conferred, the militant group would be able to control all the
relevant journals, publishing outlets, appointments, institutes, and
censorship organs, and put its competitors out of business.

For more than a decade Narkompros had steadfastly resisted such
plans, whether they came from proletarians or the artistic left, and
the Central Committee had also failed to respond to RAPP's insistent
appeals. During the Cultural Revolution, however, militant groups in
a variety of areas succeeded, albeit temporarily, in gaining the mo-
nopolistic and repressive powers they had long sought.

The Cultural Revolution was a time of great tribulation for the old
intelligentsia. With Lunacharsky's departure from Narkompros in
September 1929, that institution lost the will and power to protect
the old cultural intelligentsia, and so did such major employers
of bourgeois technical specialists as Gosplan (the state planning
agency) and Vesenkha. Young Communists took over the direction of
scholarly institutes and journals. Nonparty writers were often unable
to publish. Nonparty professors had to stand for "reelection" by their
students, and nonparty engineers were imprisoned for anti-Soviet activity (a charge often based only on failure to fulfill impossible targets set by the First Five-Year Plan).

But for young Communists it was a time of unprecedented opportunity. They provided much of the real enthusiasm behind the rhetoric of transforming nature, creating the New Man, and "catching up
and overtaking" the industrialized West. In concrete terms, they had
an opportunity to move upward into responsible jobs. And notwith-
standing the priority given to Communists and proletarians, many

educated young nonparty people and many skilled workers were drafted as *vydvizhentsy* into higher education, management, and administration. A new "proletarian intelligentsia"—mainly young, and a substantial proportion genuinely working class or peasant in origin—was being forced through a vastly expanded system of technical and higher education at breakneck speed.

Like all revolutions, the Cultural Revolution produced disorder. The "cultural army"—as the Komsomol called its corps of cultural revolutionaries—inclined more toward guerrilla tactics than soldierly discipline, and the militant Communist intellectuals were flagrantly guilty of *sektanstvo* (sectarianism) and *gruppovshchina* (factionalism). The collapse of established authorities brought "harebrained schemers" to the fore, even in such normally pedestrian areas as labor training and technical education. The education system, which had simultaneously undergone great expansion and radical structural reorganization, was in chaos. Inevitably the aftermath of revolution brought policies intended to restore order, discipline, and authority in the cultural sphere.

The restoration of order, which began in 1931–1932, proceeded along many lines simultaneously. With regard to industry and the training of engineers, the impetus for change seems to have come from Ordzhonikidze's Commissariat of Heavy Industry (the successor to Vesenkha), whose primary interest clearly lay in maximum industrial efficiency and use of competent specialists regardless of their class origin or party status. It was acknowledged that radical restructuring of the technical education system, "shock tempos" for the training of proletarian engineers and technicians, and harassment of the old technical intelligentsia had had a negative impact on industrial efficiency; and an All-Union Committee headed by the Old Bolshevik Gleb Krzhizhanovskii, the former president of Gosplan, was set up to repair the damage.[2] Measures for reorganization of the technical education system were drafted by bourgeois professors and engineers acting as government consultants, and they were uninhibited in expressing their scorn for Communist officials and industrial managers who had meddled in academic and technical matters beyond their understanding, and for the ill-prepared pro-

[2] Resolution of TsIK and SNK SSSR of 15 September 1933, and "Statute on the All-Union Committee on Technical Education under TsIK SSSR," Presidium of TsIK, 17 October 1933, in Vsesoiuznyi komitet po vysshemu tekhnicheskomu obrazovaniiu pri TsIK SSSR, *Biulleten'*, 1933 no. 9–10, p. 7. It is clear from the *Biulleten'* that the committee began work considerably before its formal establishment, probably sometime in 1932.

letarian and Communist students who had been pushed through higher technical school during the Cultural Revolution.[3]

In September 1931 the party Central Committee took the lead in restoring order in the schools by issuing a resolution denouncing the theory, promulgated by radicals during the Cultural Revolution, of "the withering away of the school." It was the first in a long series of resolutions through which the Central Committee attempted to reestablish discipline, orderly procedures, and traditional teaching methods in the schools.[4] Confronted by organizational chaos and ineffective teaching, protests from teachers and parents, and mutual accusations of political deviation among the educationalists themselves, the party leadership decided to seek safer ground. Its resolutions aimed to replace the unpopular progressive school by a disciplined school with formal procedures and academic orientation— the kind of school, in fact, that teachers and white-collar parents and ambitious lower-class parents had wanted for the past decade.

Social discrimination in school enrollment had been practiced to some extent in the 1920s and reached its height during the Cultural Revolution. It was a cumbersome process that became harder to justify as the number of school and university places increased. There was, moreover, no possible way of conciliating the old intelligentsia without giving their children unrestricted access to academic secondary and higher education. Thus in the first half of the 1930s, while large numbers of proletarian and peasant children remained in secondary and higher schools, the policy of forcing them in and other children out was gradually abandoned, not to be revived even in moderate form until the days of Khrushchev.[5] The distinction between "bourgeois intelligentsia" and "Red specialists" was dropped, and Stalin began to speak of a new classless "Soviet intelligentsia."

[3] See, for example, Front nauki i tekhniki, 1932 no. 7–8, p. 121; no. 10, p. 94; no. 11–12, p. 111.

[4] For the first resolution of the Central Committee, "On the elementary and middle school," 5 September 1931, see KPSS v rezoliutsiiakh i resheniiakh s"ezdov, konferentsii i plenumov TsK (Moscow, 1970), 4:569ff. (in this edition, the date of the resolution is wrongly given as 25 August 1931). For subsequent resolutions of the Central Committee—"On teaching programs and regimes in the elementary and middle school" (25 August 1932), "On textbooks for the elementary and middle school" (12 February 1933), "On the structure of the elementary and middle school in the USSR" (May 1934), "On the publication and sale of textbooks for the elementary, incomplete middle, and middle school" (7 August 1935), and "On the organization of teaching work and internal discipline in the elementary, incomplete middle, and middle school" (3 September 1935)—see Direktivy VKP(b) i postanovleniia sovetskogo pravitel'stva o narodnom obrazovanii (Moscow and Leningrad, 1947), 1:159ff.

[5] Discrimination in university admissions on the grounds of social origin was formally dropped at the end of 1935. See Direktivy VKP(b) i postanovleniia sovetskogo pravitel'stva o narodnom obrazovanii, 2:89.

In this process the old cultural intelligentsia was an equal beneficiary with the old technical intelligentsia. The rise in status of the
bourgeois cultural intelligentsia followed the fall of the proletarian
makers of Cultural Revolution. In 1931–1932 the party leadership
had clearly indicated its impatience with Communist scholasticism,
Communist "harebrained scheming," and local Communist dictatorships in the arts and scholarly disciplines which were unpopular,
unproductive, and insubordinate to the Central Committee's authority.[6] Communist intellectuals of the Cultural Revolution cohort—for
example, Leopold Averbakh, the leader of RAPP—were seen as too
ambitious or suspected of involvement in anti-Stalin maneuvering in
the internal politics of the party. They lacked the humility that nonparty status required; and perhaps, although the idea seems far-
fetched, they did represent some potential political threat to Stalin.
A great many of the former cultural revolutionaries were arrested in
the purges of 1937–1938; some, including Averbakh and his associates, were publicly denounced as Trotskyite traitors.[7]

When the period of "proletarian hegemony" ended in 1932 with
the dissolution of RAPP, a decision was made to organize an all-
inclusive Union of Soviet Writers in which literary factions would
be dissolved and bourgeois non-Communists admitted on equal
terms with Communists. Even the bourgeois avant-gardists, whose
reputations as troublemakers almost rivaled that of the proletarians,
were admitted and for a few years not attacked. The formula of "socialist realism" which the union adopted was not originally conceived as a party line, any more than the union was conceived as an
instrument of total party control over literature. Both were initially
intended to cancel out the old RAPP line of proletarian and Communist exclusiveness and make room for literary diversity—their disciplinary uses came later, with the mounting political tension of 1935–
1936.

The writer Maxim Gorky, who returned permanently to the USSR
in 1931, played a central role in the literary reorganization. Having
left Russia in the early 1920s after disagreements with Lenin on the
October Revolution and the treatment of the intelligentsia during the
Civil War, Gorky returned to be honored by Stalin and to provide a
symbol of reconciliation. Gorky was a stranger to the new generation

[6] See Stalin's letter to the editors, "On some questions of the history of Bolshevism,"
in *Proletarskaia revoliutsiia*, 1931 no. 6; reprinted in Stalin, *Sochineniia* (Moscow,
1947), 13:84–102.

[7] For accusations against the RAPPists Leopold Averbakh and Vladimir Kirshon, see
Literaturnaia gazeta, 20 April 1937, p. 1. It should be noted that Averbakh actually
had been a Trotskyite in 1923–1924 and the playwright Kirshon, his close friend, was
related by marriage to Genrikh Iagoda, chief of the GPU.

of Communist intellectuals who had achieved prominence during his absence (and RAPP, for example, was notably unenthusiastic about his prospective return, which was anticipated from 1928), but he was an old friend and patron of such leading bourgeois figures as the scientist Ivan Pavlov, the theater producer Konstantin Stanislavsky, and the grand old men of the Academy of Sciences. His return was followed by a rapid rise in the fortunes of all of these men. The Academy of Sciences—still the stronghold of traditional scholarship, despite the much-resented election of Communists such as Lunacharsky and Bukharin as academicians in 1929–1930[8]—recovered a position of honor, and after a few years absorbed most of the institutes of the Communist Academy.

The reconciliation was not a temporary or purely declarative one. From the early 1930s until the end of the Stalin period, part of the old cultural intelligentsia and most of the preeminent prerevolutionary cultural institutions (the Academy of Sciences, Moscow University, the Bolshoi Theater and its opera and ballet companies, the Moscow Arts Theater, and so on) enjoyed the special favor of the Soviet government and the Communist Party. The intellectuals and the institutions were, of course, subject to censorship, and Communist administrators were appointed to the institutions. Yet, in contrast to the situation during the Cultural Revolution and indeed throughout NEP, the institutions were not prevented from cultivating a dedicated apolitical professionalism—almost the spirit of a self-contained, privileged, and exclusive caste—provided they followed some ritual observances of respect for the regime and avoided political or social comment. Eminent cultural and scientific figures were not forced to become Communists, and in the 1930s few of them did so. (Even Lysenko and Makarenko, who were outsiders in their professions seeking recognition, did not find it necessary to join the party.) Within the mass of the "new Soviet intelligentsia," an old cultural intelligentsia, of bourgeois demeanor and largely unreconstructed anti-Communist habits of mind, was allowed to retain its separate identity and even, through teaching and example, perpetuate itself in the younger generation.

This reconciliation, because it lacked practical or utilitarian justification, was unlike the reconciliation with the technical intelligentsia. The cultural reconciliation was a luxury investment, involving self-imposed limitation of Communist ideological influence. Even if we assume conscious intention on the part of the leadership

---

[8] See Loren R. Graham, *The Soviet Academy of Sciences and the Communist Party, 1927–1932* (Princeton, 1967), pp. 114–15.

to dazzle the Soviet people with circuses in a time of bread rationing and to impress the West with Soviet *kul'turnost'*, the choice remains remarkable. When we note the numerous instances of Stalin's personal intervention in the fate of prestigious apolitical poets, his consultations with bourgeois scholars on matters of mutual academic interest, his derogatory comments on Communist literati, and the competitive anxiety of other party leaders to demonstrate that they too were on visiting terms with the great non-Communist writer Maxim Gorky, it is difficult to avoid the conclusion that the leadership respected "real culture" and was inwardly convinced that it was to be found among nonproletarians and non-Communists.

The cultural intelligentsia as a privileged group

This was a period of straitened resources, when industrialization and military preparation were urgent investment priorities, yet the Soviet state supported culture on a lavish scale. From the first half of the 1930s, the intelligentsia—Communist and nonparty, technical and cultural—became an unambiguously privileged group within the society.[9] Privilege was expressed in salaries, access to special stores and resorts, housing priority, children's access to higher education, honors and awards. These were essentially the same privileges offered to the upper levels of bureaucracy, the military, security police, and industrial management. All of these groups had their hierarchies of privilege, but basic privileged status was obtained through possession of formal credentials such as union membership and academic position; in other words, it was normally conferred on an individual by the profession and not by the party. No distinctions were drawn between branches of the intelligentsia on the grounds of their relative utility to the state, but there were distinctions based on the traditional social status of various groups. Thus engineers and opera singers were highly privileged, while people in the useful but traditionally low-status occupations of librarian and schoolteacher were not.

Established cultural institutions were subsidized on a much more generous scale than they had been under NEP, and they had an honorable place in the grandiose plan for the rebuilding of Moscow prepared under Lazar Kaganovich's supervision. The first major repairs of their buildings since the Revolution were undertaken in the 1930s. The Academy of Sciences, which was moved from Leningrad

[9] On the privileges, see Elagin, *Ukroshchenie iskusstv*, pp. 286–90.

to Moscow in the mid-1930s, got new buildings, including those originally intended for the Communist Academy. The climax came in the last years of Stalin's rule with the building of a Stalinist-baroque palace on Lenin Hills for Moscow University—an institution devoted largely to the humanities and pure sciences, which during the Cultural Revolution had been treated as an almost useless "survival of the past" and temporarily dissolved as a corporate entity.[10]

It is well known that under Stalin the cultural intelligentsia was subject to the constant harassment of censorship. No cultural figure, no matter how distinguished, was exempt from the possibility of having his books or films banned, exhibitions canceled, or theatrical productions closed after one performance, although in normal circumstances, connections in the party leadership and bureaucracy offered some protection. Even Aleksandr Fadeev, the powerful secretary of the Writers' Union in the 1940s, who was a party member of long standing, had to rewrite his novel *Molodaia gvardiia* and apologize for its original faults.[11] But censorship did not change the basic situation of the cultural intelligentsia as a highly privileged group within the society. Successful film directors, writers, actors with the Moscow theaters, and concert violinists enjoyed great prestige and reaped enormous material benefits. Iurii Elagin (a musician in the Vakhtangov Theater orchestra during the 1930s) compares their status with that of the aviators and polar explorers whose exploits were celebrated almost daily in the press. He even claims that the banners carried by alternating columns of children in the Revolution Day parade of 1937 read "We want to be aviators" and "We want to be violinists."[12]

Artists at the top of their profession had access to the highest Soviet elite. Biographers of the party leader Valerian Kuibyshev, for example, note the friendship that developed between him and Gorky through the proximity of their dachas, and also list, as a matter of course, the writers and artists of somewhat lesser status with whom Kuibyshev had social contact.[13] Patronage and social relations were closely, though not necessarily, linked. Stalin himself sometimes acted as a patron, as when he arranged a job for the playwright Mikhail Bulgakov at the Moscow Arts Theater. Bukharin, who is reported by Nadezhda Mandelstam to have been a patron of her hus-

[10] See *Moskovskii universitet za 50 let sovetskoi vlasti* (Moscow, 1967), pp. 68–69.

[11] Harold Swayze, *Political Control of Literature in the USSR, 1946–1959* (Cambridge, Mass., 1962), pp. 45–47.

[12] Elagin, *Ukroshchenie iskusstv*, p. 303.

[13] G. V. Kuibysheva, O. A. Lezhava, N. V. Nelidov, and A. F. Khavin, *Valerian Vladimirovich Kuibyshev* (Moscow, 1966), p. 352.

band in the early 1930s, was also an amateur painter whose work was exhibited in Moscow until 1936. A. S. Enukidze, secretary of the soviets' Central Executive Committee (TsIK) in the first half of the 1930s, was well known as a patron of the cultural intelligentsia and, like the Red Army leader and amateur singer Kliment Voroshilov, had a particular interest in the Bolshoi Opera.[14] (We have less information on patronage during the postwar period, but attacks on writers' reliance on patronage and *protektsiia* in the 1940s suggest that the phenomenon persisted.)[15]

Party leaders, GPU/NKVD chiefs, and top military personnel faithfully attended premieres at the Moscow Arts and Vakhtangov theaters, the Meyerhold Theater, and the Bolshoi Opera and Ballet. They were habitués of the salons of Zinaida Raikh (Meyerhold's wife) and Natalia Sats (niece by marriage of Lunacharsky, director of the Moscow Children's Theater, and an intimate of General Mikhail Tukhachevskii); they attended the luxurious supper parties of the non-Communist writer Count Aleksei Tolstoi—with Gorky and the aircraft designer Andrei Tupolev, one of the three Soviet citizens rumored to have inexhaustible and self-renewing accounts at the State Bank.[16]

The 1930s, in other words, saw the formation of a Soviet high society in which the artistic intelligentsia mingled with the top *nachal'stvo* (big brass). The intelligentsia were not simply providing jesters for the Stalinist court, though that was part of their role. They provided *kul'turnost'*, which was becoming a mark of status in the society. Although the Soviet Union, after 1938, had a governing elite that in large part was technically educated and professionally experienced in industry, the political leaders did not choose a similar route for their children. Children of the elite must be "cultured." Thus the tendency was to send sons to diplomatic training schools, military academies, institutes of journalism, or prestigious nontechnical schools such as the philological and physical-mathematical faculties of Moscow University, and daughters to institutes of literature, journalism, music, and ballet.[17] The middle ranks of society followed the pattern

[14] These examples belong to the folklore of the Moscow intelligentsia and are by their nature difficult to document. The Mandelstam case is reported in Nadezhda Mandelstam, *Hope against Hope* (New York, 1970); the Bulgakov case in E. Proffer, ed., *The Early Plays of Mikhail Bulgakov* (Bloomington, Ind. [1972]), pp. xviii–xx.

[15] Swayze, *Political Control of Literature*, p. 40.

[16] Elagin, *Ukroshchenie iskusstv*, p. 143.

[17] A partial list—unreliable because it is based on information obtained in interviews and from various memoir sources—of the education and professions of children of the political elite includes Stalin's younger son and daugher, air force and literature; Molotov's daughter, Gnesin Musical Institute; Litvinov's sons and daughter, science and literature; Zhdanov's son, science and scientific administrative work in Cen-

of the elite. Factory managers and local party secretaries—themselves products of technical and party schools—acknowledged the social imperatives of upward mobility by having their daughters take singing lessons and their sons study foreign languages, mathematics, and pure science.[18]

Establishment of cultural orthodoxies

Western and Soviet scholars alike have assumed that the party's primary interest in the cultural field was inculcation of Marxist and Communist values. As we have seen, however, inculcation of values was at least a two-way process. Western scholarship has been based on the further assumption that the party aimed at direct, total control of culture through the enforcement of orthodoxy. But what were the orthodoxies to which the intelligentsia had to conform?

The party required acknowledgment of the insights of Marxism-Leninism in social science works, applied the criterion of *partiinost'* (party spirit) to the work of Communist intellectuals, and encouraged artistic tributes to Stalin. But even in literature and the social sciences—areas particularly susceptible to political judgment—the criteria and desiderata could provide only limited guidance as long as the party did not require party membership of the intelligentsia and gave equal or greater honor to cultural figures who were neither Communist nor Marxist.

In most situations, the orthodoxies of immediate practical relevance to the professions were not political. They were local professional orthodoxies, established by a process of interaction between the professionals and the party's cultural administrators which was only in a few cases affected by intervention or explicit direction from the party leadership. For a writer, conformity meant respect for Gorky, respect for the Russian classics, emulation of the style of Pushkin or Nekrasov in poetry, Tolstoy in the novel, and so on. In the theater, conformity was emulation of Stanislavsky. For painters, the nineteenth-century "wanderers" (*peredvizhniki*) provided the orthodox model; for composers, Tchaikovsky and Rimsky-Korsakov. Orthodoxies were based on cultural authorities, alive or dead, whose work and obiter dicta became the bases of a system beyond reproach

---

tral Committee apparat; a Kamenev son, air force cadet; Lunacharsky's son and daughter, both journalism, after college education respectively in literature and science; Khrushchev's daughter, science journalism; Kosygin's daughter, foreign languages.

[18] For illustration, see Lena and family in Iurii Trifonov's novel *Studenty*, which won the Stalin Prize in 1951.

or criticism. The orthodoxies could be changed, but only by creative reinterpretation—forgotten aspects of the Gorky legacy, for example, or new insight into Makarenko's educational practice.

Members of the cultural intelligentsia could, of course, commit ideological crimes, just as they could play for high stakes by claiming special ideological virtue. But from the late 1930s, theaters were in much more danger of being criticized for anti-Stanislavskian principles than for anti-Marxist ones; geneticists were more likely to be attacked for not understanding Lysenko than for not understanding dialectical materialism; even writers were more likely to offend by flouting Gorky's principles of realism than by misrepresenting the process of socialist transformation in the countryside. In the purges, members of the avant-garde movements of the 1920s were denounced as "formalists" in 1936 and suffered disproportionately. An analysis of the *Letopis' zhurnal'nykh statei* (Yearbook of journal articles) for 1937–1938 suggests that in dangerous times, when the intelligentsia sought the protection of absolutely reliable authority, the figure they invoked was not Marx or Lenin or even Stalin, but Maxim Gorky.[19] To pay conspicuous tribute to Stalin—by representing his person in a play or film or by writing a scholarly work on the history of Bolshevism in the Caucasus, for example—was to go beyond normal conformity into an area of high possible reward but extremely high risk.

Established cultural authorities, then, had some protective function for the professions. But they also filled a need of the bureaucracy, particularly the censors. Lower-level officials, ignorant of scholarship and the arts but required to supervise them, needed formal criteria to identify right and wrong. This need was particularly

[19] Between July 1937 and December 1938, Gorky was the subject of 333 scholarly articles listed under *literaturovedenie* (essays on literary subjects) in the *Letopis'*, or 15 percent of the total. Pushkin, with 220 articles, was in second place. Four articles were published on Marx, Engels, or Marxist literary criticism; 18 on Lenin; 7 on Stalin. The Stalin articles and many of the Lenin ones were on the image of Stalin (Lenin) in folklore, the other Lenin articles being of the "Lenin on Gorky," "Lenin on Belinskii" type. (The first half of 1937 has been omitted from these calculations because of distortion attributable to the Pushkin centenary: of 840 articles published on literature from January to June 1937, 429 were on Pushkin, 68 on Gorky, 2 on Marx and Engels, 4 each on Lenin and Stalin.) In the category of *khudozhestvennaia literatura* (poems, plays, novels, short stories) published in the journals in 1937 and 1938, Stalin was the subject of 121 works (mainly poems by Central Asian and other non-Russian writers and folk balladists), Pushkin was the subject of 65 works, Lenin of 62, and Gorky of 8.

An analysis of the *Letopis'* for 1948 (minus two of the weekly issues) done for comparative purposes shows Gorky still in first place as the subject of 45 articles, or 9 percent of the total, as against 8 on Pushkin, 1 on Marx-Engels, 3 on Lenin, and none on Stalin. In the *khudozhestvennaia literatura* category for that year, Stalin was the subject of 25 works, Lenin of 10, Gorky of 4, Pushkin of 4, and Marx-Engels of 2.

acute from 1935 to 1939, when officials were simultaneously required to increase vigilance and to discard the old criteria—which
rank-and-file Communists instinctively understood—of social origin
and "class tendency." Orthodoxy by reference to established cultural
authorities replaced the earlier orthodoxy of party membership and
working-class origin.

Cultural authorities emerged through negotiation between professions, cultural bureaucrats, and, in some cases, the party leadership.
The group that exerted the most pressure varied with the circumstances. Within the professions, where old factional rivalries were
only formally abolished, pressure might come from a bourgeois establishment using its connections to the leadership, from Communists of the Cultural Revolution generation using their remaining
connections, or from a group of enthusiastic professional outsiders
who had the good fortune to appeal to official Communist sensibilities. Here I can only suggest the complexities and range of possi-
bilities by a brief survey of the major cultural authorities of the Stalin era.

Cultural authorities

Maxim Gorky, the prototypical cultural authority, received that
status on his return to the Soviet Union in 1931, when both the profession and the party leadership were dissatisfied with RAPP and
looking for an alternative. He probably would not have returned
without the leadership's assurances that he would have authority
without administrative responsibility or party membership.[20] He acted as cultural arbiter, patron (particularly of the non-Communist
cultural intelligentsia), and entrepreneur. The definition of "socialist
realism" was largely Gorky's, as was the firm establishment in Soviet
ideology of the concept of a classless and apolitical "classical heritage" in culture. Gorky not only provided the model for non-Communist cultural authority but also brought forward candidates for the
position in various professions, among them Konstantin Stanislavsky
in theater, Anton Makarenko in education, and Ivan Pavlov in the
life sciences.

Stanislavsky was a pure professional, with a prerevolutionary rep-

---

[20] The Soviet literature on Gorky is massive. Of particular interest here are L. By-
kovtseva, *Gor'kii v Moskve*, 2d ed. (Moscow, 1966), and Valentina Khodasevich's
memoirs of Gorky's last years in *Novyi mir*, 1968 no. 3. No adequate study of Gorky's
role in the 1930s has been written in the West, though there is a useful short chapter
in Boris Thomson, *The Premature Revolution* (London, 1972), pp. 186–205.

utation and no interest in politics or social causes. In the early 1930s he availed himself of Gorky's protection to rehabilitate his Moscow Arts Theater after a decade of criticism by Communist avant-gardists which culminated in the onslaughts of RAPP: he now styled the theater *"imeni Gor'kogo"* (named for Gorky) and staged a series of new productions of Gorky's plays (which Stanislavsky had also produced before the Revolution).[21] Stanislavsky himself remained aloof, showed no desire to become a Soviet cultural authority, and devoted the last years before his death in 1938 to elaborating his theatrical system, the Stanislavsky method. He emerged as a cultural authority around 1937–1938 through no actions of his own and without any formal laying on of hands by Stalin or the Central Committee. The conjunction of circumstances that made him an authority included the disgrace of Meyerhold, the avant-garde and pro-Communist director who was Stanislavsky's old rival, and anxiety within the theatrical profession produced by the purges. At a meeting of theater producers held early in 1939, speakers attributed the new "Stanislavskian orthodoxy" to the fact that the profession was disoriented by the attacks on Meyerhold—whom many had taken as a model for Communist theater—and to the desire of provincial theaters and censors to have a safe and reliable standard of conformity for self-protection.[22]

In the development of Makarenko as a cultural authority we find an extremely rich mixture of professional and institutional interests.[23] Makarenko was both an educationalist and a writer, a self-educated man of working-class origin, not a member of the Communist Party, who was somewhat hostile to what he saw as the intellectual establishment in both of his chosen professions. In the 1920s he organized colonies for delinquent children in the Ukraine—first, unhappily, under the republican education commissariat, which he saw as a haven for impractical intellectuals; later under the GPU, whose methods he admired. Gorky visited the GPU children's commune in the late 1920s and encouraged Makarenko to write about his experi-

[21] *Moskovskii khudozhestvennyi teatr v sovetskuiu epokhu: Materialy i dokumenty* (Moscow, 1962).

[22] The stenographic report (excluding Meyerhold's famous outburst against repression in cultural life) was published in *Rezhisser v sovetskom teatre: Materialy pervoi vsesoiuznoi konferentsii* (Moscow and Leningrad, 1940). See especially the report by S. M. Mikhoels and subsequent discussion, pp. 73ff.

[23] The English-language studies of Makarenko as educational theorist shed little light on his literary career or on his emergence as a public figure. A useful Russian source, in addition to the seven-volume *Sochineniia* published in the 1950s, is N. A. Morozova, *A. S. Makarenko: Seminarii* (Leningrad, 1961). On the controversy surrounding Makarenko in the late 1930s, I have benefited from the research of a Columbia University graduate student, Gary Davis.

ences. In the early 1930s Gorky helped him publish his first book, *Pedagogicheskaia poema* (Pedagogical poem, the basis for the popular movie *Road to Life*). In 1937, after the dissolution of all the GPU children's communes, Makarenko came to Moscow to seek his fortune as a professional writer.

The Writers' Union admitted him because of Gorky's (now posthumous) approval, but treated him rather patronizingly as a crude if talented amateur of the Nikolai Ostrovskii (*How the Steel Was Tempered*) type. Makarenko's dislike of establishment intellectuals increased. Unlike Stanislavsky, Makarenko wanted and sought authority. He systematized and publicized his educational theories, and collected a group of supporters among Komsomol activists, former RAPPists, and persons earlier associated with the GPU educational network—essentially a Communist group with the ethos of the Cultural Revolution.[24]

The first circumstances that aided Makarenko's achievement of cultural authority were the discrediting of a competing group (the pedologists) and the decimation of the educational bureaucracy by the purges.[25] The resulting vacuum was one that a living Makarenko was perhaps not suitable to fill (though one should not underestimate the instinctive approval Communists felt for successful self-educated practical men whose discoveries could confound the academicians). But Makarenko died in 1939, and his name evidently became a rallying point for those who disliked the increasingly formal and traditional organization of the Soviet schools. After a lively discussion of the "Makarenko heritage" in 1939–1940 in both the educational and literary professions, *Pravda* gave editorial endorsement to Makarenko as an educational theorist.[26] The endorsement may have constituted leadership intervention, although it is notable that it was not followed by any change in concrete educational policies. The alternative possibility is that *Pravda* did not prejudge the

[24] This characterization of Makarenko's support is based on analysis of articles listed in *Letopis' zhurnal'nykh statei* for 1938–1940 and on interviews in Moscow. It should be pointed out that among Communists of the Cultural Revolution cohort, Makarenko had critics as well as supporters—notably the group of former Communist Academy personnel associated with the journal *Literaturnyi kritik*.

[25] The pedologists' fall came with the Central Committee resolution of 4 July 1936, "On pedological distortions in the system of the education commissariats," in *Direktivy VKP(b) i postanovleniia sovetskogo pravitel'stva o narodnom obrazovanii*, 1: 190ff. The educational bureaucracy was found to contain a "counterrevolutionary Narkompros center" headed by the commissar of education of the RSFSR, A. S. Bubnov, and his deputy, M. S. Epshtein. On Bubnov's arrest, see A. Binevich and Z. Serebrianskii, *Andrei Bubnov* (Moscow, 1964), pp. 78–79.

[26] *Pravda*, 27 August 1940, p. 4.

issue but settled for what emerged as majority opinion among professional educational theorists.

In the postwar period, the orthodoxies already established held
their positions, with Makarenko—who may be seen as achieving
probationary status in 1940—rising to the full status of cultural authority around 1950.[27] The important development of these years was
the creation of cultural authorities in the natural sciences. Here the
late bourgeois physiologist Pavlov was closest to the Gorky model.
Pavlov, an outspoken critic of the Communists during the 1920s,
when he was already a scientist of international reputation, was acclaimed and honored in the Soviet Union in the years before his
death in 1936 but remained non- and probably anti-Communist. In
the mid-1930s, according to Boris Nicolaevsky, Bukharin spoke of
consulting with Gorky and Pavlov on the possible creation of an "intelligentsia party" that would give expert advice to the Soviet government.[28] In 1950, apparently by decision of the party leadership
(which the scientific community took as an affront), Pavlov became a
cultural authority, and an unchallengeable system was created in his
name.[29]

The more notorious case of Lysenko inevitably raises the question
whether the party leadership's attitude toward professional values
and *kul'turnost'* had changed.[30] However great the scientists' objection to a "Pavlovian orthodoxy," Pavlov himself had been highly respected. Trofim Lysenko was not respected, and his establishment as
a cultural authority outraged the scientists. It was the climax of a
long campaign waged by Lysenko (a non-Communist) and his supporters for official and scholarly recognition. In the 1930s the factors
in Lysenko's favor had been the panaceas he offered in the area of
agricultural science, where help was desperately needed. He presented an image of homespun practicality that appealed to Communists, who believed in science but were suspicious of intellectuals;
and, like Makarenko, he was good copy for Soviet journalists. Against
him had been the party leadership's strong commitment to support
the scientific establishment and the scientists' refusal to give him
professional acceptance. Stalin's "Bravo, Comrade Lysenko!" in 1935
did not make Lysenko a cultural authority, though it brought him

[27] See Morozova, *A. S. Makarenko*, p. 45.

[28] Boris Nicolaevsky, *Power and the Soviet Elite* (New York, 1965), pp. 14–15.

[29] Loren Graham, *Science and Philosophy in the Soviet Union* (New York, 1972), p. 375.

[30] On Lysenko, see David Joravsky, *The Lysenko Affair* (Cambridge, Mass., 1970); and Zhores A. Medvedev, *The Rise and Fall of T. D. Lysenko*, trans. I. Michael Lerner (New York, 1969).

closer;[31] neither did the Great Purges, despite the repression of some of his academic opponents.

What, then, had changed by 1948? The first possibility is that Lysenko's appeal to the party leadership had increased; the second, that the leadership's respect for professional opinion had diminished; the third, that the scientists had become less vehement in their opposition. There is some evidence to support all these hypotheses. It was a time of postwar exhaustion, cultural stagnation stirred only by random bursts of aggression from the leadership, rigidity and inflexibility at the top, and, on Stalin's part, a weakening grasp of reality and increasing paranoia. Dynamic transformation was not part of the reality of postwar Russia, but it was, perhaps for this very reason, an obsessive theme in the rhetoric. Stalin's unsuccessful reforestation campaign (celebrated in art by Leonid Leonov's novel *The Forest* and Shostakovich's cantata *Song of the Forests*, and enthusiastically supported by Lysenko) was meant to demonstrate Soviet mastery over nature. Similar points were being made in official commendation of Soviet scientific achievements, among them Lysenko's mutations, Pavlov's conditioned reflexes, and Olga Lepeshinskaia's experiments with the creation of living cells.[32] Lysenko's appeal had therefore increased because he provided evidence of the nature-transforming powers in which the leadership wanted to believe.

In the years immediately preceding Lysenko's success, the party leadership had been engaged in a disciplinary operation against the cultural intelligentsia—the *zhdanovshchina*. A range of eminent cultural figures of all types, from the Communist philosopher G. F. Aleksandrov to the apolitical composers Shostakovich and Prokofiev, had been subjected to sudden violent abuse from the Politburo member Andrei Zhdanov.[33] This onslaught undoubtedly influenced the scientists' behavior when the pressure turned on them, especially since they had lost their most distinguished and diplomatic anti-Lysenko negotiator when Academician Nikolai Vavilov was arrested in 1940.[34]

But, taking into account an evident suspension of respect for pro-

---

[31] Joravsky, *Lysenko Affair*, p. 83.

[32] Lepeshinskaia was an Old Bolshevik member of the pre-revolutionary emigration and one of the first Communists to be appointed (against bitter faculty and student protest) to the medical school of Moscow University at the beginning of the 1920s. On her work as a cytologist in the 1940s, see Graham, *Science and Philosophy*, p. 276.

[33] George S. Counts and Nucia Lodge quote extensively from the decrees and official statements on culture in this period in *The Country of the Blind: The Soviet System of Mind Control* (Boston, 1949).

[34] Joravsky, *Lysenko Affair*, p. 107.

fessional values on the part of the political leadership, we still have to decide whether the *zhdanovshchina* indicated a basic change of orientation. It caused panic among the intelligentsia, and it was accompanied by the so-called anti-cosmopolitan campaign, which cost the lives and freedom of a number of Jewish intellectuals and of others who had been in close personal contact with foreigners during the war and immediately afterward. But with the exception of these special categories, the intelligentsia were not facing a threat to their existence or a new cultural revolution. The attacks on leading cultural figures were not followed by arrest and often not even by demotion. The intelligentsia were no longer permitted to communicate with foreigners, but otherwise their status and privileges remained intact. There was no threat of collective replacement, no new pressure on the intelligentsia to join the party, and no new impediment to their doing so.

The old cultural orthodoxies remained in force and, as in previous periods of political tension, were observed with particular diligence. Veneration of persons was, in fact, increased by the extravagant blossoming of the Stalin cult—which had its own important impact on the cultural scene, but not at the level of basic party/intelligentsia relations. In his articles on linguistics, Stalin sent out a very ambiguous message attacking the "Arakcheev regime" established in linguistics by disciples of the late Marxist scholar N. Ia. Marr.[35] Since Stalin borrowed his position from the traditional non-Marxist linguists, he could be seen as defending bourgeois professional values. On the other hand, since he attacked "Arakcheev regimes" in scholarship, he could be seen as renouncing the whole institution of cultural authorities and cultural orthodoxies. Neither interpretation was easy to reconcile with the contemporary party endorsement of Lysenko and Pavlov, so Stalin's political message, if he had one, sank without trace. At this period it seems that the regime was hardly capable of making major policy initiatives or generating radical structural change. In culture, as elsewhere, it was a time of tense inaction while the political leadership waited for Stalin to die.

Both the Lysenko case and the *zhdanovshchina* show that the party could on occasion repudiate professional values by falling back on a kind of Communist populism, as if scientific and cultural policy could be based on the encouragement of worker-inventors, *praktiki*, and aged peasants making folk epics on the life of Stalin. The populist greeting was offered to the cloth-capped and surly Lysenko, to

---

[35] "Otnositel'no marksizma i iazykoznanii," *Pravda*, 20 June 1950; reprinted in Stalin, *Sochineniia*, ed. Robert H. McNeal, 3 vols. (Stanford, 1967), 3:114–48.

Makarenko, Nikolai Ostrovskii, and the image of the young Gorky tramping Russia in rags; the same spirit was reflected in Zhdanov's advice to the composers in 1948 to learn from the simple folk songs of the people.

But this populist spirit was not dominant in the culture of the Stalin period because the regime had made the basic decision to put its money on *kul'turnost'* and to honor the old non-Communist and nonproletarian cultural intelligentsia. In Western discussion of Stalinist culture, the question *Kto kogo?* has not been asked because the power relationship between party leadership and intelligentsia seems obvious. Yet power and cultural authority were in different hands under Stalin: the party had the political power to discipline the old intelligentsia but lacked the will or resources to deny its cultural authority. In cultural terms, then, who was assimilating whom?

(1975)

Index

Library of Congress Cataloging-in-Publication Data

Fitzpatrick, Sheila.
  The cultural front : power and culture in revolutionary Russia / Sheila Fitzpatrick.
    p. cm.—(Studies in Soviet history and society)
  Includes bibliographical references and index.
  ISBN 0-8014-2196-9.—ISBN 0-8014-9516-4 (pbk.)
  1. Soviet Union—Intellectual life—1917–1970. 2. Soviet Union—Politics and
government—1917–1936. 3. Soviet Union—Politics and government—1936–
1953. I. Title. II. Series.
DK266.4.F58 1992
947.084—dc20   92-52752